TECHNIQUES OF EVENT
HISTORY MODELING
New Approaches to
Causal Analysis

TECHNIQUES OF EVENT HISTORY MODELING
New Approaches to Causal Analysis

Hans-Peter Blossfeld
Götz Rohwer
University of Bremen, Germany

LEA

LAWRENCE ERLBAUM ASSOCIATES, PUBLISHERS

1995   Mahwah, New Jersey

Lawrence Erlbaum Associates, Inc., Publishers
10 Industrial Avenue
Mahwah, New Jersey 07430

Cover design by Kate Dusza

Library of Congress Cataloging-in-Publication Data

Blossfeld, Hans-Peter.
    Techniques of event history modeling : new approaches to causal
analysis / Hans-Peter Blossfeld, Götz Rohwer.
        p. cm.
    Supplement and update to Event history analysis / Hans-Peter
Blossfeld. 1988.
    Includes bibliographical references and index.
    ISBN 0-8058-1959-2.—ISBN 0-8058-1960-6 (pbk.)
    1. Event history analysis Computer simulation. I. Rohwer,
Götz. II. Blossfeld, Hans-Peter. Event history analysis. III.
Title.
H61.B493   1995
001.4'3—dc20   95-23513
                                       CIP

Books published by Lawrence Erlbaum Associates are printed on
acid-free paper, and their bindings are chosen for strength and durability.

Contents

Preface

In this book we want to give a comprehensive introductory account of event history modeling techniques and their usefulness for causal analysis in the social sciences. In the literature a distinction between discrete-time and continuous-time models is often made (Allison 1982, 1984; Blossfeld, Hamerle, and Mayer 1989; Hamerle and Tutz 1989; Yamaguchi 1991). This volume is intended to introduce the reader to the application of continuous-time models. It is both a student textbook and a reference book for research scientists.

There were three main goals in writing this book. The first was to demonstrate that event history models are an extremely useful approach to uncover causal relationships or to map out a system of causal relations. Event history models are linked very naturally to a causal understanding of social processes because they relate change in future outcomes to conditions in the past.

The second objective of this book was to introduce the reader to the computer program Transition Data Analysis (TDA). This program, written by Götz Rohwer, estimates the sorts of models most frequently used with longitudinal data, in particular, event history data. The guiding principle in constructing TDA was the desire to make a broad range of event history analysis techniques as simple and convenient to apply as possible. TDA is now widely used in many research and university centers that analyze longitudinal data in Europe and the United States. It can be run on DOS-based personal computers and UNIX workstations. Attached to this book is a disk with an executable version of the TDA program for DOS-based machines, a file with the data used in the examples throughout the book, and a series of files containing the TDA set ups for the examples.[1] Thus, the reader is offered the unique opportunity to easily run and modify all the application examples on a computer. In fact, we advise the event history analysis beginner to go through the application examples of the book on his or her own computer step by step. Based on our teaching experience from many workshops and introductory classes, this seems to be the most efficient and straightforward way to get familiar with these complex analysis techniques.

We have tried to emphasize the strengths and weaknesses of event history modeling techniques in each example. In particular, we have tried to complement each practical application with a short exposition of the underlying statistical concepts. The examples start with an introduction of the substantive background for the specific model. Then we demonstrate how to organize the input data and use the commands to control the TDA operation. Finally, a substantive interpretation of the obtained results is given.

The third goal was to supplement and update the textbook *Event History*

---

[1] Appendix B describes the accompanying disk and explains how to install the software.

vii

Analysis by Blossfeld, Hamerle, and Mayer (1989). It is a supplement because it substantially extends the practical application of event history analysis, and it is an update because it adds several important new models and concepts that have been developed in an extremely active research area since the late 1980s. Nevertheless, our book heavily builds on the Blossfeld, Hamerle, and Mayer volume with regard to statistical theory, which will not be repeated to the same extent here. It also takes up several of the examples given there for the computer programs SPSS, BMDP, GLIM, RATE, or SAS, so that the earlier volume provides a link to such computer applications. Therefore, based on the complementary character of these two volumes, we recommend a combination of both books for courses in applied event history analysis.

Acknowledgments

We have received financial support for our work from several sources in different countries. Early drafts of this book were written at the European University Institute in Florence, Italy. In particular, we would like to express our appreciation to the European University Institute for the financial support we received for the project "Household Dynamics and Social Inequality." The concluding draft of the book was done at the University of Bremen, Germany. We would like to thank *Institut für empirische und angewandte Soziologie* (EMPAS) for generously supplementing our computer equipment and funds, as well as the Deutsche Forschungsgemeinschaft (DFG) for supporting our work through the research project "Haushaltsdynamik und soziale Ungleichheit im internationalen Vergleich," which is part of the Sonderforschungsbereich 186 "Statuspassagen und Risikolagen im Lebensverlauf."

The TDA program has been in development for several years and is still a work in progress. Many people have helped and we would like thank them all. Additional information can be found in Appendix A to this book.

To produce the camera-ready copy for this book, we used Donald Knuth's typesetting program TEX in connection with Leslie Lamport's LATEX and Tomas Rokicki's DVIPS PostScript driver. Most of the figures in this book were created by TDA's plot module.

The data used in our examples were taken from the German Life History Study (GLHS) and were anonymized for data protection purposes. The GLHS study was conducted by Karl Ulrich Mayer, as principal investigator at the Max Planck Institute for Human Development and Education in Berlin. The original data collection was funded by the Deutsche Forschungsgemeinschaft (DFG) within its Sonderforschungsbereich 3 "Mikroanalytische Grundlagen der Gesellschaftspolitik." We would like to thank Professor Mayer for his kind permission to use a sample of 600 job episodes in the GLHS as a basis for our practical examples.

We are also indebted to the students in our statistics classes and to the participants in several international workshops for their comments on earlier versions of the book. First drafts were used in statistics classes on event history analysis at the European University Institute in Florence and at the University of Bremen. More developed versions of the manuscript were employed in workshops for advanced research scientists at the University of Haifa (Israel), the Johann-Wolfgang-Goethe University in Frankfurt am Main (Germany), the University of Cologne (Germany), the University of Southampton (England), the Universidad Complutense de Madrid (Spain), the Karl-Franzens University in Graz (Austria), and the Université de Genève (Switzerland).

We also wish to express our thanks to Sonja Drobnič, Andreas Timm, and Immo Wittig at the University of Bremen, who have provided superb collegial support. It is a special pleasure to thank Julie Winkler-Vinjukova and Katherine Bird who, as native speakers, did an expert job of copy-editing our drafts. Beate Ernicke, Simon Koch, Jo Mowitz, Marion Ostermeier, and Dave Salierno, the copy editor of Lawrence Erlbaum Associates, proofread the final versions of the manuscript. Although these colleagues eliminated some of our errors, only we are responsible for those that remain.

Hans-Peter Blossfeld
Götz Rohwer

Chapter 1
Introduction

Over the last 20 years, social scientists have been collecting and analyzing event history data with increasing frequency. This is not an accidental trend, nor does it reflect a prevailing type of fashion in survey research or statistical analysis. Instead, it indicates a growing recognition among social scientists that event history data are often the most appropriate empirical information one can get on the substantive process under study.

James Coleman (1981:6) characterized this kind of substantive process in the following general way: (1) there are units—which may be individuals, organizations, societies, or whatever—that change from one discrete state to another; (2) these changes (or events) can occur at any point in time and are not restricted to predetermined points in time; and (3) there are time-constant and/or time-dependent factors influencing the events.

Illustrative examples of this type of substantive process can be given for a wide variety of social research fields (Blossfeld, Hamerle, and Mayer 1989): in *labor market studies*, workers move between unemployment and employment, or between full- and part-time work;[1] in *demographic analyses*, men and women enter into consensual unions, marriages, or into father-/motherhood, or are getting a divorce;[2] in *sociological mobility studies*, employees shift through different occupations, social classes, or industries;[3] in *studies of organizational ecology*, firms, unions, or organizations are founded or closed down;[4] in *political science research*, governments break down or countries go through a transition from one political regime to another; in *migration studies*, people move between dif-

---

[1] See, e.g., Blossfeld in press; Carroll and Mayer 1986; Mayer and Carroll 1987; DiPrete and Whitman 1988; Heckman and Borjas 1980; Galler and Pötter 1990; Diekmann and Preisendörfer 1988; Sørensen and Tuma 1981; Becker 1993; Carroll and Mosakowski 1987; Brüderl 1991a; DiPrete 1993; Andreß 1989; Hachen 1988; Esping-Andersen, Leth-Sørensen, and Rohwer 1994, Drobnič and Wittig in press.

[2] See, e.g., Blossfeld 1995; Huinink 1987, 1993, 1995; Lauterbach 1994; Diekmann and Weick 1993; Diekmann 1989; Manting 1994; Bernasco 1994; Hoem 1983, 1986, 1991; Hoem and Rennermalm 1985; Blossfeld, De Rose, Hoem, and Rohwer 1993; Mayer and Schwarz 1989; Hannan and Tuma 1990; Wu 1990; Teachman 1983; Papastefanou 1987; Sørensen and Sørensen 1985; Mayer, Allmendinger, and Huinink 1991; Liefbroer 1991; Rindfuss and Hirschman 1984; Rindfuss and John 1983; Michael and Tuma 1985; Grundmann 1992; Leridon 1989; Klijzing 1992.

[3] See, e.g., Sørensen and Blossfeld 1989; Mayer, Featherman, Selbee, and Colbjørnsen 1989; Featherman, Selbee, and Mayer 1989; Allmendinger 1989a, 1989b; Esping-Andersen 1990, 1993.

[4] See, e.g., Hannan and Freeman 1989; Freeman, Carroll, and Hannan 1983; Carroll and Delacroix 1982; Brüderl, Diekmann, and Preisendörfer 1991; Preisendörfer and Burgess 1988; Lomi 1995.

ferent regions or countries;[5] in *marketing applications*, consumers switch from one brand to another or purchase the same brand again; in *criminology studies*, prisoners are released and commit another criminal act after some time; in *communication analysis*,[6] communication processes such as interpersonal and small group processes are studied;[7] in *educational studies*, students drop out of school before completing their degrees;[8] in *analyses of ethnic conflict*, events like racial claims, expressing a grievance, or attacking members of another ethnic group are studied;[9] and so on.

Technically speaking, in all of these examples, units of analysis occupy a state in a theoretically meaningful state space and transitions between these states can virtually occur at any time.[10] Given an event history data set, the typical problem of the social scientist is to use appropriate statistical methods for describing this process of change, and to discover social conditions of the events and to assess their importance.

This book has been written to help the applied social scientists to achieve this goal. In this introductory chapter we discuss different observation plans and their consequences for causal modeling. We also summarize the fundamental concepts of event history analysis and show that the change in the transition rate is a natural way to represent the causal effect. The remaining chapters are organized as follows:

- Chapter 2 describes event history data sets and their organization. Also shown is how to use such data sets with TDA.

- Chapter 3 discusses basic nonparametric methods to describe event history data, mainly the life table and the Kaplan-Meier (product-limit) estimation methods.

- Chapter 4 deals with the basic exponential transition rate model. Although this very simple model is almost never appropriate in practical applications, it serves as an important starting point for all other transition rate models.

- Chapter 5 describes a simple generalization of the basic exponential model, called the *piecewise constant exponential model*. In our view, this is one of the most useful models for empirical research, and so we devote a full chapter to discussing it.

---

[5] See, e.g., Pickles and Davies 1986; Wagner 1989a, 1989b, 1990; Bilsborrow and Akin 1982; Courgeau 1990.

[6] See, e.g., Krempel 1987.

[7] See, e.g., Snyder 1991.

[8] See, e.g., Willett and Singer 1991; Singer and Willett 1991; Becker 1993; Meulemann 1990.

[9] See, e.g., Olzak 1992.

[10] See, e.g., Cox and Oakes 1984; Tuma and Hannan 1984; Hutchison 1988a, 1988b; Kiefer 1988.

- Chapter 6 discusses time-dependent covariates. The examples are restricted to exponential and piecewise exponential models, but the topic—and part of the discussion—is far more general. In particular, we introduce the problem of how to model parallel and interdependent processes.

- Chapter 7 introduces a variety of models with a parametrically specified duration-dependent transition rate, in particular Gompertz-Makeham, Weibull, log-logistic, log-normal, and sickle models.

- Chapter 8 discusses the question of goodness-of-fit checks for parametric transition rate models. In particular, the chapter describes simple graphical checks based on transformed survivor functions and generalized residuals.

- Chapter 9 introduces semi-parametric transition rate models based on an estimation approach proposed by D. R. Cox (1972).

- Chapter 10 discusses problems of model specification and, in particular, transition rate models with unobserved heterogeneity. The discussion is mainly critical and the examples are restricted to using a gamma mixing distribution.

1.1   Causal Modeling and Observation Plans

In event history modeling, design issues regarding the type of substantive process are of crucial importance. It is assumed that the methods of data analysis (e.g. estimation and testing techniques) cannot only depend on the particular type of data (e.g. cross-sectional data, panel data, etc.) as has been the case in applying more traditional statistical methodologies. Rather, the characteristics of the specific kind of social process itself must "guide" both the *design of data collection* and *the way that data are analyzed and interpreted* (Coleman 1973, 1981, 1990).

To collect data generated by a continuous-time, discrete-state substantive process, different observation plans have been used (Coleman 1981; Tuma and Hannan 1984). With regard to the extent of detail about the process of change, one can distinguish between cross-sectional data, panel data, event count data, event sequence data, and event history data.

In this book, we do not discuss *event count data* (see Barron 1993), which simply record the number of different types of events for each unit (e.g. the number of upward, downward, or lateral moves in the employment career in a period of 10 years), or *event sequence data*, which document the sequence of states occupied by each unit, as they are rarely used in the social sciences. On the other hand, cross-sectional data and panel data are standard sociological data types (Tuma and Hannan 1984). It is, therefore, particularly intriguing

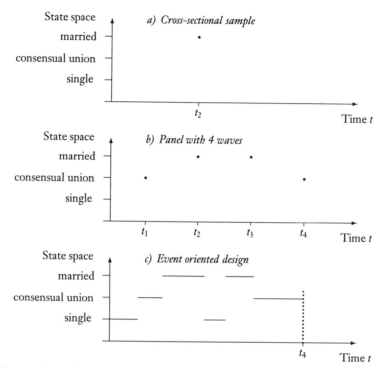

Figure 1.1.1 Observation of an individual's family career on the basis of a cross-sectional survey, a panel study, and an event history-oriented design.

to compare event history data with cross-sectional and panel data. We use the example shown in Figure 1.1.1. In this figure, an individual's family career is observed in a cross-sectional survey, a panel survey, and an event-oriented survey.

1.1.1 Cross-Sectional Data

Let us first discuss the *cross-sectional observation*. In the social sciences, this is the most common form of data for assessing the determinants of behavior. The family history of the individual in Figure 1.1.1 is represented by one single point in time: his or her marital state at the time of interview. Thus, a cross-sectional sample is only a "snapshot" of the substantive process being studied. The point in time when researchers take that "picture" is normally not determined by hypotheses about the dynamics of the substantive process itself, but by external considerations like getting research funds, finding an appropriate institute to conduct the survey, and so on.

Coleman (1981) has demonstrated that one must be cautious in drawing inferences about explanatory variables on the basis of such data because, implicitly or explicitly, social researchers must assume that the substantive process under study is in some kind of *statistical equilibrium*. Statistical equilibrium or *stability of the process* means that although individuals (or any other unit of analysis) may change their states over time, the state probabilities are fairly trendless or stable. Therefore, an equilibrium of the process requires that the inflows to and the outflows from each of the discrete states be equal over time to a large extent. It is only in such cases that one can reasonably assess the estimates of *logit* and *log-linear analyses*, as shown by Coleman (1981).

However, these estimates are ambiguous because they only represent the net differences in the effects of independent variables (Coleman 1981). Consider, for example, that we are studying a process with two states ("being unemployed" and "being employed"), which is in equilibrium (i.e. the unemployment rate is time-constant or trendless); and let us further assume that the covariate "educational attainment" increases the probability of movement from unemployment to employment (UE → E) and increases the probability of movement from employment to unemployment (E → UE) for each individual. In a cross-sectional logistic regression analysis using the probability of being employed as the dependent variable, the estimated coefficient for "educational attainment" only expresses the net difference of both directional effects. Therefore, if the positive effect of educational attainment on UE → E offsets the positive effect on E → UE, the "net coefficient" of "educational attainment" in the logistic regression will be about zero and not significant. In other words, a *zero effect of a covariate in a cross-sectional logistic regression analysis* could mean both (1) that there is *no effect at all* of the respective covariate on UE → E and on E → UE, or (2) that the *directional effects on UE → E and on E → UE offset each other*. Consequently, if the net effect of "educational attainment" in a cross-sectional logistic regression using the probability of becoming employed is positive, then, the following four different interpretations are possible: (1) that the positive effect on UE → E is greater than the positive effect on E → UE, (2) that the negative effect on UE → E is smaller than the negative effect on E → UE, (3) that there is only a positive effect on UE → E and no effect on E → UE, and (4) that there is no effect on UE → E and only a negative effect on E → UE. Similarly, for negative effects in the cross-sectional logistic regression, the four interpretations simply have to be reversed.

However, if there is no equilibrium in the process, *cross-sectional coefficients may not only be ambiguous, but even present a completely misleading picture*. In a recent study on unemployment incidence, Rosenthal (1991), for example, demonstrated how confusing cross-sectional estimates can be if the unemployment rate increases or decreases in a specific region and if the process of change is, therefore, not in equilibrium.

In the social sciences one can expect that stability is very rare. For example, life history studies (Mayer 1990; Blossfeld 1989, 1995, in press) show that change across age, cohort, and historical period is an enduring and important feature in all domains of modern individuals' lives (Mayer and Tuma 1990); organizational studies demonstrate that most social organizations seem to follow a program of growth and not of stability; and most modern societies reveal an accelerating rate of change in almost all of their subsystems (cf. the rapid changes in family systems, job structures, educational systems, etc.; see Heinz 1991a, 1991b, 1992; Mayer 1990; Blossfeld 1989, 1995, in press). But even in areas considered to be fairly stable, one must ask the crucial methodological question: To what extent is the process under study close to an equilibrium (Tuma and Hannan 1984)? This question can only be answered if longitudinal data are applied because longitudinal data are the only type of data that indicate whether a steady state actually exists, or how long it will take until a system returns to a new equilibrium after some external upheaval.

Beyond the crucial assumption of process stability, cross-sectional data have many inferential limitations with regard to causal modeling. We want to address at least some of the more important problems here.[11]

Direction of causality. There are only a few situations in which the direction of causality can be established based on cross-sectional data (Davies 1987). For example, consider the strong positive association between parental socioeconomic characteristics and educational attainment of sons and daughters, controlling for other important influences (Shavit and Blossfeld 1993). A convincing interpretation of this effect might be that being born into a middle class family increases the likelihood of attaining a university degree because one is unable to think of any other plausible explanation for the statistical association. However, such recursive relationships, in which all the causal linkages run "one way" and have no "feedback" effects, are rare in social science research. For example, there is very often an association between the age of the youngest child and female labor force participation in modern industrialized societies (Blossfeld and Rohwer in press). The common interpretation is that there is a one-way causality with young children tending to keep mothers at home. However, it is quite possible that the lack of jobs encourages women to enter into marriage and motherhood, suggesting a reversed relationship (Davies 1987).

The ambiguity of causation seems to be particularly important for the modeling of the *relationship between attitudes and behavior*. There are two interesting aspects of this relationship: There is a direct effect in which behavior affects attitudes, and there is a "feedback" process where attitudes change behavior

---

[11] These problems are however not mutually exclusive.

(Davies 1987).[12] The well-known disputes among sociologists, as to whether value change engenders change in social structure, or whether structural change leads to changing values of individuals, often originate from the fact that cross-sectional surveys can only assess the net association of these two processes.

Various strengths of reciprocal effects. Connected with the inability of establishing the direction of causality in cross-sectional surveys is the drawback that these data cannot be used to discover the different strengths of reciprocal effects. For example, many demographic studies have shown that first marriage and first motherhood are closely interrelated (Blossfeld and Huinink 1991). To understand what has been happening with regard to family formation in modern societies, it might be of interest not only to know the effect of marriage on birth rates, but also the effect of pregnancy or first birth on getting married (Blossfeld and Huinink 1991; Blossfeld 1995); and, perhaps, how these effects have changed over historical time (Manting 1994).

Observational data. Most sociological research is based on nonexperimental observations of social processes, and these processes are highly selective. For example, Lieberson (1985), in a study examining the influence of type of school (private vs. public) on test performance among students, distinguished at least three types of nonrandom processes: (1) there is *self-selectivity*, in which the units of analysis sort themselves out by choice (e.g. specific students choose specific types of schools); (2) there is *selective assignment by the independent variable* itself, which determines, say, what members of a population are exposed to specific levels of the independent variable (e.g. schools select their students based on their past achievement); and (3) there is also *selectivity due to forces exogenous to variables under consideration* at the time (socioeconomic background, ethnicity, gender, previous school career, changes of intelligence over age, etc.); and many of these sources are not only *not observed*, but effectively *unmeasurable*. Although no longitudinal study will be able to overcome all the problems of identification of causal effects, cross-sectional data offer the worst of all opportunities to disentangle the effects of the causal factors of interest on the outcome from other forces operating at the same time because these data are least informative about the process of change. Cross-sectional analysis therefore requires a particularly careful justification, and the results must always be appropriately qualified (Davies 1987; Pickles and Davies 1989).

Previous history. There is one aspect of observational data that deserves special attention in the social sciences. Life courses of individuals (and other units of analysis like organizations, etc.) involve complex and cumulative time-related layers of selectivity (Mayer 1991; Mayer and Müller 1986; Mayer

---

[12] The relationship between attitudes and behavior suggests that there is some kind of inertia (or positive feedback), which means that the probability of a specific behavior increases as a monotonic function of attitudes and attitudes depend on previous behavior (Davies and Crouchley 1985).

and Schöpflin 1989). Therefore, there is a strong likelihood that specific individuals have been entering a specific origin state. In particular, life course research has shown that the past is an indispensible factor in understanding the present (Heinz 1991a, 1991b, 1992; Mayer 1990). Cross-sectional analysis may be performed with some proxy-variables as well as with assumptions of the causal order and interdependencies between the various explanatory variables. However, it is often not possible to appropriately trace back the time-related selective processes operating in the previous history because these data are simply not available. Thus, the normal control approaches in cross-sectional statistical techniques will rarely be successful in isolating the influence of some specific causal force (Lieberson 1985).

Age and cohort effects. Cross-sectional data cannot be used to distinguish age and cohort effects (Tuma and Hannan 1984; Davies 1987). However, in many social science applications it is of substantive importance to know whether the behavior of people (e.g. their tendency to vote for a specific party) is different because they belong to different age groups or whether they are members of different birth cohorts (Blossfeld 1986, 1989).

Historical settings. Cross-sectional data are not able to take into account the fact that processes emerge in particular historical settings. For example, in addition to individual resources (age, education, labor force experience, etc.), there are at least two ways in which a changing labor market structure affects career opportunities. The first is that people start their careers in different structural contexts. It has often been assumed that these specific historic conditions at the point of entry into the labor market have a substantial impact on people's subsequent careers. This kind of influence is generally called a cohort effect (Glenn 1977). The second way that changing labor market structure influences career opportunities is that it improves or worsens the career prospects of all people within the labor market at a given time. For example, in a favorable economic situation with low unemployment, there will be a relatively wide range of opportunities. This kind of influence is generally called a period effect (Mason and Fienberg 1985). With longitudinal data, Blossfeld (1986) has shown that *life-course, cohort, and period effects* can be identified based on substantively developed measures of these concepts (Rodgers 1982), and that these effects represent central mechanisms of career mobility that must be distinguished.

Multiple clocks, historical eras, and point-in-time events. From a theoretical or conceptual point of view, multiple clocks, historical eras, and point-in-time events very often influence the substantive process being studied (Mayer and Tuma 1990). For example, in demographic studies of divorce, types of clocks, such as age of respondent, time of cohabitation, duration of marriage, ages of children, as well as different phases in the state of the business cycle, or changes in national (divorce) laws are of importance (Blossfeld, De Rose,

Hoem, and Rohwer 1993). With respect to cross-sectional data, such relationships can hardly be studied without making strong untestable assumptions.

Contextual processes at different levels. Social scientists are very often interested in the influences of contextual processes at different aggregation levels (Huinink 1989). Contextual process effects refer to situations where changes in the group contexts themselves influence the dependent variable. For example, career mobility of an individual may be conceptualized as being dependent on changes in resources at the *individual level* (e.g. social background, educational attainment, experience, etc.), the success of the firm in which he/she is employed (e.g. expansion or contraction of the organization) at the *intermediate level*, and changes in the business cycle at the   *macro level* (Blossfeld 1986; DiPrete 1993). Cross-sectional data do not provide an adequate opportunity for the study of such influences at different levels (Mayer and Tuma 1990).

Duration dependence. Another problem of cross-sectional data is that they are *inherently ambiguous with respect to their interpretation at the level of the unit of observation.* Suppose we know that, in West Germany, 30.6 percent of employed women were working part-time in 1970 (Blossfeld and Rohwer in press). At the one extreme, this might be interpreted to imply that *each* employed woman had a 30.6 percent chance of being employed part-time in this year, but on the other, one could infer that 30.6 percent of the employed women always worked part-time and 69.4 percent were full-timers only. In other words, cross-sectional data do not convey information about the *time women spent in these different employment forms.* They are therefore open to quite different substantive interpretations (Heckman and Willis 1977; Flinn and Heckman 1982). In the first case, each woman would be expected to move back and forth between part-time and full-time employment. In the second, there is no mobility between part-time and full-time work, and the estimated percentages describe the proportions of two completely different groups of employed women. From an analytical point of view, it is therefore important to have data about durations in a state. Also, repeated cross-sectional analysis using comparable samples of the same population (e.g. a series of microcensuses or cross-sectional surveys) can only show net change, not the flow of individuals.

Variability in state dependencies. In many situations cross-sectional data are problematic because the rate of change is strongly state dependent and *entries into and exits from these states are highly variable over time* (e.g. over the life course and historical period or across cohorts). For example, it is well known that the roles of wives and mothers (the latter in particular) have been central in women's lives. Therefore, the *family cycle concept* has frequently been used in sociology to describe significant changes in the circumstances that affect the availability of women for paid work outside the home. The basic idea is that there is a set of ordered stages primarily defined by variations in family composition and size that could be described with cross-sectional data. However, this view often leads to the tendency to assume that what happens to different women in various phases in the family cycle at one point in time is similar to the pattern that women experience when they make these transitions in different historical times (which has been called the *"life course fallacy"*). Moreover, there is the well-known problem that individuals and families often fail to conform to the assumption of a single progression through a given number of stages in a predetermined order. At least three reasons for this may exist (Murphy 1991): (1) the chronology of timing of events may not conform to the ideal model, for example childbearing may start before marriage; (2) many stages are not reached, for example, by never-married persons; and (3) the full set of stages may be truncated by events such as death or marital breakdown. Such complex constellations between the family cycle and women's labor force participation could hardly be meaningfully described or studied on the basis of cross-sectional data (see also Blossfeld in press).

Changes in outcomes. Cross-sectional models very often have a *tendency to overpredict change* and consistently *overestimate the importance of explanatory variables* (Davies 1987). The reason for this phenomenon is that these analyses cannot be based on how *changes* in explanatory variables engender *changes* in outcomes. They are only concerned with how *levels* of explanatory variables "explain" an *outcome* at a specific point in time. However, if an outcome at time t (e.g. choice of mode of travel to work in June) is dependent on a previous outcome (e.g. established choice of mode of travel to work), and if both outcomes are positively influenced in the same way by an explanatory variable (e.g. merits of public transport), then the effect of the explanatory variable will reflect both the true positive influence of the explanatory variable on the outcome at time t and a positive spurious element due to that variable acting as a proxy for the omitted earlier outcome (established mode of travel to work). Thus, a cross-sectional analysis of the travel to work choice (e.g. public vs. private transport) would have a tendency to overpredict the effect of policy changes (e.g. fare increases or faster buses) because there is a strong behavioral inertia (Davies 1987).

These examples show that cross-sectional data have many severe inferential limitations for social scientists. Therefore, it is not surprising that causal conclusions based on cross-sectional data have often been radically altered after the processes were studied with longitudinal data (Lieberson 1985).

Longitudinal studies also have a much greater power than cross-sectional ones, both in the estimation of bias from missing data, and in the means for correcting it. This is because in longitudinal studies one often has data from previous points in time, thus enabling the characteristics of non-responders or lost units to be assessed with some precision. It is noteworthy that almost all the substantive knowledge concerning the biases associated with missing data, which all studies must seek to minimize, is derived from longitudinal studies (Medical Research Council 1992).

Although longitudinal data are no panacea, they are obviously more effective in causal analysis and have less inferential limitations (Magnusson, Bergmann, and Törestad 1991; Arminger, Clogg, and Sobel 1995; Clogg and Arminger 1993; Blossfeld 1995, in press; Mayer 1990; Mayer and Tuma 1990). They are indispensable for the study of processes over the life course (of all types of units) and their relation to historical change. Therefore, research designs aimed at a causal understanding of social processes should be based on longitudinal data at the level of the units of analysis.

1.1.2   Panel Data

The temporal data most often available to sociologists are *panel data*, for which the same persons or units are re-interviewed or observed at a series of discrete points in time (Chamberlain 1984; Hsiao 1986; Arminger and Müller 1990; Engel and Reinecke 1994). Figure 1.1.1 shows a four-wave panel in which the family career of the respondent was observed at four different points in time. This means that there is only information on states of the units at pre-determined survey points, but the course of the events between the survey points remains unknown.

Panel data normally contain more information than cross-sectional data, but involve well-known distortions created by the method itself (see, e.g., Magnusson and Bergmann 1990; Hunt 1985).

Panel bias. Respondents often answer many questions differently in the second and later waves than they did the first time; perhaps this is because they are less inhibited, or they mulled over or discussed the issues between questioning dates.

Modification of processes. Panels tend to influence the very phenomena they seek to observe—this changes the natural history of the processes being observed.

Regression to the mean. During the first panel wave, some panel members answer specific questions a bit differently than they normally would, due to chance circumstances at the time of measurement. For example, when a respondent has some problems during the first observation, he/she may perform poorly on some topics, but will report more accurately at the next panel wave. This phenomenon, known as "regression to the mean," can easily be mistaken by researchers for specific trends.

Attrition of the sample. In panel studies the composition of the sample normally diminishes selectively as time goes by. Therefore, what researchers observe in the panel may not give a true view of what has happened to their original sample.

Non-responses and missing data. In a cross-sectional analysis, one can afford to throw out a small number of cases with "non-responses" and "missing data," but in a long-term longitudinal study, throwing out incomplete cases at each round of observations can eventually leave a severely pruned sample having very different characteristics from the original one.

Fallacy of cohort centrism. Very often panel studies are focused on members of a specific cohort (cf., e.g., the British National Child Study). In other words, these panels study respondents that were born in, grew up in, and have lived in a particular segment of history. There is therefore a danger that researchers might assume that what happens to a particular group of people over time reveals general principles of the life course (fallacy of cohort centrism). Many events may simply be specific for that generation.

Fallacy of period centrism. Many panel studies include just a few waves and, therefore, cover only a short period of historical time (cf. the German Socio-Economic Panel, which now covers 10 years). At the time of a particular observation, special conditions may exist and this can result in an individual responding differently than he/she normally would (fallacy of historical period).

Confounded age, period, and cohort effects. In any long-term panel study in sociology, three causal factors—individual's age, cohort, and period effect—are confounded (cf. the Panel Study of Income Dynamics). Analytical techniques are necessary to unconfound these three factors and reveal the role of each. As discussed in more detail later, panel data do have some specific problems unconfounding the three major factors. However, for gaining scientific insights into the interplay of processes governing life courses from birth to death, they appear to be a better approach than applying cross-sections. But a mechanical and atheoretical cohort analysis is a useless exercise, and statistical innovations alone will not solve the age-period-cohort problem (Blossfeld 1986; Mayer and Huinink 1990).

Most of the previously mentioned difficulties concerning panel studies can be dealt with by sophisticated statistical procedures or more panel waves. However, panel data also lead to a series of deficiencies with respect to the estimation of transition rates (Tuma and Hannan 1984): First, there is the problem of "embeddability," which means that there may be difficulties in embedding a matrix of observed transition probabilities within a continuous-time Markov process (Singer and Spilerman 1976a); second, there is the problem that there may be no unique matrix of transition rates describing the data (Singer and Spilerman 1976b); and third, there is the drawback that the observed matrix of transition probabilities may be very sensitive to sampling and measurement error (Tuma and Hannan 1984). Multiple waves with irregular spacing or shorter intervals between waves can reduce these problems. However, as Hannan and Tuma (1979) have noted, the more panel and event history data resemble each other, the less problematic modeling becomes.

Lazarsfeld (1948, 1972) was among the first sociologists to propose panel analysis of discrete variables. In particular, he wanted to find a solution to the problem of ambiguity in causation. He suggested that if one wants to know whether a variable X induces change in another variable Y, or whether Y induces change in X, observations of X and Y at two points in time would be necessary. Lazarsfeld applied this method to dichotomous variables whose time-related structure he analyzed in a resulting sixteenfold table. Later on, Goodman (1973) applied log-linear analysis to such tables. For many years, such a cross-lagged panel analysis for qualitative and quantitative variables (Campbell and Stanley 1963; Shingles 1976) was considered to be a powerful quasi-experimental method of making causal inferences. It was also extended to multiwave-multivariable panels to study more complex path models with structural-equation models (Jöreskog and Sörbom 1993). However, it appears that the strength of the panel design for causal inference was hugely exaggerated (Davis 1978). Causal inferences in panel approaches are much more complicated than has been generally realized. Several reasons are responsible for this:

Time until the effect starts to occur. It is important to realize that the role of time in causal explanations does not only lie in specifying a *temporal order* in which the effect follows the cause in time. It additionally implies that a *temporal interval* is necessary for the cause to have an impact (Kelly and McGrath 1988). In other words, if the cause has to precede the effect in time, it takes some finite amount of time for the cause to produce the effect. The time interval may be very short or very long, but can never be zero or infinity (Kelly and McGrath 1988). Some effects take place almost instantaneously. For example, if the effect occurs at microsecond intervals, then the process must be observed in these small time units to uncover causal relations. However, some effects may occur in a time interval too small to be measured by any given methods, so that cause and effect *seem to occur* at the same point in time. Apparent simultaneity is often the case in those social science applications where basic observation intervals are relatively crude (e.g. days, months, or even years), such as, for example, yearly data about first marriage and first childbirth (Blossfeld, Manting, and Rohwer 1993). For these parallel processes, the events "first marriage" and "first childbirth" may be functionally interdependent, but whether these two events are observed simultaneously or successively depends on the degree of temporal refinement of the scale used in making the observations. Other effects need a long time until they start to occur. Thus, there is a *delay* or *lag* between cause and effect that must be specified in an appropriate causal analysis. However, in most of the current sociological theories and interpretations of research findings this interval is left unspecified. In most cases, at least implicitly, researchers assume that the effect takes place almost immediately. Of course, if this is the case, then there seems to be no need for theoretical statements about the time course of causal effects. A single measurement of the effect at some point in time after a cause has been imposed might be sufficient for catching it (see Figure 1.1.2a). However, if there is a reason to assume that there is a lag between cause and effect, then a single measurement of the outcome is inadequate for describing the process (see Figure 1.1.2b); and the interpretation arrived at on the basis of that single measurement will be a function of the point in time chosen to measure the effect.

Thus, a *restrictive assumption of panel designs* is that either cause and effect occur almost simultaneously, or the interval between observations is of approximately the same length as the true causal lag. The greater the discrepancy, the greater the likelihood that the panel analysis will fail to discover the true causal process. Thus, as expressed by Davis (1978), if one does not know the causal lag exactly, panel analysis is not of much utility to establish causal direction or time sequencing of causal effects. Unfortunately, we rarely, if ever, have enough information about the detailed structure of a social process to specify the true lag precisely.

Temporal shapes of the unfolding effect. In addition to the question of how long the delay between the timing of the cause and the beginning of the unfolding of the effect is, there might be *different shapes of how the effect develops in time*. While the problem of time-lags is widely recognized in social science literature, there is almost no information with respect to the temporal shapes of effects (Kelly and McGrath 1988). Social scientists seem to be quite ignorant with respect to the fact that causal effects could be highly time-dependent, too. The panels of Figure 1.1.2 illustrate several possible shapes these effects may trace over time. In Figure 1.1.2a, there is an almost all-at-once change that is then maintained; in Figure 1.1.2b, the effect occurs with some lengthy time-lag and is then time-invariant; in Figure 1.1.2c, the effect starts almost immediately and then gradually increases; in Figure 1.1.2d, there is an almost all-at-once increase, which reaches a maximum after some time and then decreases; finally, in Figure 1.1.2e, a cyclical effect pattern over time is described.

If the effect increases or decreases monotonically or linearly, oscillates in cycles, or shows any other complicated time-related pattern, then the strength of the observed effect is dependent on the timing of the panel waves. A panel design might be particularly problematic if there are non-monotonic cycles of the effect because totally opposite conclusions about the effects of the explanatory variable can be arrived at, depending on whether the panel places measurement points at a peak or at an ebb in the curve (see Figures 1.1.2d and 1.1.2e).

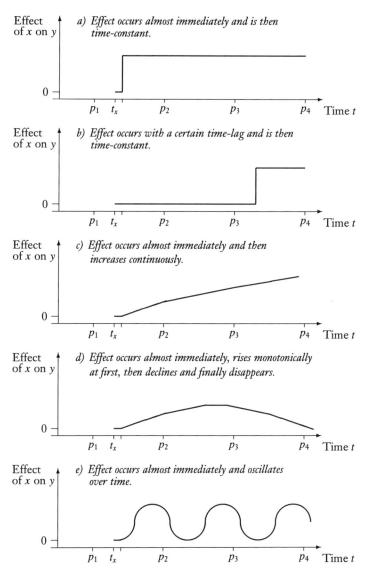

Figure 1.1.2 Different temporal shapes of how a change in a variable x, occurring at point in time t_x, effects a change in a variable y.

Reciprocal effects with different time-paths. In cases of reciprocal causality, additional problems will arise if the time structure of the effects of X_1 on X_2 and of X_2 on X_1 are different with respect to lags and shapes. In these situations, a panel design might turn out to be completely useless for those wishing to detect such time-related recursive relationships.

Observational data and timing of measurement of explanatory variables. Most sociological research is based on observational data, meaning that manipulation of the timing of the independent variables is generally not possible. For example, if the researcher is going to study the effects of job mobility on marriage behavior, it is impossible to force respondents to change their jobs, say, at the time of the first panel wave. Thus, the longer the interval between panel waves, the more uncertainty there will be regarding the exact point in time when an individual moved to another job and therefore about the *point we evaluate in the time-path of the effect* (Coleman 1981). The situation may be even more problematic if changes in independent variables are repeatable and several changes are possible between two successive panel waves, as might be the case with job shifts observed in yearly intervals (cf. Sandefur and Tuma 1987). In such panel studies, even the causal order of explanatory and dependent events may become ambiguous.

Observational data and the timing of control variables. Observational studies take place in natural settings and, therefore, offer little control over changes in other important variables and their timing. If these influences change arbitrarily and have time-related effect patterns, then panel studies are useless in disentangling the effect of interest from time-dependent effects of other parallel exogenous processes.

Continuous changes of explanatory and control variables. In observational studies, explanatory and control variables may not only change stepwise from one state to another, but can often *change continuously* over time. For example, individuals continuously change age, constantly acquire general labor force experience or job-specific human capital if they are employed (Blossfeld and Huinink 1991), are exposed to continuously changing historical conditions (Blossfeld 1986), are steadily changing their social relationships in marital or consensual unions (Blossfeld, De Rose, Hoem, and Rohwer 1993), and so on. Even in cases where these continuous changes are not connected with lags or time-related effect patterns, there are deficiencies of panel data concerning their capabilities of detecting time dependence in substantive processes. This is why panel analysis can often not appropriately identify age, period, and cohort effects (Blossfeld 1986).

Therefore, the use of panel data causes an identification problem due to omitted factors whose effects are summarized in a disturbance term. These factors are not stable over time, which means that the disturbance term cannot be uncorrelated with the explanatory variables. Panel analysis therefore critically depends on solutions to the problem of autocorrelation. This problem can be reasonably well tackled by increasing the number of panel waves and modifying their spacing. Panel analysis is particularly sensitive to the *length of the time intervals between waves relative to the speed of the process* (Coleman 1981). They can be too short, so that too few events will be observed, or too long, so that it is difficult to establish a time-order between events (Sandefur and Tuma 1987). A major advantage of the continuous-time observation design in event history analysis is therefore that it makes the timing between waves irrelevant (Coleman 1968).

1.1.3 Event History Data

For many processes in the social sciences, a continuous measurement of qualitative variables seems to be the only adequate method of assessing empirical change. This is achieved by utilizing an *event oriented observation design*, which records all the changes in qualitative variables and their timing. As shown in Figure 1.1.1, the major advantage of event history data is that they provide the *most complete data possible on changes in qualitative variables* that may occur at any point in time. The observation of events therefore provides an attractive alternative to the observation of states for social scientists.

Event history data, mostly *collected retrospectively* via *life history studies*, cover the whole life course of individuals. An example for such a study is the German Life History Study (GLHS; Mayer and Brückner 1989). Retrospective studies have the advantage of normally being *cheaper* to collect than panel data. They are also systematically *coded to one framework of codes and meanings* (Dex 1991). But retrospective (in contrast to prospective) studies suffer from several limitations that have been increasingly acknowledged (Medical Research Council 1992):

Non-factual data. It is well known that retrospective questions concerning motivational, attitudinal, cognitive, or affective states are particularly problematic because the respondents can hardly recall the timing of changes in these states accurately (Hannan and Tuma 1979). This type of data is not verifiable even in principle because these states exist only in the minds of the respondents and are only directly accessible, if at all, to the respondent concerned (Sudman and Bradburn 1986). For these non-factual data, panel studies have the advantage of being able to repeatedly record current states of the same individual over time. Thus, for studies aiming to model the relationship between attitudes and behavior over time, panel observations of attitudinal states, combined with retrospective information on behavioral events since the last sweep, appear to be an appropriate design.

Recall problems with regard to behavior or facts. Behavioral or factual questions ask the respondents about characteristics, things they have done, or things that have happened to them, which in principle are verifiable by an external observer. Most surveys (cross-sectional, panel, or event oriented) elicit retrospective information on behavior or facts (e.g. by asking people about their education, social origin, etc.), so that the disadvantages of retrospection are only a matter of degree. However, event history studies are particularly ambitious (see Mayer and Brückner 1989). They try to collect continuous records of qualitative variables that have a high potential for bias because of their strong reliance on memory. However, research on the accuracy of retrospective data shows that individuals' marital and fertility histories, family characteristics and education, health service usage, and employment history can be collected to a reasonable degree of accuracy. A very good overview concerning the kinds of data that can be retrospectively collected, the factors affecting recall accuracy, and the methods improving recall has been presented by Dex (1991).

Unknown factors. Retrospective designs cannot be used to study factors involving variables that are not known to the respondent (e.g. emotional and behavioral problems when the respondent was a child). In such cases, panel studies are indispensable (Medical Research Council 1992).

Limited capacity. There is a limit to respondents' tolerance for the amount of data that can be collected on one occasion (Medical Research Council 1992). A carefully corsetted panel design can therefore provide a broader coverage of variables (if these are not unduly influenced by variations at the time of assessment).

Only survivors. Due to their nature, retrospective studies must be based on survivors. Thus, those subjects who have died or migrated from the geographical area under study will necessarily be omitted. If either is related to the process (as often may be the case), biases will arise. This problem is particularly important for retrospective studies involving a broad range of birth cohorts, like the German Life History Study (GLHS) or international migration studies (Blossfeld 1987a).

Misrepresentation of specific populations. Retrospective studies also systematically misrepresent specific populations. For example, Duncan (1966) has shown that if men are asked about their fathers, men from earlier generations who had no sons, or whose sons died or emigrated are not represented in a retrospective father-son mobility table.

To avoid the aforementioned problems concerning retrospective event history data, a mixed design employing a follow-up (or "catch-up") and a follow-back strategy appears to combine the strengths of panel designs with the virtues of retrospective studies. Therefore, in modern panel studies, event histories are collected retrospectively for the period before the panel started and between the successive panel waves. Sometimes, complete administrative records also contain time-related information about events in the past. All of these procedures (retrospective, combined follow-up and back-up, or available registers) offer a comparatively superior opportunity for modeling social processes, regardless of which method is selected.

One aim of our book is to show that event history models are a useful approach to uncovering causal relationships or mapping out a system of causal relations. As becomes apparent later on in the book, event history models are linked very naturally to a causal understanding of social processes because they relate change in future outcomes to conditions in the past and try to predict future changes on the basis of past observations (Aalen 1987).

1.2 Event History Analysis and Causal Modeling

The investigation of causal relationships is an important but difficult scientific endeavor. As shown earlier, opportunities for assessing causal inferences vary strongly with the type of observation available to the sociologist. This is because they determine *the extent* to which the researcher is forced to make *untested* assumptions. In this section, we discuss the role of time in causal inferences, and also show how the idea of causal relations can be represented in the statistical concepts of event history analysis.

Correlation and Causation

To begin with, statements about causation should be distinguished from statements about association. In making correlational inferences, one can be satisfied to observe how the values of one variable are associated with the values of other variables over the population under study and, perhaps, over time. In this context, time is only important insofar as it determines the population under analysis or specifies the operational meaning of a particular variable (Holland 1986). Statements about associations describe what has happened. They are quite different from causal statements designed to say something about how events are produced or conditioned by other events.

Sometimes social scientists argue that because the units of sociological analysis continuously learn and change and involve actors with goals and beliefs, sociology can at best only provide systematic descriptions of phenomena at various points in history. This position is based on the view that causal statements about events are only possible if they are regulated by "eternal," time-less laws (Kelly and McGrath 1988). Of course, the assumption that such laws can be established with regard to social processes can reasonably be disputed. However, we are not forced to accept a simple contrast: either describing contingent events or assuming "eternal" laws. Many social phenomena show *systematic temporal variations* and *patterned regularities* under specific conditions that themselves are a legitimate focus of our efforts to understand social change (Kelly and McGrath 1988). Thus, sociology can do more than just describe the social world. This book therefore emphasizes the usefulness of techniques of event history modeling as "new" approaches to the investigation of causal explanations.[13]

---

[13] We speak of a "new" approach just to emphasize the contrast to traditional "causal analysis"

Causal Mechanisms and Substantive Theory

The identification of causal mechanisms has been one of the classic concerns in sociology. Causal statements are made to explain the occurrence of events, to understand why particular events happen, and to make predictions when the situation changes (Marini and Singer 1988). Although sociologists sometimes seem to be opposed to using the word *cause*, they are far less reluctant to apply very similar words like *force*, *agency*, or *control*, when trying to understand social phenomena.

There is consensus in the fact that causal inferences cannot simply and directly be made from empirical data, regardless of whether they are collected through ingenious research designs or summarized by particularly advanced statistical models. Thus, using event history observation plans and event history analysis models per se will not allow us to prove causality, as is the case for all other statistical techniques. However, as already shown in section 1.1, event-oriented observation designs offer richer information and, as we try to demonstrate in this book, event history models provide more appropriate techniques for exploring causal relations.

It seems useful to treat causality as being a property of theoretical statements rather than the empirical world itself (Goldthorpe 1994). In sociology, causal statements are based primarily on substantive hypotheses that the researcher develops about the social world. In this sense, causal inference is theoretically driven (Freedman 1991) and it will always reflect the changing state of sociological knowledge in a field.[14] Of course, descriptive statements are also dependent on theoretical views guiding the selection processes and providing the categories underlying every description. The crucial point, however, is that causal statements need a theoretical argument specifying the particular mechanism of how a cause produces an effect or, more generally, in which way interdependent forces affect each other in a given setting over time.

Therefore, the important task of event history modeling is not to demonstrate causal processes directly, but to establish relevant empirical evidence that can serve as a link in a chain of reasoning about causal mechanisms (Goldthorpe 1994). In this respect, event history models might be particularly helpful instruments because they allow a time-related empirical representation of the structure of causal arguments.

---

based on structural equation models, which are basically time-less models.   See the discussion in Bollen (1989), Campbell, Mutran, and Parker (1987), or Faulbaum and Bentler (1994). Structural equation models normally fit a deterministic structure across the observed points in time and do not distinguish between a completed past, the present, and a conditionally open future.

[14] Causal relations are always identified against the background of some field, and specification of a field is critical to the identification of an observed relation (Marini and Singer 1988).

Attributes, Causes, and Time-Constant Variables

Holland (1986) tried to establish some links between causal inference and statistical modeling. In particular, he emphasized that for a conception of causality it is essential that each unit of a population must be exposable to any of the various levels of a cause, at least hypothetically. He argued, for example, that the schooling a student receives can be a cause of the student's performance on a test, whereas the student's race or sex cannot. In the former case it seems possible to contemplate measuring the causal effect, whereas in the latter cases, where we have the enduring attributes of a student, all that can be discussed is association (see also Yamaguchi 1991).

We agree with Holland that it is essential for causal statements to imply counterfactual reasoning: *if* the cause *had been* different, there *would have been* another outcome, at least with a certain probability. In this sense, counterfactual statements reflect imagined situations. It is not always clear, however, which characteristics of a situation can sensibly be assumed to be variable (i.e. can be used in counterfactual reasoning) and which characteristics should be regarded as fixed. At least to some degree, the distinction depends on the field of investigation. For example, from a sociological point of view what is important with regard to sex is not the biological attributes per se, but the social meaning attached to these attributes. The social meaning of these attributes can change regardless of whether their biological basis changes or not. For example, societal rules might change to create more equality between the races or sexes. We therefore think that in sociological applications counterfactuals can also be meaningfully applied to such attributes. They can be represented as *time-constant* "variables" in statistical models to investigate their possible impact on some outcome to be explained. It is, however, important to be quite explicit about the sociological meaning of causal statements that involve references to biological or ethnic attributes. There is, for example, no eternal law connecting gender and/or race with wage differentials. But probably there are *social* mechanisms that connect gender and ethnic differences with different opportunities in the labor market.

Causes and Time-Dependent Variables

The meaning of the counterfactual reasoning of causal statements is that causes are states that could be different from what they actually are. However, the consequences of conditions that could be different from their actual state are obviously not observable.[15] To find an empirical approach to causal statements, the researcher must look at conditions that actually do change in time. These changes are events. More formally, an event is a change in a variable, and

---

[15] Holland (1986) called this "the fundamental problem of causal inference." It means that it is simply impossible to observe the effect that *would have* happened on the same unit of analysis, *if* it were exposed to another condition at the same time.

this change must happen at a specific point in time. This implies that the most obvious empirical representation of causes is in terms of variables that can change their states over time. In chapter 6, we see that this statement is linked very naturally with the concept of *time-dependent covariates*. The role of a time-dependent covariate in event history models is to indicate that a (qualitative or metric) causal factor has changed its state at a specific time and that the unit under study is exposed to another causal condition. For example, in the case of gender the causal events might be the steps in the acquisition of gender roles over the life course or the exposure to sex-specific opportunities in the labor market at a specific historical time. Thus, a time-constant variable "gender" should ideally be replaced in an empirical analysis by time-changing events assumed to produce sex-specific differences in the life history of men and women. Of course, in empirical research that is not always possible, so one very often has to rely on time-constant "variables" as well. However, it is important to recognize that for these variables the implied *longitudinal causal relation* is not examined. For example, if we observe an association among people with different levels of educational attainment and their job opportunities, then we can normally draw the conclusion that changes in job opportunities are a result of changes in educational attainment level. The implied idea is the following: If we started having people with the lowest educational attainment level and followed them over the life course, they would presumably differ in their rates to attaining higher levels of educational attainment and this would produce changes in job opportunities. Whether this would be the case for *each* individual is not very clear from a study that is based on people with *different* levels of educational attainment. In particular, one would expect that the causal relationship between education and job opportunities would radically be altered if all people acquired a higher (or the highest) level of educational attainment.[16] Thus, the two statements—the first about associations across different members of a population and the second about dependencies in the life course for each individual member of the population—are quite different; one type of statement can be empirically true while the other one can be empirically false. Therefore, statements of the first type cannot be regarded as substitutes for statements of the second type. However, since all causal propositions have consequences for longitudinal change (see Lieberson 1985), only time-changing variables provide the most convincing empirical evidence of causal relations.[17]

---

[16] A longitudinal approach would provide, however, the opportunity to study these kinds of changes in the causal relationships over time.

[17] There is also another aspect that is important here (see Lieberson 1985): Causal relationships can be symmetric or asymmetric. In examining the causal influence of a change in a variable X on a change in a dependent variable Y, one has to consider whether shifts to a given value of X from either direction have the same consequences for Y. For example, rarely do researchers consider whether an upward shift on the prestige scale, say from 20 to 40, will lead to a different outcome of Y (say family decisions) than would a downward shift of X from 60 to 40. In other words, most researchers assume symmetry. However, even if a change is reversible, the causal *process* may not

Time Order and Causal Effects

We can summarize our view of causal statements in the following way:

$$\Delta X_t \longrightarrow \Delta Y_{t'}$$

meaning that a *change* in variable X_t at time t is a cause of a *change* in variable $Y_{t'}$ at a later point in time, t'. It is not implied, of course, that X_t is the only cause that might affect $Y_{t'}$. So we sometimes speak of *causal conditions* to stress that there might be, and normally is, a quite complex set of causes.[18]

Thus, if causal statements are studied empirically, they must intrinsically be related to time. There are three important aspects. First, to speak of a change in variables necessarily implies reference to a time axis. We need at least two points in time to observe that a variable has changed its value. Of course, at least approximately, we can say that a variable has changed its value *at a specific point in time*.[19] Therefore, we use the symbols ΔX_t and ΔY_t to refer to changes in the values of the time-dependent variable X_t and the state variable Y_t at time t. This leads to the important point that causal statements relate *changes* in two (or more) variables.

Second, there is a time ordering between causes and effects. The cause must *precede* the effect in time: $t < t'$, in the formal representation given above. This seems to be generally accepted.[20] As an implication, there must be a *temporal interval* between the change in a variable representing a cause and a change in the variable representing a corresponding effect. This time interval may be *very short* or *very long*, but can never be *zero* or *infinity* (Kelly and McGrath 1988). Thus, *the cause and its effect logically cannot occur at the same point in time*. Any appropriate empirical representation of causal effects in a statistical model must

---

be. The question is: If a change in a variable X causes a change in another one, Y, what happens to Y if X returns to its earlier level? "Assuming everything else is constant, a process is *reversible*, if the level of Y also returns to its initial condition; a process is irreversible if Y does not return to its earlier level. Observe that it is the *process*—not the *event*—that is being described as reversible or irreversible" (Lieberson 1985:66).

[18] It is important to note here that the effect of a variable X is always measured relative to other causes. A conjunctive plurality of causes occurs if various factors must be jointly present to produce an effect. Disjunctive plurality of causes, on the other hand, occurs if the effect is produced by each of several factors alone, and the joint occurrence of two or more factors does not alter the effect (see the extensive discussion in Marini and Singer 1988).

[19] Statements like this implicitly refer to some specification of "point in time." The meaning normally depends on the kind of events that are to be described, for instance, a marriage, the birth of a child, or to become unemployed. In this book, we always assume a continuous time axis for purposes of mathematical modeling. This should however be understood as an idealized way of representing social time. We are using mathematical concepts to speak about social reality, so we disregard the dispute about whether time *is* "continuous" (in the mathematical sense of this word) or not.

[20] See, for instance, the discussion in Eells (1991, Ch. 5).

therefore take into account that there may be various delays or lags between the events assumed to be causes and the unfolding of their effects.

This immediately leads to a third point. There may be a variety of different temporal shapes (functional forms) in which the causal effect Y_t unfolds over time. Some of these possibilities have been depicted in Figure 1.1.2. Thus, an appropriate understanding of causal relations between variables should take into account that the causal relationship itself may change over time. This seems particularly important in sociological applications of causal reasoning. In these applications we generally cannot rely on the assumption of eternal, time-less laws, but have to recognize that the causal mechanisms may change during the development of social processes.

Actors and Probabilistic Causal Relations

It seems agreed that social phenomena are always directly or indirectly based on actions of individuals. This clearly separates the social from the natural sciences. Sociology therefore does not deal with associations among variables per se, but with variables that are associated via acting people. There are at least three consequences for causal relations. First, in methodological terms, this means that if individuals relate causes and effects through their actions, then research on social processes should at best be based *on individual longitudinal data* (Coleman and Hao 1989; Coleman 1990). This is why life history data on individuals, and not aggregated longitudinal data, provide the most appropriate information for the analyses of social processes. Only with these data can one trace the courses of action at the level of each individual over time. Second, in theoretical terms, it means that the explaining or understanding of social processes requires a time-related specification of (1) the past and present conditions under which people act,[21] (2) the many and possibly conflicting goals that they pursue at the present time, (3) the beliefs and expectations guiding the behavior, and (4) the actions that probably will follow in the future.[22] Third, if it is people who are doing the acting, then causal inference must also take into account the free will of individuals. This introduces an essential element of indeterminacy into causal inferences. This means that in sociology we can only reasonably account for and model the generality but not the determinacy

---

[21] These conditions are, of course, heavily molded by social structural regularities in the past and the present. Sociology must always be a historical discipline (Goldthorpe 1991).

[22] Sometimes it is argued that, because human actors act intentionally and behavior is goal-oriented, the intentions or motives of actors to bring about some effect in the future causes the actor to behave in a specific way in the present (Marini and Singer 1988). This does not however contradict a causal view. One simply has to distinguish intentions, motives, or plans as they occur in the present from their impact on the behavior that follows their formation temporally, and from the final result, as an outcome of the behavior. An expectation about a future state of affairs should clearly be distinguished from what eventually happens in the future. Therefore, the fact that social agents can behave intentionally, based on expectations, does not reverse the time order underlying our causal statements.

of behavior. The aim of substantive and statistical models must therefore be to capture common elements in the behavior of people, or patterns of action that recur in many cases (Goldthorpe 1994). This means that in sociological applications randomness has to enter as a defining characteristic of causal models. We can only hope to make sensible causal statements about how a given (or hypothesized) change in variable X_t in the past affects the probability of a change in variable $Y_{t'}$ in the future. Correspondingly, the basic causal relation becomes

$$\Delta X_t \longrightarrow \Delta \Pr(\Delta Y_{t'}) \quad t < t' \tag{1.1}$$

This means that a change in the time-dependent covariate X_t will *change the probability* that the dependent variable $Y_{t'}$ will change in the future ($t' > t$). In sociology, this interpretation seems more appropriate than the traditional deterministic approach. The essential difference is not that our knowledge about causes is insufficient because it only allows probabilistic statements, but that *the causal effect to be explained is a probability*. Thus, probability in this context is not just a technical term anymore, but is considered as a theoretical one: it is the propensity of social agents to change their behavior.

Causal Statements and Limited Empirical Observations

A quite different type of randomness related to making inferences occurs if causal statements are applied to real-world situations in the social sciences. There are at least four additional reasons to expect further randomness in empirical studies. These are basically the same ones that occur in deterministic approaches and are well known from traditional regression modeling (Lieberson 1991). The first one is *measurement error*, a serious problem in empirical social research, which means that the observed data deviate somewhat from the predicted pattern without invalidating the causal proposition. The second reason is particularly important in the case of non-experimental data. It is often the case that *complex multivariate causal relations* operate in the social world. Thus, a given outcome can occur because of the presence of more than one influencing factor. Moreover, it may also not occur at times because the impact of one independent variable is outweighed by other influences working in the opposite direction. In these situations, the observed influence of the cause is only approximate, unless one can control for the other important factors. The third motive is that sociologists often do *not know* or are *not able to measure* all of the important factors. Thus, social scientists have to relinquish the idea of a complete measurement of causal effects, even if they would like to make a deterministic proposition. Finally, sometimes *chance* affects observed outcomes in the social world. It is not important here to decide whether chance per se exists or whether it is only a surrogate for the poor state of our knowledge of additional influences and/or inadequate measurement.

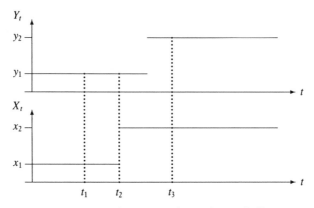

Figure 1.2.1 Observation of a simple causal effect.

In summary, these problems imply that social scientists can only hope to make empirical statements with a probabilistic character. This situation can lead to problems, as is discussed in chapter 10. Without strong assumptions about missing information and errors in the available data, it is generally not possible to find definite statements about causal relations (Arminger 1990).

A Simplistic Conception of Causal Relations

At this point it is important to stress that the concept of causal relation is a rather special abstraction implying a time-related structure that does not immediately follow from our sensory impressions. Consider the following example in Figure 1.2.1 where we characterize the necessary time-related observations of a unit being affected by a causal effect. This figure shows that an empirical representation of the most simple causal effect (i.e. (1) where the condition X_t changes (from one state $X_{t_1} = x_1$ to another one $X_{t_2} = x_2$) and (2) is then constant afterwards, (3) the change in Y_t (from $Y_{t_2} = y_1$ to $Y_{t_3} = y_2$) takes place almost instantaneously and (4) is then also time-constant afterwards) needs at least three points in time where the researcher must note the states of the independent and dependent variables, respectively.[23] This is because, if we assume that a change in the independent variable X_t has taken place at t_2, then, to be able to fix the particular change in the condition in the past, we need to know the state of the independent variable X_t at an earlier time, t_1 (see Figure 1.2.1). For the dependent variable Y_t we need an observation before the effect has started to occur. Assuming everything else is constant, this observation can be made, at the latest at point t_2, because the effect has to *follow* the cause in time. To evaluate whether the hypothesized effect has indeed taken place at a later

---

[23] This example is instructive because Lazarsfeld (1948, 1972) and many others after him have argued that for causal inferences two observations of the units would be sufficient.

time, t_3, we must again note the state of the dependent variable Y_t. Thus, a *simplistic representation of a causal effect* exists when we compare the change in the observations for the independent variable in the past and the present with the change in the observations for the dependent variable in the present and in the future and link both changes with a substantive argument.[24]

However, as already demonstrated in section 1.1, this is only a simple and fairly unrealistic example of a causal effect. In the case of observational data in the social sciences, where there are many (qualitative and metric) causal variables that might change their values at any point in time, when their causal effects might have various delays and different shapes in time (see Figure 1.1.2), then the quantity of the observed causal effect as shown in Figure 1.2.1 will strongly depend on when the measurements at the three points in time are taken.

Thus, what can we say about the causal effect(s) at any given point in time if the situation is more complex? A paradox occurs: the concept of causal effect depends intrinsically on comparisons between changes in both the independent and dependent variables in at least three points in time. Yet the concept of causal effect should itself reflect a state of a unit of observation at any point in time as being an appropriate one in real empirical situations. Thus, what is still needed in our discussion is a concept that represents the quantity of the causal effect at any point in time.

Causal Effects and Changes in Transition Rates

If the dependent variable is discrete and can change its state at any time, then the transition rate framework offers a time-point-related representation for the causal effect. We briefly want to develop this idea.

Let us first start with the dependent variable, Y_t, and its changes in the future (as a consequence of a change in a causal factor). In particular, we are interested in changes of states occupied by the units of analysis. The state space is assumed to be discrete, and so the possible changes are discrete. We assume that a unit enters at time t_0 into the (origin) state j, that is $Y_{t_0} = j$. The basic form of change to be explained in the transition rate framework is the probability of a change in Y_t from an origin state j to a destination state k (while $t > t_0$).

Now, we need a concept that allows describing the development of the process at every point in time, while the process is going on, and that, for its definition, only relies on information about the past development of the process. The crucial concept that can be used for this purpose is the *transition rate*. To define this concept, let us first introduce a random variable T to represent the duration, beginning at t_0, until a change in the dependent variable, that is a transition from (origin) state j to (destination) state k, occurs. To simplify the

---

[24] Indeed such a simplistic idea of the causal effect is the basis of all panel designs, as shown in section 1.1.

notation we will assume that $t_0 = 0$. Then, the following probability can be defined:

$$\Pr(t \leq T < t' \mid T \geq t) \quad t < t' \tag{1.2}$$

This is the probability that an event occurs in the time interval from t to t', given that no event (transition) has occurred before, that is, in the interval from 0 to t. This probability is well defined and obviously well suited to describe the temporal evolution of the process. The definition refers to each point in time while the process is evolving, and thereby can express the idea of change during its development. Also, the definition only relies on information about the past of the process, what has happened up to the present point in time, t. Therefore, the concept defined in (1.2) can sensibly be used to describe the process before it has finished for all individuals in the population. Assume that we know the probabilities defined in (1.2) for all points in time up to a certain point t^*. Then we have a description of the process up to this point, and this description is possible without knowing how the process will develop in the future (i.e. for $t > t^*$).

Because our mathematical model is based on a continuous-time axis, one can in the expression (1.2) let $t' - t$ approach zero. However, as the length of the time interval approaches zero, the concept of change in the dependent variable would simply disappear because the probability that a change takes place in an interval of zero length is zero:

$$\lim_{t' \to t} \Pr(t \leq T < t' \mid T \geq t) = 0$$

To avoid this, we regard the *ratio* of the transition probability to the length of the time interval to represent the probability of future changes in the dependent variable per unit of time (Coleman 1968), that is, we consider

$$\Pr(t \leq T < t' \mid T \geq t) \big/ (t' - t)$$

This allows us to define the limit

$$r(t) = \lim_{t' \to t} \frac{\Pr(t \leq T < t' \mid T \geq t)}{t' - t} \tag{1.3}$$

and we arrive at the central concept of the *transition rate*. Because of the various origins of transition rate framework in the different disciplines, the transition rate   is also called the *hazard rate, intensity rate, failure rate, transition intensity, risk function*, or *mortality rate*.

The transition rate concept obviously provides the possibility of giving a local, time-related description of how the process (defined by a single episode) evolves over time. We can interpret $r(t)$ as the *propensity* to change the state, from origin j to destination k, at t. But one should note that this propensity is defined in relation to a risk set, the risk set at t (i.e. the set of individuals who can experience the event because they have not already had the event before t).

Having introduced the basic concept of a transition rate, we can finally formulate our basic modeling approach. The preliminary description in (1.1) can now be restated in a somewhat more precise form as

$$r(t) = g(t, x) \tag{1.4}$$

This is the basic form of a transition rate model. The central idea is to make the transition rate, which describes a process evolving in time, dependent on time and on a set of covariates, x. Obviously, we also need the "variable" time (t) on the right-hand side of the model equation. However, it must be stressed that a sensible causal relation can only be assumed for the dependency of the transition rate on the covariates. The causal reasoning underlying the modeling approach (1.4) is

$$\Delta X_t \longrightarrow \Delta r(t') \quad t < t'$$

As a causal effect, the changes in some covariates in the past may lead to changes in the transition rate in the future, which in turn describe the propensity that the units under study will change in some presupposed state space. As discussed earlier, this causal interpretation requires that we take the temporal order in which the process evolves very seriously. At any given point in time, t, the transition rate $r(t)$ can be made dependent on conditions that happened to occur in the past (i.e. before t), but not on what is the case *at t* or in the future after t.

There are many possibilities to specify the functional relationship $g(.)$ in (1.4). Some of these possibilities are discussed extensively in subsequent chapters. We particularly discuss how the formal dependence of the transition rate on time, t, can be interpreted from a causal point of view in chapters 6 and 7.

It is sometimes argued that sociologists should give up the causal analytical point of view in favor of a systems view because the operation of causal forces is mutually interdependent and variables change each other more or less simultaneously in many systems (Marini and Singer 1988). However, even in systems of interdependent processes time does not run backwards, and change in one of the interdependent variables will take (at least a small amount of) time to produce a change in another one. Thus, in systems of variables there cannot be any simultaneity of causes and their effects. This allows us to demonstrate in chapter 6 that a causal approach to interdependent systems is possible with the help of the transition rate concept. In other words, the systems view is not a substitute for a proper causal approach in our field (Kelly and McGrath 1988).

Additional Statistical Concepts

Because the transition rate is indeed an abstraction, it is necessary to relate it back to quantities that are directly observable, that is, to frequencies of state occupancies at particular points in time. To support such inferences, some additional statistical concepts are useful.

We begin with the basic concept to describe the probability distribution of T, that is, the distribution function

$$F(t) = \Pr(T \le t)$$

It is the probability that the episode's duration is less than or equal to t, or put otherwise, the probability that an event happens in the time interval from 0 to t. Equivalently, we can describe the probability distribution of T by a *survivor function*, defined by

$$G(t) = 1 - F(t) = \Pr(T > t)$$

This is the probability that the episode's duration is at least t, that the event by which the current episode comes to an end occurs later than t.

Both concepts, the distribution function and the survivor function, are mathematically equivalent. However, in describing event histories one generally prefers the survivor function because it allows for a more intuitive description. We can imagine a population of individuals (or other units of analysis) all beginning a certain episode with origin state j at the same point in time $t = 0$. Then, as time goes on, events occur (i.e. individuals leave the given origin state). Exactly this process is described by the survivor function. If N is the size of the population at $t = 0$, then $N \cdot G(t)$ is the number of individuals who have not yet left the origin state up to t. Sometimes this is called the "risk set" (i.e. the set of individuals who remain exposed to the "risk" of experiencing the event that ends the current episode).

Finally, because T is a continuous random variable, its distribution can also be described by a density function, $f(t)$, which is related to the distribution function by

$$F(t) = \int_0^t f(\tau) \, d\tau$$

The meaning of the density function is similar to (1.3). In fact, we can write its definition in the following way:

$$f(t) = \lim_{t' \to t} \frac{F(t') - F(t)}{t' - t} = \lim_{t' \to t} \frac{\Pr(t \le T < t')}{t' - t}$$

On the right-hand side, before going to the limit, we have the probability that the event occurs in the time interval from t to t'. $f(t)$ is approximately proportional to this probability, if the time interval becomes very short.

Distribution function, survivor function, and density function are quite familiar concepts to describe the probability distribution of a random variable. However, these functions do not make explicit that our random variable T has a quite specific meaning: the duration of an episode. Our mathematical concepts are intended to describe a *process evolving in time*. In defining such a process, we refer to a population of individuals (or other units of analysis) who are seen as "bearing" the process. These individuals evolve over time, and their behavior generates the process. With respect to these individuals, and while the process is evolving, there is always a distinction in past, present, and future. This is particularly important for a causal view of the process. The past conditions the present, and what happens in the present shapes the future. The question is how these temporal aspects of the process can be made explicit in our concepts to describe the process. As we have seen, the development of an episode can be represented by a random variable T, and statistics offers familiar concepts to describe the distribution of the variable. However, these concepts have hidden the temporal nature of the process. This becomes clear if we ask the question, *when* does a description of the distribution of T become available? At the earliest, this is when the current episode has ended for all individuals of the population. Therefore, although a description of the distribution of T provides a description of the process *as it had evolved*, to make a causal assessment of how the process evolves, we need a quite different description. We need a concept that allows describing the development of the process at every point in time, while the process is going on, and that, for its definition, only relies on information about the past development of the process.

Now we can investigate the relationship with the transition rate again. By definition, we have

$$\Pr(t \leq T < t' \mid T \geq t) = \frac{\Pr(t \leq T < t')}{\Pr(T \geq t)}$$

Therefore, definition (1.3) can also be written as

$$r(t) = \lim_{t' \to t} \frac{\Pr(t \leq T < t')}{t' - t} \frac{1}{\Pr(T \geq t)} = \frac{f(t)}{G(t)} \tag{1.5}$$

This shows that the transition rate is a conditional density function, i.e. the density function $f(t)$ divided through the survivor function $G(t)$.

The transition rate allows for a local description of the development of a process. To calculate $r(t)$ one needs information about the local probability density for events at t, given by $f(t)$, and about the development of the process up to t, given by $G(t)$. Of course, if we know the transition rate for a time interval, say t to t', we have a description of how the process evolves during this time interval. And if we know the transition rate for all (possible) points in time, we eventually have a description of the whole process, which is mathematically equivalent to having a complete description of the distribution of T.

There is a simple relationship between the transition rate and the survivor function. First, given the survivor function $G(t)$, we can easily derive the transition rate as (minus) its logarithmic derivative:[25]

$$\frac{d \log(G(t))}{dt} = \frac{1}{G(t)} \frac{dG(t)}{dt} = \frac{1}{G(t)} \frac{d}{dt} (1 - F(t)) = -\frac{f(t)}{G(t)} = -r(t)$$

Using this relation, the other direction is provided by integration. We have

$$-\int_0^t r(\tau) \, d\tau = \log(G(t)) - \log(G(0)) = \log(G(t))$$

since $G(0) = 1$. It follows the basic relation, often used in subsequent chapters, that

$$G(t) = \exp\left(-\int_0^t r(\tau) \, d\tau\right) \tag{1.6}$$

Finally, one should note that $r(t)$ is a transition *rate*, not a transition probability. As shown in (1.5), $r(t)$ is similar to a density function. To derive proper probability statements, one has to integrate over some time interval, as follows:

$$\begin{aligned}
\Pr(t \leq T < t' \mid T \geq t) &= \frac{G(t) - G(t')}{G(t)} = 1 - \frac{G(t')}{G(t)} \\
&= 1 - \exp\left(-\int_t^{t'} r(\tau) \, d\tau\right)
\end{aligned}$$

One easily verifies however that $1 - \exp(-x) \approx x$ for small values of x. Therefore, the probability that an event happens in a *small* time interval (t, t') is approximately equal to $r(t)$:

$$\Pr(t \leq T < t' \mid T \geq t) \approx (t' - t) r(t)$$

---

[25] Throughout this book, we use log(.) to denote the natural logarithm.

Chapter 2
Event History Data Structures

This chapter discusses event history data structures. We first introduce the basic terminology used for event history data and then give an example of an event history data file. Finally, we show how to use it in conjunction with TDA.

2.1 Basic Terminology

Event history analysis studies *transitions* across a set of discrete states, including the length of *time intervals* between entry to and exit from specific states. The basic analytical framework is a state space and a time axis. The choice of the *time axis* or *clock* (e.g. age, experience, marriage duration, etc.) used in the analysis must be based on theoretical considerations and affects the statistical model. In this book, we discuss only methods and models using a *continuous* time axis. An *episode, spell, waiting time,* or *duration*—terms that are used interchangeably—is the time span a unit of analysis (e.g. an individual) spends in a specific state. The *states* are *discrete* and usually small in number. The definition of a set of possible states, called the *state space* $\mathcal{Y}$, is also dependent on substantive considerations. Thus, a careful, theoretically driven choice of the time axis and design of state space are important because they are often serious sources of misspecification. In particular, misspecification of the model may occur because some of the important states are not observed. For example, in a study analyzing the determinants of women's labor market participation in West Germany, Blossfeld and Rohwer (in press) have shown that one arrives at much more appropriate substantive conclusions if one differentiates the state "employed" into "full-time work" and "part-time work." One should also note here that a small change in the focus of the substantive issue in question, leading to a new definition of the state space, often requires a fundamental reorganization of the event history data file.

The most restricted event history model is based on a process with only a *single episode* and *two states* (one *origin* and one *destination* state). An example may be the duration of *first* marriage until the end of the marriage, for whatever reason. In this case each individual who entered into first marriage (origin state) started an episode, which could be terminated by a transition to the destination state "not married anymore." In the *single episode* case each unit of analysis that entered into the origin state is represented by one episode. If more than one destination state exists, we refer to these models as *multistate models*. Models for the special case with a single origin state but two or more destination states are also called *models with competing events* or *risks*. For example, a housewife might become "unemployed" (meaning entering into the state "looking for work"), or start being "full-time" or "part-time employed." If more than one event is possible (i.e. if there are repeated events or transitions over the observation period), we use the term *multi-episode models*. For example, an employment career normally consists of a series of job shifts. Figure 1.1.1c (p. 4) describes a *multistate-multi-episode* process. The individual moves repeatedly between several different states. As shown in Blossfeld, Hamerle, and Mayer (1989), most of the basic concepts for the one-episode and one-event case can simply be extended and applied to more complex situations with *repeated episodes* and/or *competing events*. In this book, we mainly stick to the more complex notation for the multistate-multi-episode case. Thus, if one has a sample of $i = 1, \ldots, N$ multistate-multi-episode data, a complete description of the data[1] is given by

$$(u_i, m_i, o_i, d_i, s_i, t_i, x_i) \qquad i = 1, \ldots, N$$

where u_i is the identification number of the individual or any other unit of analysis the ith episode belongs to; m_i is the serial number of the episode; o_i is the origin state, the state held during the episode until the ending time; d_i is the destination state defined as the state reached at the ending time of the episode; and s_i and t_i are the starting and ending times, respectively. In addition, there is a covariate vector x_i associated with the episode. We always assume that the starting and ending times are coded such that the difference $t_i - s_i$ is the duration of the episode, and is positive and greater than zero. There is also an ordering of the episodes for each individual, given by the set of serial numbers of the episodes. Although it is not necessary that these serial numbers be contiguous, it is required that the starting time of an episode be not less than the ending time of a previous episode.

Observations of event histories are very often *censored*. Censoring occurs when the information about the duration in the origin state is incompletely recorded. Figure 2.1.1 gives examples of different types of censoring created by an observation window (see also Yamaguchi 1991; Guo 1993). The horizontal axis indicates historical time and the observation period is usually of finite length, with the beginning and end denoted by τ_a and τ_b, respectively.

- *Episode A* is fully censored on the left, which means that the starting and ending times of this spell are located before the beginning of the observation window. Left censoring is normally a difficult problem because it is not possible to take the effects of the unknown episodes into account. It is only easy to cope with, if the assumption of a Markov process is justified (i.e. if the transition rates do not depend on the duration in the origin state).

---

[1] A complete history of state occupancies and times of changes is often called a "sample path" (see Tuma and Hannan 1984).

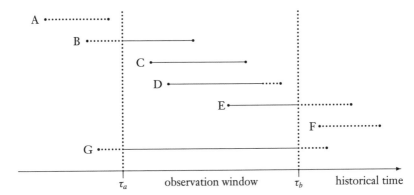

Figure 2.1.1 Types of censoring in an observation window.

- *Episode B* is partially censored on the left, so that the length of time a subject has already spent in the origin state is unkown. In this case we have the same problems as for A-type episodes.

  However, sometimes (e.g. in a first panel wave) we have additional retrospective information about the time of entry into the origin state of Episode B. In this case, usually called a *left truncated* observation (see Guo 1993), we can reconstruct the full duration of episode B, but do not have information about episodes of type A. This creates a sample selection bias for the period before the observation window. The earlier the starting time of the episode and the shorter the durations, the less likely it is that these episodes will appear in the observation window. One solution to this problem is that one starts to analyze the process at the beginning of the observation window and evaluates only the part of the duration that reaches into the observation window, beginning with time τ_a and ending with t_i. This means that the analysis is conditional on the fact that the individual has survived up to τ_a (see Guo 1993).

- *Episode C* is complete. There is no censoring on the left or right.

- *Episode D* is a special case. This episode is censored on the right within the observation window. If the censoring is a result of a random process, then event history analysis methods can take these episodes into account without any problems, as is shown later (Kalbfleisch and Prentice 1980: type II censoring). Technically speaking, it can be treated in the same way as Episode E. However, this type of censoring might occur because of attrition or missing data in a panel study. Such dropouts or missing data are normally not random, and the characteristics of the lost individuals are very often related to the process under study. Such selectivity bias creates problems and cannot easily be corrected in an event history analysis.

- *Episode E* is right censored because the observation is terminated at the right-hand side of the observation window. This type of censoring typically occurs in life course studies at the time of the retrospective interview, or in panel studies at the time of the last panel wave. Because the end of the observation window, τ_b, is normally determined independently from the substantive process under study, this type of right censoring is unproblematic. It can be handled with event history methods (Kalbfleisch and Prentice 1980: type I censoring).

- *Episode F* is completely censored on the right. Entry into and exit from the duration occurs after the observation period. This type of censoring normally happens in retrospective life history studies in which individuals of various birth cohorts are observed over different spans of life. To avoid sample selection bias, such models have to take into account variables controlling for the selection, for example, by including birth cohort dummy variables.

- *Episode G* represents a duration that is left and right censored.[2] Such observations happen, for example, in panel studies in which job mobility is recorded. In such cases one knows that a person is in a specific job at the first sweep and in the same job up to the second one, but one has no information about the actual beginning and ending times.

In the examples in this book, which are based on the German Life History Study (GLHS), we do not have left censored data because all the life histories of the birth cohorts 1929–31, 1939–41, and 1949–51 were collected retrospectively from the time of birth up to the date of the interview (1981–1983, see Mayer and Brückner 1989; Mayer 1987, 1988, 1991). Thus, we do not have data of the type A, B, and G. Type D censoring can only occur because of missing data, not because of attrition, because the GLHS is a retrospective study. Because we are studying different birth cohorts in our analyses (data of type E and F), we have to control for the fact that members of these birth cohorts could only be observed over various age spans (1929–31: up to the age of 50; 1939–41: up to the age of 40; and 1949–51: up to the age of 30).

---

[2] A special case of such data type are "current-status" data. These data comprise information on whether an event has or has not been reached at the time of a survey, and information on age at the time of the survey. If the event has occurred, one has incomplete information on when it occurred. On the other hand, we do not know when it will happen (if ever) for those respondents who have not experienced the event at the time of the survey (see Diamond and McDonald 1992).

2.2 Event History Data Organization

Event history data are more complex than cross-sectional ones because for each episode information about an *origin state* and a *destination state*, as well as the *starting* and *ending times*, are given. In most studies, there are also *repeated episodes* from *various parallel processes* (e.g. job, marital, or residential histories, etc.) at *different levels* (e.g. job history of an individual, histories of the firm where the individual worked at the mesolevel, and/or structural changes in the labor market at the macrolevel) for each unit of analysis. Therefore, large event history data sets have often been stored in data bank systems. In this book, we do not discuss the advantages and disadvantages of different data bank systems for event histories in terms of efficiency, convenience, data handling, and retrieval. For the purpose of this book it is, however, important to stress that event history data have to be organized as a *rectangular data file* in order to analyze the data with standard programs like SPSS, SAS, or GLIM (e.g. see Blossfeld, Hamerle, and Mayer 1989), or the program that is used throughout this book, TDA.

In an event-oriented data set *each record of the file is related to a duration in a state or episode* (see Carroll 1983). As shown previously, type and number of states for each unit of analysis are dependent on the substantive question under consideration. Changes in the state space usually lead to a new definition of episodes and very often entail a fundamental reorganization of the data file.

If, for each unit of analysis, only one episode is considered (e.g. entry into first marriage), then the number of records in the data file corresponds to the number of units. In an analysis concerned with repeated events (e.g. consecutive jobs in an individual's career), whose number may vary among individuals, the sum of these person-specific episodes represents the number of records in the data set.

In the examples throughout this book, we use event history data from the German Life History Study (GLHS). The GLHS provides detailed retrospective information about the life histories of men and women from the birth cohorts 1929–31, 1939–41, and 1949–51, collected in the years 1981–1983 (Mayer and Brückner 1989). For our didactical task in this book, we only use an event history data file of 600 job episodes from 201 respondents (arbitrarily selected and anonymized). Each record in this file represents an employment episode, and the consecutive jobs of a respondent's career are stored successively in the file. For some individuals there is only a single job episode, whereas for others there is a sequence of two or more jobs.

The data file, *rrdat.1*, contains 12 variables that are described briefly in Box 2.2.1. "Column" refers to the position of the variable in the data file, which

Box 2.2.1   Variables in data file *rrdat.1*

Variable	Column	Label	Description
V1	C1	ID	ID of individual
V2	C2	NOJ	Serial number of the job
V3	C3	TStart	Starting time of the job
V4	C4	TFin	Ending time of the job
V5	C5	SEX	Sex (1 men, 2 women)
V6	C6	TI	Date of interview
V7	C7	TB	Date of birth
V8	C8	T1	Date of entry into the labor market
V9	C9	TM	Date of marriage (0 if no marriage)
V10	C10	PRES	Prestige score of job i
V11	C11	PRESN	Prestige score of job i + 1
V12	C12	EDU	Highest educational attainment

Box 2.2.2   First records of data file *rrdat.1*

C1	C2	C3	C4	C5	C6	C7	C8	C9	C10	C11	C12
1	1	555	982	1	982	351	555	679	34	-1	17
2	1	593	638	2	982	357	593	762	22	46	10
2	2	639	672	2	982	357	593	762	46	46	10
2	3	673	892	2	982	357	593	762	46	-1	10
3	1	688	699	2	982	473	688	870	41	41	11
3	2	700	729	2	982	473	688	870	41	44	11
3	3	730	741	2	982	473	688	870	44	44	11
3	4	742	816	2	982	473	688	870	44	44	11
3	5	817	828	2	982	473	688	870	44	-1	11

is "free format," meaning that the numerical entries are separated by a blank character.

V1   identifies the individuals in the data set. Because the data file contains information about 201 individuals, there are 201 different ID numbers. The numbers are arbitrarily chosen and are not contiguous.

V2   gives the serial number of the job episode, always beginning with job number 1. For instance, if an individual in our data set has had three jobs, the data file contains three records for this individual entitled job number 1, 2, and 3. Note that only job episodes are included in this data file. If an individual has experienced an interruption between two consecutive jobs, the difference between the ending time of a job and the starting time of the next job may be greater than 1 (see Figure 2.2.1b).

V3   is the starting time of the job episode, in century months.[3] The date given in this variable records the first month in a new job.

V4   is the ending time of the job episode, in century months. The date given in this variable records the last month in the job.

---

[3] A century month is the number of months from the beginning of the century; 1 = January 1900.

V5   records the sex of the individual, coded 1 for men and 2 for women.

V6   is the date of the interview, in century months. Using this information, one can decide whether an episode is right censored or not. If the ending time of an episode (*V4*) is less than the interview date, the episode ended with an event (see Figure 2.2.1c), otherwise the episode is right censored (see Figures 2.2.1a and 2.2.1b).

V7   records the birth date of the individual, in century months. Therefore, *V3* minus *V7* is the age, in months, at the beginning of a job episode.

V8   records the date of first entry into the labor market, in century months.

V9   records whether/when an individual has married. If the value of this variable is positive, it gives the date of marriage (in century months). For still unmarried individuals at the time of the interview, the variable is coded 0.

V10 records the prestige score of the current job, that is, the job episode in the current record of the data file.

V11 records the prestige score of the consecutive job, if there is a next job, otherwise a missing value (-1) is coded.

V12 records the highest educational attainment before entry into the labor market. In assigning school years to school degrees, the following values have been assumed (Blossfeld 1985, 1992): Lower secondary school qualification (*Hauptschule*) without vocational training is equivalent to 9 years, middle school qualification (*Mittlere Reife*) is equivalent to 10 years, lower secondary school qualification with vocational training is equivalent to 11 years, middle school qualification with vocational training is equivalent to 12 years. *Abitur* is equivalent to 13 years, a professional college qualification is equivalent to 17 years, and a university degree is equivalent to 19 years.

Box 2.2.2 shows the first nine records of data file *rrdat.1*. Note that all dates are coded in *century months*. Thus, 1 means January 1900, 2 means February 1900, 13 means January 1901, and so on. In general:

$$\text{YEAR} \;=\; (\text{DATE} - 1) \;/\; 12 + 1900$$
$$\text{MONTH} \;=\; (\text{DATE} - 1) \;\% \; 12 + 1$$

where DATE is given in century months, and MONTH and YEAR refer to calendar time. "/" means *integer division* and "%" is the *modulus operator*.[4] For instance, the first individual (ID = 1) has a single job episode. The starting time is given as century month 555, corresponding to March 1946, and the ending time is 982 = October 1981. Because this is equal to the interview month, the episode is right censored.

The panels in Figure 2.2.1 demonstrate the three basic types of job careers included in the example data file.

---

[4] Given two integer numbers, *n* and *m*, *n* % *m* is the remainder after dividing *n* by *m*. For instance: 13 % 12 = 1.

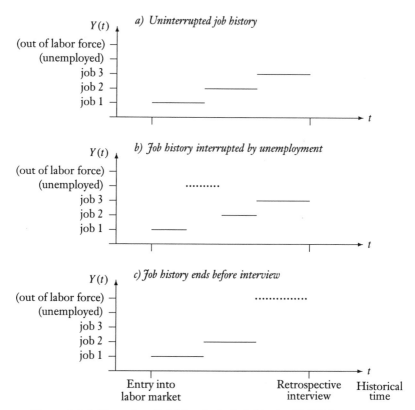

Figure 2.2.1 Examples of job histories included in the GLHS data set.

a) For some respondents, the file *rrdat.1* contains an uninterrupted job history from the time of entry into the labor market until the time of the retrospective interview. If there is more than one job for respondents, the ending time of job *n* (column *C4*) and the starting time of job *n* + 1 (column *C3*) are contiguous. For example, the first individual in the data set (*ID* = *1*, see Box 2.2.2), who is a man (*C5* = *1*), has had only one job from first entry into the labor market (*C3* = *555*) up to the time of the interview (*C4* = *982* equals *C6* = *982*). So this episode is right censored.

b) Some respondents' job histories were interrupted by an unemployment episode, or because the respondents were out of the labor market for some period. In these cases the example data set *rrdat.1* only contains the job episodes, and there may be gaps between the ending time of job *n* and the starting time of job *n* + 1 (see Figure 2.2.1b).

Box 2.2.3   Command file *ehb1.cf*

```
        dfile = rrdat.1;        data file

        v1  (ID)    = c1 ;    ID of individual
        v2  (NOJ)   = c2 ;    Serial number of the job
        v3  (TStart) = c3 ;   Starting time of the job
        v4  (TFin)  = c4 ;    Ending time of the job
        v5  (SEX)   = c5 ;    Sex (1 men, 2 women)
        v6  (TI)    = c6 ;    Date of interview
        v7  (TB)    = c7 ;    Date of birth
        v8  (T1)    = c8 ;    Date of entry into the labor market
        v9  (TM)    = c9 ;    Date of marriage (0 if no marriage)
        v10 (PRES)  = c10;    Prestige score of job i
        v11 (PRESN) = c11;    Prestige score of job i + 1
        v12 (EDU)   = c12;    Highest educational attainment
```

c) Finally, for some respondents, the observed job history may have ended before the time of the interview because the employment career stopped or was interrupted (due to unemployment or being out of the labor force) and re-entry did not take place before the time of the interview. For example, the second individual (ID = 2), who is a woman ($C5$ = 2), had a continuous career of three jobs, then an interruption ($C4$ = 892), and did not re-enter the labor market before the time of interview ($C6$ = 982) (see Figure 2.2.1c).

Using Event History Data Files with TDA

We now use TDA to read the data file *rrdat.1*. For this purpose, we use a short command file (*ehb1.cf*), shown in Box 2.2.3.[5] As explained in Appendix A, a command file is a short text file containing commands to be executed by TDA. A command file can be created with any editor. Our first example, shown in Box 2.2.3, contains 13 commands. Each command must be terminated by a semicolon; anything following a semicolon (in the same line) will be ignored (so can be used for comments). A command can run through several lines of a command file. In fact, each piece of text, up to a terminating semicolon, will be interpreted by TDA as a single command. If there is no terminating semicolon, TDA will exit with an error message. "White space" (blank, tabulator, and new line characters) can be used to make a command file more easily readable; they will be ignored by TDA.

The example command file in Box 2.2.3 contains two types of commands. The first of these, the *dfile* command, simply provides the name of the data file, *rrdat.1*, in our example. The name of the file is given without a preceding path, so TDA will assume that the file can be found in the current working directory.

---

[5] All command files are contained on the accompanying disk. The naming convention to identify these command files is: *ehxn.cf*, where the single letter x is one of the series $a,b,c,...$ referring to the successive chapters, and n numbers the command files in each chapter.

Otherwise a full path name must be provided. The remaining 12 commands define the variables to be created by TDA. The syntax for these commands is

VName (Label) = expression;

VName is the name of the variable; possible variable names are *V1...V32000*. Then follows, optionally, a label. The expression on the right-hand side of the command tells TDA how to build the variable. In our example, we have used the keywords $C1, C2,...$, which are references to columns (variables) in a data file. For instance, *C1* is a reference to the first column (variable) in a data file, *C2* refers to the second column (variable), and so on. Therefore, in our example, the command

v1 (ID) = c1;

means that TDA will create a variable with the name *V1* and label *ID* by using the first column (variable) in the data file *rrdat.1* defined by the *dfile* command.

As a default, TDA assumes a free-format data file where consecutive entries in a record are separated by (at least) one blank character. The numerical entries in the data file's records are then uniquely identified by the keywords $C1, C2,...$ If the data file has a fixed format without special characters to separate numerical entries (values of variables), one needs an additional command to tell TDA about the structure of the data file's record (see Appendix A). However, our example data file is free-format, and so we do not need any additional information.

Given any set of commands defining variables, TDA tries to create an internal data matrix. This will be a rectangular matrix with rows corresponding to records (episodes) of the input data file and columns corresponding to variables. The number of columns will be identical to the number of variables defined in the command file. The number of cases depends on the number of records (episodes) in the input data file. In general, if no selection commands have been used, the number of rows in the internal data matrix will be the same as the number of records in the data file. In our example, the internal data matrix will consist of 600 episodes (rows) and 12 variables (columns).

However, TDA needs to know the maximum number of cases for the internal data matrix in advance. This maximum number of cases can be controlled with the command

noc = maximum_number_of_cases_for_data_matrix;

The default value is *noc=1000* (i.e. a maximum of 1000 records is read from the data file to build the internal data matrix). In our example with only 600 records (episodes) in the input data file, this will be sufficient.[6] But if a data file contains more than 1000 records, one must define the appropriate maximum number of cases with the *noc* command.

---

[6] In fact, one could add the command *noc=600* to save space.

Executing TDA with a Command File

Having prepared a command file, one can get TDA to execute the commands. There are two different ways to do this. First, one can invoke TDA with the command

tda cf=fname

where *fname* is the name of a command file (optionally preceded by a path statement). TDA tries to find the command file, reads the commands given in the file, and tries to execute the commands, possibly exiting with error messages. Any output (except of output files requested with specific commands in a command file) will be written to the computer's standard output (i.e. to the screen of the user's terminal). Optionally, one can redirect TDA's standard output into a user-defined file. This can be done in the following way:

tda cf=fname > ofile

Again, *fname* is the name of a command file. *ofile* is an arbitrary file name provided by the user. TDA (in fact, the "shell" that is running TDA) will then create a new file with the name *ofile* (overwriting any already existing file with the same name) and write its output into this file. The output file *ofile* can be viewed on the screen, loaded by an editor, or sent to a printer.

When executing command file *ehb1.cf*, TDA will create an internal data matrix consisting of 600 cases and 12 variables. If the user wants any further actions, these must be specified by additional commands. For instance, one can request simple descriptive statistics of the variables by using the *dstat* command; or one can request one or multi-dimensional frequency tables by using the *freq* command. As an example, add the command

freq = v2;

to the command file to obtain the frequency distribution of variable *V2* (i.e. the distribution of the number of job episodes in the input data file).

It is important to understand that the commands we have used in command file *ehb1.cf* only define an internal data matrix. This data matrix can be used for many different statistical procedures and is interpreted differently depending on the type of procedure (e.g. as a set of cross-sectional data, a set of panel data, or a set of event history data). If one intends to use the data matrix as a set of event history data, TDA must be explicitly informed about how to *interpret* the data matrix as a set of episodes. In fact, there are two different ways of interpreting the data matrix as a set of episodes: single episode data and multi-episode data.

Single Episode Data

To interpret the internal data matrix as a set of single episode data, TDA needs four pieces of information, provided by the following commands:

org=   name of the variable containing the episode's origin state.
des=   name of the variable containing the episode's destination state.
ts=   name of the variable containing the episode's starting time.
tf=   name of the variable containing the episode's ending time.

Given this information, each row of the internal data matrix will be interpreted as a separate episode. The implicit assumption is that all individual episodes are statistically independent.[7]

Before defining episode data, two basic dimensions must be specified: the state space and the time axis. The *state space* is the set of possible origin and destination states. TDA builds a state space from all values found in the variables defined with the *org* and *des* commands.[8] Values can be arbitrarily assigned. For instance, if we are only interested in job duration, the origin state of each job episode may be coded 0 and the destination state may be coded 1. This implies that we do not distinguish between different ways to leave a job. There is just a single transition: from 0 (being in a job) to 1 (leaving that job). Of course, some episodes may be right censored. In these cases, individuals are still in the origin state at the observed ending time of the episode. TDA's convention for recognizing right censored episodes is therefore that the destination state equals the origin state.

In addition to a state space, one needs a *time axis*. For instance, in our example data file, the jobs are coded in historical time defined in century months. The implied origin of this time axis is the beginning of January 1900. TDA always assumes a *process time axis* that begins at time zero. The definition of starting and ending times with the *ts* and *tf* commands must conform to this assumption. The easiest way, for example, is to define the time of entry into the episode as zero and the ending time as the episode's duration.[9] In fact, in the single episode case TDA *always* assumes that episodes begin at time zero. If the starting time defined with the *ts* command is greater than zero, it is assumed that the episode is only partially observed, beginning at the point in time given by the *ts* command and ending at the point in time given by the *tf* command.[10] In addition, one should note two basic conditions that must be matched by the *TS* and *TF* variables: the values of these variables must be non-negative, and for each episode the value of the *TF* variable must be greater than the value of the *TS* variable (i.e. each episode must have a positive duration). In fact,

---

[7] This may not be true if some individuals contribute more than a single episode and if the dependencies are not sufficiently controlled for by covariates (see section 4.3).

[8] Note that, in TDA, possible values for state variables are only non-negative integer values.

[9] It should be noted here that the time of entry into the origin state is sometimes hard to determine. For example, consider the case when people start a consensual union, begin a friendship, or are looking for a marriage partner.

[10] In this way it is easily possible to use left-truncated episodes; see, for example, Episode B in Figure 2.1.1, where the observation does not cover the whole episode, but retrospective information about the episode's starting time is available.

Box 2.2.4   Command file *ehb2.cf*

```
dfile = rrdat.1;      data file

v1  (ID)     = c1 ;   ID of individual
v2  (NOJ)    = c2 ;   Serial number of the job
v3  (TStart) = c3 ;   Starting time of the job
v4  (TFin)   = c4 ;   Ending time of the job
v5  (SEX)    = c5 ;   Sex (1 men, 2 women)
v6  (TI)     = c6 ;   Date of interview
v7  (TB)     = c7 ;   Date of birth
v8  (T1)     = c8 ;   Date of entry into the labor market
v9  (TM)     = c9 ;   Date of marriage (0 if no marriage)
v10 (PRES)   = c10;   Prestige score of job i
v11 (PRESN)  = c11;   Prestige score of job i + 1
v12 (EDU)    = c12;   Highest educational attainment

# Define origin and destination state. Origin state is 0.
# Destination state is 0 if right censored, or 1.
v13 (ORG)    = 0;
v14 (DES)    = if eq(v4,v6) then 0 else 1;

# Definition of starting and ending time on a process time axis.
v15 (TSP) = 0;
v16 (TFP) = v4 - v3 + 1; one month added

# commands to define single episode data
org =  v13;   define origin state
des =  v14;   define destination state
ts  =  v15;   define starting time
tf  =  v16;   define ending time
```

TDA always calculates the (observed) duration of an episode as the value of *TF* minus the value of *TS*. So the user has to provide variables that conform to these conventions.

Command file *ehb2.cf*, shown in Box 2.2.4, illustrates the definition of single episode data with our example data set. The state space is $\mathcal{Y} = \{0, 1\}$, 0 = "being in a job episode," 1 = "having left the job." This is achieved by defining two new variables, *V13* and *V14*. *V13*, to be used as the origin state, is simply set to zero. *V14*, to be used as the destination state, is assigned zero or one, depending on whether the episode is right censored or not. An episode is right censored if its ending time (*V4*) is equal to the interview date (*V6*). Therefore, if *V4* is equal to *V6*, variable *V14* becomes zero, otherwise one.

Because we are only interested in job duration in this example, starting and ending times are given on a process time axis, that is, the starting time is always zero and the ending time equals the (observed) duration of the episode. This is achieved by defining variables *V15* and *V16* for the starting and ending times, respectively. *V15*, the starting time, is set to zero. *V16* is calculated as

Box 2.2.5 Result of using command file *ehb2.cf* (Box 2.2.4)

```
    Single episode data

    Origin state: V13     Destination state: V14
    Starting time: V15    Ending time: V16
                                      Mean
    SN  Org Des    Episodes   Weighted  Duration   TS Min    TF Max
    -----------------------------------------------------------------
     1   0   0        142       142.00    128.18     0.00     428.00
     1   0   1        458       458.00     49.30     0.00     350.00
     1   0  Sum       600       600.00     67.97     0.00     428.00
```

the difference between historical ending time (*V4*) and historical starting time (*V3*). To avoid zero durations, we have added one month to the job duration, or the *observed* duration if the episode is right censored. For example, it might happen that an individual enters a job on the first day of a month and then leaves it during that same month. Because observed ending times refer to the last month where an individual occupies the current job, starting and ending times would be equal and the duration would be zero. Thus, we assume that any employment duration in the last month can be treated as a full month.

Executing command file *ehb2.cf* with TDA can be achieved in the following way:

   tda cf=ehb2.cf > out

Part of the output file (*out*) is shown in Box 2.2.5. First, TDA recognized that we have defined single episode data. Then a table is printed, showing which transitions have been found in the input data. In our example, we have 458 episodes ending with an event and 142 right censored episodes. *TS Min* shows the minimum value found in the *TS* variable (in fact, in our example all job episodes begin at time zero). *TS Max* shows the maximum value found in the *TF* variable (the maximum ending time or job duration is 428 months for censored durations, and 350 months for completed episodes). The column labeled *Mean Duration* shows the mean value of *TF-TS* and is, of course, no proper estimate if some episodes are right censored. Finally, the first column, labelled *SN*, shows the serial (sequence) number of the episodes. In the case of single episode data, all episodes are assigned the serial number 1.

Multi-Episode Data

For multi-episode data, one needs two additional pieces of information. First, one must know which episodes belong to which individual; second, one must have knowledge about the serial (sequence) number of the episodes. Therefore, one needs the following six commands to define multi-episode data:

Box 2.2.6 Command file *ebb3.cf* for multi-episode data

```
dfile = rrdat.1;       data file

v1  (ID)     = c1 ;    ID of individual
v2  (NOJ)    = c2 ;    Serial number of the job
v3  (TStart) = c3 ;    Starting time of the job
v4  (TFin)   = c4 ;    Ending time of the job
v5  (SEX)    = c5 ;    Sex (1 men, 2 women)
v6  (TI)     = c6 ;    Date of interview
v7  (TB)     = c7 ;    Date of birth
v8  (T1)     = c8 ;    Date of entry into the labor market
v9  (TM)     = c9 ;    Date of marriage (0 if no marriage)
v10 (PRES)   = c10;    Prestige score of job i
v11 (PRESN)  = c11;    Prestige score of job i + 1
v12 (EDU)    = c12;    Highest educational attainment

# Definition of origin and destination states.
v13 (ORG)    = 1 + 2 * (v2 - 1);
v14 (DES)    = if lt(v4,v6) then v13 + 1 else v13;

# Definition of a common process time axis.
v15 (TFC)    = if eq(v2,1) then v3 else pre(v15);
v16 (TSP)    = v3 - v15;
v17 (TFP)    = v4 - v15 + 1;

id  =  v1;     define ID of individuals
sn  =  v2;     define serial number of episode
org =  v13;    define origin state
des =  v14;    define destination state
ts  =  v16;    define starting time
tf  =  v17;    define ending time
```

id= name of the variable containing the individual's ID number.
sn= name of the variable containing the serial number of the episode.
org= name of the variable containing the episode's origin state.
des= name of the variable containing the episode's destination state.
ts= name of the variable containing the episode's starting time.
tf= name of the variable containing the episode's ending time.

All episodes that have the same value of the *ID* variable belong to the same individual identified by this *ID*. The successive episodes in these sets of episodes are distinguished by their serial number given in the *SN* variable. The serial numbers must be positive integers and they should be contiguous.

To specify a set of multi-episode data, one again has to decide on an appropriate state space and a time axis. There are usually several options. For our example data, it would be possible, for instance, to use the following state space:

1   1st job: origin state
2   1st job: destination state

Box 2.2.7 Example of multi-episode data for three individuals

```
ID SN TStart TFin  ORG  DES  TFC  TSP  TFP
-------------------------------------------
 1  1   555   982   1    1   555    0  428
 2  1   593   638   1    2   593    0   46
 2  2   639   672   3    4   593   46   80
 2  3   673   892   5    6   593   80  300
 3  1   688   699   1    2   688    0   12
 3  2   700   729   3    4   688   12   42
 3  3   730   741   5    6   688   42   54
 3  4   742   816   7    8   688   54  129
 3  5   817   828   9   10   688  129  141
```

Box 2.2.8a Result (first part) of using command file *ebb3.cf* (Box 2.2.6)

```
Multi-episode data

Case ID: V1            Spell number: V2
Origin state: V13      Destination state: V14
Starting time: V16     Ending time: V17

Frequencies of spell numbers
  SN   N of Units   Weighted    N of Spells    Weighted
-------------------------------------------------------
   1        39        39.00          201        201.00
   2        55        55.00          162        162.00
   3        45        45.00          107        107.00
   4        30        30.00           62         62.00
   5        12        12.00           32         32.00
   6         9         9.00           20         20.00
   7         7         7.00           11         11.00
   8         3         3.00            4          4.00
   9         1         1.00            1          1.00
 Sum       201       201.00          600        600.00
```

3   2nd job: origin state
4   2nd job: destination state
5   3rd job: origin state
6   3rd job: destination state
    and so on.

As in the case of single episode data, right censored episodes are identified by the fact that their destination state equals their origin state.

To define a time axis, one has at least two options. One can reset the clock at the beginning of each new episode, or one can use a common process time axis where the first episode for each individual begins at time zero (e.g. the general labor force experience as time axis). We use this latter option to illustrate the

Box 2.2.8b Result (second part) of using command file *ehb3.cf* (Box 2.2.6)

SN	Org	Des	Episodes	Weighted	Mean Duration	TS Min	TF Max
1	1	1	16	16.00	233.44	0.00	428.00
1	1	2	185	185.00	52.73	0.00	326.00
1	1	Sum	201	201.00	67.11	0.00	428.00
2	3	3	36	36.00	150.17	13.00	450.00
2	3	4	126	126.00	52.30	3.00	406.00
2	3	Sum	162	162.00	74.05	3.00	450.00
3	5	5	38	38.00	121.74	9.00	463.00
3	5	6	69	69.00	50.36	8.00	403.00
3	5	Sum	107	107.00	75.71	8.00	463.00
4	7	7	24	24.00	85.33	52.00	465.00
4	7	8	38	38.00	37.71	9.00	329.00
4	7	Sum	62	62.00	56.15	9.00	465.00
5	9	9	9	9.00	110.22	66.00	441.00
5	9	10	23	23.00	22.61	39.00	348.00
5	9	Sum	32	32.00	47.25	39.00	441.00
6	11	11	8	8.00	45.75	151.00	379.00
6	11	12	12	12.00	43.75	46.00	324.00
6	11	Sum	20	20.00	44.55	46.00	379.00
7	13	13	7	7.00	114.14	132.00	427.00
7	13	14	4	4.00	52.75	112.00	368.00
7	13	Sum	11	11.00	91.82	112.00	427.00
8	15	15	3	3.00	65.00	129.00	440.00
8	15	16	1	1.00	72.00	213.00	285.00
8	15	Sum	4	4.00	66.75	129.00	440.00
9	17	17	1	1.00	34.00	285.00	319.00

setup of multi-episode data with our example data set. The example command file, *ehb3.cf*, is shown in Box 2.2.6.

To define the common process time axis "general labor force experience," we have first defined a new variable, *V15*, with the command

$$v15\ (TFC) = if\ eq(v2,1)\ then\ v3\ else\ pre(v15);$$

meaning that for all sets of episodes that belong to the same ID, *V15* equals the starting time of the episode with serial number 1.[11] This variable is then subtracted from the original starting and ending times to get their values on

---

[11] Explicitly formulated, the definition is: if *V2* is equal to 1, *V15* should be equal to *V3*; otherwise *V15* should be equal to its predecessor. Of course, this definition relies on the fact that in our example data file the episodes are ordered with respect to their serial numbers.

the process time axis. Again, we have added one month to the ending times to get positive durations. Box 2.2.7 shows, for the first three individuals in our example data set, how the process time axis is created from the calendar time axis.

Part of TDA's standard output from the execution of command file *ehb3.cf* is shown in Boxes 2.2.8a and 2.2.8b. There are two tables. The first table (Box 2.2.8a) shows the distribution of episodes across individuals. In our example, we have 201 individuals: 39 individuals have only one job episode, 55 individuals have two job episodes, and so on. Finally, there is only one individual who has nine job episodes.

The second table (Box 2.2.8b) shows which types of episodes (transitions) are found in the input data. The table is similar to the table shown in Box 2.2.5; the main difference is that in the case of multi-episode data one has to distinguish episodes with respect to their serial (sequence) number and their changing starting times.

Chapter 3
Nonparametric Descriptive Methods

In this chapter we discuss nonparametric estimation methods that can be used to describe the characteristics of the process under study. Because these methods do not make any assumptions about the distribution of the process, they are particularly suited for first exploratory data analyses. TDA contains procedures to calculate life tables and Kaplan-Meier (or product limit) estimates. Both of these methods are helpful for graphical presentations of the survivor function (and their transformations) as well as the transition rate. The life table method is the more traditional procedure and has been used in the case of large data sets because it needs less computing time and space. However, compared to the Kaplan-Meier estimator, the life table method has the disadvantage that the researcher has to define discrete time intervals, as is shown later. Given modern computers, there seems to be no reason anymore to prefer the life table method on the basis of computer time or storage space. We therefore give only a few examples for the life table method and discuss the Kaplan-Meier estimator in more detail.

3.1 Life Table Method

The life table method enables the calculation of nonparametric estimates of the survivor function, the density function, and the transition rate for durations given in a set of episodes.[1] There are two drawbacks to this method. First, it is necessary to group the durations into fixed intervals. The results therefore depend more or less on these arbitrarily defined time intervals. Second, it is only sensible to use this method if there is a relatively large number of episodes, so that estimates conditional for each interval are reliable. However, if this second requirement is fulfilled, the method gives good approximations that can be easily calculated.

Time intervals are defined by split points on the time axis

$$0 \leq \tau_1 < \tau_2 < \tau_3 < \ldots < \tau_L$$

With the convention that $\tau_{L+1} = \infty$, there are L time intervals, each including the left limit, but not the right one.

$$I_l = \{t \mid \tau_l \leq t < \tau_{l+1}\} \qquad l = 1, \ldots, L$$

---

[1] An extensive discussion of the life table method has been given by Namboodiri and Suchindran (1987).

Given these time intervals, the calculation of life tables by TDA is always done using episode durations. In the following description we therefore assume that all episodes have starting time zero. In addition, we assume that the time intervals start at zero (i.e. $\tau_1 = 0$).[2]

The calculation depends somewhat on the type of input data. The following possibilities are recognized by TDA. (1) If there are sample weights defined with the *cwt* command (see Appendix A), these weights are used in all calculations.[3] This is an especially useful option for large data sets where durations are heavily tied. (2) If the input data are split into groups, a separate life table is calculated for each of the groups. (3) If there is more than one origin state, the life table calculation is done separately for each subset of episodes having the same origin state. Consequently, the life table calculation is always conditional on a given origin state. (4) If, for a given origin state, there is only a single destination state, an ordinary life table is calculated. If there are two or more destination states, a so-called multiple-decrement life table is produced.

To explain the formulas used for the life table calculation, we proceed in two steps. We first consider the case of a single transition (i.e. only a single origin and a single destination state); then we take into account the possibility of competing risks (i.e. two or more destination states). In both cases, to simplify notation, we assume a sample of N episodes all having the same origin state.

Single Transitions

All formulas used in the calculation of single transition life tables are based on the following quantities, defined for each interval I_l, $l = 1, \ldots, L$.

$$E_l \;=\; \text{the number of episodes with events in } I_l$$

$$Z_l \;=\; \text{the number of censored episodes ending in } I_l$$

The next important point is the definition of a *risk set*, $\mathcal{R}_l$, for each of the time intervals, that is, the set of units (episodes) that are at risk of having an event during the lth interval.[4] To take into account episodes that are censored during the interval, this is done in two steps. First the number of episodes, N_l, that enter the lth interval, is defined recursively by

$$N_1 = N, \quad N_l = N_{l-1} - E_{l-1} - Z_{l-1}$$

In a second step one has to decide how many of the episodes that are censored during an interval should be contained in the risk set for that interval. A

---

[2] With TDA, if the definition of time intervals starts at a value greater than zero, an additional interval $[0, \tau_1)$ is created internally and taken into account in all calculations; however, this additional interval is not used in the printout of results.

[3] For a discussion of using weight in longitudinal data analyses, see Hoem 1985, 1989.

[4] We generally denote the risk set by the symbol $\mathcal{R}$, the number of units contained in the risk set by the symbol R.

standard assumption is that one half of their number should be contained but, clearly, this is a somewhat arbitrary assumption.[5] To provide the possibility of changing this assumption, we assume a constant ω $(0 \leq \omega \leq 1)$ for the definition of the fraction of censored episodes that should be contained in the risk set.[6] The number of elements in the risk set is defined, then, by

$$R_l = N_l - \omega Z_l$$

Using these basic quantities, it is easy to define all other concepts used in the life table setup. First the conditional probabilities for having an event in the lth interval, q_l, and for surviving the interval, p_l, are

$$q_l = \frac{E_l}{R_l} \quad \text{and} \quad p_l = 1 - q_l$$

As an implication, one gets the following estimator for the survivor function[7]

$$G_1 = 1, \quad G_l = p_{l-1} G_{l-1}$$

Having estimates of the survivor function, the density function is evaluated approximately at the midpoints of the intervals as the first derivative

$$f_l = \frac{G_l - G_{l+1}}{\tau_{l+1} - \tau_l} \qquad l = 1, \ldots, q - 1$$

Of course, if the last interval is open on the right side, it is not possible to calculate the survivor function for this interval. Also, estimates of the transition rate, r_l, are calculated at the midpoints of the intervals. They are defined by

$$r_l = \frac{f_l}{\bar{G}_l} \qquad \text{where} \qquad \bar{G}_l = \frac{G_l + G_{l+1}}{2}$$

and this can also be written as

$$r_l = \frac{1}{\tau_{l+1} - \tau_l} \frac{q_l}{1 - q_l/2} = \frac{1}{\tau_{l+1} - \tau_l} \frac{E_l}{R_l - E_l/2}$$

Finally, it is possible to calculate approximate standard errors for the estimates of the survivor and density function, and for the transition rates, by the formulas

$$\text{SE}\,(G_l) \;=\; G_l \left[\sum_{i=1}^{l-1} \frac{q_i}{p_i\, R_i} \right]^{1/2}$$

---

[5] See the discussion given by Namboodiri and Suchindran (1987, p. 58ff).

[6] For life table calculations done with TDA, the constant ω may be defined with the command *cfrac=...*; the default value is one half.

[7] Note that the survivor function is calculated at the beginning of each interval. Most programs use this convention in the printout of life tables. An exception is SPSS, where the survivor function in the life table output is given at the end of each interval (see Blossfeld, Hamerle, and Mayer 1989).

$$\text{SE}(f_l) \;=\; \frac{q_l\,G_l}{\tau_{l+1} - \tau_l} \left[\sum_{i=1}^{l-1} \frac{q_i}{p_i\,R_i} + \frac{p_i}{q_i\,R_i} \right]^{1/2}$$

$$\text{SE}(r_l) \;=\; \frac{r_l}{\sqrt{q_l\,R_l}} \left[1 - \left[\frac{r_l\,(\tau_{l+1} - \tau_l)}{2} \right]^2 \right]^{1/2}$$

Given large samples, it may be assumed that the values of the survivor, density, and rate functions, divided by their standard errors, are approximately standard normally distributed. In these cases it is then possible to calculate confidence intervals.

As an example of life table estimation with TDA, we examine the length of durations between successive job shifts. This means that there is only one type of event: a "job shift" from the origin state "being in a job" to the destination state "having left the job." Unrealistically, we assume in this application that all job episodes in the data file *rrdat.1* (see Boxes 2.2.1 and 2.2.2) can be considered as independent from each other (single episode case) and that there is no important heterogeneity among the individuals.[8] Thus, we are going to estimate "average" survivor and transition rate functions across all the job spells and individuals.

In Box 3.1.1 the command file (*ehc1.cf*) for the life table estimation with TDA is shown. The upper part of this file is identical to command file *ehb2.cf*, shown in Box 2.2.4, which was used to define single episode data. Only two commands have to be added to request a life table estimation. First, the command

   $tp = 0 \; (30) \; 500;$

is used to define time intervals, each having a width of 30 months, beginning at time zero and going up to time 500. The second command is

   $ltb = ehc1.ltb;$

which requests a life table estimation and defines the name of an output file. Recognizing this command, TDA performs a life table estimation and writes the resulting table(s) into the user-defined output file.

Executing command file *ehc1.cf* with TDA, one gets two output files. The first is the standard output, which, as a default, is displayed on the terminal's screen with some basic information about the job; the second is the file *ehc1.ltb* containing the estimated life table. The contents of the second output file are shown in Box 3.1.2. The life table is divided into two panels. The upper panel shows the time intervals and the basic quantities for each of the time intervals. The second panel again shows the time intervals and gives estimates of the survivor function, the duration density function, and the transition rate, each

---

[8] Of course, this is a very strong assumption because the individuals are represented in the data file (*rrdat.1*) with varying numbers of job spells. Thus, there are dependencies between the episodes of each individual.

Box 3.1.1 Command file *ehc1.cf* (life table estimation)

```
dfile = rrdat.1;        data file

v1  (ID)     = c1 ;     ID of individual
v2  (NOJ)    = c2 ;     Serial number of the job
v3  (TStart) = c3 ;     Starting time of the job
v4  (TFin)   = c4 ;     Ending time of the job
v5  (SEX)    = c5 ;     Sex (1 men, 2 women)
v6  (TI)     = c6 ;     Date of interview
v7  (TB)     = c7 ;     Date of birth
v8  (T1)     = c8 ;     Date of entry into the labor market
v9  (TM)     = c9 ;     Date of marriage (0 if no marriage)
v10 (PRES)   = c10;     Prestige score of job i
v11 (PRESN)  = c11;     Prestige score of job i + 1
v12 (EDU)    = c12;     Highest educational attainment

# Define origin and destination state. Origin state is 0.
# Destination state is 0 if right censored, or 1.
v13 (ORG)    = 0;
v14 (DES)    = if eq(v4,v6) then 0 else 1;

# Definition of starting and ending time
# on a process time axis.
v15 (TSP) = 0;
v16 (TFP) = v4 - v3 + 1; one month added

# commands to define single episode data
org =  v13;   define origin state
des =  v14;   define destination state
ts  =  v15;   define starting time
tf  =  v16;   define ending time
```

```
# add commands for life table estimation
tp  = 0 (30) 500;   time intervals: 0, 30, 60, ...
ltb = ehc1.ltb;     life table is written to ehc1.ltb
```

with its estimated standard errors. An estimate of the median is calculated, if possible, by linear interpolation of the survivor function.

We want to give a short example of how the numbers in the life table of our example are related to the formulas developed earlier.

In the third column of the life table in Box 3.1.2, the number of episodes entering into the successive intervals is given. In the first interval, all 600 episodes entered: $N_1 = N = 600$. The numbers of the following intervals $l = 2, 3, \ldots$ are calculated as

$$N_l = N_{l-1} - E_{l-1} - Z_{l-1}$$

where E_l, the number of events in the lth interval, is printed in column 6 and Z_l, the number of censored episodes in the lth interval, is printed in column 4.

Box 3.1.2   Result of using command file *ebc1.cf* (Box 3.1.1)

```
Life table. SN 1. Origin state 0.
Cases: 600  weighted: 600

Start of              Number  Number  Exposed      D-State 1
Interval Midpoint Entering Censored  to Risk Events    Prob
    0.00   15.00      600       28     586.0     223 0.38055
   30.00   45.00      349       23     337.5     113 0.33481
   60.00   75.00      213       15     205.5      51 0.24818
   90.00  105.00      147       16     139.0      25 0.17986
  120.00  135.00      106       15      98.5      24 0.24365
  150.00  165.00       67        5      64.5       9 0.13953
  180.00  195.00       53        9      48.5       4 0.08247
  210.00  225.00       40        5      37.5       3 0.08000
  240.00  255.00       32        5      29.5       0 0.00000
  270.00  285.00       27        7      23.5       2 0.08511
  300.00  315.00       18        5      15.5       2 0.12903
  330.00  345.00       11        1      10.5       2 0.19048
  360.00  375.00        8        3       6.5       0 0.00000
  390.00  405.00        5        4       3.0       0 0.00000
  420.00  435.00        1        1       0.5       0 0.00000

Start of              Survivor        D-State 1       D-State 1
Interval Midpoint Function Error Density    Error    Rate    Error
    0.00   15.00 1.00000 0.00000 0.01268 0.00067 0.01567 0.00102
   30.00   45.00 0.61945 0.02006 0.00691 0.00058 0.01340 0.00124
   60.00   75.00 0.41205 0.02077 0.00341 0.00045 0.00944 0.00131
   90.00  105.00 0.30979 0.01995 0.00186 0.00036 0.00659 0.00131
  120.00  135.00 0.25407 0.01922 0.00206 0.00040 0.00925 0.00187
  150.00  165.00 0.19217 0.01822 0.00089 0.00029 0.00500 0.00166
  180.00  195.00 0.16535 0.01774 0.00045 0.00022 0.00287 0.00143
  210.00  225.00 0.15172 0.01754 0.00040 0.00023 0.00278 0.00160
  240.00  255.00 0.13958 0.01748 0.00000      ** 0.00000      **
  270.00  285.00 0.13958 0.01748 0.00040 0.00027 0.00296 0.00209
  300.00  315.00 0.12770 0.01790 0.00055 0.00037 0.00460 0.00324
  330.00  345.00 0.11122 0.01900 0.00071 0.00047 0.00702 0.00493
  360.00  375.00 0.09004 0.02045 0.00000      ** 0.00000      **
  390.00  405.00 0.09004 0.02045 0.00000      ** 0.00000      **
  420.00  435.00 0.09004 0.02045 0.00000      ** 0.00000      **
Median duration: 47.28
```

In our example:

$$N_1 = 600$$
$$N_2 = 600 - 223 - 28 = 349$$
$$N_3 = 349 - 113 - 23 = 213$$

Under the assumption that censored episodes are equally distributed within each interval ($w = 0.5$), one is able to estimate the number of episodes at risk in each interval. For the lth interval:

$$\hat{R}_l = N_l - 0.5\,Z_l$$

In our example:

$$\hat{R}_1 = 600 - 0.5 \cdot 28 = 586.0$$
$$\hat{R}_2 = 349 - 0.5 \cdot 23 = 337.5$$

The conditional probability of having an event in the lth interval, calculated as

$$\hat{q}_l = \frac{E_l}{\hat{R}_l}$$

is printed in column 7. In our example:

$$\hat{q}_1 = \frac{223}{586.0} = 0.38055$$
$$\hat{q}_2 = \frac{113}{337.5} = 0.33481$$

The conditional probability of experiencing no event in the lth interval is then

$$\hat{p}_l = 1 - \hat{q}_l$$

In our example:

$$\hat{p}_1 = 1 - 0.38055 = 0.61945$$
$$\hat{p}_2 = 1 - 0.33481 = 0.66519$$

Based on these estimates, one can compute estimates of the survivor function (column 3 of the lower panel of the life table):

$$\hat{G}_1 = 1$$
$$\hat{G}_l = \hat{p}_{l-1} \cdot \hat{p}_{l-2} \cdots \hat{p}_1$$

In our example:

$$\hat{G}_1 = 1$$
$$\hat{G}_2 = 0.61945 \cdot 1 = 0.61945$$
$$\hat{G}_3 = 0.66519 \cdot 0.61945 \cdot 1 = 0.41205$$

Finally, we also have to consider the length of the intervals, $\tau_{l+1} - \tau_l$ (for the lth interval). The duration density function is given as

$$\hat{f}_l = \frac{\hat{G}_l - \hat{G}_{l-1}}{\tau_{l+1} - \tau_l}$$

In our example:

$$\hat{f}_1 = \frac{1.00000 - 0.61945}{30 - 0} = 0.01268$$

$$\hat{f}_2 = \frac{0.61945 - 0.41205}{60 - 30} = 0.00691$$

The "average" transition rate, evaluated at the midpoint of each interval, is printed in column 7 of the lower panel in the life table:

$$\hat{r}_l = \frac{1}{\tau_{l+1} - \tau_l} \frac{E_l}{\hat{R}_l - 0.5\,E_l}$$

In our example:

$$\hat{r}_1 = \frac{1}{30 - 0} \frac{223}{586.0 - 0.5 \cdot 223} = 0.01567$$

$$\hat{r}_2 = \frac{1}{60 - 30} \frac{113}{337.5 - 0.5 \cdot 113} = 0.01340$$

The standard errors for the survivor function are printed in column 4, the standard errors for the duration density function are printed in column 6, and the standard errors for the rate function are printed in column 8 of the lower panel in the life table. Finally, the median duration in a job is 47.28 months. This means that half of the respondents left their jobs after about 4 years.

Life tables, as shown in Box 3.1.2, are very complex and are not easily interpreted. It is therefore better to plot the interval-related information of the survivor, density, and rate functions. An example of a TDA command file *ehc2.cf*, which can be used to generate a plot of the survivor function, is shown in Box 3.1.3. Similar command files can be used to generate plots for the density and rate functions.[9]

In the TDA command file in Box 3.1.3 the life table contained in file *ehc1.ltb* is used as an input file. Because we are interested in the survivor function, we skip the upper panel (the first 15 records) of the life table (in Box 3.1.2) and read only records 16 to 30. Then we define just two variables, *V1* and *V2*, which are needed for the plot, by referring to columns *C1* and *C3* of the data file. The remaining commands define the plot. The *postscript* command defines the name of the output file containing the PostScript description of the plot. The commands *pxlen* and *pylen* define the physical size of the plot, the commands

    pxa(60,5) = 0,300;
    pya(1,10) = 0,1;

define the user coordinates. The x axis is defined in the range 0 to 300 (months), with a big tick mark every 60 months subdivided by 5 small tick marks. The y

---

[9] These command files are not shown here but are contained on the accompanying disk. The command files are *ehc2a.cf* and *ehc2b.cf*, respectively.

Box 3.1.3   Command file *ehc2.cf* to plot a survivor function

```
dfile = ehc1.ltb;          data file
drec  = 16 - 30;           select second part of life table
v1(Time)     = c1;         time axis (begin of interval)
v2(Survivor) = c3;         survivor function

postscript = ehc2.ps;      PostScript output file

pxlen = 80;                physical width (in mm)
pylen = 40;                physical height (in mm)
pxa(60,5) = 0,300;         user coordinates on X axis
pya(1,10) = 0,1;           user coordinates on Y axis
pyfmt = 4.2;               print format

plot = v1,v2;              plot variable v1 vs v2
pltext(80,0.8) = 'Life Table Survivor Function';
```

axis is defined in the range 0 to 1, with just two labelled tick marks subdivided into 10 small intervals. Finally, we define two plot objects. The first plot object, specified by the command

   plot = v1, v2;

is a plot of variable *V1* (x axis coordinates) vs. variable *V2* (y axis coordinates). The second plot object is the string *Life Table Survivor Function* to be plotted at the user coordinates (80,0.8).

Executing TDA with command file *ehc2.cf* creates the output file *ehc2.ps*. This is a PostScript file that can be sent to a printer for a hard copy of the plot, or can be used as part of a PostScript document. The resulting plot, in addition to plots of the density function and the transition rate, is shown in Figure 3.1.1.

The plot of the survivor function shows estimates of the proportions of respondents who have not yet changed their job up to a specific duration. For example, after 10 years (or 120 months) about 25 percent of respondents are still in their job, while about 75 percent have already left. The density function of the job durations, which steeply declines with duration, is an estimate of the probability of a job shift per unit time in the *l*th interval. The transition rate, which also steeply declines with increasing duration, is an estimate of the probability per unit time that a respondent who has survived to the beginning of a given interval will leave his/her job within that interval. It is computed as the number of job moves per unit time in the interval, divided by the average number of individuals who have not yet moved at the mid-point of the interval. Thus, the transition rate applies to those still "at risk" of a job move (i.e. to those to whom a job shift could happen). This means that, in principle, the density function (i.e. the probability of a job shift per unit time in the *l*th interval) can be low even though the transition rate is high, simply because so few individuals are still at risk.

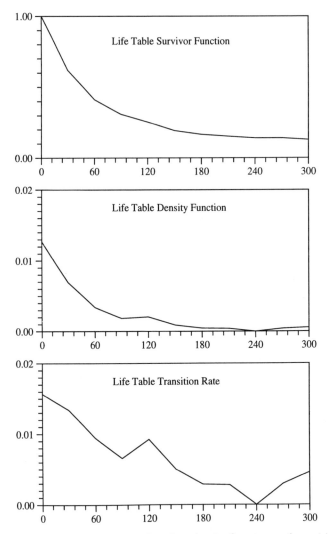

Figure 3.1.1 Plots of the survivor function, density function, and transition rate generated with command files *ehc2.cf*, *ehc2a.cf*, and *ehc2b.cf*, respectively.

Life Table Estimation for Different Groups

Life tables are particularly useful for comparisons of the behavior of subgroups. We therefore extend the example in Box 3.1.1 and demonstrate how separate life tables for men and women can be estimated with TDA. This can be achieved by adding a command to define groups. In this example, we define two groups,

Box 3.1.4   Part of command file *ehc3.cf* (life table estimation)

```
... (first part identical to first part of Box 3.1.1)

# add indicator variables for men and women
# and define two groups
v17 (Men)   = v5[1];    v17 = 1 if v5 = 1, otherwise 0
v18 (Women) = v5[2];    v18 = 1 if v5 = 2, otherwise 0
grp = v17,v18;          define two groups

# add commands for life table estimation
tp  = 0 (30) 500;  time intervals: 0, 30, 60, ...
ltb = ehc3.ltb;    life tables are written to ehc3.ltb
```

men and women. For each group we need an indicator variable that takes any value not equal to zero if the case (data matrix row) is a member of the group, and is zero otherwise. Box 3.1.4 shows part of command file *ehc3.cf*, which is just a modification of command file *ehc1.cf*. *V17* and *V18* are the indicator variables for men and women. The command *grp=V17,V18* defines the two groups based on these two indicator variables. The commands to request life table estimation are basically the same. Only the name of the output file has been changed to *ehc3.ltb*.

The result of using command file *ehc3.cf* is the output file *ehc3.ltb*, now containing two separate life tables, one for men and one for women. To save space, these tables are not shown here. Instead, Figure 3.1.2 shows a plot of the survivor functions.[10] It is easy to see that at the beginning the process for men and women is quite similar. But after a duration of about three years the survivor function of women decreases more steeply than the survivor function for men. Thus, women tend to leave their jobs sooner than men do. After 20 years about 20 % of men, but only about 5 % of women are still in their jobs. The median job durations are about 57 months for men and about 40 months for women.

Examples of the Application of Survivor Functions in Social Research

In modern social research, survivor functions have been increasingly used to study social change. They are particularly suited to the analysis of how changing historical conditions affect life course transitions of successive birth cohorts.[11] They enable the description of the age-graded character of roles and behaviors and, by documenting shifts in the timing when individuals enter or leave spe-

---

[10] The plot was generated with command file *ehc4.cf*, supplied on the accompanying disk.

[11] See Mayer and Schwarz 1989; Hogan 1978, 1981; Marini 1978, 1984, 1985; Elder 1975, 1978, 1987.

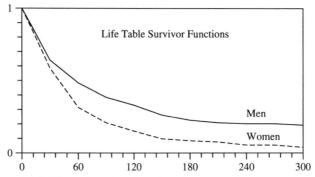

Figure 3.1.2 Plots of survivor functions for men and women, generated with command file *ehc4.cf*.

cific social institutions or positions, the changes of life phases (Blossfeld and Nuthmann 1990; Becker and Blossfeld 1991).

Example 1: "Vulnerable" Phases in the Educational Careers of German Students

An example of the application of survivor functions in educational research is given in Blossfeld (1990, 1992). He studies the process of entry into vocational training in Germany and shows that the particular organizational structure of the German educational system creates what he calls a "vulnerable" life phase for students. *Vulnerability* means that the time span between having left the general educational system and entry into vocational training is limited to a short period of about two or three years, during which prevailing historical events, economic conditions, and demographic constellations strongly determine the opportunities of each generation to acquire vocational training.

The survivor functions in Figure 3.1.3 demonstrate this "vulnerable" phase for three different birth cohorts and for men and women. They show the proportions of school leavers who did not yet enter the German vocational training system for every point in time after leaving the general educational system. The curves are very different for the three birth cohorts and for men and women. In particular, the economic and political breakdown in the immediate postwar period (1945–50) had a strong negative effect on enrollment in vocational training for the 1929–31 cohort. Confronted with the existing historical conditions, school leavers of this birth cohort did not rank entering vocational training highly because they had more urgent problems to deal with (e.g. making a living), and it would have been very difficult to find trainee positions at all (Mayer 1987, 1988, 1991). Compared to this immediate postwar period, the later social and economic development until the mid-1970s led to a constant rise in the standard of living, a decrease in unemployment, and a

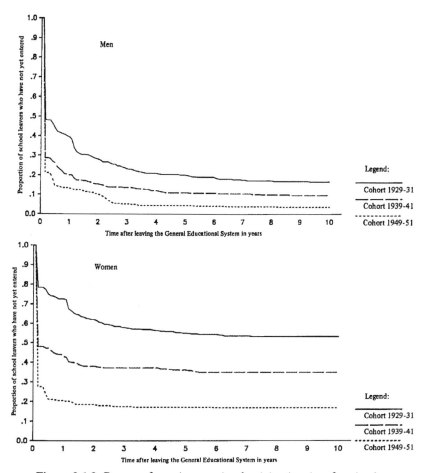

Figure 3.1.3 Process of entering vocational training (survivor functions).

substantial growth in the number of trainee positions offered in the private sector.

The upper part of Figure 3.1.3 shows that about 50 % of men in the 1929–31 birth cohort started vocational training immediately after leaving the general educational system. An additional 27 % of these men undertook vocational training within three years of leaving the general educational system. But about 23 % never entered vocational training. In comparison, about 71 % and 79 % of the men in the 1939–41 and 1949–51 birth cohorts, respectively, began vocational training immediately, and an additional 14 % of the men in both cohorts started within three years. Thus, only about 15 % of the men in the

1939–41 cohort and about 7 % of the men in the 1949–51 cohort never entered vocational training.

For women (lower part of Figure 3.1.3), these differences were even more pronounced. Within three years of leaving the general educational system, only 40 % of the women in the 1929–31 cohort, but 60 % of the women in the 1939–41 cohort, and 80 % of the women in the 1949–51 cohort undertook vocational training. In other words, with regard to educational opportunities, women, in particular, carried the burden of the immediate postwar social and economic crises, but they also profited more than men from the rapid economic recovery in the 1960s and early 1970s.

In summary, this description based on survivor functions reveals that in the German vocational training system entries are hard to postpone beyond a "vulnerable" life phase of about two or three years after leaving the general educational system. Individuals' careers are directed to vocational training relatively early and are hard to change later on. The tremendous increase in the proportion of trainee positions until the early 1970s had therefore almost no effect on the process of entering vocational training for the 1929–31 cohort (Figure 3.1.3). It was not possible for the members of this cohort to "stop" their life course and to "resume" their educational careers when the trainee positions finally became available. In the German educational system a temporary lack of trainee positions is therefore not only a short-term problem, but leads to long-term life-course effects for many people. There is a long-term disadvantage because it is difficult to acquire vocational degrees in later life stages when one is more removed from the institutions of vocational training and has additional social commitments (such as maintaining one's own home, marriage, and children), making entrance into the institutions of vocational training more and more unlikely. Hence, in terms of educational opportunities, there are disadvantaged generations in Germany, such as the cohorts born around 1930, who completed their training in the immediate postwar period, or the large birth cohorts that crowded into vocational training at the beginning of the 1980s.

Example 2: Changes in Women's Ages at Family Formation

Another illustration of the utility of survivor functions for describing social change is given by Blossfeld and Jaenichen (1992). They discussed the changes in the process of women's entry into marriage and motherhood across successive birth cohorts in Germany. Tables 3.1.1 and 3.1.2 show the percentages of women who have not yet entered first marriage or first birth for each birth cohort and specific ages. These percentages are based on life table estimates of survivor functions for each cohort for the events of entry into marriage and first birth.

As shown in Table 3.1.1, age at first marriage fell sharply from the 1919–23 cohort to the 1944–48 cohort, and has since been rising again until the youngest

Table 3.1.1 Changes in the timing of entry into marriage, as measured by proportions unmarried at specific ages (percentages).

Birth	Proportion of unmarried women at age							
Cohort	20	24	28	32	36	40	44	48
1964–68	89	–	–	–	–	–	–	–
1959–63	78	40	–	–	–	–	–	–
1954–58	73	32	19	–	–	–	–	–
1949–53	65	24	11	7	–	–	–	–
1944–48	65	15	7	4	3	–	–	–
1939–43	80	21	8	5	3	3	–	–
1934–38	76	23	9	6	5	5	4	–
1929–33	86	32	13	7	6	5	5	4
1924–28	90	40	16	11	8	6	5	5
1919–23	90	46	20	13	10	9	7	7

Table 3.1.2 Changes in the timing of entry into motherhood as measured by proportions childless at specific ages (percentages).

Birth	Proportion of childless women at age							
Cohort	20	24	28	32	36	40	44	48
1964–68	92	–	–	–	–	–	–	–
1959–63	90	57	–	–	–	–	–	–
1954–58	84	55	30	–	–	–	–	–
1949–53	78	47	21	15	–	–	–	–
1944–48	77	32	16	11	9	–	–	–
1939–43	87	41	18	13	10	10	–	–
1934–38	83	45	18	13	11	11	11	–
1929–33	92	54	28	19	16	16	16	16
1924–28	87	56	26	19	15	14	14	14
1919–23	91	57	30	19	15	15	15	15

birth cohort. The greatest movements occurred among women aged 20–24, where the unmarried proportion dropped from 46 % to 15 % and subsequently increased again to 40 %. The result is that as far as the youngest cohorts, 1964–68 and 1959–63, can be followed, they have more or less the same age pattern at entry into marriage as we find for the oldest cohorts, 1924–28 and 1919–23.

Looking at ages at first birth in Table 3.1.2, we observe a similar trend. Again, it is the 1944–48 cohort that entered motherhood at the youngest ages. For this cohort not only marriages but entries into motherhood were highly concentrated. And again, we find more or less the same time pattern of entry into motherhood for the youngest cohorts, 1964–68 and 1959–63, and the oldest cohorts, 1924–28 and 1919–23, at least as far as the youngest cohorts can be followed.

Both tables show that in Germany the delay of entry into marriage and motherhood seems to be less dramatic than has been shown for other countries, such as the Scandinavian ones, especially Sweden (see Blossfeld 1995; Hoem 1986, 1991; Hoem and Rennermalm 1985). In Germany, more or less the same entrance pattern of ages into marriage and motherhood is observed as was already established 50 years ago. However, it is also clear that in Germany the earlier movement toward younger and universal marriage and motherhood had come to a halt at the end of the 1960s and the beginning of the 1970s. But this reversal of the timing of marriage and motherhood is not in line with the monotonic trend in women's educational attainment across cohorts (Blossfeld and Shavit 1993). It is therefore questionable whether changes in marriage and motherhood can be attributed mainly to women's growing economic independence (see Blossfeld 1995), as argued for example by Becker (1981).

3.2   Product-Limit Estimation

Another method for the nonparametric estimation of the survivor function and its derivatives is the product-limit, also called the Kaplan-Meier (1958), method. One of the advantages of this approach, compared with the life table method, is that it is not necessary to group the episode durations according to arbitrarily defined time intervals. Instead, the product-limit method is based on the calculation of a risk set at every point in time where at least one event occurred. In this way the information contained in a set of episodes is optimally used. The only drawback of this method results from the fact that all episodes must be sorted according to their ending (and starting) times, but with efficient sorting algorithms the method can be employed with fairly large sets of episodes.

This section describes the product-limit estimation method and its implementation in TDA. The options, depending on the type of input data, are essentially the same as with the life table method: (1) If there are sample weights defined with the *cwt* command, these weights are used in all calculations. (2) If the input data are split into groups, separate product-limit estimates are calculated for each of the groups. (3) If there is more than a single origin state, one or more product-limit estimates are calculated for each subset of episodes having the same origin state. (4) If there is more than a single destination state, separate product-limit estimates are calculated for each transition found in the input data.

The following description proceeds in two steps. First, we consider the case of a single transition, then the case of two or more destination states.

Single Transitions

We assume a sample of N episodes, all having the same origin state and either having the same destination state or being right censored. If groups are defined, it is assumed that all episodes belong to the same group. For the moment we also assume that all episodes have the starting time zero.[12]

The first step is to consider the points in time where at least one of the episodes ends with an event. There are, say, q such points in time.

$$\tau_1 < \tau_2 < \tau_3 < \ldots < \tau_q$$

The second step is to define three basic quantities, all defined for $l = 1, \ldots, q$, with the convention that $\tau_0 = 0$.

$E_l = $ the number of episodes with events at τ_l

$Z_l = $ the number of censored episodes ending in $[\tau_{l-1}, \tau_l)$

$R_l = $ the number of episodes in the risk set at τ_l, denoted $\mathcal{R}_l$, i.e. the number of episodes with starting time less than τ_l and ending time $\geq \tau_l$

Note that the implied definition of the risk set allows the handling of episodes with starting times greater than zero. Also note that the risk set at τ_l includes episodes that are censored at this point in time. It is assumed that a censored episode contains the information that there was no event up to *and including* the observed ending time of the episode. As sometimes stated, censoring takes place an infinitesimal amount to the right of the observed ending time.

Given these quantities, the product-limit estimator of the survivor function is defined as

$$\hat{G}(t) = \prod_{l:\tau_l < t} \left(1 - \frac{E_l}{R_l} \right)$$

This is a step function with steps at the points in time, τ_l. The commonly used formula to calculate estimates of standard errors for the survivor function is

$$\text{SE}(\hat{G}(t)) = \hat{G}(t) \left[\sum_{l:\tau_l < t} \frac{E_l}{R_l (R_l - E_l)} \right]^{1/2}$$

---

[12] Note that this assumption is not necessary for product-limit calculations with TDA. For instance, it is possible to perform product-limit estimations with left-truncated data, or with a set of episodes that are split into parts. However, in the context of duration analysis the assumption of zero starting times in order to get sensible results applies in almost all cases.

Box 3.2.1 Part of command file *ehc5.cf* (Kaplan-Meier estimation)

```
... (first part identical to first part of Box 3.1.1)

# add commands for Kaplan-Meier estimation
ple = ehc5.ple; estimates are written to output file ehb5.ple
```

In addition to survivor function estimates, the product-limit method gives a simple estimate of the cumulated transition rate.

$$\hat{H}(t) = -\log\left(\hat{G}(t)\right)$$

This is again a step function. It is especially useful for simple graphical checks of distributional assumptions about the underlying durations. Some examples are given in chapter 8.

Unfortunately, unlike the life table estimation, the product-limit method does not provide direct estimates of transition rates. Of course, it is possible to get estimates by numerical differentiation of $\hat{H}(t)$, but this requires that one first applies a smoothing procedure to the cumulative rate.[13]

In illustrating the application of the product-limit estimator with TDA in Box 3.2.1, we again apply the job change example in which we assumed that there are only single episodes and two states ("being in a job" and "having left the job"). The difference between the TDA command file for the life table method in Box 3.1.1 and the TDA command file for the product-limit estimator is small. Just the *ltb* and *tp* commands in Box 3.1.1 have to be replaced by the *ple* command in Box 3.2.1. The command *ple=ehc5.ple* requests the product limit estimates to be written into the file named *ehc5.ple*. The command file *ehc5.cf* can be executed with the command

tda cf=ehc5.cf > output_file

Part of the result of this run is shown in Box 3.2.2. The first two columns are to simplify access to the table, if it is used as an input data file for plots. The first column assigns a unique identification number to each table (here the number is 0); the second column simply counts the data lines (in this case we have a maximum of 131 data lines).

The column labeled *Time* shows the points in time where at least one event takes place. The number of events (job moves) is given in the next column. For example, at a job duration of 6 months we observe 10 job moves, and at a job duration of 42 months we observe 1 event. Then come the number of censored episodes with ending times less than the actual value of the *Time* column and greater or equal to the preceding value in the *Time* column. For example, at the job duration of 3 months, there is a censored episode that is

---

[13] TDA offers spline functions to smooth the cumulative rate. Using this option automatically provides first derivatives. However, this option is not illustrated here.

Box 3.2.2 Result of command file *ehc5.cf* (Box 3.2.1)

```
SN 1. Transition: 0,1 - Product-Limit Estimation
```

ID	Index	Time	Number Events	Number Censored	Exposed to Risk	Survivor Function	Std. Error	Cum. Rate
0	0	0.00	0	0	600	1.00000	0.00000	0.00000
0	1	2.00	2	0	600	0.99667	0.00235	0.00334
0	2	3.00	5	1	597	0.98832	0.00439	0.01175
0	3	4.00	9	2	590	0.97324	0.00660	0.02712
0	4	5.00	3	0	581	0.96822	0.00717	0.03230
0	5	6.00	10	1	577	0.95144	0.00880	0.04978
0	6	7.00	9	0	567	0.93634	0.00999	0.06578
0	7	8.00	6	1	557	0.92625	0.01070	0.07661
0	8	9.00	7	3	548	0.91442	0.01146	0.08947
0	9	10.00	8	1	540	0.90087	0.01225	0.10439
. . . .								
0	41	42.00	1	1	273	0.50399	0.02093	0.68519
0	42	43.00	2	0	272	0.50029	0.02094	0.69257
0	43	44.00	5	1	269	0.49099	0.02096	0.71133
0	44	45.00	1	1	263	0.48912	0.02096	0.71514
. . . .								
0	125	275.00	1	11	26	0.13452	0.01751	2.00607
0	126	293.00	1	5	20	0.12779	0.01788	2.05736
0	127	312.00	1	3	16	0.11980	0.01846	2.12190
0	128	326.00	1	1	14	0.11125	0.01902	2.19601
0	129	332.00	1	2	11	0.10113	0.01980	2.29132
0	130	350.00	1	1	9	0.08990	0.02054	2.40910
0	131	428.00	0	8				

```
Median Duration: 43.03
Duration times limited to: 350
Cases: 600  weighted: 600
```

Box 3.2.3 Command file *ehc6.cf* to plot a survivor function

```
dfile = ehc5.ple;            data file

postscript = ehc6.ps;        PostScript output file
pxlen = 80;                  physical width (in mm)
pylen = 40;                  physical height (in mm)
pxa(60,5) = 0,300;           user coordinates on X axis
pya(1,10) = 0,1;             user coordinates on Y axis

plabel  = 'Product-Limit Survivor Function';

v1(Time)     = c3;           time axis (begin of interval)
v2(Survivor) = c7;           survivor function

plot = v1,v2;                plot variable v1 vs v2
```

less than 3 months long and greater than or equal to 2 months. Given this information, the risk set printed in the fifth column is easily calculated. For example, at the job duration of 3 months, 597 episodes (600 episodes minus 2 events at job duration 2 minus 1 censored episode up to job duration 3) are still at risk. The last three columns show estimates of the survivor function, its standard errors, and the cumulated transition rate as defined previously. For example, after about 4 years (or 45 months) a proportion of 0.48912 of workers are still in the same job. The survivor function of the product-limit estimator is only defined up to the highest event time. The highest event time in Box 3.2.2 is 350 months. Eight additional censored cases with longer job durations follow. Under these circumstances, the estimated survivor function can no longer approach zero and can only be interpreted up until 350 months. Finally, if possible, an estimate of the median is calculated by linear interpolation of the survivor function. In Box 3.2.2 the estimate of the median of job duration is 43.03 months.

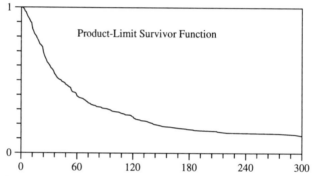

Figure 3.2.1 Plot of survivor function (product-limit estimation) generated with command file *ehc6.cf*.

Again, the survivor function in Box 3.2.2 is not very comprehensible. The shape of the function can be evaluated more easily, if it is plotted against job duration. An example command file, *ehc6.cf*, to plot the product-limit estimator of the survivor function with TDA, is shown in Box 3.2.3. Because it is basically identical to command file *ehc2.cf* (Box 3.1.3), we do not give further explanation. The resulting plot is shown in Figure 3.2.1. A comparison with the life table estimate of the survivor function, shown in Figure 3.1.1, shows fairly identical results. This is in accordance with our experience in practical research applications that show that the difference between life table and product-limit estimations is normally very small.

3.3   Comparing Survivor Functions

In analyzing episode data, one often has to compare survivor functions and test if there are significant differences. Basically two different methods are available. The first relies on the calculation of confidence intervals for each of

Box 3.3.1 Part of command file *ehc7.cf* (comparing survivor functions)

```
    ... (first part identical to first part of Box 3.1.1)

    # Define indicator variables for men and women
    v17 (Men)   = v5[1];   v17 = 1 if v5 = 1
    v18 (Women) = v5[2];   v18 = 1 if v5 = 2

    # add commands for Kaplan-Meier estimation
    ple = ehc7.ple; estimates are written to output file ehc7.ple

    # define two groups (men and women) and request a comparison
    # of survivor functions
    grp = v17,v18;
    csf;
```

the survivor functions and then checks if they overlap or not. This is possible with both the life table and the product-limit methods. Both methods provide estimates of standard errors for the survivor function. Another possibility is to calculate specific test statistics to compare two or more survivor functions. This section describes both possibilities.

Defining Groups of Episodes

To make any comparisons, there must be two or more groups of episodes. This is easily done using indicator variables that define membership in a group. In TDA, the syntax is

$grp = G1, G2, G3,...;$

with $G1$, $G2$, and so on, the names of variables contained in the data matrix. The set of episodes given in the current data matrix is then split into m groups, with m the number of indicator variables defined with the *grp* command. The first group, defined by $G1$, contains all episodes where the value of this variable is not zero, the second group is defined by $G2$ in the same way, and so on.

To illustrate grouping in the case of product-limit estimation, we extend the example in Box 3.2.1. The new command file, *ehc7.cf*, is a small modification of command file *ehc5.cf* already shown in Box 3.2.1. The additional commands are shown in Box 3.3.1.

Using this modified command file, a product-limit estimation is done separately for men and women. Consequently, the output file *ehc7.ple* contains two tables, one with estimates for men, another one for women. Figure 3.3.1 shows a plot of these two survivor functions, together with 95 % confidence intervals.[14] After about 3 years, the confidence bands of the survivor functions

---

[14] The plot has been generated with command file *ehc8.cf*, which is part of the accompanying disk.

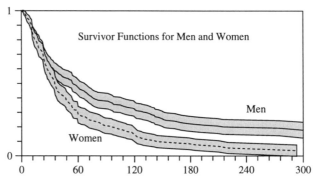

Figure 3.3.1 Plots of survivor functions (product-limit estimation) for men and women with 95 % confidence intervals (grey-scaled). The plot has been generated with command file *ehc8.cf*.

of men and women no longer intersect. Thus, there are statistically significant differences in the job exit behavior of men and women for greater durations.

Construction of Test Statistics

Many different test statistics have been proposed to compare two or more survivor functions. We describe four that can be calculated by TDA. All of them are based on product-limit estimates of survivor functions.

It is assumed that m groups have been defined that do not intersect. The whole sample is implicitly defined as the set of all episodes that are contained in one of these groups. Then, in exactly the same way as explained in connection with the product-limit method, all calculations are done for each transition in the whole sample separately. Therefore, we only consider a sample of episodes that have the same origin state and are censored or have the same destination state.

In general, a sample defined this way consists of m groups and the following table can be calculated.

$$
\begin{array}{llllllll}
\tau_1 & R_{11} & E_{11} & R_{12} & E_{12} & \ldots & R_{1m} & E_{1m} \\
\tau_2 & R_{21} & E_{21} & R_{22} & E_{22} & \ldots & R_{2m} & E_{2m} \\
& & & & \vdots & & & \\
\tau_q & R_{n1} & E_{q1} & R_{q2} & E_{q2} & \ldots & R_{qm} & E_{qm}
\end{array}
$$

These are the basic quantities for the product-limit estimation, for the whole sample, and for each group separately. $\tau_1 < \tau_2 < \ldots < \tau_q$ are the points in time where at least one episode contained in the sample has an event. E_{lg} is the number of episodes contained in group g and having an event at τ_l; R_{lg} is defined as the number of elements in the risk set at τ_l for the episodes contained in group g (i.e. all episodes belonging to group g that have starting times less than τ_l and ending times equal to or greater than τ_l). Altogether, these quantities are sufficient for a product-limit estimation in each of the m groups.

Given this, the four test statistics can be defined and they are denoted S_v ($v = 1, \ldots, 4$). Because the calculations only differ in different weights, we give their definitions first. The weights are denoted $W_l^{(v)}$, and they are defined for $l = 1, \ldots, q$ by

$$W_l^{(1)} = 1$$

$$W_l^{(2)} = R_l \qquad (3.1)$$

$$W_l^{(3)} = \sqrt{R_l}$$

$$W_l^{(4)} = \prod_{i=1}^{l} \frac{R_i - E_i + 1}{R_i + 1}$$

The next step is to construct for each of the four test statistics one (m)-vector $U^{(v)}$ and one (m, m)-matrix $V^{(v)}$. The definitions are[15]

$$U_g^{(v)} = \sum_{l=1}^{q} W_l^{(v)} \left(E_{lg} - R_{lg} \frac{E_{l0}}{R_{l0}} \right)$$

$$V_{g_1 g_2}^{(v)} = \sum_{i=1}^{n} W_l^{(v)2} \frac{E_{l0} (R_{l0} - E_{l0})}{R_{l0} - 1} \frac{R_{l g_1}}{R_{l0}} \left(\delta_{g_1 g_2} - \frac{R_{l g_2}}{R_{l0}} \right)$$

Finally, the test statistics are defined by

$$S_v = U^{(v)\prime} V^{(v)-1} U^{(v)} \qquad (3.2)$$

All of them follow a χ^2-distribution with $m - 1$ degrees of freedom given the null hypothesis that there are no significant differences. Note that, accordingly, the rank of $V^{(v)}$ is only $m - 1$. Therefore, in the calculation of (3.2), one can use a generalized inverse or omit the last dimension without loss of generality. TDA follows the latter of these two possibilities.[16]

Unfortunately, there is no uniform convention to name the different test statistics, so we state the names used by TDA and give some remarks about other naming conventions. In the order given by (3.1), we have:

1. **Log-Rank (Savage).** Other names are *Generalized Savage Test* (Andreß 1985, p. 158; 1992). The same name is used by BMDP, with *Mantel-Cox* added. SAS calculates this test statistic under the name *Logrank*.

---

[15] δ_{ij} is the Kronecker symbol, which is one, if $i = j$ and zero otherwise.

[16] If there are anymore rank deficiencies in the V-matrices, TDA will report this in its standard output. Optionally the U-vectors and V-matrices are printed into the protocol file; see the TDA manual for more information.

Box 3.3.2   Results of command file *ehc7.cf* (Box 3.3.1)

```
Group   Variable  Label     Episodes   Weighted
------------------------------------------------
   1      V17      Men          348     348.00
   2      V18      Women        252     252.00
 Sum                            600     600.00


                               Episodes          Weighted
 SN  Org Des  Group  Label  Events  Censored   Events   Censored
----------------------------------------------------------------
   1   0   1    1    Men      245      103     245.00    103.00
   1   0   1    2    Women    213       39     213.00     39.00
 Sum                         458      142     458.00    142.00


Product-limit estimation
Table of PL estimates printed to: ehc7.ple


Comparison of group-specific survivor functions

 SN  Org Des   Test Statistic              T-Stat   DF   Signif
----------------------------------------------------------------
   1   0   1    Log-Rank (Savage)          20.6032   1   1.0000
   1   0   1    Wilcoxon (Breslow)          9.3647   1   0.9978
   1   0   1    Wilcoxon (Tarone-Ware)     14.3267   1   0.9998
   1   0   1    Wilcoxon (Prentice)        10.6951   1   0.9989
```

2. **Wilcoxon (Breslow).** BMDP gives the name *Generalized Wilcoxon (Breslow)*, SAS uses only the label *Wilcoxon*.

3. **Wilcoxon (Tarone-Ware).** This test statistic was proposed by Tarone and Ware (1977) and is named accordingly. It is also calculated by BMDP, using the label *Tarone-Ware*.

4. **Wilcoxon (Prentice).** Finally, we have a test statistic explained by Lawless (1982, p. 423) with reference to R. L. Prentice. Because it is some type of a Wilcoxon test, we use this name.

The TDA command to request the calculation of test statistics to compare survivor functions is simply *csf* as shown in Box 3.3.1. The resulting test statistics are written into the standard output. For the example command file *ehc7.cf*, discussed earlier, this is shown in Box 3.3.2. All test statistics are based on the null hypothesis that the survivor functions of men and women do not differ. They are χ^2-distributed with $m - 1$ degrees of freedom (in the example we have two groups, men and women: $m = 2$). In our example, all four test statistics are significant. In other words, the null hypothesis that survivor functions of men and women do not differ must be rejected. However, it is easy to see that there is a great difference between the Log-Rank (or Savage) test statistic and the three different versions of the Wilcoxon test statistics.

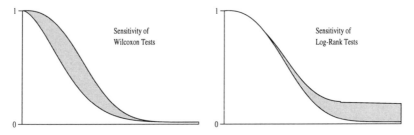

Figure 3.3.2 Regions of sensitivity for Wilcoxon and Log-Rank tests.

The reason for this is that the Wilcoxon tests stress differences of the survivor functions at the beginning of the duration, while the Log-Rank (or Savage) test statistic stresses increasing differences at the end of the process time (see Figure 3.3.2).

Multiple Destination States

We now turn to the case of multiple transitions. Here we have a situation of competing risks conditional on a given origin state. There are different concepts to describe such a situation. The simplest generalization of the single transition case leads to product-limit estimates for pseudosurvivor functions.[17]

The method is analogous to the single transition case. One starts with N_j episodes having the same origin state j. Then, for each possible destination state k, one looks at the points in time, $\tau_{jk,l}$, where at least one transition to destination state k takes place. There are, say, $l = 1, \ldots, q_{jk}$ such points in time.

Let $E_{jk,l}$ denote the number of events at $\tau_{jk,l}$, and let $\mathcal{R}_{j,l}$ denote the risk set at the same point in time. Note that the risk set does not depend on the destination state, but is defined as in the single transition case as the set of all episodes with origin state j, with a starting time less than $\tau_{jk,l}$, and with an ending time equal to or greater than $\tau_{jk,l}$. The product-limit estimate of the pseudosurvivor functions may then be formally defined by

$$\tilde{G}_{jk}(t) = \prod_{l:\tau_{jk,l}<t} \left(1 - \frac{E_{jk,l}}{R_{j,l}}\right)$$

Obviously, a calculation of this estimate can use the same algorithm as in the single transition case. In the calculation for a specific destination state, one only has to treat *all* episodes that do not end in this destination as if they were censored.

---

[17] This generalization is commonly used with the product-limit estimation method. See, for instance, the discussion in Lawless (1982, p. 486f), and Tuma and Hannan (1984, p. 69f).

Box 3.3.3 Command file *ehc9.cf*

```
dfile = rrdat.1;        data file

v1  (ID)      = c1 ;    ID of individual
v2  (NOJ)     = c2 ;    Serial number of the job
v3  (TStart)  = c3 ;    Starting time of the job
v4  (TFin)    = c4 ;    Ending time of the job
v5  (SEX)     = c5 ;    Sex (1 men, 2 women)
v6  (TI)      = c6 ;    Date of interview
v7  (TB)      = c7 ;    Date of birth
v8  (T1)      = c8 ;    Date of entry into the labor market
v9  (TM)      = c9 ;    Date of marriage (0 if no marriage)
v10 (PRES)    = c10;    Prestige score of job i
v11 (PRESN)   = c11;    Prestige score of job i + 1
v12 (EDU)     = c12;    Highest educational attainment

# Define origin and destination states. Origin state is 0.
# Destination state is 1 for upward moves,
# 2 for lateral moves, and 3 for downward moves.
v13 (ORG)     = 0;
v14 (DES)     = if eq(v4,v6) then 0 else
                if ge(v11/v10 - 1,0.2) then 1 else
                if lt(v11/v10 - 1,0.0) then 3 else 2;

# Definition of starting and ending time
# on a process time axis.
v15 (TSP) = 0;
v16 (TFP) = v4 - v3 + 1; one month added

# commands to define single episode data
org = v13;    define origin state
des = v14;    define destination state
ts  = v15;    define starting time
tf  = v16;    define ending time

# add command for Kaplan-Meier estimation
ple = ehc9.ple; estimates are written to ehc9.ple
```

As an illustration, we use (in command file *ehc9.cf* in Box 3.3.3) our example data set, *rrdat.1*, and construct three destination states defined by

$$v14\ (DES) = if\ eq(v4,v6)\ then\ 0\ else$$
$$if\ ge(v11/v10 - 1,0.2)\ then\ 1\ else$$
$$if\ lt(v11/v10 - 1,0.0)\ then\ 3\ else\ 2;$$

Variable DES (*V14*) takes the values 1, 2, and 3 for upward, lateral, and downward moves, respectively, or the value 0 for right censored episodes. Executing the command file *ehc9.cf*, shown in Box 3.3.3, with TDA generates the output file *ehc9.ple* containing three tables with product-limit estimates for the three destination states. Parts of these tables are shown in Boxes 3.3.4a–c.

Box 3.3.4a Part 1 (upward moves) of output file *ehc9.ple*

```
SN 1. Transition: 0,1 - Product-Limit Estimation

                 Number Number  Exposed  Survivor   Std.     Cum.
ID Index  Time Events Censored to Risk  Function   Error     Rate
 0    0   0.00    0      0        600   1.00000 0.00000 0.00000
 0    1   2.00    1      0        600   0.99833 0.00167 0.00167
 0    2   4.00    2     12        590   0.99495 0.00291 0.00506
 0    3   6.00    3     12        577   0.98978 0.00415 0.01028
 0    4   7.00    1      7        567   0.98803 0.00450 0.01204
 0    5   8.00    1      9        557   0.98626 0.00483 0.01384
 ...........................................................
 0   50 160.00    1     13         62   0.73352 0.03124 0.30990
 0   51 170.00    1      2         59   0.72109 0.03310 0.32699
 0   52 326.00    1     44         14   0.66958 0.05838 0.40110
 0   53 428.00    0     13
Cases: 600  weighted: 600
```

Box 3.3.4b Part 2 (lateral moves) of output file *ehc9.ple*

```
SN 1. Transition: 0,2 - Product-Limit Estimation

                 Number Number  Exposed  Survivor   Std.     Cum.
ID Index  Time Events Censored to Risk  Function   Error     Rate
 1    0   0.00    0      0        600   1.00000 0.00000 0.00000
 1    1   3.00    2      4        597   0.99665 0.00236 0.00336
 1    2   4.00    4      4        590   0.98989 0.00411 0.01016
 1    3   5.00    2      5        581   0.98649 0.00475 0.01361
 1    4   6.00    4      3        577   0.97965 0.00582 0.02056
 1    5   7.00    3      5        567   0.97446 0.00651 0.02587
 ...........................................................
 1   83 184.00    1      1         53   0.41806 0.03161 0.87212
 1   84 194.00    1      2         50   0.40970 0.03206 0.89232
 1   85 209.00    1      8         41   0.39971 0.03280 0.91701
 1   86 350.00    1     31          9   0.35530 0.05102 1.03480
 1   87 428.00    0      8
Median Duration: 122.24
Duration times limited to: 350
Cases: 600  weighted: 600
```

Figure 3.2.3 shows the survivor functions for these three directional moves.[18] One observes that workers move down faster than they move up. After a duration of approximately 120 months (or 10 years) in a job, only about 23 % have experienced an upward move, while about 38 % moved down.

----

[18] The TDA command file that has been used to generate the plot, *ehc10.cf*, is supplied on the accompanying disk.

Box 3.3.4c Part 3 (downward moves) of output file *ehc9.ple*

```
SN 1. Transition: 0,3 - Product-Limit Estimation

            Number Number  Exposed  Survivor  Std.    Cum.
ID Index  Time Events Censored to Risk Function Error   Rate
 2    0   0.00    0      0      600   1.00000 0.00000 0.00000
 2    1   2.00    1      1      600   0.99833 0.00167 0.00167
 2    2   3.00    3      1      597   0.99332 0.00333 0.00671
 2    3   4.00    3      6      590   0.98827 0.00441 0.01180
 2    4   5.00    1      5      581   0.98656 0.00472 0.01353
 2    5   6.00    3      2      577   0.98144 0.00555 0.01874
 . . . . . . . . . . . . . . . . . . . . . . . . . . . . . . . . . . . .
 2   82 275.00    1     11       26   0.47048 0.04215 0.75400
 2   83 293.00    1      5       20   0.44696 0.04614 0.80529
 2   84 312.00    1      3       16   0.41902 0.05102 0.86983
 2   85 332.00    1      4       11   0.38093 0.05891 0.96514
 2   86 428.00    0     10
Median Duration: 215.96
Duration times limited to: 332
Cases: 600  weighted: 600
```

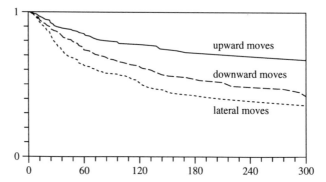

Figure 3.2.3 Plot of survivor functions (product-limit estimation) for upward, lateral, and downward moves. The plot was generated with command file *ehc10.cf*.

Multi-Episode Data (or Repeating Events)

The presentation of the life table method and the product-limit estimation in this book has been limited to the special case of single episodes (with competing risks). For didactical reasons we assumed in our practical examples that the episodes in the data set *rrdat.1* are statistically independent from each other and that the population is homogeneous. Of course, this is not the case because in the GLHS complete job histories of men and women up to the time of the interview are recorded. Thus, individuals with a higher number of jobs are represented in the file *rrdat.1* more often than individuals with a lower number. One solution to this problem is therefore that one only looks at episodes of a certain job number. For example, one could study job behavior in only the first job, second job, and so on. Another solution would be that one compares survivor functions for several—say the first four—jobs (using the variable "serial number of job" as a group variable) and tests whether the survivor functions are equal. If they do not significantly differ, one could pool them and continue as in the single episode case.

Generally, great differences in the number of episodes between observation units suggests that the sample is quite heterogeneous. However, even in the case of single episodes homogeneous populations are assumed. Neglected (or unobserved) heterogeneity between observation units can lead to apparent time-dependence (see chapter 10) and wrong substantive conclusions. One should therefore be careful and only estimate survivor functions for actually homogeneous groups by disaggregating the sample according to theoretically important variables. Unfortunately, in practical applications, this approach is normally of limited use due to the huge sample size that would be necessary for studying a great number of various subpopulations separately. Thus, comparisons of survivor functions between subgroups and the possibility to detect time-dependence based on transformations of survivor functions (see chapter 8) usually possess only a heuristic character. In many cases it is easier to include population heterogeneity and differences in the event histories of individuals into transition rate models, as is shown in the following chapters.

Chapter 4
Exponential Transition Rate Models

In practical research, the analysis of event history data with nonparametric estimation methods is associated with several disadvantages. First, as discussed in the previous chapter, with an increasing number of subgroups normally a point is rapidly reached, at which it is no longer sensible to estimate and compare survivor functions due to the small number of cases left in the various subgroups. Second, even in the case where it is feasible to estimate a rising number of survivor functions for important subgroups, comparisons of these functions quickly become complex and interpretation difficult. Third, in the case of quantitative characteristics (e.g. income, age, etc.), variables must be grouped (e.g. "high income group" vs. "low income group," etc.), with a loss of information, to be able to estimate and compare survivor functions. Finally, multi-episode processes can hardly be analyzed with nonparametric methods. Over the last 20 years, transition rate models have therefore increasingly been used in practical research for the analysis of event history data instead of nonparametric methods.

Transition rate models are a general statistical technique through which one can analyze how the transition rate is dependent on a set of covariates. As discussed in section 1.2, viewing the transition rate as a function of change in covariates is naturally linked with a causal approach to the study of social processes. In general, this modeling approach requires that covariates be measured on an interval or ratio scale, but nominal and ordinal covariates can be incorporated into the models through the use of "dummies" (i.e. by substituting the original variables by a set of 0-1-variables). If permitted by measurement, there is also the interesting possibility of controlling for various factors by introducing their metric versions as proxies in the analysis.[1] Well-known examples are the inclusion of social inequality   via metric prestige scores (Treiman 1977; Handl, Mayer, and Müller 1977; Wegener 1985; Shavit and Blossfeld 1993) or the approximation of qualification levels by the average number of school years necessary to obtain a specific level of educational attainment (Blossfeld 1985; Shavit and Blossfeld 1993). The previous history of the process can also be easily taken into account in transition rate models. For example, in the job duration example, the history of the process might be incorporated through

---

[1] In this case it is assumed that qualitative states reflect points (or intervals) on an underlying metric scale. If the states are ordered, one might argue that the sequence of states corresponds to segments of an underlying continuous variable.

a variable "general labor force experience" (measured in number of months worked) or a variable "number of previously held jobs." The application of these metric versions of important factors makes it possible to study or control for a great number of effects without significantly increasing the number of parameters to be estimated in the models. Finally, and most importantly, transition rate models also permit the analysis of the impact of duration dependence and the influence of one or more parallel processes by the use of (qualitative and/or quantitative) time-dependent covariates.

In this chapter, we discuss the application of the basic exponential model. We start by describing the characteristics of the exponential transition rate model and its estimation using the maximum likelihood method. Then we estimate exponential models without covariates and with time-constant covariates and give detailed interpretations. We also demonstrate how to deal with multiple destination states and multiple episodes as well as the application of equality constraints. Extensions of the basic exponential model are discussed in the next two chapters.

4.1 The Basic Exponential Model

The exponential model is the most simple transition rate model. It assumes that the duration variable T can be described by an exponential distribution with density, survivor, and transition rate function given, respectively, by

$$
\begin{aligned}
f(t) &= a \exp(-at) \qquad a > 0 \\
G(t) &= \exp(-at) \\
r(t) &= a
\end{aligned}
$$

A general definition of the model, for transitions from origin state j to destination state k, can be given as

$$
r_{jk}(t) \equiv r_{jk} = \exp\left(\alpha_{jk0} + A_{jk1}\,\alpha_{jk1} + \ldots\right) = \exp\left(A_{jk}\,\alpha_{jk}\right)
$$

r_{jk} is the time-constant transition rate from origin state j to destination state k. The exit rate (i.e. the rate of leaving the origin state for any one of the possible destination states) is

$$
r_j = \sum_{k \in \mathcal{D}_j} r_{jk}
$$

with $\mathcal{D}_j$ denoting the set of all possible destination states that can be reached from origin state j. The survivor function for the duration in origin state j can easily be formulated with the help of this exit rate:

$$
G_j(t) = \exp\left(-\int_0^t r_j\,d\tau\right) = \exp\left(-tr_j\right)
$$

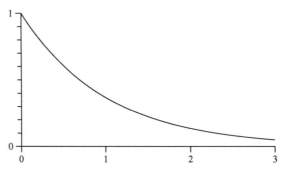

Figure 4.1.1 Density and survivor function of the standard ($r = 1$) exponential distribution.

The exponential model assumes that the transition rate $r_{jk}(t)$ from origin state j to destination state k can vary with different constellations of covariates, but is time-constant: $r_{jk}(t) = r_{jk}$.[2] In other words, it is assumed that the process is not time-dependent. The relationship between the transition rate and the (row) vector of covariates A_{jk} is specified as log-linear to make sure that estimates of the transition rate cannot become negative.[3] The (column) vector of unknown parameters α_{jk} and the vector of observed covariates A_{jk} are specific with regard to the origin state j and the destination state k. The vector of parameters also includes a constant term, α_{jk0}, which can be estimated even if no covariates are included in the model. The covariates in the vector A_{jk} are assumed to be measured at the beginning of each episode and to be time-constant.

Figure 4.1.1 shows the density and survivor function of a standard exponential distribution where the transition rate is $r = 1$. In this case, both functions are identical. In general, the density function is the survivor function multiplied by the transition rate (see section 1.2). By definition, the distribution is only defined on a non-negative time axis.

4.1.1   Maximum Likelihood Estimation

The exponential model, like all parametric transition rate models,[4] is estimated using the maximum likelihood method. To explain the general setup of the likelihood for parametric transition rate models, we proceed in three steps: first we consider the case of a single transition, then situations with one origin state but possibly two or more destination states, and finally situations with more than one origin state.

---

[2] This formulation includes the special case of a single origin state and a single destination state.

[3] We generally adopt the convention of writing covariates as row vectors and the associated coefficients as column vectors.

[4] See chapters 5, 6, and 7.

The notation to set up the likelihood is as follows. $\mathcal{O}$ is the set of origin states, and $\mathcal{D}_j$ is the set of possible destination states for episodes with origin $j \in \mathcal{O}$. $\mathcal{N}_j$ and $\mathcal{Z}_j$ are, respectively, the set of all episodes and the set of all censored episodes having an origin state j. $\mathcal{E}_{jk}$ is the set of all episodes with origin state j and destination state k that have an event ($j \neq k$). To simplify notation, the dependence on parameters is not explicitly shown.

In the case of a single transition (j, k), the likelihood may be written as

$$\mathcal{L}_{jk} = \prod_{i \in \mathcal{E}_{jk}} f(t_i) \prod_{i \in \mathcal{Z}_j} G(t_i) = \prod_{i \in \mathcal{E}_{jk}} r(t_i) \prod_{i \in \mathcal{N}_j} G(t_i)$$

where $f(t)$ is the density function and $G(t)$ is the survivor function for the single transition (j, k). The contribution to the likelihood of an episode with an event at t_i is given by the density function, evaluated at the ending time t_i and with appropriate covariate values. The contribution of a censored episode is given by the survivor function evaluated at the censored ending time t_i, but possibly depends on covariates changing their values during the episode. Remember that at the moment, we assume that all episodes have the starting time zero. The likelihood can be expressed, then, by using only the transition rate and the survivor function.

The next step is to look at the case with a single origin state j but possibly more than one destination state. The destination state space is $\mathcal{D}_j$. Using the notation introduced in Rohwer (1994: TDA-WP 5-1), the likelihood may be written as

$$\mathcal{L}_j = \prod_{k \in \mathcal{D}_j} \prod_{i \in \mathcal{E}_{jk}} \tilde{f}_{jk}(t_i) \prod_{i \in \mathcal{Z}_j} G_j(t_i)$$

The contribution of an episode with an event at t_i is again given by the density function, but is now transition-specific, according to the underlying model. It is, in fact, a subdensity function, $\tilde{f}_{jk}(t)$, with the interpretation that $\tilde{f}_{jk}(t)\, dt$ is the probability of leaving the origin state j for the destination state k in a small time interval at t. The contribution to the likelihood of a right censored episode is the value of the survivor function at t_i, denoted by $G_j(t_i)$, that is, the probability that the episode starting in state j has no event until t_i.

It is now possible to factor the likelihood in a product of transition-specific terms. First, the likelihood may be rewritten as

$$\mathcal{L}_j = \prod_{k \in \mathcal{D}_j} \prod_{i \in \mathcal{E}_{jk}} r_{jk}(t_i) \prod_{i \in \mathcal{N}_j} G_j(t_i)$$

This can be rewritten by using so-called pseudosurvivor functions, defined by

$$\tilde{G}_{jk}(t) = \exp\left(-\int_0^t r_{jk}(\tau)\, d\tau\right)$$

Using this definition, the survivor function $G_j(t)$ can be written as a product of pseudosurvivor functions:

$$G_j(t) = \prod_{k \in \mathcal{D}_j} \tilde{G}_{jk}(t)$$

Inserting this, the likelihood becomes

$$\mathcal{L}_j = \prod_{k \in \mathcal{D}_j} \prod_{i \in \mathcal{E}_{jk}} r_{jk}(t_i) \prod_{k \in \mathcal{D}_j} \prod_{i \in \mathcal{N}_j} \tilde{G}_{jk}(t_i)$$

or, with terms rearranged:

$$\mathcal{L}_j = \prod_{k \in \mathcal{D}_j} \left\{ \prod_{i \in \mathcal{E}_{jk}} r_{jk}(t_i) \prod_{i \in \mathcal{N}_j} \tilde{G}_{jk}(t_i) \right\}$$

The third step, to account for more than a single origin state, is again simple. In the context of duration analysis one treats the origin states as given, and the models are formulated as conditional on given origin states. Therefore, the total likelihood is the product of the likelihood for each of the origin states, $\mathcal{L}_j$. Consequently, one can write

$$\mathcal{L} = \prod_{j \in \mathcal{O}} \prod_{k \in \mathcal{D}_j} \prod_{i \in \mathcal{E}_{jk}} r_{jk}(t_i) \prod_{i \in \mathcal{N}_j} \tilde{G}_{jk}(t_i)$$

All models described in this book are estimated using the logarithm of this likelihood, that is

$$\ell = \sum_{j \in \mathcal{O}} \sum_{k \in \mathcal{D}_j} \sum_{i \in \mathcal{E}_{jk}} \log \left\{ r_{jk}(t_i) \right\} + \sum_{i \in \mathcal{N}_j} \log \left\{ \tilde{G}_{jk}(t_i) \right\} \tag{4.1}$$

The fact that the total likelihood can be expressed as a product of transition-specific factors implies that, in the case of several transitions, a model for each transition can be estimated separately.[5] The estimation for a transition (j, k) is done using all episodes starting in origin state j; the episodes ending in destination state k are regarded as having an event, and *all other* episodes are included as censored.

Moreover, the possibility of factoring the total likelihood offers an easy way to estimate models with different specifications of transition rates for different transitions. A different model can be assumed for each transition, and then each of these models can be estimated separately.

All parametric transition rate models offered by TDA are estimated by maximizing the log likelihood (4.1). TDA's default method is a modified Newton algorithm using first and second derivatives of the log likelihood.[6]

---

[5] Of course, this is only possible if there are no constraints on parameters across different transitions. To provide for this possibility is the main reason for using the likelihood (4.1).

[6] Some other algorithms are also available; see Rohwer (1994: TDA-WP 1-2).

Box 4.1.1 Command file *ehd1.cf* (exponential model without covariates)

```
dfile = rrdat.1;      data file

v1  (ID)     = c1 ;   ID of individual
v2  (NOJ)    = c2 ;   Serial number of the job
v3  (TStart) = c3 ;   Starting time of the job
v4  (TFin)   = c4 ;   Ending time of the job
v5  (SEX)    = c5 ;   Sex (1 men, 2 women)
v6  (TI)     = c6 ;   Date of interview
v7  (TB)     = c7 ;   Date of birth
v8  (TI)     = c8 ;   Date of entry into the labor market
v9  (TM)     = c9 ;   Date of marriage (0 if no marriage)
v10 (PRES)   = c10;   Prestige score of job i
v11 (PRESN)  = c11;   Prestige score of job i + 1
v12 (EDU)    = c12;   Highest educational attainment

# Define origin and destination state. Origin state is 0.
# Destination state is 0 if right censored, or 1.
v13 (ORG)    = 0;
v14 (DES)    = if eq(v4,v6) then 0 else 1;

# Definition of starting and ending time
# on a process time axis.
v15 (TSP) = 0;
v16 (TFP) = v4 - v3 + 1; one month added

# commands to define single episode data
org = v13;   define origin state
des = v14;   define destination state
ts  = v15;   define starting time
tf  = v16;   define ending time
```

```
# command to request estimation of an exponential model
rate = 2;      model selection

# commands to request a printout of estimated transition rate
prate = ehd1.prs;   print to output file: ehd1.prs
tab   = 0,300,10;   time axis for the table
```

4.1.2 Models without Covariates

We begin with a simple exponential model and then gradually introduce complexity. To illustrate the interpretation of the basic exponential model, we first estimate a model without any covariates (i.e. we only analyze the average job change behavior of individuals). For didactic purposes we further assume that the episodes in the data file *rrdat.1* are independent of each other and that there

Box 4.1.2 Results of using command file *ehd1.cf* (Box 4.1.1)

```
Single episode data

Origin state: V13      Destination state: V14
Starting time: V15     Ending time: V16

                                    Mean
SN  Org Des  Episodes  Weighted  Duration  TS Min  TF Max
-----------------------------------------------------------
 1   0   0      142      142.00   128.18    0.00   428.00
 1   0   1      458      458.00    49.30    0.00   350.00
 1   0  Sum     600      600.00    67.97    0.00   428.00


-----------------------------------------------------------
Model: Exponential

Maximum likelihood estimation
Maximum of log likelihood: -2514.02
Norm of final gradient vector: 1.8e-13
Last absolute change of function value: 0.0e+00
Last relative change in parameters: 0.0e+00

Idx SN Org Des MT Var  Label   Coeff  Error   T-Stat  Signif
-----------------------------------------------------------
  1  1   0   1  A --   Const -4.4891 0.0467 -96.0715  1.0000
```

is only one origin state ("being in a job") and one destination state ("having left the job"). Thus the exponential model to be estimated is

$$r(t) \equiv r = \exp(\alpha_0)$$

Box 4.1.1 shows how to estimate this exponential model with TDA. Most of the command file, *ehd1.cf*, is again identical to previously used command files and deals with reading the input data file (*rrdat.1*) and defining variables as well as episode data. The additional commands are

  rate = 2;

to request the estimation of an exponential transition rate model, and the *prate* and *tab* commands to print the estimated rate, density, and survivor functions into an output file (*ehd1.prs*, in our example). Because the model is to be estimated without covariates, no other commands are necessary.

Part of TDA's standard output, when called with *ehd1.cf*, is shown in Box 4.1.2. The value of the log likelihood function is -2514.02, and the estimated coefficient is $\hat{\alpha}_0 = -4.4891$. The estimated average rate of job change is therefore

$$r = \exp(-4.4891) = 0.0112.$$

This can also be seen in Box 4.1.3, which shows the output file *ehd1.prs*. This file is simply a table of the estimated survivor function, density function, and transition rate, tabulated according to command *tab = 0,300,10.*[7]

Because for exponentially distributed durations the number of events N within a specified time interval is characterized by a Poisson distribution with an expected value of

$$E(N) = rt = 0.0112 \cdot t$$

we expect an annual average number of job changes of $0.0112 \cdot 12 \approx 0.13$.

An estimate of the average duration in a job may be obtained in the exponential model via the relationship (see Blossfeld, Hamerle, and Mayer 1989)

$$E(T) = \frac{1}{r} = \frac{1}{0.0112} \approx 89 \text{ months}$$

This means that on the average about seven and a half years pass before individuals change their jobs.

Based on the survivor function

$$G(t) = \exp(-rt)$$

one can get an estimate of the median duration M, defined by $G(M) = 0.5$. Inserting the estimated rate:

$$G(\hat{M}) = \exp(-0.0112\,\hat{M}) = 0.5$$

our estimate is $\hat{M} \approx 62$ months. Because the exponential distribution is skewed to the right (see Figure 4.1.1), the median is smaller than the mean of the job duration. In general, for the exponential model, the median (M) is about 69.3 % of the mean $(E(T))$:

$$0.5 = \exp\left(-\frac{1}{E(T)} M\right)$$

The probability that an individual is still employed in the same job after ten years is $G(120) = \exp(-0.0112 \cdot 120) = 0.26$, or 26 %, and the probability that he/she has left the job by this time is $1 - G(120) = 1 - 0.26 = 0.74$, or 74 %.

4.1.3 Time-Constant Covariates

The simple model without covariates treats the data as a sample of homogeneous individual job episodes, meaning that, in estimating such a model, we abstract from all sources of heterogeneity between individuals and their job episodes. Of course, social scientists are normally more interested in finding

---

[7] Such a table can be used, in particular, to create plots of the estimated transition rate. Examples are given in chapters 5 and 7 for transition rates that are non-constant functions of time.

Box 4.1.3 Table of estimated rates (output file *ehd1.prs*)

```
        Estimated Rates
        Model: Exponential

        Idx SN Org Des MT Var  Label        Coeff  Covariate
        ----------------------------------------------------------
          1  1   0   1  A      Const      -4.4891   1.0000

        ID        Time    Surv.F   Density     Rate
        -----------------------------------------------------
         0      0.0000    1.0000   0.0000    0.0000
         0     10.0000    0.8938   0.0100    0.0112
         0     20.0000    0.7988   0.0090    0.0112
         0     30.0000    0.7140   0.0080    0.0112
         0     40.0000    0.6381   0.0072    0.0112
         0     50.0000    0.5703   0.0064    0.0112
         0     60.0000    0.5098   0.0057    0.0112
         0     70.0000    0.4556   0.0051    0.0112
         0     80.0000    0.4072   0.0046    0.0112
         0     90.0000    0.3639   0.0041    0.0112
         0    100.0000    0.3253   0.0037    0.0112
         0    110.0000    0.2907   0.0033    0.0112
         0    120.0000    0.2598   0.0029    0.0112
         0    130.0000    0.2322   0.0026    0.0112
         0    140.0000    0.2076   0.0023    0.0112
         0    150.0000    0.1855   0.0021    0.0112
         0    160.0000    0.1658   0.0019    0.0112
         0    170.0000    0.1482   0.0017    0.0112
         0    180.0000    0.1325   0.0015    0.0112
         0    190.0000    0.1184   0.0013    0.0112
         0    200.0000    0.1058   0.0012    0.0112
         0    210.0000    0.0946   0.0011    0.0112
         0    220.0000    0.0845   0.0009    0.0112
         0    230.0000    0.0755   0.0008    0.0112
         0    240.0000    0.0675   0.0008    0.0112
         0    250.0000    0.0603   0.0007    0.0112
         0    260.0000    0.0539   0.0006    0.0112
         0    270.0000    0.0482   0.0005    0.0112
         0    280.0000    0.0431   0.0005    0.0112
         0    290.0000    0.0385   0.0004    0.0112
         0    300.0000    0.0344   0.0004    0.0112
```

differences (i.e. in investigating how the transition rate describing the process under study depends on observable characteristics of the individuals and their environment).

To do so, one has to include covariates into the model. The most simple way is to include time-constant covariates. This means that the values of these covariates are fixed *at the beginning* of the episodes under study, that is, they do not change their values while the process is going on. As noted by Yamaguchi (1991), basically two groups of time-constant covariates can be distinguished:

(1) *Ascribed statuses* that are (normally) constant throughout individuals' lives, such as race, gender, or social origin; (2) *statuses attained prior to* (or at the time of) entry into the process time and that remain constant thereafter.[8] Examples are the highest educational attainment at time of marriage or age at marriage in the analysis of divorce from first marriage. It should be noted that very often selection bias exists with regard to such states at entry, and this must be carefully considered in event history models.

A special case of time-constant covariates is *information about the history of the process itself*, evaluated at the beginning of the episodes under study. For instance, in the job duration example, the dependence between successive job episodes might be controlled for by including information about the number of previous jobs (and unemployment episodes) and their durations.[9] To include such information is important from a substantive point of view because life course research has shown that, in the case of repeated events, the past course of the process is a crucial factor in understanding the present. But it is also important from a statistical point of view because model estimation is based on the assumption of conditionally independent episodes (i.e. conditional on the covariates that are accounted for in the model specification).[10]

To estimate a model with time-constant covariates, we use the command file *ehd2.cf*, a small modification of *ehd1.cf*. The modifications are shown in Box 4.1.4. We define the additional covariates required and then include these covariates into the model specification.

First, to include an individual's highest educational attainment at the beginning of each job, we use EDU (*V12*) as a metric proxy variable. This variable is already contained in our data file, *rrdat.1*, and measures the average number of school years necessary to obtain a certain educational attainment level. Second, to distinguish between the three birth cohorts, two dummy variables, COHO2 (*V20*) and COHO3 (*V21*), are defined in the following way:

	COHO2	COHO3
Cohort 1929-31	0	0
Cohort 1939-41	1	0
Cohort 1949-51	0	1

Third, a variable LFX (*V22*) is constructed to measure, approximately, "general labor force experience" at the beginning of each job episode. This variable is

---

[8] In the case of multi-episode processes, the status must be attained prior to the *first* entry into the process.

[9] Heckman and Borjas (1980) called the effect of the number of previous occupancy of labor force states (e.g. jobs) "occurrence dependence" and the effect of the durations in previous states (e.g. general labor force experience) "lagged duration dependence."

[10] Maximum likelihood estimation assumes independent episodes. The better the dependencies between the episodes are controlled for in the case of repeated events, the less biased are the estimated parameters. However, in practical research it is very difficult to achieve this goal completely. Therefore, it is always a source of possible misspecification; see chapter 10.

Box 4.1.4 Part of command file *ehd2.cf* (exponential model with covariates)

```
   ... (first part identical to first part in Box 4.1.1)

   # define additional variables to include into the model
   v20 (COHO2) = ge(v7,468) . le(v7,504); cohort 2
   v21 (COHO3) = ge(v7,588) . le(v7,624); cohort 3
   v22 (LFX)   = v3 - v8;                 labor force experience
   v23 (PNOJ)  = v2 - 1;                  previous number of jobs

   # command to request estimation of an exponential model
   rate = 2;    model selection

   # command to include covariates into model, for transition
   # from origin state 0 to destination state 1.
   # (V12 and V10 already defined)
   xa (0,1)    =    v12,v20,v21,v22,v23,v10;
```

computed as the difference, in months, between the beginning of the respective job episode (*V3*) and the time of first entry into the labor force (*V8*).[11] Fourth, we define a variable PNOJ (*V23*) to capture information about the number of previously held jobs. The value of this covariate is simply the serial number of the current job minus one. Finally, we use a variable PRES (*V10*) to capture the prestige score of the current job. This information is already contained in our data file.

Model specification now requires two commands. The first is, again, the model selection command *rate=2* to select an exponential model. In addition, we need a command to include covariates. The TDA command is

$$xa\ (org,des) = list\_of\_variables;$$

meaning that the list of variables given on the right-hand side should be included in the model specification for the transition from origin state *org* to destination state *des*. Because in our current example, there is only a single transition, from origin state 0 ("being in a job") to destination state 1 ("having left the job"), we include our covariates in the following way:

$$xa(0,1) = v12,\ v20,\ v21,\ v22,\ v23,\ v10;$$

Using TDA's default specification, a log-linear link function between the transition rate and the vector of explaining time-constant covariates, the model that will be estimated is

$$r(t) \equiv r = \exp(A\alpha)$$

---

[11] Of course, this variable is only a very rough proxy because it assumes that individuals have been continuously employed. In a "real" job shift analysis, one would construct the variable "general labor force experience" for each individual on the basis of the number of months he/she had actually worked.

Box 4.1.5 Results of using command file *ehd2.cf* (Box 4.1.4)

```
Model: Exponential

Maximum likelihood estimation
Maximum of log likelihood: -2465.99
Norm of final gradient vector: 7.8e-04
Last absolute change of function value: 1.5e-09
Last relative change in parameters: 8.9e-04

Idx SN Org Des MT Var  Label   Coeff    Error    T-Stat   Signif
----------------------------------------------------------------
  1  1   0   1  A  --   Const  -4.4894  0.2795  -16.0624  1.0000
  2  1   0   1  A V12   EDU     0.0773  0.0247    3.1292  0.9982
  3  1   0   1  A V20   COHO2   0.6080  0.1136    5.3547  1.0000
  4  1   0   1  A V21   COHO3   0.6108  0.1185    5.1526  1.0000
  5  1   0   1  A V22   LFX    -0.0032  0.0009   -3.3900  0.9993
  6  1   0   1  A V23   PNOJ    0.0596  0.0442    1.3507  0.8232
  7  1   0   1  A V10   PRES   -0.0280  0.0055   -5.0641  1.0000
```

Estimation results for this model are shown in Box 4.1.5. First of all, we get a value of the log likelihood function: -2465.99. Thus, one can compare this model with the exponential model without covariates (in Box 4.1.2) using a likelihood ratio test. Under the null hypothesis that the additionally included covariates do not significantly improve the model fit, the likelihood ratio test statistic (LR) follows approximately a χ^2-distribution with m degrees of freedom where m is the number of additionally included covariates. These test statistics can be calculated as two times the difference of the log likelihoods:

$$LR = 2 \left(\text{LogLik(present model)} - \text{LogLik(reference model)} \right)$$

For our example, the test statistic is

$$LR = 2 \left((-2465.99) - (-2514.02) \right) = 2 \cdot 48.03 = 96.06.$$

with six degrees of freedom (the six additionally included covariates). Given a significance level of 0.05, we conclude that the null hypothesis should be rejected. At least one of the included covariates significantly improves the model fit.

In addition, the maximum likelihood estimation provides standard errors for the estimated coefficients. These standard errors are useful to assess the precision of the estimates of the model parameters. In particular, one can check whether the estimated coefficients are significantly different from zero. Dividing the estimated coefficients (column *Coeff* in Box 4.1.5) by the estimated standard error (column *Error*) produces a test statistic (column *T-Stat*) that is approximately standard normally distributed if the model is correct and the sample is large. Assuming this, one can apply a formal test (see Blossfeld, Hamerle, and Mayer 1989). If one uses, for instance, a 0.05 significance level and a two-sided test, then a covariate A_j has a significant (non-zero) effect, if the following relationship is satisfied:

$$\left| \frac{\hat{\alpha}_j}{\hat{\sigma}(\hat{\alpha}_j)} \right| > 1.96$$

$\hat{\alpha}_j$ is the estimated coefficient for covariate A_j, $\hat{\sigma}_j$ is the associated standard error. In Box 4.1.5 all covariates with the exception of PNOJ ("previous number of jobs") have a significant effect.[12]

The effect of a covariate can easily be interpreted when one examines the percentage change in the rate, given that only one covariate changes its value. The formula (see Blossfeld, Hamerle, and Mayer 1989) is

$$\Delta \hat{r} = (\exp(\hat{\alpha}_j)^{\Delta A_j} - 1) \cdot 100 \, \%$$

ΔA_j is the change in variable A_j. $\Delta \hat{r}$ is the resulting percentage change in the estimated rate. $\exp(\alpha_j)$, the antilogarithm of the coefficient α_j, is referred to in the literature as the "alpha effect" (see Tuma and Hannan 1984).[13] It takes the value 1 when the covariate has no effect ($\alpha_j = 0$); it is smaller than 1 if $\alpha_j < 0$ and greater than 1 if $\alpha_j > 0$. If the value of the covariate is increased by just one unit, then the rate changes by

$$\Delta \hat{r} = (\exp(\hat{\alpha}_j) - 1) \cdot 100 \, \%$$

In Box 4.1.5, the coefficient of the covariate EDU ("educational attainment level") has a positive sign. Therefore, each additional school year increases the job shift rate by about $\exp(0.0773) - 1) \cdot 100 \, \% = 8 \, \%$. This means that better educated workers are more mobile than less educated ones. However, this estimate is hard to interpret because theory suggests that educational attainment should have a positive effect on upward moves and a negative effect on downward moves, while the effects of educational attainment on lateral moves are theoretically still quite open (Blossfeld and Mayer 1988; Blossfeld 1989). Thus, a reasonable substantive interpretation of the effect of variable EDU can only be achieved if we estimate models with directional moves (see next section).

Each younger birth cohort is more mobile. Compared to the reference group (individuals born 1929-31), the job change rate of people born 1939-41 (COHO2) is about 83.7 % higher: $(\exp(0.6080) - 1) \cdot 100 \, \%$, and of the people born in 1949-51 (COHO3), about 84.2 % higher: $(\exp(0.6108) - 1) \cdot 100 \, \%$.

The effect of labor force experience (LFX) is negative. Thus, in our example, each additional year of labor force experience decreases the job shift rate by 3.2 %. This is in accordance with the human capital theory, which predicts

---

[12] TDA calculates a significance level, given in column *Signif*, as: $2 \cdot \Phi(T\text{-}Stat) - 1$. Φ is the standard normal distribution function.

[13] A table containing these alpha effects can be requested with the TDA command *rrisk*.

that with increasing general labor force experience, additional investments into human capital decline and, as a consequence, job moves decrease.[14]

Also the number of previously held jobs (PNOJ) has a positive effect, but this variable is not significant. Therefore, in our example, this part of the job history has no effect on the job change rate.

Finally, the prestige score of the current job (PRES) influences the job change rate negatively. An increase by 10 units on the magnitude prestige scale (Wegener 1985) decreases the job change rate by about 24 %.[15]

It is important to note that the effects of the covariates are not independent of each other. They are related *multiplicatively*. For example, a simultaneous change in prestige by 10 units and in labor force experience by one year decreases the job change rate by 27.3 %:

$$\left(\exp(-0.0280)^{10} \cdot \exp(-0.0032)^{12} - 1 \right) \cdot 100\% \approx -27.3\%$$

For selected subgroups one can also predict the average job duration, the median of the duration, the average number of events in a given duration interval, and the probability of remaining in the same job up to a given point in time. For example, for an individual with Abitur (EDU = 13) of the birth cohort 1929-31 (COHO2 = 0 and COHO3 = 0), just entering the labor market (LFX = 0 and PNOJ = 0) into a job with prestige level PRES = 60 on the Wegener scale, we can calculate the following rate:

$$r = \exp(-4.4894 + 0.0773 \cdot 13 - 0.028 \cdot 60) \approx 0.0057$$

Consequently, we expect an average job duration of about 175 months, or 15 years ($1/0.0057 \approx 175$), for individuals with these characteristics. Analogously, the median job duration for this group of individuals can be calculated as about 69.3 % of the mean duration, which is about 10 years ($175 \cdot 0.693 \approx 121$). Finally, the probability that individuals with the assumed characteristics are still employed in the same job after 8 years is about 58 %. This is calculated by using the survivor function $G(96) = \exp(-0.0057 \cdot 96) \approx 0.58$. Similar predictions can be made for other subgroups too, so that one obtains a quite differentiated picture of job change behavior in the sample.

4.2 Models with Multiple Destinations

So far we have only considered single transitions. More important are situations where, from a given origin state, individuals can move to any one of a set of many possible destination states ("competing risks"). Defining an appropriate state

---

[14] Also, in this case, the effect on directional moves can be better interpreted in substantive terms (see next section).

[15] Again, in substantive terms this result is more easily interpreted for directional moves. For example, vacancy competition theory (Sørensen 1977, 1979) argues that upward moves are increasingly less likely the higher the job is located in the pyramid of inequality (see next section).

Box 4.2.1 Part of command file *ehd3.cf*

```
... (first part identical to first part of Box 4.1.1)

# Define a single origin state (0)
# and three destination states:
# 1 = upward move
# 2 = lateral move
# 3 = downward move

v13 (ORG)   = 0;
v14 (DES)   = if eq(v4,v6) then 0 else
                 if ge(v11/v10 - 1,0.2) then 1 else
                 if lt(v11/v10 - 1,0) then 3 else 2;

# Definition of starting and ending time
# on a process time axis.
v15 (TSP) = 0;
v16 (TFP) = v4 - v3 + 1; one month added

# commands to define single episode data
org =  v13;   define origin state
des =  v14;   define destination state
ts  =  v15;   define starting time
tf  =  v16;   define ending time

# define additional variables to include into the model
v20 (COHO2) =   ge(v7,468) . le(v7,504); cohort 2
v21 (COHO3) =   ge(v7,588) . le(v7,624); cohort 3
v22 (LFX)   =   v3 - v8;          labor force experience
v23 (PNOJ)  =   v2 - 1;           previous number of jobs

# command to request estimation of an exponential model
rate = 2;   model selection

# commands to include covariates into model
xa (0,1) = v12,v20,v21,v22,v23,v10; transition 0 -> 1
xa (0,2) = v12,v20,v21,v22,v23,v10; transition 0 -> 2
xa (0,3) = v12,v20,v21,v22,v23,v10; transition 0 -> 3
```

space is a matter of substantive consideration. For example, as shown in the previous section, it is very hard to interpret the effect of educational attainment on the rate of job movement because theory predicts contradictory effects of educational attainment on upward and downward moves. Furthermore, the effect of educational attainment on lateral moves is theoretically still quite open. Thus, in the causal analysis of transitions, the specification of the state space might turn out to be a serious source of misspecification (see chapter 10). Origin and destination states must be carefully selected and the effects of covariates must be related to the specific transitions in a theoretically meaningful way.

In this section, we extend the exponential model with time-constant covariates to study transitions from the origin state "being in a job" to a better job (upward shift), a worse job (downward shift), and to a job of about the same reward level (lateral shift). In other words, we are estimating a model with one origin state and multiple destination states or competing risks. Part of the command file (*ehd3.cf*) is shown in Box 4.2.1. The first part, only specifying the data file *rrdat.1* and providing definitions of the basic variables, is identical with the command file in Box 4.1.1 and is omitted in Box 4.2.1. The differences are, first, that we now have to define a new variable for the possible destination states. As before, there is only a single origin state 0 ("being in a job"). The three destination states are 1 ("better job"), 2 ("same job level"), and 3 ("worse job").[16] Second, as in Box 4.1.4, we define a set of covariates to be used in the model specification. Finally, an exponential model is selected with the *rate=2* command, and the covariates to be included in the model are specified. One should note that TDA expects a separate command for each of the possible transitions. In our example we have three possible transitions: (0,1), (0,2), and (0,3), so we use three commands to specify covariates.[17]

Using command file *ehd3.cf*, part of TDA's standard output is shown in Box 4.2.2. The first table shows the transitions found in the input data. The second table reports estimates for the rates of upward (DES = 1), lateral (DES = 2), and downward moves (DES = 3). The results for lateral moves are presented but not interpreted.

The *positive effect of education* (EDU) *on upward moves* is in accordance with status attainment theory (e.g. Blau and Duncan 1967; Sewell and Hauser 1975; Goldthorpe 1987; Erikson and Goldthorpe 1991), human capital theory (Becker 1975), and vacancy competition theory (Sørensen 1979). However, the three theories offer different explanations.[18] Status attainment theory says that increases in educational attainment always lead to better job opportunities and will have a positive effect on upward moves. Under the condition of an imperfect labor market, human capital theory predicts that upward shifts are more likely if employees are under-rewarded; and the likelihood of being under-rewarded increases with increasing personal resources (Tuma 1985). Education will therefore have a positive effect on upward moves. Finally, vacancy competition theory explains this positive effect of education in terms of the ability of higher educated persons to get better places in the labor queue and to therefore be in a better position to take advantage of opportunities.

---

[16] This is in accordance with section 3.3 (see Box 3.3.3), where we defined upward shifts as job mobility leading to an increase in the prestige score of 20 % or more, downward shifts as job mobility connected with a decrease in the prestige score, and lateral shifts as having no effect or experiencing an increase in the prestige score of up to 20 %.

[17] In this example, the same list of covariates is linked to each of the three transitions. In general, it would be possible to use different sets of covariates for each transition.

[18] This is a good example of the well-known situation in the social sciences where the causal effect can be explained by different theories. Comparing the relative merits of these competing theories is very difficult, simply because it is difficult to find a "crucial test" (see Lieberson 1985).

Box 4.2.2   Results of using command file *ehd3.cf* (Box 4.2.1)

```
Single episode data
Origin state: V13      Destination state: V14
Starting time: V15     Ending time: V16

                                    Mean
SN  Org Des   Episodes  Weighted  Duration  TS Min  TF Max
------------------------------------------------------------
 1   0   0       142      142.00    128.18    0.00   428.00
 1   0   1        84       84.00     45.05    0.00   326.00
 1   0   2       219      219.00     45.91    0.00   350.00
 1   0   3       155      155.00     56.40    0.00   332.00
 1   0 Sum       600      600.00     67.97    0.00   428.00


------------------------------------------------------------

Model: Exponential


Maximum of log likelihood: -2884.79
Norm of final gradient vector: 5.0e-09
Last absolute change of function value: 1.6e-14
Last relative change in parameters: 2.3e-06

Idx SN Org Des MT Var  Label  Coeff   Error   T-Stat Signif
------------------------------------------------------------
  1  1  0   1  A --   Const -5.1036  0.6175  -8.2648 1.0000
  2  1  0   1  A V12  EDU    0.3018  0.0430   7.0215 1.0000
  3  1  0   1  A V20  COHO2  0.6379  0.2713   2.3510 0.9813
  4  1  0   1  A V21  COHO3  0.7354  0.2765   2.6595 0.9922
  5  1  0   1  A V22  LFX   -0.0023  0.0021  -1.0898 0.7242
  6  1  0   1  A V23  PNOJ   0.1731  0.1004   1.7239 0.9153
  7  1  0   1  A V10  PRES  -0.1441  0.0141 -10.1970 1.0000
------------------------------------------------------------
  8  1  0   2  A --   Const -5.8043  0.4054 -14.3164 1.0000
  9  1  0   2  A V12  EDU    0.0033  0.0380   0.0881 0.0702
 10  1  0   2  A V20  COHO2  0.6722  0.1643   4.0926 1.0000
 11  1  0   2  A V21  COHO3  0.6843  0.1732   3.9501 0.9999
 12  1  0   2  A V22  LFX   -0.0031  0.0014  -2.2579 0.9760
 13  1  0   2  A V23  PNOJ   0.0323  0.0645   0.5010 0.3836
 14  1  0   2  A V10  PRES   0.0081  0.0081   1.0094 0.6872
------------------------------------------------------------
 15  1  0   3  A --   Const -4.9051  0.5251  -9.3405 1.0000
 16  1  0   3  A V12  EDU   -0.0167  0.0490  -0.3404 0.2664
 17  1  0   3  A V20  COHO2  0.5300  0.1935   2.7387 0.9938
 18  1  0   3  A V21  COHO3  0.5705  0.2030   2.8101 0.9950
 19  1  0   3  A V22  LFX   -0.0037  0.0017  -2.2649 0.9765
 20  1  0   3  A V23  PNOJ   0.0407  0.0775   0.5252 0.4005
 21  1  0   3  A V10  PRES  -0.0157  0.0097  -1.6208 0.8949
```

The *positive effects of the cohort dummy variables* for the birth cohorts 1939-49 (COHO2) and 1949-51 (COHO3) on all directional moves show that each younger cohort is more mobile, independently of whether we focus on upward, downward, or lateral job shifts. However, one must be careful in interpreting this result in substantive terms. We only consider these variables as technical control variables for the different lengths of job histories in the GLHS here.

The *negative effect of prestige on upward moves* can also be interpreted in the light of two different theories. For Sørensen, opportunities for even better jobs decline as the level of attainment (measured here in terms of prestige scores) already achieved increases. In this theoretical model, employees have control over the decision to leave their job. This control over the decision to leave the job is derived from job-specific skills, collective action, and so on. Thus, employees will only leave jobs when a better job is available, but the higher the attainment level already achieved, the harder it will be to find an even better job in a given structure of inequality. It should be noted that within the framework of vacancy competition theory, the size of the coefficient of prestige is also a measure of the opportunity structure of a given society: The larger the absolute magnitude of this coefficient, the fewer the opportunities for gains that are available in a society (Sørensen and Blossfeld 1989). A competing explanation is given by human capital theory, which assumes that there are costs of job searches and there is imperfect information. In this case, upward moves are more likely if employees are under-rewarded; and the likelihood of being under-rewarded decreases with increasing job rewards. In other words, the higher the prestige score of the origin job, the less upward moves are to be expected (Tuma 1985).

Also in accordance with this modified form of human capital theory (Tuma 1985) is the *negative effect of education on downward moves* (although not significant in our didactical example because of the small number of events). Downward moves should be more likely if employees are over-rewarded; and the likelihood of being over-rewarded rises with decreasing personal resources, for example, educational attainment. Another reason can be seen in the specific type of labor market organization found in Germany. For example, Blossfeld and Mayer (1988) have shown that labor market segmentation in Germany is much more the result of qualification barriers, and that educational certificates tend to protect workers against downward shifts to the secondary labor market (see also Blossfeld, Giannelli, and Mayer 1993).

Even if human capital and vacancy competition theory are able to explain some of the estimated coefficients in Box 4.2.2, there are also results that contradict these theories. Most important, vacancy competition theory regards downward moves as an exception. However, this is not the case. The number of downward moves ($n_{down} = 155$) is greater than the number of upward moves ($n_{up} = 84$).[19] Further, according to the vacancy competition model, the effect of time spent in the labor force (or labor force experience) on upward moves should

---

[19] These numbers are also a function of the technical definition of upward, downward, and lateral moves. In our example, the number of upwards moves stays however more or less the same if we lower the threshold from a 20 % increase to a 10 % or even 5 % increase in the prestige score.

Box 4.2.3 Part of command file *ehd4.cf*

```
# random selection of about 84 / 219 * noc cases:
dsel = le (rd(0,1), 84/219);

# Define a single origin state (0)
# and a single destination state: 2 = lateral move
v13 (ORG)    = 0;
v14 (DES)    = if eq(v4,v6) then 0 else
                  if ge(v11/v10 - 1,0.2) then 0 else
                  if lt(v11/v10 - 1,0) then 0 else 2;

# command to request estimation of an exponential model
rate = 2;      model selection

# commands to include covariates into model
xa (0,2) = v12,v20,v21,v22,v23,v10; transition 0 -> 2
```

not be significant once education and prestige are controlled for. Otherwise, this variable is no adequate proxy of the discrepancy between resources and current job rewards.[20] An explanation for the negative effect of the covariate "general labor force experience" on upward moves is however given by Mincer (1974). He argued that people invest in their resources as long as their expected returns exceed their expected costs. Therefore, training is concentrated mainly in the earlier phases of employment, where more time is left to recover training costs. In this way the job mobility process is time-dependent because time spent in the labor force (or general labor force experience) reduces the likelihood of new training and consequent gains in attainment.

It should also be noted that human capital theory is interesting for sociological mobility research only insofar as an imperfect labor market is assumed. As shown by Tuma (1985), human capital theory only leads to specific hypotheses about mobility if imperfect information and search costs are assumed. Otherwise the labor market would be in equilibrium, and in equilibrium job shifts only occur randomly because no one can improve his/her present situation.

Comparison of Covariate Effects Across Destinations

In comparing covariate effects across various destinations in competing risks models, one must be careful because statistical significance tests of parameters (see section 4.1.3) are normally affected by a varying number of competing events. For example, in Box 4.2.2 these tests are based on 84 upward moves, 219 lateral moves, and 155 downward moves. Thus, given a fixed size of an effect for all directional moves, the results of the significance tests are dependent

---

However, there are good theoretical reasons to classify job moves only as upward moves, if they are connected with a significant step upwards (Blossfeld 1986).

[20] Similar problems exist with regard to the effect of labor market experience on downward shifts.

Box 4.2.4 Part of command file *ehd5.cf*

```
# random selection of about 84 / 155 * noc cases:
dsel = le (rd(0,1), 84/155);

# Define a single origin state (0)
# and a single destination state: 3 = downward move
v13 (ORG)   = 0;
v14 (DES)   = if eq(v4,v6) then 0 else
              if ge(v11/v10 - 1,0.2) then 0 else
              if lt(v11/v10 - 1,0) then 3 else 0;

# command to request estimation of an exponential model
rate = 2;    model selection

# commands to include covariates into model
xa (0,3) = v12,v20,v21,v22,v23,v10; transition 0 -> 3
```

Box 4.2.5 Results of using command file *ehd4.cf* (Box 4.2.3)

```
Selection of data file records
  LE(RD(0,1),84/219)
                               Mean
SN  Org Des  Episodes Weighted Duration TS Min  TF Max
-------------------------------------------------------
 1   0   0      145    145.00    82.71   0.00   428.00
 1   0   2       90     90.00    49.33   0.00   209.00
 1   0  Sum     235    235.00    69.93   0.00   428.00

-------------------------------------------------------

Model: Exponential
Maximum of log likelihood: -552.886

Idx SN Org Des MT Var  Label  Coeff   Error   T-Stat Signif
-----------------------------------------------------------
 1   1  0   2  A  --   Const -5.3301  0.6960  -7.6583 1.0000
 2   1  0   2  A  V12  EDU   -0.0097  0.0594  -0.1627 0.1293
 3   1  0   2  A  V20  COHO2  0.6587  0.2516   2.6181 0.9912
 4   1  0   2  A  V21  COHO3  0.4869  0.2732   1.7824 0.9253
 5   1  0   2  A  V22  LFX   -0.0025  0.0023  -1.1042 0.7305
 6   1  0   2  A  V23  PNOJ  -0.0109  0.1138  -0.0961 0.0765
 7   1  0   2  A  V10  PRES   0.0014  0.0127   0.1073 0.0854
```

on the number of events. It is more likely that the statistical test provides a significant result for lateral moves than for downward moves, and it is more likely there than for upward moves.

To demonstrate the impact of the various number of events, we standardize the number of events across the three directional moves. Because the number of upward moves is smallest, we use this number as the baseline and standardize

Box 4.2.6 Results of using command file *ehd5.cf* (Box 4.2.4)

```
Selection of data file records
   LE(RD(0,1),84/155)
                                    Mean
SN  Org Des   Episodes   Weighted Duration  TS Min   TF Max
----------------------------------------------------------------
 1   0   0      235        235.00   76.25    0.00    428.00
 1   0   3       79         79.00   50.84    0.00    312.00
 1   0  Sum     314        314.00   69.86    0.00    428.00


----------------------------------------------------------------
Model: Exponential
Maximum of log likelihood: -516.503

Idx SN Org Des MT Var  Label   Coeff   Error   T-Stat Signif
----------------------------------------------------------------
 1   1   0   3  A --   Const  -5.6720  0.7092 -7.9981 1.0000
 2   1   0   3  A V12  EDU     0.0169  0.0601  0.2806 0.2210
 3   1   0   3  A V20  COHO2   0.5486  0.2714  2.0218 0.9568
 4   1   0   3  A V21  COHO3   0.5347  0.2890  1.8498 0.9357
 5   1   0   3  A V22  LFX    -0.0056  0.0027 -2.0972 0.9640
 6   1   0   3  A V23  PNOJ    0.1471  0.1122  1.3114 0.8103
 7   1   0   3  A V10  PRES   -0.0085  0.0131 -0.6488 0.4836
```

the number of events by drawing probability samples from the input data for lateral and downward job moves (Boxes 4.2.3 and 4.2.4).

In Box 4.2.3, an input episode is randomly selected by the *dsel* command, if an equally distributed random number in the interval (0,1) is less than or equal to the value 84 / 219, the number of upward moves divided by the number of lateral moves. Box 4.2.5 shows that this procedure selects 235 episodes with 90 events.

In Box 4.2.4, an input episode is randomly selected by the *dsel* command, if an equally distributed random number in the interval (0,1) is less than or equal to the value 84 / 155, the number of upward moves divided by the number of downward moves. Box 4.2.6 shows that this command file selects 314 episodes with 79 events.

The unstandardized and standardized estimation results for upward, lateral, and downward moves are again summarized in Box 4.2.7 to make comparison easier. In the case of lateral moves, the effects of the covariates COHO3 and LFX, and in the case of downward moves, the effect of covariate COHO3, are no longer significant in the standardized estimation. Thus, there is a chance that one could come to quite different substantive conclusions if the number of events in the comparisons of effects across various transitions is taken into account. As a rule, if one wants to compare the effects of covariates across competing transitions, one should always be aware that different event numbers might have an effect on statistical tests.

Box 4.2.7 Comparison of standardized and unstandardized estimates.

```
                                  Unstandardized      Standardized
                                  Number of Events   Number of Events
                                  ----------------   ----------------
   Idx SN Org Des MT Var  Label    Coeff   T-Stat     Coeff   T-Stat
   ----------------------------------------------------------------------
   Upward moves. Events: 84 (unstandardized) 84 (standardized)
   ----------------------------------------------------------------------
     1  1   0   1  A --   Const  -5.1036  -8.2648   -5.1036  -8.2648
     2  1   0   1  A V12  EDU     0.3018   7.0215    0.3018   7.0215
     3  1   0   1  A V20  COHO2   0.6379   2.3510    0.6379   2.3510
     4  1   0   1  A V21  COHO3   0.7354   2.6595    0.7354   2.6595
     5  1   0   1  A V22  LFX    -0.0023  -1.0898   -0.0023  -1.0898
     6  1   0   1  A V23  PNOJ    0.1731   1.7239    0.1731   1.7239
     7  1   0   1  A V10  PRES   -0.1441 -10.1970   -0.1441 -10.1970
   ----------------------------------------------------------------------
   Lateral moves. Events: 218 (unstandardized) 90 (standardized)
   ----------------------------------------------------------------------
     8  1   0   2  A --   Const  -5.8043 -14.3164   -5.3301  -7.6583
     9  1   0   2  A V12  EDU     0.0033   0.0881   -0.0097  -0.1627
    10  1   0   2  A V20  COHO2   0.6722   4.0926    0.6587   2.6181
    11  1   0   2  A V21  COHO3   0.6843   3.9501    0.4869   1.7824
    12  1   0   2  A V22  LFX    -0.0031  -2.2579   -0.0025  -1.1042
    13  1   0   2  A V23  PNOJ    0.0323   0.5010   -0.0109  -0.0961
    14  1   0   2  A V10  PRES    0.0081   1.0094    0.0014   0.1073
   ----------------------------------------------------------------------
   Downward moves. Events: 155 (unstandardized) 79 (standardized)
   ----------------------------------------------------------------------
    15  1   0   3  A --   Const  -4.9051  -9.3405   -5.6720  -7.9981
    16  1   0   3  A V12  EDU    -0.0167  -0.3404    0.0169   0.2806
    17  1   0   3  A V20  COHO2   0.5300   2.7387    0.5486   2.0218
    18  1   0   3  A V21  COHO3   0.5705   2.8101    0.5347   1.8498
    19  1   0   3  A V22  LFX    -0.0037  -2.2649   -0.0056  -2.0972
    20  1   0   3  A V23  PNOJ    0.0407   0.5252    0.1471   1.3114
    21  1   0   3  A V10  PRES   -0.0157  -1.6208   -0.0085  -0.6488
```

Estimations with Constraints

TDA provides the option to define equality constraints for parameters of a model to be estimated with maximum likelihood. For example, in the case of competing risks, parameter constraints might be used to study the behavior of substantively interesting parameters under the condition that some other parameters are equal for all transitions. This is, of course, only some sort of *Gedankenexperiment*.

To demonstrate equality constraints, we use the example of an estimation of an exponential model for upward, downward, and lateral moves (Box 4.2.1) and constrain the parameters of the cohort dummy variables COHO2 and COHO3 to be equal for all three directional moves. The new command file, part of which is shown in Box 4.2.8, is called *ehd6.cf*. TDA's command to define

Box 4.2.8 Part of command file *ehd6.cf*

```
# command to request estimation of an exponential model
rate = 2;      model selection

# commands to include covariates into model
xa (0,1)    =    v12,v20,v21,v22,v23,v10; transition 0 -> 1
xa (0,2)    =    v12,v20,v21,v22,v23,v10; transition 0 -> 2
xa (0,3)    =    v12,v20,v21,v22,v23,v10; transition 0 -> 3

# define equality constraints
con = (3) - (10) = 0;
con = (3) - (17) = 0;
con = (4) - (11) = 0;
con = (4) - (18) = 0;
```

constraints is *con=...* and follows after covariates have been assigned to the A-vectors for the three transitions. The equations

$$con = (3) - (10) = 0;$$
$$con = (3) - (17) = 0;$$
$$con = (4) - (11) = 0;$$
$$con = (4) - (18) = 0;$$

require the parameters (3) and (10), (3) and (17), (4) and (11), as well as (4) and (18) to be equal. The TDA number of parameters can easily be seen in Box 4.2.9. In the first column of the table of parameter estimates (*Idx*), TDA assigns a serial number to each of the parameters. Parameter numbers 3 and 4 refer to the parameters of the cohort dummy variables COHO2 and COHO3 for *upward moves*; parameter numbers 10 and 11 refer to the parameters for the cohort dummy variables COHO2 and COHO3 for *lateral moves*; and parameter numbers 17 and 18 refer to the parameters of the cohort dummy variables COHO2 and COHO3 for *downward moves*. Thus, the constraints make each set of the parameters for the birth cohort 1939-41 (COHO2) and for the birth cohort 1949-51 (COHO3) equal for the three transitions. This can be seen in Box 4.2.9. The constrained estimates for COHO2 = 0.6182 and for COHO3 = 0.6543. The other parameter estimates in Box 4.2.9 are pretty much the same as in Box 4.2.2.

Continuous Time, Continuous State Space Models

Our job mobility example with directional moves has the disadvantage that a continuous state space of inequality (measured in terms of prestige levels of jobs) has to be collapsed into a set of ordered destination states ("better job," "job of same level," and "worse job"). Thus, for job moves, the exact size of the increases in prestige scores could not be evaluated. To solve this problem, Petersen (1988a) suggested a method for analyzing what he calls continuous

Box 4.2.9 Results of using command file *ebd6.cf* (Box 4.2.8)

```
Model: Exponential

Equality constraints
Con 1   :  (3) - (10)  = 0
Con 2   :  (3) - (17)  = 0
Con 3   :  (4) - (11)  = 0
Con 4   :  (4) - (18)  = 0

Maximum of log likelihood: -2885.02
Norm of final gradient vector: 3.1e-09
Last absolute change of function value: 1.2e-14
Last relative change in parameters: 2.3e-06

Idx SN Org Des MT Var  Label  Coeff    Error   T-Stat  Signif
-------------------------------------------------------------
  1  1   0   1  A --   Const  -5.0782  0.5981  -8.4902  1.0000
  2  1   0   1  A V12  EDU     0.3006  0.0423   7.1066  1.0000
  3  1   0   1  A V20  COHO2   0.6182  0.1136   5.4404  1.0000
  4  1   0   1  A V21  COHO3   0.6543  0.1190   5.4985  1.0000
  5  1   0   1  A V22  LFX    -0.0024  0.0020  -1.1832  0.7633
  6  1   0   1  A V23  PNOJ    0.1780  0.0991   1.7962  0.9275
  7  1   0   1  A V10  PRES   -0.1435  0.0140 -10.2516  1.0000
-------------------------------------------------------------
  8  1   0   2  A --   Const  -5.7656  0.3950 -14.5984  1.0000
  9  1   0   2  A V12  EDU     0.0017  0.0376   0.0445  0.0355
 10  1   0   2  A V20  COHO2   0.6182  0.1136   5.4404  1.0000
 11  1   0   2  A V21  COHO3   0.6543  0.1190   5.4985  1.0000
 12  1   0   2  A V22  LFX    -0.0031  0.0013  -2.3396  0.9807
 13  1   0   2  A V23  PNOJ    0.0341  0.0641   0.5328  0.4058
 14  1   0   2  A V10  PRES    0.0083  0.0080   1.0365  0.7000
-------------------------------------------------------------
 15  1   0   3  A --   Const  -4.9621  0.5197  -9.5479  1.0000
 16  1   0   3  A V12  EDU    -0.0152  0.0491  -0.3092  0.2428
 17  1   0   3  A V20  COHO2   0.6182  0.1136   5.4404  1.0000
 18  1   0   3  A V21  COHO3   0.6543  0.1190   5.4985  1.0000
 19  1   0   3  A V22  LFX    -0.0036  0.0016  -2.2089  0.9728
 20  1   0   3  A V23  PNOJ    0.0362  0.0774   0.4683  0.3604
 21  1   0   3  A V10  PRES   -0.0161  0.0097  -1.6623  0.9035
```

time, continuous state space failure time processes. In these processes the dependent variable is continuous, but stays constant for finite periods of time in contrast to diffusion processes. He shows that the likelihood for this type of process can be written as the product of the transition rate of a change in the state variable $Y(t)$ and the density for the new value of $Y(t)$, given that a change in $Y(t)$ has occurred. For the first term, transition rate models for the analysis of duration data apply, as shown previously. For the second term, transition rate models for the outcomes of continuous dependent variables can be used. It is simple to introduce covariates into both model equations. Petersen (1988a) illustrated this method, analyzing first the rate of upward shifts in socioeconomic status and then the new value of socioeconomic status, given that an upward shift has occurred.

Another methodological solution for the analysis of continuous time, continuous-outcome processes has been suggested by Hannan, Schömann, and Blossfeld (1990). They analyzed wage trajectories across job histories of men and women and estimated (1) the wage rate at time of first entry into the labor market, (2) wage changes when workers changed jobs, and (3) wage growth within jobs. Especially for estimating the wage growth within jobs a stochastic differential equation model was applied.

4.3   Models with Multiple Episodes

As demonstrated in this chapter, transitions to a destination job are modeled as a function of the time since entry into an origin job in most studies of social mobility research (e.g.   Sørensen and Tuma 1981; Sørensen 1984; Carroll and Mayer 1986; Tuma 1985; Sørensen and Blossfeld 1989). The career trajectory of an individual is therefore divided into a series of job spells (single episodes), each starting with time equal to 0. The process time is job-specific labor force experience. The effects of causal variables are mostly regarded as independent of the different job episodes and are therefore estimated as constant across episodes.[21]   Blossfeld and Hamerle (1989a; Hamerle 1989, 1991) called this type of job-shift model *uni-episode analysis with episode-constant coefficients.*[22]

Another way to model job mobility is to regard job transitions as being dependent on the time a person spent in the labor force since entry into the labor market.   Process time in this case is the amount of *general labor force experience.*[23] Starting and ending times of the job spells in a person's career are then given as the time since entry into the labor market.[24] The coefficients of covariates may be estimated as constant or as changing across episodes. One can term this type of job shift analysis *multi-episode models with episode-constant or episode-changing coefficients* (Blossfeld and Hamerle 1989a).

In the case of an exponential model, for which we assume that general labor force experience does not affect job shift rates, an interesting application of

---

[21] In the case of exponential models, for example, interaction terms between the serial number of the job (or a set of dummy variables for it) and the other time-constant covariates could be used to study changes of such covariate effects across spells.

[22] In the literature these models normally also include job duration dependence (see chapters 5, 6, and 7). But in this case, time-dependence means that the event of a job shift primarily depends on the time spent in each of these jobs (or job-specific labor force experience), regardless of the specific location of the job in an individual's job career (which is general labor force experience).

[23] Again, definitions of different clocks or process times are particularly important in the case of models with time-dependence (chapter 7) and semi-parametric (Cox) models (chapter 9).

[24] In time-dependent models, the event of a job shift depends on the specific location of the spell in a person's life course. Consequently, the job spells of a person's career are not treated as autonomous entities.

a multi-episode model could be to study how covariate effects change across episodes. Such a model is estimated with command file *ehd7.cf*, shown in Box 4.3.1.

However, before we begin to describe this command file, we should make some more general comments. It is important to note here that compared to American workers, German workers have considerably fewer jobs and change jobs less frequently. The average time in a given job for a man in Germany is about 6 years (Carroll and Mayer 1986), while in the United States it is only 2.2 years (Tuma 1985). The stable nature of job trajectories in Germany implies that a job change is more likely to be substantively meaningful than is a job shift in the United States. But, on the other hand, it also means that the distribution of job episodes is clustered more to the left of the mean with extreme values to the right (see Box 2.2.8a). This has consequences for the analysis of career mobility as a multi-episode process: (1) The smaller the number of job transitions for a given serial job number, the more likely it is to produce statistically insignificant results; hence, a comparison of episode-specific parameters across spell numbers based on significant coefficients may be misleading; (2) the number of serial job episodes used to study career mobility as a multi-episode process is limited. In such a model, it is not wise to include episodes of serial numbers with a very small number of job transitions. Therefore, based on the distribution of job transitions, as displayed in Box 2.2.8a, only the first four job episodes are used for our estimation of the multi-episode model. This ensures that the number of job spells and transitions in each episode is great enough to compare the estimates across episodes in a meaningful way. Additionally, it guarantees that only a few job spells are lost in the analysis. On the basis of this decision, about 89 % (532/600) of all job spells and 91 % (418/458) of all job moves (or events) are included in this multi-episode model.

Now we explain command file *ehd7.cf*, shown in Box 4.3.1. First, we select episodes with the *dsel* command. The command *dsel = le(c2,4)* tells TDA to include only job episodes with a serial number (stored in column $C2$ in the data file *rrdat.1*) less than or equal to 4.

Then, compared to the command file for the exponential model with single episodes in Box 4.1.1, we now need two additional pieces of information. One must know which episodes belong to which employee (the case ID stored in column 1 of the data file and assigned the variable $V1$), and one must have knowledge about the serial number of the episodes (stored in column 2 of the data file and assigned the variable $V2$). Thus, the following two additional commands are used to define multi-episode data in our example:

$id = v1;$
$sn = v2;$

All job spells with the same value of the ID variable belong to the same worker. The episodes (jobs) belonging to each individual are distinguished by their

Box 4.3.1 Command file *ehd7.cf* (multi-episode exponential model)

```
    dfile = rrdat.1;        data file
    dsel = le(c2,4);        select up to four jobs

    v1  (ID)     = c1 ;     ID of individual
    v2  (NOJ)    = c2 ;     Serial number of the job
    v3  (TStart) = c3 ;     Starting time of the job
    v4  (TFin)   = c4 ;     Ending time of the job
    v5  (SEX)    = c5 ;     Sex (1 men, 2 women)
    v6  (TI)     = c6 ;     Date of interview
    v7  (TB)     = c7 ;     Date of birth
    v8  (T1)     = c8 ;     Date of entry into the labor market
    v9  (TM)     = c9 ;     Date of marriage (0 if no marriage)
    v10 (PRES)   = c10;     Prestige score of job i
    v11 (PRESN)  = c11;     Prestige score of job i + 1
    v12 (EDU)    = c12;     Highest educational attainment

    # Define a single origin state (0)
    # and a single destination state (1):
    v13 (ORG)    = 0;
    v14 (DES)    = lt(v4,v6);

    # Definition of starting and ending time on a process time axis
    v15 (TSP) = 0;
    v16 (TFP) = v4 - v3 + 1; one month added

    # commands to define multi-episode data
    id  = v1;       define case id
    sn  = v2;       define episode number
    org = v13;      define origin state
    des = v14;      define destination state
    ts  = v15;      define starting time
    tf  = v16;      define ending time

    # command to request estimation of an exponential model
    rate = 2;       model selection

    # define additional variables to include into the model
    v20 (COHO2) =   ge(v7,468) . le(v7,504); cohort 2
    v21 (COHO3) =   ge(v7,588) . le(v7,624); cohort 3
    v22 (LFX)   =   v3 - v8;             labor force experience
    v23 (PNOJ)  =   v2 - 1;              previous number of jobs

    # commands to include covariates into model
    xa (0,1,1)  =   v12,v20,v21,    v10; 0 -> 1, first spell
    xa (0,1,2)  =   v12,v20,v21,v22,v10; 0 -> 1, second spell
    xa (0,1,3)  =   v12,v20,v21,v22,v10; 0 -> 1, third spell
    xa (0,1,4)  =   v12,v20,v21,v22,v10; 0 -> 1, fourth spell
```

serial number given by the SN variable. As discussed in chapter 2, the serial numbers must be positive integers and they should be contiguous.

Box 4.3.2a Result (first part) of using command file *ehd7.cf* (Box 4.3.1)

```
Multi-episode data

Case ID: V1          Spell number: V2
Origin state: V13    Destination state: V14
Starting time: V15   Ending time: V16

Frequencies of spell numbers
  SN   N of Units   Weighted   N of Spells   Weighted
  --------------------------------------------------------
   1        39        39.00         201        201.00
   2        55        55.00         162        162.00
   3        45        45.00         107        107.00
   4        62        62.00          62         62.00
 Sum       201       201.00         532        532.00

                                        Mean
 SN  Org Des   Episodes   Weighted   Duration  TS Min   TF Max
 -------------------------------------------------------------
  1   0   0        16        16.00     233.44    0.00    428.00
  1   0   1       185       185.00      52.73    0.00    326.00
  1   0  Sum      201       201.00      67.11    0.00    428.00
 -------------------------------------------------------------
  2   0   0        36        36.00     150.17    0.00    407.00
  2   0   1       126       126.00      52.30    0.00    350.00
  2   0  Sum      162       162.00      74.05    0.00    407.00
 -------------------------------------------------------------
  3   0   0        38        38.00     121.74    0.00    329.00
  3   0   1        69        69.00      50.36    0.00    332.00
  3   0  Sum      107       107.00      75.71    0.00    332.00
 -------------------------------------------------------------
  4   0   0        24        24.00      85.33    0.00    340.00
  4   0   1        38        38.00      37.71    0.00    146.00
  4   0  Sum       62        62.00      56.15    0.00    340.00
 -------------------------------------------------------------
  A   0   0       114       114.00     138.73    0.00    428.00
  A   0   1       418       418.00      50.84    0.00    350.00
  A   0  Sum      532       532.00      69.68    0.00    428.00
```

A further difference of the command files in Boxes 4.1.1 and 4.3.1 is in the assignment of covariates. If episode-specific parameters of covariates for the first four jobs of an individual should be estimated, one has to specify which covariates should be included in the episode-specific A-vectors. The syntax of the TDA command is

$$xa\ (j,k,n) = list\_of\_covariates;$$

to link the list of covariates on the right-hand side to the model parameters (model term A) for the transition from origin state j to destination state k and for episodes with serial number n. For example, in Box 4.3.1, the command

$$xa\ (0,1,4) = v12,v20,v21,v22,v10;$$

Box 4.3.2b   Result (second part) of using command file *ehd7.cf* (Box 4.3.1)

```
Model: Exponential

Maximum likelihood estimation
Algorithm 5: Newton (I)

Convergence reached in 6 iterations
Number of function evaluations: 7

Maximum of log likelihood: -2233.7
Norm of final gradient vector: 7.0e-06
Last absolute change of function value: 1.6e-11
Last relative change in parameters: 2.5e-04

Idx SN Org Des MT Var  Label  Coeff   Error   T-Stat  Signif
------------------------------------------------------------
  1  1   0   1  A --   Const -5.0179  0.4174 -12.0225  1.0000
  2  1   0   1  A V12  EDU    0.0622  0.0327   1.9052  0.9432
  3  1   0   1  A V20  COHO2  0.7221  0.1888   3.8245  0.9999
  4  1   0   1  A V21  COHO3  0.6638  0.1792   3.7050  0.9998
  5  1   0   1  A V10  PRES  -0.0095  0.0091  -1.0452  0.7041
------------------------------------------------------------
  6  2   0   1  A --   Const -3.7352  0.5778  -6.4644  1.0000
  7  2   0   1  A V12  EDU    0.1261  0.0516   2.4442  0.9855
  8  2   0   1  A V20  COHO2  0.3423  0.2157   1.5867  0.8874
  9  2   0   1  A V21  COHO3  0.2704  0.2334   1.1582  0.7532
 10  2   0   1  A V22  LFX   -0.0062  0.0018  -3.3525  0.9992
 11  2   0   1  A V10  PRES  -0.0510  0.0110  -4.6237  1.0000
------------------------------------------------------------
 12  3   0   1  A --   Const -4.2628  0.7397  -5.7631  1.0000
 13  3   0   1  A V12  EDU    0.0522  0.0749   0.6976  0.5146
 14  3   0   1  A V20  COHO2  0.1975  0.2972   0.6645  0.4936
 15  3   0   1  A V21  COHO3  0.7143  0.3289   2.1719  0.9701
 16  3   0   1  A V22  LFX   -0.0039  0.0020  -1.9843  0.9528
 17  3   0   1  A V10  PRES  -0.0223  0.0139  -1.6008  0.8906
------------------------------------------------------------
 18  4   0   1  A --   Const -2.2232  1.3489  -1.6481  0.9007
 19  4   0   1  A V12  EDU    0.0438  0.1329   0.3295  0.2583
 20  4   0   1  A V20  COHO2  1.1354  0.3830   2.9643  0.9970
 21  4   0   1  A V21  COHO3  0.3163  0.4492   0.7041  0.5186
 22  4   0   1  A V22  LFX   -0.0052  0.0027  -1.9131  0.9443
 23  4   0   1  A V10  PRES  -0.0654  0.0205  -3.1986  0.9986
```

assigns the list of covariates given on the right-hand side to the transition from origin state 0 ("being in a job") to destination state 1 ("having left the job") and for episodes with serial number 4. Note that the covariate LFX (*V22*), general labor force experience measured at the beginning of each new job episode, cannot be included as a covariate for the *first* job episode because this variable is zero for all first episodes (or workers). With the exception of this variable, all other covariates are time-constant because they do not change their value after the beginning of the process time, which is the *time of entry into the first job*. Variable LFX ("general labor force experience at the beginning of each new job") is a special form of a (process-related) time-dependent covariate because it changes its value at the beginning of each job. Using this covariate in a multi-episode exponential model whose process time is defined by the clock "general labor force experience" would be meaningless. If, on the one hand, the assumption of the exponential model is correct, then this covariate cannot have a significant effect because the process does not depend on history, and the rate of job change is constant across the process time (i.e. general labor force experience). If, on the other hand, the covariate "general labor force experience" had a significant effect, then the assumption of an exponential distribution would be wrong, and one should use a model with a time-dependent transition rate. The transition rate would then become a function of time so that events become either less likely (negative duration dependence) or more likely (positive duration dependence) as the clock, general labor force experience, progresses. Thus, this multi-episode model can serve as a test for the assumption that the job history process is *time stationary* or *time homogeneous* (i.e. transitions do not depend on time).

Estimation results using command file *ehd7.cf* (Box 4.3.1) are shown in the Boxes 4.3.2a and 4.3.2b. The table in Box 4.3.2a shows some descriptive statistics for the individuals' first four jobs, and Box 4.3.2b provides the job-number-specific estimates for the covariates. It is easy to see that the covariate "general labor force experience" (LFX) has significant effects on the rate of job change for episode numbers two and three, and is almost significant for the fourth job. This means that the job history is not time stationary or time homogeneous, but that the movement rate becomes less likely as general labor force experience increases.

It is interesting to see how the effects of covariates change across the number of episodes. For mobility out of the first job, only the cohort dummy variables are statistically significant. The parameters for COHO2 and COHO3 are quite similar in size. Thus, the greatest difference is between the reference group (birth cohort 1929–31) and the two younger birth cohorts (born in 1939–41 and 1949–51). After having left the first job and entered the second one, the educational attainment level has a positive impact and prestige of the job has a negative impact on job mobility. In the third job, only the birth cohort 1949–51 (COHO3) behaves differently. Members of this cohort move to a fourth job significantly more often. Finally, in the fourth job, the birth cohort 1939–41 (COHO2) is more mobile and the prestige level (PRES) reduces job mobility. Of course, all of these estimates are based on a small number of events, and the interpretation given here only serves for didactical purposes.

Chapter 5

Piecewise Constant Exponential Models

In most applications of transition rate models, the assumption that the forces of change are constant over time is not theoretically justified. It is therefore important for an appropriate modeling of social processes to be able to include time-dependent covariates in transition rate models. Before discussing this topic more deeply in chapter 6, we survey the *piecewise constant exponential model*. This is a simple generalization of the standard exponential model (chapter 4), but it is extremely useful in many practical research situations. It is particularly helpful when researchers are not in a position to measure and include important time-dependent covariates explicitly or when they do not have a clear idea about the form of the time-dependence of the process. In both these situations, a small modification of the exponential model leads to a very flexible instrument of analysis. The basic idea is to split the time axis into time periods and to assume that transition rates are constant in each of these intervals but can change between them.

5.1   The Basic Model

If there are L time periods, the piecewise constant transition rate is defined by L parameters. There are two different options to include covariates in TDA, which are demonstrated in this section. The first is to assume that only a baseline rate, given by period-specific constants, can vary across time periods but the covariates have the same (proportional) effects in each period.[1] And the second option allows for period-specific effects of covariates. We begin by demonstrating the first option.

The TDA command to request this first version of the piecewise constant exponential model is

$rate = 3;$

In addition, one has to define time periods by split points on the time axis

$$0 = \tau_1 < \tau_2 < \tau_3 < \ldots < \tau_L$$

With $\tau_{L+1} = \infty$, one gets L time periods

$$I_l = \{t \mid \tau_l \leq t < \tau_{l+1}\} \qquad l = 1, \ldots, L$$

---

[1] The exponential model and the piecewise constant exponential model, in which the covariates have the same effects across the time periods, are both special cases of the more general proportional transition rate models (see chapter 9).

The TDA command to define time periods is

$$tp = \tau_1, \tau_2, \ldots, \tau_L;$$

Given these time periods, the transition rate from origin state j to destination state k is

$$r_{jk}(t) = \exp\left\{\bar{\alpha}_l^{(jk)} + A^{(jk)}\alpha^{(jk)}\right\} \quad \text{if} \quad t \in I_l \tag{5.1}$$

For each transition (j, k), $\bar{\alpha}_l^{(jk)}$ is a constant coefficient associated with the lth time period. $A^{(jk)}$ is a (row) vector of covariates, and $\alpha^{(jk)}$ is an associated vector of coefficients assumed not to vary across time periods. Note that with this model the vector of covariates cannot contain a separate constant.

Maximum Likelihood Estimation

The maximum likelihood estimation of this model is done following the outline given in section 4.1.1. To simplify notation we omit indices for transitions and define $l[t]$ to be the index of the time period containing t (so $t \in I_{l[t]}$ always). Also the following notation is helpful:

$$\delta[t, l] = \begin{cases} 1 & \text{if } t \in I_l \\ 0 & \text{otherwise} \end{cases}$$

$$\Delta[s, t, l] = \begin{cases} t - \tau_l & \text{if } s \le \tau_l, \ \tau_l < t < \tau_{l+1} \\ \tau_{l+1} - \tau_l & \text{if } s \le \tau_l, \ t \ge \tau_{l+1} \\ \tau_{l+1} - s & \text{if } t \ge \tau_{l+1}, \ \tau_l < s < \tau_{l+1} \\ 0 & \text{otherwise} \end{cases}$$

The conditional survivor function may then be written as

$$G(t \mid s) = \exp\left\{-\sum_{l=1}^{L} \Delta[s, t, l] \exp(\bar{\alpha}_l + A\alpha)\right\}$$

Using this expression, the log likelihood can be written as

$$\ell = \sum_{i \in \mathcal{E}} (\bar{\alpha}_{l[t_i]} + A_i\alpha) - \sum_{i \in \mathcal{N}}\sum_{l=1}^{L} \Delta[s_i, t_i, l] \exp(\bar{\alpha}_l + A_i\alpha)$$

To maximize this likelihood, TDA uses first and second derivatives and calculates default starting values by assuming the same rate in each time period. As an initial estimate, the constant rate of a correspondingly defined exponential model (without covariates) is used. In most practical situations this is sufficient to reach convergence of the maximum likelihood iterations.

5.2   Models without Covariates

As an illustration of the piecewise constant exponential model, we continue
with the example in Box 4.1.1 (section 4.1), but now allow for the possibility
that the transition rate varies across time periods.

Box 5.2.1   Part of command file *ehe1.cf* (piecewise constant exponential model)

```
... (first part identical to first part in Box 4.1.1)

# command to request estimation of a
# piecewise constant exponential model
rate = 3;           model selection
tp   = 0 (12) 96;   time periods

# commands to request a printout of estimated transition rate
prate = ehe1.prs;   print to output file: ehe1.prs
tab   = 0,300,2;    time axis for the table
```

Generally, time periods can be arbitrarily defined, but there is some trade-
off.   If one chooses a large number of time periods, one will get a better
approximation of the unknown baseline rate, but this implies a large number of
coefficients to be estimated. On the other hand, if one chooses a small number
of periods, there are less estimation problems, but there is probably a poorer
approximation of the baseline rate. Therefore, in most cases some compromise
is needed.

Another important requirement is that there should be some episodes with
ending times within the interval for all time periods. Otherwise it is generally
not possible to reach sensible estimates. Note that TDA, unlike some other
programs, does not automatically set coefficients to zero if they cannot be
estimated.

However, we already have some information about the length of episodes in
our example data set. We know that the mean duration of episodes with an
event is about 49 months, and that the mean duration of censored episodes is
about 128 months (see Box 2.2.5). Therefore, it seems appropriate to use eight
time periods, each having a length of one year, plus an additional open-ended
interval. To define these time periods the command is

$tp = 0(12)96;$ or $tp = 0,12,24,36,48,60,72,84,96;$

Using the command *rate=3* to request the estimation of a piecewise constant
exponential model, and adding the command *tp=0(12)96* to the command file
in Box 4.1.1, results in a new command file, *ehe1.cf*, shown in Box 5.2.1.

Using this command file TDA estimates a piecewise constant exponential
model. Part of the program's output is shown in Box 5.2.2. The estimated
parameters for the baseline transition rate at first increase, from -4.6829 to
-3.7854, and then decrease. In our application example this means that with

Box 5.2.2 Estimation results of command file *ehe1.cf* (Box 5.2.1)

```
Model: Exponential with time periods

                    Begin         Number of weighted
Time Period      of Period    Starting Times  Ending Times
---------------------------------------------------------
        1          0.0000         600.00          76.00
        2         12.0000           0.00         104.00
        3         24.0000           0.00         108.00
        4         36.0000           0.00          55.00
        5         48.0000           0.00          44.00
        6         60.0000           0.00          38.00
        7         72.0000           0.00          22.00
        8         84.0000           0.00           9.00
        9         96.0000           0.00         144.00

Maximum likelihood estimation
Maximum of log likelihood: -2456.61
Norm of final gradient vector: 1.0e-04
Last absolute change of function value: 5.7e-08
Last relative change in parameters: 9.6e-04

Idx SN Org Des MT Var  Label      Coeff   Error    T-Stat  Signif
-----------------------------------------------------------------
  1  1   0   1  A --   Period-1  -4.6829  0.1260  -37.1691  1.0000
  2  1   0   1  A --   Period-2  -4.0420  0.1021  -39.6029  1.0000
  3  1   0   1  A --   Period-3  -3.7854  0.1026  -36.8954  1.0000
  4  1   0   1  A --   Period-4  -4.3178  0.1508  -28.6410  1.0000
  5  1   0   1  A --   Period-5  -4.2955  0.1622  -26.4792  1.0000
  6  1   0   1  A --   Period-6  -4.3690  0.1857  -23.5278  1.0000
  7  1   0   1  A --   Period-7  -4.7274  0.2425  -19.4915  1.0000
  8  1   0   1  A --   Period-8  -5.6864  0.4082  -13.9289  1.0000
  9  1   0   1  A --   Period-9  -5.1650  0.1195  -43.2137  1.0000
```

increasing duration in a specific job the force of job mobility (or the job shift rate) is non-monotonic. This can be seen more easily when the estimation result in Box 5.2.2 is plotted in Figure 5.2.1.[2]

In substantive terms this bell-shaped rate pattern might be interpreted as an interplay of two opposing causal forces (increases in job-specific investments and decreases in the need to resolve mismatches) that cannot easily be measured, so that the duration in a job has to serve as a proxy variable for them. The argument is that when people are matched to jobs under the condition of imperfect information and high search costs, mismatches can occur. Particularly during the first months of each new employment, there will be an intensive adjustment process in which the respective expectations of the employer and the employee are confronted with reality. German labor law, for example, al-

---

[2] The TDA command file, *ehe1a.cf*, which plots the estimated rates of the piecewise constant exponential model, is included on the accompanying disk.

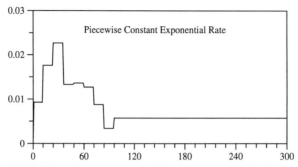

Figure 5.2.1 Piecewise constant transition rate, estimated with command file *ehe1.cf*. The PostScript file was generated with command file *ehe1a.cf*.

lows for a probationary period of six months during which it is relatively easy for employers to fire somebody if they are not satisfied. But employees also quit their job more readily at the beginning of each new employment because their job-specific investments are still low. Consequently, one would expect that the rate of moving out of the job increases at the beginning of each new employment. However, as mismatches have been increasingly resolved and investments in job-specific human capital are continuously rising, a point will be reached at which both of these forces will become equally strong. This is where the peak of the transition rate of moving out of the job is reached (Figure 5.2.1). In our example this point is reached after about 2 years of employment in a new job. After this job duration, further increases in job-specific investments will more and more outweigh the force of resolving mismatches, so that the job shift rate will decline with increasing duration.

5.3 Models with Proportional Covariate Effects

The problem with the analysis without covariates in the previous section is that important heterogeneity between the individuals has not been taken into account. Thus, in the next step we study whether the non-monotonic pattern of the job shift rate will still be there if time-constant covariates are included. This can be done by a simple modification of command file *ehe1.cf* (Box 5.2.1). The new command file is *ehe2.cf*, and the additional commands are shown in Box 5.3.1. There is a set of commands to define the required covariates (which are not already available in the data file), and a single command to include these covariates into the model specification.

The estimation results of using command file *ehe2.cf* are shown in Box 5.3.2. Based on these parameter estimates, one can draw at least two conclusions: First, the non-monotonic rate pattern of the piecewise constant exponential model without covariates (Box 5.2.2) has not changed. Thus, this pattern

Box 5.3.1   Part of command file *ehe2.cf*

```
# define additional variables to include into the model
v20 (COHO2) =   ge(v7,468) . le(v7,504);   cohort 2
v21 (COHO3) =   ge(v7,588) . le(v7,624);   cohort 3
v22 (LFX)   =   v3 - v8;                    labor force experience
v23 (PNOJ)  =   v2 - 1;                     previous number of jobs

# commands to request estimation of a
# piecewise constant exponential model
rate = 3;          model selection
tp   = 0 (12) 96;  time periods

# command to include covariates into model, for transition from
# origin state 0 to destination state 1.
xa (0,1) = v12,v20,v21,v22,v23,v10;
```

Box 5.3.2   Estimation results of command file *ehe2.cf* (Box 5.3.1)

```
Model: Exponential with time periods

Maximum of log likelihood: -2417.18
Norm of final gradient vector: 4.7e-07
Last absolute change of function value: 2.7e-12
Last relative change in parameters: 8.1e-06

Idx SN Org Des MT Var  Label      Coeff    Error    T-Stat  Signif
------------------------------------------------------------------
  1  1   0   1  A --   Period-1  -4.6053   0.3019  -15.2522  1.0000
  2  1   0   1  A --   Period-2  -3.9236   0.2922  -13.4281  1.0000
  3  1   0   1  A --   Period-3  -3.6302   0.2904  -12.5000  1.0000
  4  1   0   1  A --   Period-4  -4.1514   0.3101  -13.3852  1.0000
  5  1   0   1  A --   Period-5  -4.1106   0.3157  -13.0201  1.0000
  6  1   0   1  A --   Period-6  -4.1584   0.3292  -12.6327  1.0000
  7  1   0   1  A --   Period-7  -4.5272   0.3609  -12.5459  1.0000
  8  1   0   1  A --   Period-8  -5.4741   0.4876  -11.2257  1.0000
  9  1   0   1  A --   Period-9  -4.9094   0.2887  -17.0067  1.0000
 10  1   0   1  A V12  EDU        0.0683   0.0249    2.7409  0.9939
 11  1   0   1  A V20  COHO2      0.4841   0.1155    4.1931  1.0000
 12  1   0   1  A V21  COHO3      0.3823   0.1228    3.1146  0.9982
 13  1   0   1  A V22  LFX       -0.0037   0.0009   -3.9943  0.9999
 14  1   0   1  A V23  PNOJ       0.0618   0.0442    1.3987  0.8381
 15  1   0   1  A V10  PRES      -0.0266   0.0055   -4.8228  1.0000
```

of time-dependence cannot be explained by the additionally included time-constant covariates.[3] Second, the parameter estimates for the time-constant covariates resemble the estimates for the basic exponential model in Box 4.1.5.

---

[3] In chapter 10 we give some examples of how unobserved time-constant heterogeneity can produce time-dependent rates.

Thus, the parameter estimates for the time-constant covariates in the exponential model seem to be quite robust.[4]

5.4   Models with Period-Specific Effects

In this section we further generalize the piecewise constant exponential model by also allowing the effects of the time-constant covariates (i.e. their associated parameters) to vary across time periods.[5] This model was first proposed by Tuma (1980).

To request estimation of an exponential model with period-specific effects, the TDA model selection command is

   rate = 16;

In addition, one has to define time periods by split points on the time axis in exactly the same way as for the standard exponential model with time periods, using the command

   $tp = \tau_1, \tau_2, \ldots, \tau_L;$

Given these time periods, the transition rate from origin state j to destination state k is

$$r_{jk}(t) = \exp\left\{\bar{\alpha}_l^{(jk)} + A^{(jk)}\alpha_l^{(jk)}\right\} \quad \text{if} \quad \tau_l \leq t < \tau_{l+1} \qquad (5.2)$$

For each transition (j, k), $\bar{\alpha}_l^{(jk)}$ is a constant coefficient associated with the lth time period. The (row) vector of covariates is $A^{(jk)}$, and $\alpha_l^{(jk)}$ is an associated vector of coefficients, showing the effects of these covariates in the lth time period.

Obviously, the standard exponential model with time periods defined in (5.1) (see section 5.1) is a special case of the model defined in (5.2). In fact, estimating the latter model with constraints that require the $\alpha_l^{(jk)}$ parameters to be equal across time periods would give identical results to the standard exponential model with time periods.

Maximum Likelihood Estimation.   The maximum likelihood estimation of this model is similar to the standard piecewise constant exponential model described earlier. Using the same abbreviations, $l[t]$ and $\Delta[s, t, l]$, the conditional survivor function is

$$G(t \mid s) = \exp\left\{-\sum_{l=1}^{L} \Delta[s, t, l] \exp(\bar{\alpha}_l + A\alpha_l)\right\}$$

---

[4] We shall see that the parameter estimates for the time-constant covariates are surprisingly stable across a broad range of different models.

[5] One should note that this is not the same as a standard exponential model with interaction effects between covariates and time periods. Such interaction effects with process time would lead to heavily biased estimation results.

Box 5.4.1 Part of command file *ehe3.cf*

```
# ehe3.cf    piecewise constant exponential model with covariates
#            (period-specific effects)

# command to request estimation of an extended
# piecewise constant exponential model
rate = 16;         model selection
tp   = 0,24,60;    time periods

# command to include covariates into model, for transition from
# origin state 0 to destination state 1.
xa (0,1) = v12,v20,v21,v22,v23,v10;
```

and using this expression, the log likelihood can be written as

$$\ell = \sum_{i \in \mathcal{E}} (\bar{\alpha}_{l[t_i]} + A_i \alpha_{l[t_i]}) - \sum_{i \in \mathcal{N}} \sum_{l=1}^{L} \Delta[s_i, t_i, l] \exp(\bar{\alpha}_l + A_i \alpha_l)$$

Initial estimates to begin the iterative process of maximizing the log likelihood are calculated in the same way as for the standard piecewise constant exponential model.

Example. In the context of our job mobility example, the piecewise constant exponential model with period-specific effects is particularly interesting because it provides the opportunity to assess hypotheses based on the *filter* or *signaling theory* (Arrow 1973; Spence 1973, 1974). This labor market theory contends that in the hiring process easily observable characteristics (such as educational qualifications, number of previously held jobs, or years of labor force experience) serve as signals for employers. In particular, these characteristics are used by employers to infer differences in productivity among people applying for a given job. Thus, they are very important for employment decisions as well as in a starting phase of each new job. With increasing job duration, however, the employer is able to gain more direct information on the employee and is increasingly less forced to rely on such signals to evaluate the competence or productivity of employees. Thus, the expectation is that, for job decisions, the importance of such signals declines with increasing duration in a job. On the other hand, one can also assume that job decisions of an employee, especially at the beginning of each new job, depend strongly on the image (or prestige) of the job position, and that the relevance of these characteristics for his/her job decisions declines with increasing experience in the job. In summary, both arguments lead to the hypothesis that the effects of those time-constant covariates that serve as signals decline over job duration.

In the following example, we therefore divide the duration in a job into periods and estimate period-specific effects of covariates with a piecewise constant exponential model. We use a new command file, *ehe3.cf*, which is however ba-

Box 5.4.2   Estimation results of command file *ehe3.cf* (Box 5.4.1)

```
Model: Exponential with period-specific effects

                    Begin          Number of weighted
    Time Period    of Period    Starting Times   Ending Times
    -----------------------------------------------------------
          1          0.0000         600.00         180.00
          2         24.0000           0.00         207.00
          3         60.0000           0.00         213.00

Maximum likelihood estimation
Maximum of log likelihood: -2434.9
Norm of final gradient vector: 1.8e-08
Last absolute change of function value: 1.2e-13
Last relative change in parameters: 5.7e-06

Idx SN Org Des MT Var  P Label     Coeff    Error   T-Stat  Signif
------------------------------------------------------------------
  1  1   0   1  A --   1 Period-1  -4.4627  0.4522  -9.8688  1.0000
  2  1   0   1  A --   2 Period-2  -3.7235  0.4451  -8.3647  1.0000
  3  1   0   1  A --   3 Period-3  -5.0902  0.5780  -8.8058  1.0000
  4  1   0   1  A V12  1 EDU        0.1016  0.0384   2.6455  0.9918
  5  1   0   1  A V12  2 EDU        0.0548  0.0435   1.2590  0.7920
  6  1   0   1  A V12  3 EDU        0.0470  0.0494   0.9508  0.6583
  7  1   0   1  A V20  1 COHO2      0.5849  0.2038   2.8692  0.9959
  8  1   0   1  A V20  2 COHO2      0.5112  0.1864   2.7426  0.9939
  9  1   0   1  A V20  3 COHO2      0.4116  0.2192   1.8776  0.9396
 10  1   0   1  A V21  1 COHO3      0.4666  0.2061   2.2638  0.9764
 11  1   0   1  A V21  2 COHO3      0.2824  0.1939   1.4562  0.8547
 12  1   0   1  A V21  3 COHO3      0.6422  0.2518   2.5505  0.9892
 13  1   0   1  A V22  1 LFX       -0.0059  0.0017  -3.4044  0.9993
 14  1   0   1  A V22  2 LFX       -0.0031  0.0014  -2.1951  0.9718
 15  1   0   1  A V22  3 LFX       -0.0017  0.0018  -0.9437  0.6547
 16  1   0   1  A V23  1 PNOJ       0.1668  0.0742   2.2486  0.9755
 17  1   0   1  A V23  2 PNOJ       0.0326  0.0697   0.4683  0.3604
 18  1   0   1  A V23  3 PNOJ      -0.0445  0.0917  -0.4856  0.3727
 19  1   0   1  A V10  1 PRES      -0.0336  0.0089  -3.7938  0.9999
 20  1   0   1  A V10  2 PRES      -0.0265  0.0091  -2.9246  0.9966
 21  1   0   1  A V10  3 PRES      -0.0121  0.0113  -1.0723  0.7164
```

sically the same as command file *ehe2.cf* already used for the standard piecewise constant exponential model. Therefore, Box 5.4.1 only shows the commands for model selection and specification, which have been changed. One should however note the new specification of time periods. Because our model estimates parameters for all covariates in each time period separately, we have to use a reasonably small number of periods to get sensible estimates with the 600 job episodes in our example data set.[6] Thus, we only define three periods by using three split points, namely, 0, 24, and 60 months.

---

[6] It is obvious that a model that tries to estimate changing effects of covariates across a number of

Part of the estimation result is shown in Box 5.4.2. It supports our hypothesis that the effects of the signaling or filter variables, such as educational attainment (EDU), general labor force experience at the beginning of each job (LFX), number of previously held jobs (PNOJ), or prestige of the job (PRES), are strong in the first phase of each job (period up to two years), and then decline in importance across later periods. In the third period (job duration greater than 5 years), none of these signaling or filter variables is significant anymore.

---

time periods requires, in general, large data sets, even in the case of moderate numbers of periods and covariates.

Chapter 6
Exponential Models with Time-Dependent Covariates

In our view, the most important step forward in event history analysis, with respect to the empirical study of social change, has been to explicitly measure and include time-dependent covariates in transition rate models. In such cases, covariates can change their values over process time. Time-dependent covariates can be qualitative or quantitative, and may stay constant for finite periods of time or change continuously.

Three basic approaches can be distinguished to include time-dependent covariates in transition rate models. Time-dependent covariates can be included (1) by using a piecewise constant exponential model as shown in the previous chapter, (2) by applying the method of episode splitting in parametric and semi-parametric transition rate models, and (3) by specifying the distributional form of the time-dependence and directly estimating its parameters using the maximum likelihood method. In this chapter we begin with a general discussion of time-dependent covariates in the framework of parallel and interdependent processes, and then focus on the method of episode splitting.[1] Parametric models of time-dependence are presented in chapter 7.

6.1 Parallel and Interdependent Processes

In applying time-dependent covariates, the effects of change over time in one phenomenon on change in another one can be studied (Tuma and Hannan 1984).[2] From a substantive point of view, it is therefore useful to conceptualize time-dependent covariates as observations of the sample path of parallel processes (Blossfeld, Hamerle, and Mayer 1989).[3] These processes can operate at different levels. For example:

---

[1] See, e.g., Petersen 1986a, 1986b; Blossfeld, Hamerle, and Mayer 1989. The method of episode splitting can also be applied in the case of parametric models of time-dependence (see chapter 7) or semi-parametric (Cox) models (see chapter 9). Because the logic of including time-dependent covariates for all parametric models is the same, we only demonstrate this method for exponential models.

[2] In this book, we only focus on continuous-time, discrete-state dependent processes.

[3] A complete history of state occupancies and times of changes is referred to as a *sample path* (Tuma and Hannan 1984).

1. there can be *parallel processes at the level of the individual in different domains of life* (e.g., one may ask how upward and downward moves in an individual's job career influence his/her family trajectory), cf. Blossfeld and Huinink (1991);

2. there may be *parallel processes at the level of some few individuals interacting with each other* (e.g., one might study the effect of the career of the husband on his wife's labor force participation), see Bernasco (1994);

3. there may be *parallel processes at the intermediate level* (e.g., one can analyze how organizational growth influences career advancement or changing household structure determines women's labor force participation), see Blossfeld (in press);

4. there may be *parallel processes at the macrolevel* (e.g., one may be interested in the effect of changes in the business cycle on family formation or career advancement), see Blossfeld (1987b) and Huinink (1989, 1992, 1993);

5. there may be *any combination of such processes of type* (1) *to* (4). For example, in the study of life-course, cohort and period effects, time-dependent covariates at different levels must be included simultaneously (Blossfeld 1986; Mayer and Huinink 1990). Such an analysis combines processes at the individual level (life-course change) with two kinds of processes at the macrolevel: (1) variations in structural conditions across successive (birth, marriage, entry, etc.) cohorts, and (2) changes in historical conditions affecting all cohorts in the same way.

In dealing with such systems of parallel processes, the issue of reverse causation is normally addressed in the methodological   literature (see, e.g., Kalbfleisch and Prentice 1980; Tuma and Hannan 1984; Blossfeld, Hamerle, and Mayer 1989; Yamaguchi 1991; Courgeau and Lelièvre 1992). Reverse causation refers to the (direct or indirect) effect of the dependent process on the independent covariate process. Reverse causation is seen as a problem because the effect of a time-dependent covariate on the transition rate is confounded with a feedback effect of the dependent process on the values of the time-dependent covariate.[4] However, in the literature, two types of time-dependent covariates have been described as not being subject to reverse causation (Kalbfleisch and Prentice 1980):

1. *Defined time-dependent covariates*, whose total time path (or functional form of change over time) is *determined in advance in the same way for all subjects* under study. For example, process time, like age or duration in a state (e.g. job-specific labor force experience), is a defined time-dependent covariate because its values are predetermined for all the subjects. Thus, by definition, the values

---

[4] In other words, the value of the time-dependent covariate carries information about the state of the dependent process.

of these time-dependent covariates cannot be affected by the dependent process under study.

2. *Ancillary time-dependent covariates*, whose time path is the output of a stochastic process that is *external* to the units under study. Again, by definition, the values of these time-dependent covariates are not influenced by the dependent process itself. Examples of time-dependent covariates that are *approximately external* in the analysis of individual life courses are variables that reflect *changes at the macrolevel* of society (unemployment rates, occupational structure, etc.) or the *population level* (composition of the population in terms of age, sex, race, etc.), provided that the contribution of each unit is small and does not really affect the structure in the population (Yamaguchi 1991). For example, consider the changes in the occupational structure. Although a job move by an individual might contribute to the change in the occupational structure, its effect on the job structure is negligibly small.[5]

In contrast to defined or ancillary time-dependent covariates, *internal time-dependent covariates* are referred to as being problematic for causal analysis with event history models (e.g.   Kalbfleisch and Prentice 1980; Tuma and Hannan 1984; Blossfeld,   Hamerle, and Mayer 1989; Yamaguchi 1991; Courgeau and Lelièvre 1992). An internal time-dependent covariate X_t describes a stochastic process, considered in a causal model as being the cause, that is in turn affected by another stochastic process Y_t, considered in the causal model as being the effect.   Thus, there are direct effects in which the processes autonomously affect each other (X_t affects Y_t and Y_t affects X_t), and there are "feedback" effects in which these processes are affected by themselves via the respective other process (Y_t affects Y_t via X_t and X_t affects X_t via Y_t). In other words, such processes are interdependent and form what has been called a dynamic system (Tuma and Hannan 1984). Interdependence is typical at the individual level for processes in different domains of life and at the level of few individuals interacting with each other (e.g. career trajectories of partners). For example, the empirical literature suggests that the employment trajectory of an individual is influenced by his/her marital history and marital history is dependent on the employment trajectory.

In dealing with dynamic systems, at least two main approaches have been suggested.   We consider both and call them the "system approach" and the "causal approach."

---

[5] As noted by Yamaguchi (1991), selection bias may exist for the effects of ancillary time-dependent covariates. For example, if regional unemployment rates or crime rates reflect the composition of the population in each region, a transition rate model will lead to biased estimates and erroneous conclusions if it fails to include (or control for) these differences.

6.2 Interdependent Processes: The System Approach

The system approach in the analysis of interdependent processes, suggested in the literature (see, e.g., Tuma and Hannan 1984; Courgeau and Lelièvre 1992), defines change in the system of interdependent processes as a new "dependent variable." Thus, instead of analyzing one of the interdependent processes with respect to its dependence on the respective others, the focus of modeling is a system of state variables.[6] In other words, interdependence between the various processes is taken into account only implicitly.

We first demonstrate the logic of this approach for a system of *qualitative* time-dependent variables and give some examples, then discuss its limitations, and finally describe the causal approach, which, we believe, is more appropriate for an analysis of coupled processes from an analytical point of view.

Suppose there are J interrelated qualitative time-dependent variables (processes): $Y_t^A, Y_t^B, Y_t^C, \ldots, Y_t^J$. A new time-dependent variable (process) Y_t, representing the system of these J variables, is then defined by associating each discrete state of the ordered J-tuple with a particular discrete state of Y_t. As shown by Tuma and Hannan (1984), as long as change in the whole system only depends on the various states of the J qualitative variables and on exogenous variables, this model is identical to modeling change in a single qualitative variable.[7] Thus, the idea of this approach is to simply define a new *joint* state space, based on the various state spaces of the coupled qualitative processes, and then to proceed as in the case of a single dependent process.

For example, suppose we have repeated episodes from two interdependent processes, "employment trajectory" and "marital history," represented by two dichotomous variables Y_t^A and Y_t^B, where Y_t^A takes the values 1 ("not employed") or 2 ("employed") and Y_t^B takes the values 1 ("not married") or 2 ("married"). Then, as shown in Figure 6.2.1, a new variable Y_t, representing the bivariate system, has $L = 4$ different states:[8]

$1 \equiv (1, 1)$ "not employed and not married"
$2 \equiv (1, 2)$ "not employed and married"

---

[6] There have also been other suggestions for the analysis of dynamic systems based on this approach (e.g. Klijzing 1993).

[7] The basic model for the development of Y_t is a Markov model. It makes two assumptions: First, it assumes that the episodes defined with respect to Y_t are independent of previous history. Thus, when the past of the process makes the episodes dependent, it is crucial to include these dependencies as covariates in transition rate models at the beginning of each new episode of the Y_t process (Courgeau and Lelièvre 1992). Second, the model assumes that transitions to a destination state of the system are not allowed to depend on the episode's duration, but only on the type of states. However, this is not a necessary assumption. The model for the system could also be formulated as a semi-Markov model allowing for duration dependence in the various origin states.

[8] The number of distinct values L of the system variable Y_t is given by the product of the distinct values for each of the J variables. When the system is formed by J dichotomous variables, then the number of distinct values is $L = 2^J$. Of course, some of these combinations may not be possible and must then be excluded.

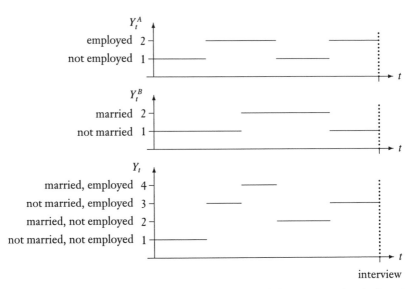

Figure 6.2.1 Hypothetical sample paths of two coupled processes, Y_t^A and Y_t^B, and the sample path of the combined process, Y_t.

$3 \equiv (2, 1)$ "employed and not married"
$4 \equiv (2, 2)$ "employed and married"

In general, with L different states in the combined process, there are $L(L-1)$ possible transitions. However, if one excludes the possibility of simultaneous changes in two or more of the processes,[9] the number of possible transitions is reduced by the number of simultaneous transitions. Then, in our example of two dichotomous variables, eight transition rates describe the joint process completely, as can be seen in Figure 6.2.2. Each of these origin and destination specific rates can be estimated in a model without covariates or with respect to its dependence on exogenous covariates.

In the case of coupled processes, and if one considers only irreversible events, for example, first marriage and first pregnancy, the diagram of possible transitions can further be simplified to four possible transitions, as shown in Figure 6.2.3. As demonstrated by Courgeau and Lelièvre (1992), one can use equality tests comparing origin and destination specific transition rates to determine whether (see Figure 6.2.3):[10]

---

[9] If the modeling approach is based on a continuous time axis, this could then formally be justified by the fact that the probability of simultaneous state changes is zero; see Coleman (1964).

[10] In this example, a problem might arise when the analysis is only based on observed behavior. For example, it might happen that a couple first decides to marry, then, following this decision, the woman becomes pregnant, and finally the couple marries. In this case, we would observe pregnancy occurring before marriage and assume that pregnancy increases the likelihood of marriage.

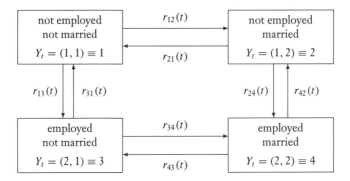

Figure 6.2.2 States and transitions for the system Y_t consisting of employment and marital histories.

1. the two processes are independent: $r_{12} = r_{34}$ and $r_{13} = r_{24}$;
2. one of the two processes is exogenous and the other endogenous:[11]
   a) $r_{12} = r_{34}$ and $r_{13} \neq r_{24}$: pregnancy affects marriage positively: $r_{13} < r_{24}$, pregnancy affects marriage negatively: $r_{13} > r_{24}$, or
   b) $r_{12} \neq r_{34}$ and $r_{13} = r_{24}$: marriage affects pregnancy positively: $r_{12} < r_{34}$, marriage affects pregnancy negatively: $r_{12} > r_{34}$, or
3. the processes are interdependent (or endogenous) and affect each other: $r_{12} \neq r_{34}$ and $r_{13} \neq r_{24}$.

These equality tests can easily be conducted, as long as there are no covariates involved and only baseline transition rates for specific origin and destination states have to be estimated. However, if the episodes are heterogeneous and a greater number of covariates has to be taken into account to make the episodes in each origin state independent of each other, the number of possible equality tests will quickly rise, presenting practical problems for comparisons (Courgeau and Lelièvre 1992).

Thus, although the system approach provides some insight into the behavior of the dynamic system as a whole, it has several disadvantages: (1) From a

---

However, the time order between the processes is the other way around: The couple decides to marry and then the woman gets pregnant. Because the time between decisions and behavior is probably not random and is different for various couples, an analysis that only uses behavioral observations can lead to false conclusions. Courgeau and Lelièvre (1992) have introduced the notion of "fuzzy time" for the time span between decisions and behavior. Note, however, that this issue does not alter the key temporal issues embedded within the causal logic (see section 1.2). There is clearly a time order with regard to decisions and behavior. However, as this example demonstrates, only using the time order of behavioral events without taking into account the timing of decisions could lead to serious misspecification.

[11] Courgeau and Lelièvre (1992) called this specific case "unilateral dependence" or "local dependence."

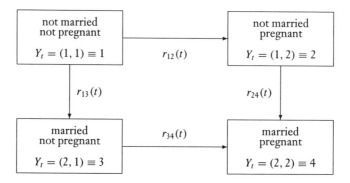

Figure 6.2.3 States and transitions for the system Y_t consisting of first marriage and first pregnancy.

causal analytical point of view, *it does not provide direct estimates of effects of coupled processes* on a process under study. In other words, using the system approach one normally does not know to what extent one or more of the other coupled processes affect the process of interest, controlling for other exogenous variables and the history of the dependent process. It is only possible to compare transition rates for general models without covariates, as shown in the pregnancy-marriage example above. (2) In particular, a *mixture of qualitative and quantitative processes*, in which the transition rate of a qualitative process depends on the levels of one or more metric variables, turns out to be a problem in this approach.[12] Tuma and Hannan (1984) suggested in these situations to collapse each quantitative variable into a set of ordered states. But in many situations this is not very useful. (3) This approach is also unable to handle *interdependencies* between coupled processes *occurring only in specific phases of the process* (e.g. processes might be interdependent only in specific phases of the life course) or interdependencies that are dynamic over time (e.g. an interdependence might be reversed in later life phases; see Courgeau and Lelièvre 1992). (4) Finally, the number of origin and destination states of the combined process Y_t, representing the system of J variables, may lead to practical problems. Even when the number of variables and their distinct values is small, the *state space of the system variable is large*. Therefore, event history data sets must contain a great number of events, even if only the most general models of change (i.e. models without covariates) are to be estimated. In summary, the system approach has many limitations for analyzing interdependent processes. We therefore suggest using a different perspective in modeling dynamic systems, which we call the "*causal approach.*"

---

[12] Tuma and Hannan (1984) called this type of coupling between processes "cross-state dependence."

6.3   Interdependent Processes: The Causal Approach

The underlying idea of the *causal approach* in analyzing interdependent processes can be outlined as follows (Blossfeld 1994): Based on theoretical reasons, the researcher *focuses on one* of the interdependent processes and considers it *the dependent one*. The future changes of this process are linked to the *present state and history* of the whole dynamic system as well as to   other exogenous variables (see Blossfeld 1986; Gardner and Griffin 1986; Blossfeld and Huinink 1991). Thus, in this approach the variable Y_t, representing the system of joint processes at time t, is not used as a multivariate dependent variable. Instead, the history and the present state of the system are seen as a condition for change in (any) one of its processes.

The question of how to find a more precise formulation for the causal approach remains. Two ideas may be helpful. First, it seems somewhat misleading to regard processes as causes. As argued in section 1.2, only events, or changes in a state variable, can sensibly be viewed as possible causes. Consequently, we would not say that a process Y_t^B is a cause of a process Y_t^A, but that *a change* in Y_t^B could be a cause (or provide a new condition) of a change in Y_t^A. This immediately leads to a second idea: that each event needs some time to become the cause of an effect (see section 1.2). This time span may be very short, but it, nonetheless, does not seem sensible to assume an instantaneous reaction, at least not in the social world where most effects are mediated by decision-making agents.[13]

Combining both ideas, a causal view on parallel and interdependent processes becomes easy, at least in principle. Given two parallel processes, Y_t^A and Y_t^B, a change in Y_t^A at any (specific) point in time t' may depend on the history of both processes *up to, but not including,* t'. Or stated in another way: What happens with Y_t^A at any point in time t' is *conditionally* independent of what happens with Y_t^B at t', conditional on the history of the joint process $Y_t = (Y_t^A, Y_t^B)$ up to, but not including, t'. Of course, the same reasoning can be applied if one focuses on Y_t^B instead of Y_t^A as the "dependent variable." We call this the *principle of conditional independence* for parallel and interdependent processes.[14]

The same idea can be developed more formally. Beginning with a transition rate model for the joint process, $Y_t = (Y_t^A, Y_t^B)$, and assuming the principle of conditional independence, the likelihood for this model can be factorized into a product of the likelihoods for two separate models: a transition rate model for Y_t^A, which is dependent on Y_t^B as a time-dependent covariate, and a transition rate model for Y_t^B, which is dependent on Y_t^A as a time-dependent covariate.[15]

---

[13] See also Kelly and McGrath (1988).

[14] The terminology is adapted from Gardner and Griffin (1986) and Pötter (1993).

[15] The mathematical steps leading to this factorization are, in principle, very easy but unfortunately need a complex terminology. The mathematical apparatus is therefore not given here. The mathematics can be found in Gardner and Griffin (1986), Pötter (1993), and Rohwer (1995). An

This result has an important implication for the modeling of event histories. From a *technical point of view*, there is *no need to distinguish between defined, ancillary, and internal covariates* because all of these time-dependent covariate types can be treated equally in the estimation procedure. A distinction between defined and ancillary covariates on the one hand and internal covariates on the other is however sensible from a *theoretical perspective* because only in the case of internal covariates does it make sense to examine whether parallel processes are independent, whether one of the parallel processes is endogenous and the other ones are exogenous, or whether parallel processes form an interdependent system (i.e. they are all endogenous).[16]

In the next section we show how qualitative time-dependent covariates, whose sample paths follow a step function, can be included in transition rate models on the basis of the episode splitting method. This procedure leads to direct estimates of how parallel qualitative processes affect the rate of change in another qualitative process and allows the conducting of significance tests of their parameters (see section 4.1.3). Then, in section 6.5, we demonstrate that a generalization of the episode splitting technique can also be used to include quantitative time-dependent covariates. In particular, this method offers an efficient strategy for approximating (1) the effects of any type of duration dependence in a state, (2) the effects of any sort of parallel quantitative process, as well as (3) complex temporal shapes of effect patterns of covariates over time.

6.4   Episode Splitting with Qualitative Covariates

Estimating the effects of time-dependent processes on the transition rate can easily be achieved by applying the method of episode splitting. The idea of this method can be described as follows: Time-dependent qualitative covariates change their values only at discrete points in time. At all points in time, when (at least) one of the covariates changes its value, the original episode is split into subepisodes—called *splits* (of an episode) or *subepisodes*. For each subepisode a new record is created containing:

1. information about the origin state of the original episode;

2. the values of all the covariates at the beginning of the subepisode;

3. the starting and ending times of the subepisode (information about the duration would only be sufficient in the case of an exponential model);

---

important implication is that because not only the states, but also functions of time (e.g. duration) can be included conditionally, the distinction between state and rate dependence proposed by Tuma and Hannan (1984) loses its meaning (see Pötter 1993).

[16] Thus, in a technical sense there was nothing wrong with the traditional approach, which simply ignored the "feedback" effects and analyzed the impact of processes on the basis of time-dependent covariates as if they were external. However, from a theoretical perspective it was not necessary to "justify" (on theoretical grounds) or to "conclude" (from some preliminary empirical analyses) that a dependent process only has a small effect on the independent one(s) that can be ignored.

4. information indicating whether the subepisode ends with the destination state of the original episode or is censored. All subepisodes, apart from the last one, are regarded as right censored. Only the last subepisode is given the same destination state as the original episode.

Consider one of the original episodes (j, k, s, t), with single origin and destination states j and k, and with starting and ending times s and t, respectively. It is assumed that the episode is defined on a process time axis so that $s = 0$. Now assume that this episode is split into L subepisodes[17]

$$(j, k, s, t) \equiv \{(j_l, k_l, s_l, t_l) \mid l = 1, \ldots, L\} \tag{6.1}$$

The likelihood of this episode can be written as the product of a transition rate $r(t)$, and a survivor function $G(t)$. Obviously, only $G(t)$ is influenced by the process of episode splitting. However, $G(t)$ can be written as a product of the conditional survivor functions for each split of the episode:

$$G(t) = \prod_{l=1}^{L} G(t_l \mid s_l)$$

with conditional survivor functions defined by

$$G(t_l \mid s_l) = \frac{G(t_l)}{G(s_l)} = \exp\left\{-\int_{s_l}^{t_l} r(\tau) \, d\tau\right\}$$

On the right-hand side, the transition rate $r(\tau)$ could be specific for each split (j_l, k_l, s_l, t_l) and may depend on covariate values for this split.[18]

It would now be possible to rewrite the general likelihood function for transition rate models given in section 4.1.1 by inserting the product of conditional pseudosurvivor functions. However, one does not really need to do this. One can write a general likelihood function for transition rate models as

$$\mathcal{L} = \prod_{j \in \mathcal{O}} \prod_{k \in \mathcal{D}_j} \prod_{i \in \mathcal{E}_{jk}} r_{jk}(t_i) \prod_{i \in \mathcal{N}_j} \tilde{G}_{jk}(t_i \mid s_i) \tag{6.2}$$

Written this way, the likelihood can also be used with a sample of original (not split) episodes, where all starting times are zero, and with a sample of splits. Of

---

[17] $j_l = j$ for $l = 1, \ldots, L$; $k_l = j$ for $l = 1, \ldots, L - 1$; and $k_L = k$.

[18] These formulations assume that there is only a single transition, from a given origin state to one possible destination state. It is easy however to generalize the result for a situation with many possible destination states. The survivor function then becomes

$$\tilde{G}_{jk}(t) = \prod_{l=1}^{L} \tilde{G}_{jk}(t_l \mid s_l)$$

with conditional pseudosurvivor functions defined by

$$\tilde{G}_{jk}(t_l \mid s_l) = \frac{\tilde{G}_{jk}(t_l)}{\tilde{G}_{jk}(s_l)} = \exp\left\{-\int_{s_l}^{t_l} r_{jk}(\tau) \, d\tau\right\}$$

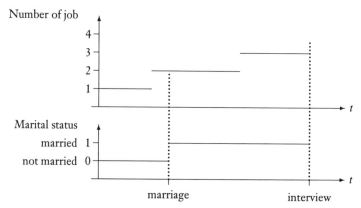

Figure 6.4.1 Modeling the effect of marriage on job mobility as a time-dependent covariate.

course, it is the responsibility of the user to do any episode splitting in such a way that the splits add up to a sample of meaningful episodes.

The maximum likelihood estimation of transition rate models in TDA is always done using the likelihood (6.2).[19] Therefore, the program can easily be used with the episode splitting method. In fact, TDA supports two different approaches to episode splitting. The first is called *external episode splitting* because in a first step, based on the original data file, a new external file containing the splits is created, which is then used as an input file for actually estimating the parameters of the model.[20] The second approach is called *internal episode splitting* because the splitting of episodes is done internally. Therefore, splitting and estimation can be achieved in one step. We consider both approaches and give some examples.

External Episode Splitting

Suppose we study job mobility and want to examine whether first marriage has an effect on the job shift rate. In this case we must first create a time-dependent dummy variable that changes its value from 0 to 1 at the time of first marriage. We must add this information to the original job episodes as a new variable by splitting the original job episodes into two subepisodes where the marriage date lies between the starting and ending times of a job (see the second job in Figure 6.4.1).

---

[19] Consequently, using a data set of episode splits will give identical estimation results if the same set of covariates is included in the model.

[20] This is the traditional method (see Blossfeld, Hamerle, and Mayer 1989) because episode splitting is considered to be part of data preparation, which is normally more efficiently done with FORTRAN, PASCAL, C, and so on.

Box 6.4.1   Command file *ehf1.cf*

```
dfile = rrdat.1;        data file
v1  (ID)     = c1 ;     ID of individual
v2  (NOJ)    = c2 ;     Serial number of the job
v3  (TStart) = c3 ;     Starting time of the job
v4  (TFin)   = c4 ;     Ending time of the job
v5  (SEX)    = c5 ;     Sex (1 men, 2 women)
v6  (TI)     = c6 ;     Date of interview
v7  (TB)     = c7 ;     Date of birth
v8  (T1)     = c8 ;     Date of entry into the labor market
v9  (TM)     = c9 ;     Date of marriage (0 if no marriage)
v10 (PRES)   = c10;     Prestige score of job i
v11 (PRESN)  = c11;     Prestige score of job i + 1
v12 (EDU)    = c12;     Highest educational attainment

# Define origin and destination state. Origin state is always 0.
# Destination state is 0 if right censored, or 1.
v13 (ORG)    = 0;
v14 (DES)    = if eq(v4,v6) then 0 else 1;

# Definition of starting and ending time on a process time axis.
v15 (TSP) = 0;
v16 (TFP) = v4 - v3 + 1; one month added

# define additional variables
v20 (COHO2) =   ge(v7,468) . le(v7,504);   cohort 2
v21 (COHO3) =   ge(v7,588) . le(v7,624);   cohort 3
v22 (LFX)   =   v3 - v8;                    labor force experience
v23 (PNOJ)  =   v2 - 1;                     previous number of jobs

# commands to define single episode data
org =  v13;   define origin state
des =  v14;   define destination state
ts  =  v15;   define starting time
tf  =  v16;   define ending time

# define variable for episode splitting
v24 (MarrDate) = if le(v9,0) then 10000 else v9 - v3;

# commands to split episodes and to write the new data to
# output file rrdat.s1;
split = v24;
pdate = rrdat.s1;

# using the keep command to select variables for the output file
keep = v15,v16,v12,v20,v21,v22,v23,v10,v24,v5;
```

If we use the external episode splitting approach with TDA, this can be done in two steps. First, one has to create a data file containing the split episodes. As an example we use command file *ehf1.cf* shown in Box 6.4.1. Most commands

Box 6.4.2   First records of *rrdat.s1* (generated with *ehf1.cf* in Box 6.4.1)

ID	SN	ORG	DES	TSS	TFS	TS	TF	EDU	COH2	COH3	LFX	PNOJ	PRES	MDate	Sex
C1	C2	C3	C4	C5	C6	C7	C8	C9	C10	C11	C12	C13	C14	C15	C16
1	1	0	0	0	124	0	428	17	0	0	0	0	34	124	1
1	2	0	0	124	428	0	428	17	0	0	0	0	34	124	1
2	1	0	1	0	46	0	46	10	0	0	0	0	22	169	2
3	1	0	1	0	34	0	34	10	0	0	46	1	46	123	2
4	1	0	0	0	89	0	220	10	0	0	80	2	46	89	2
4	2	0	1	89	220	0	220	10	0	0	80	2	46	89	2
5	1	0	1	0	12	0	12	11	1	0	0	0	41	182	2
6	1	0	1	0	30	0	30	11	1	0	12	1	41	170	2
7	1	0	1	0	12	0	12	11	1	0	42	2	44	140	2
8	1	0	1	0	75	0	75	11	1	0	54	3	44	128	2
9	1	0	1	0	12	0	12	11	1	0	129	4	44	53	2
10	1	0	1	0	55	0	55	13	0	1	0	0	55	0	2
11	1	0	1	0	68	0	68	11	0	0	0	0	44	118	1
12	1	0	0	0	50	0	137	11	0	0	68	1	44	50	1
12	2	0	1	50	137	0	137	11	0	0	68	1	44	50	1
13	1	0	0	0	195	0	195	11	0	0	205	2	44	-87	1
14	1	0	1	0	26	0	26	11	1	0	0	0	29	90	1
15	1	0	1	0	26	0	26	11	1	0	37	1	47	53	1
16	1	0	0	0	10	0	76	11	1	0	80	2	47	10	1
16	2	0	1	10	76	0	76	11	1	0	80	2	47	10	1

are already familiar from previous command files. A few commands are new. First, the command

$$V24 \ (MarrDate) = if \ le(V9,0) \ then \ 10000 \ else \ V9 - V3;$$

is used to create a new variable to be used for episode splitting. This variable contains the duration, measured from the beginning of each episode, until a marriage takes place or, if the individual is not yet married (by the interview date), the variable is given an arbitrary but very high value, 10000 in our example. The second command is

$$split = v24;$$

to inform TDA to split the episodes at the dates contained in variable *V24* (i.e. the marriage date). Given this command, each episode where *V24* contains a value less than the episode's duration is split into two parts (therefore, with *V24* = *10000*, no splitting is performed). Finally there are the commands

$$pdate = rrdat.s1;$$
$$keep = v15,v16,v12,v20,v21,v22,v23,v10,v24,v5;$$

the first one used to request that the episode splits are written into an output file, *rrdat.s1* in this example, and the second one to select variables for the output file. The first records of this new data file are shown in Box 6.4.2. This Box shows, for example, that the individual with ID = 1 married after he had been in his first job for 124 months (the total duration in this job is 428

Box 6.4.3 Command file *ehf2.cf*

```
# ehf2.cf    estimating an exponential model using the split episodes
#            in data file rrdat.s1

dfile = rrdat.s1;        data file
v1  (CASE)     = c1;
v2  (SPLIT)    = c2;
v3  (ORG)      = c3;
v4  (DES)      = c4;
v5  (TS)       = c5;
v6  (TF)       = c6;
v7  (TSP)      = c7;
v8  (TFP)      = c8;
v9  (EDU)      = c9;
v10 (COHO2)    = c10;
v11 (COHO3)    = c11;
v12 (LFX)      = c12;
v13 (PNOJ)     = c13;
v14 (PRES)     = c14;
v15 (MarrDate) = c15;
v16 (SEX)      = c16;

# define a dummy variable taking 0 before, and 1 after marriage.
# the operator ts provides the starting time of an episode or split.
v17 (MARR) = le(v15,ts);

# commands to define single episode data
org =  v3;      define origin state
des =  v4;      define destination state
ts  =  v5;      define starting time
tf  =  v6;      define ending time

# command to request estimation of an exponential model
rate = 2;            model selection

# command to include v17 as single covariate for transition from
# origin state 0 to destination state 1.
xa (0,1) = v17;
```

months). Consequently, TDA created two subepisodes out of the original job episode: a first one with TS = 0, TF = 124, ORG = 0, DES = 0, and MDate = 124; and a second one with TS = 124, TF = 428, ORG = 0, DES = 0, and MDate = 124. Note that the first subepisode is right censored, that is, it has the same origin and destination states as the origin state in the original episode, that is, 0 ("being in a job"). Only the second split is given the same destination state as in the original episode. However, in this case the original episode was also censored. This is, for example, not the case for the individual with ID = 4 in Box 6.4.2.

In a second step, this data file *rrdat.s1* serves as an input file for the cre-

Box 6.4.4   Result of command file *ehf2.cf* (Box 6.4.3)

```
Single episode data

Origin state: V3     Destination state: V4
Starting time: V5    Ending time: V6
                                      Mean
SN  Org Des  Episodes  Weighted   Duration   TS Min    TF Max
-------------------------------------------------------------------
 1   0   0      303      303.00      76.35     0.00     428.00
 1   0   1      458      458.00      38.53     0.00     350.00
 1   0  Sum     761      761.00      53.59     0.00     428.00


-------------------------------------------------------------------
Model: Exponential

Maximum likelihood estimation
Maximum of log likelihood: -2498.53
Norm of final gradient vector: 1.1e-04
Last absolute change of function value: 4.3e-08
Last relative change in parameters: 9.3e-04

Idx SN Org Des MT Var  Label    Coeff    Error    T-Stat  Signif
-------------------------------------------------------------------
 1  1   0   1  A --  Const    -4.2129   0.0639  -65.9430  1.0000
 2  1   0   1  A V17 MARR     -0.5212   0.0937   -5.5629  1.0000
```

ation of the time-dependent dummy variable MARR ($V17$, "marriage") and the estimation of its effect. For our example we use an exponential model. An appropriate command file, *ehf2.cf*, is shown in Box 6.4.3. Most commands are already familiar from previous command files, the only new command is

$$v17 \ (MARR) = le(v15,ts);$$

to create a time-dependent dummy variable, with value 0 until the marriage date and value 1 if the individual has married. The definition of this variable relies on TDA's *ts* operator, which provides the value of the current (sub)episode's starting time. Therefore, $v17$ has the value 1 if the marriage date, given in variable $V15$, is less than or equal to the starting time of a subepisode; otherwise it has the value 0.

Using command file *ehf2.cf*, part of the estimation results are shown in Box 6.4.4. Obviously, the coefficient for the time-dependent covariate $V17$ (MARR) is statistically significant and has a negative sign. This means that entry into marriage reduces the job shift rate by about 41 %, calculated as

$$\left(\exp(-0.5212) - 1 \right) \cdot 100 \% = -40.6$$

In other words, marriage makes the individuals less mobile. The question of how this result depends on other covariates now arises.

6.4.5 Part of command file *ehf3.cf*

```
define variable for episode splitting
4 (MarrDate) = if le(v9,0) then 10000 else v9 - v3;

plit episodes with v24
t = v24;

'ine a dummy variable taking 0 before, and 1 after marriage.
operator ts provides the starting time of an episode or split.
arr) = le(v24,ts);

nds to define single episode data
 r13;    define origin state
 14;    define destination state
 5;    define starting time
 5;    define ending time

#     mand to request estimation of an exponential model
rate = 2;            model selection

# command to include covariates into model, for transition from
# origin state 0 to destination state 1.
xa (0,1) = v12,v20,v21,v22,v23,v10,v25;
```

Box 6.4.6 Result of command file *ehf3.cf* (Box 6.4.5)

```
Model: Exponential

Maximum of log likelihood: -2460.25

Idx SN Org Des MT Var  Label   Coeff    Error    T-Stat  Signif
---------------------------------------------------------------
 1  1  0   1  A  --    Const  -4.3878  0.2756  -15.9222  1.0000
 2  1  0   1  A  V12   EDU     0.0770  0.0246    3.1358  0.9983
 3  1  0   1  A  V20   COHO2   0.5971  0.1137    5.2534  1.0000
 4  1  0   1  A  V21   COHO3   0.6138  0.1188    5.1651  1.0000
 5  1  0   1  A  V22   LFX    -0.0023  0.0010   -2.3731  0.9824
 6  1  0   1  A  V23   PNOJ    0.0645  0.0440    1.4674  0.8577
 7  1  0   1  A  V10   PRES   -0.0274  0.0055   -4.9533  1.0000
 8  1  0   1  A  V25   Marr   -0.3447  0.1022   -3.3716  0.9993

Estimation with internal episode splitting.
Number of splits: 761
```

Internal Episode Splitting

To investigate this question, one could use the command file *ehf2.cf*, shown in Box 6.4.3, and simply add covariates to the model specification command *xa(0,1)=. . .* We however follow a slightly different route to illustrate the method of *internal episode splitting* and use another command file, *ehf3.cf*, part of which

Box 6.4.7   Part of command file *ehf4.cf*

```
# define variable for episode splitting
v24 (MarrDate) = if le(v9,0) then 10000 else v9 - v3;

# split episodes with v24
split = v24;

# define a dummy variable taking 0 before, and 1 after marriage,
# a dummy variable for men (sex = 1), and an interaction effect.
v25 (MARR) = le(v24,ts);
v26 (MARR.MEN) = v5[1] . le(v24,ts);

# command to request estimation of an exponential model
rate = 2;            model selection

# command to include covariates into model, for transition from
# origin state 0 to destination state 1.
xa (0,1) = v12,v20,v21,v22,v23,v10,v25,v26;
```

is shown in Box 6.4.5. Basically, this is a combination of previously used command files (see Boxes 6.4.1 and 6.4.3). The command file reads the data file *rrdat.1* and defines all additionally required variables. In particular, the variable *V24* (marriage date), to be used to split the episodes with the *split* command, is defined. In fact, this variable and the variable *V25*, the dummy variable for being married or not, are defined in exactly the same way as in command file *ehf2.cf* (Box 6.4.3). Finally, an exponential model is selected and a list of variables to be included in the model specification is defined with the *xa(0,1)=...* command.

Part of the estimation results is shown in Box 6.4.6. The effect of the time-dependent covariate is still highly significant and has a negative sign. However, its absolute size is smaller than in Box 6.4.4. Controlling for the time-constant covariables, entry into marriage reduces the job shift rate by about only 29 %.[21] Thus, part of the time-constant heterogeneity between the individuals was captured by the time-dependent covariate "marriage." The estimated effects of the time-constant covariates however are very similar compared with the results in Box 4.1.5, where the time-dependent covariate "marriage" was not included.

Interaction Effects with Time-Dependent Covariates

Although we get a significant effect for the time-dependent covariate "marriage" in Box 6.4.6, it cannot be easily interpreted in theoretical terms. For example, it is well known from the empirical literature that family events have opposite influences on the job mobility rates for men and women. Marriage,

---

[21] $(\exp(-0.3447) - 1) \cdot 100\,\% \approx -29.2\,\%$.

Box 6.4.8 Result of command file *ehf4.cf* (Box 6.4.7)

```
Model: Exponential

Maximum likelihood estimation
Maximum of log likelihood: -2434.18

Idx SN Org Des MT Var  Label      Coeff   Error    T-Stat  Signif
-----------------------------------------------------------------
  1  1   0   1  A --   Const     -4.5842  0.2694  -17.0163  1.0000
  2  1   0   1  A V12  EDU        0.0943  0.0234    4.0227  0.9999
  3  1   0   1  A V20  COHO2      0.5423  0.1132    4.7916  1.0000
  4  1   0   1  A V21  COHO3      0.5304  0.1192    4.4494  1.0000
  5  1   0   1  A V22  LFX       -0.0031  0.0010   -3.1550  0.9984
  6  1   0   1  A V23  PNOJ       0.1029  0.0445    2.3126  0.9793
  7  1   0   1  A V10  PRES      -0.0264  0.0054   -4.9363  1.0000
  8  1   0   1  A V25  MARR       0.2735  0.1231    2.2209  0.9736
  9  1   0   1  A V26  MARR.MEN  -1.0231  0.1401   -7.3019  1.0000

Estimation with internal episode splitting.
Number of splits: 761
```

at least for the older cohorts, increases the rate of moving out of the job for women (because they normally take care of the household and children), while marriage for men decreases the job shift rate (because they normally carry an additional economic responsibility for the wife and children).

To examine whether these sex-specific relationships between marriage and employment career are true, we create an interaction variable for the joint effect of the time-dependent covariate marriage and the time-constant variable sex. Part of the command file is shown in Box 6.4.7. The interaction variable MARR.MEN is created by multiplying a dummy variable for men (*V5[1]*) by the variable MARR. Therefore, this variable has the value 1 as soon as a man marries.

Part of the estimation results are shown in Box 6.4.8. The estimated parameters are in accordance with our expectations. The effect of marriage on the rate of moving out of a job is *positive* for women. Marriage *increases* the job mobility rate for women by about 31 %.[22] Of course, here the time-dependent covariate marriage also serves as a proxy variable for other time-dependent processes that are connected with the marriage event, like childbirth, and so on. In a "real" analysis one would therefore also include time-dependent covariates for childbirth and additional possible interaction effects, for example, with the birth cohort.[23]

---

[22] $(\exp(0.2735) - 1) \cdot 100\,\% \approx 31.5\,\%$.

[23] New event history analyses show that younger women decreasingly change their employment behavior at the time of marriage, but increasingly at the time when the first baby is born. Thus, the important marker for employment shifted in the first family phase from marriage to the birth of the first child across cohorts (see Blossfeld in press).

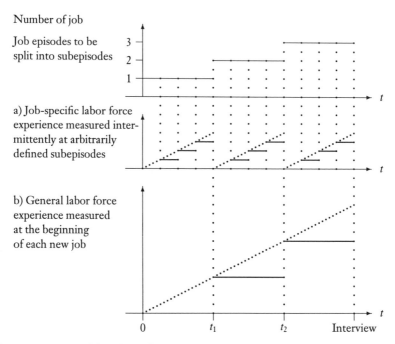

Figure 6.5.1 Modeling labor force experience as (a) time-dependent covariate *job-specific labor force experience* and (b) time-constant covariate *general labor force experience*, illustrated with three consecutive job episodes arbitrarily split into subepisodes.

On the other hand, for men the effect of marriage on the job change rate is *negative*. Marriage *decreases* the rate of moving out of a job by about 53 %.[24] In other words, marriage makes men less mobile.

This didactic example again demonstrates how important theory is for modeling event history data. The reason for the negative effect of the time-dependent covariate in Box 6.4.6 is only that the negative effect for men is stronger than the positive effect for women. In general, it is really difficult to evaluate whether an estimated model is appropriate without a strong theory. There are a few technical criteria and approaches that can be applied to assess models (see chapters 8 and 10), but our experience shows that they only give limited help in deciding about competing models. Thus, event history modeling (as is true for all causal modeling) must be guided by theoretical ideas.

---

[24] $(\exp(0.2735 - 1.0231) - 1) \cdot 100\,\% \approx -52.7\,\%$.

6.5 Episode Splitting with Quantitative Covariates

Many of the theoretical models that are of interest to sociologists relate quantitative processes to qualitative outcomes over time. For example, "job-specific labor force experience" can be considered a metric latent (or unobserved) variable. There are good reasons to measure it with the proxy variable "duration in a job." Other examples for metric causal processes are continuously changing "investments into specific marriages" in divorce studies (Blossfeld, De Rose, Hoem, and Rohwer 1993), "career success of the partner" in analyses of parallel careers of husbands and wives (Bernasco 1994), or measures of the continuously changing "business cycle" or "modernization process" in job mobility studies (see Blossfeld 1986). As long as the effects of such quantitative variables can be considered a specific function of process time (e.g. based on a Weibull, Gompertz (-Makeham), a log-logistic, a lognormal, a sickle model, etc.), available parametric models of time-dependence might be selected and estimated (chapter 7).[25]

However, if these parametric models are not appropriate, or if the sample path of the quantitative covariate is so irregular or complex over time that it is impossible to specify its shape with a parametric distribution, then the method of episode splitting can be generalized and used as an effective instrument to *approximate the sample path of a metric covariate* (Blossfeld, Hamerle, and Mayer 1989). Using this approach, the original episodes are divided arbitrarily into small subepisodes and the quantitative time-dependent covariate is intermittently measured at the beginning of each of these subepisodes (see panel (a) of Figure 6.5.1).[26] The result of this procedure is a step function approximating the changes of the metric causal variable. The approximation is, of course, the better the smaller the chosen subepisodes are and the more often the metric time-dependent causal variable is intermittently measured.

We use the variable "job-specific labor force experience" as an example. We assume that this (unobserved) variable increases linearly over the time a person spends in a job. In section 4.1.3, labor force experience was only considered in terms of "general labor force experience" measured at the beginning of each new job episode and treated as constant over the whole duration in a job. Panel (b) in Figure 6.5.1 shows that this normally leads to a very bad approximation of what might be called labor force experience, in particular for employees who do not change jobs very often. Now, we additionally include the variable "job-specific labor force experience," measured intermittently at the beginning of arbitrarily defined subepisodes within each job (see panel (a) in Figure 6.5.1). We start our example by defining subepisodes with a maximal length of 60

---

[25] In these cases, the values of the causal variables are truly known continuously, that is, at every moment in some interval (Tuma and Hannan 1984).

[26] "Continuous" measurement of quantitative processes usually means that variables are measured intermittently with a very small interval between measurements (see Tuma and Hannan 1984).

Box 6.5.1 Part of command file *ehf5.cf*

```
... (first part identical to Box 6.4.1)

# define variable for episode splitting
v31 (Split_60 ) =  60;
v32 (Split_120) = 120;
v33 (Split_180) = 180;
v34 (Split_240) = 240;
v35 (Split_300) = 300;
v36 (Split_360) = 360;
v37 (Split_420) = 420;

# commands to split episodes and to write the new data to
# output file rrdat.d60
split = v31,v32,v33,v34,v35,v36,v37;
pdate = rrdat.d60;

# using the keep command to select variables for the output file
keep = v15,v16,v12,v20,v21,v22,v23,v10;
```

Box 6.5.2 First records of data file *rrdat.d60*

```
ID SN ORG DES TSS TFS  TS   TF EDU COH2 COH3 LFX PNOJ PRES
-----------------------------------------------------------
 1  1  0   0    0  60   0  428  17   0    0    0    0   34
 1  2  0   0   60 120   0  428  17   0    0    0    0   34
 1  3  0   0  120 180   0  428  17   0    0    0    0   34
 1  4  0   0  180 240   0  428  17   0    0    0    0   34
 1  5  0   0  240 300   0  428  17   0    0    0    0   34
 1  6  0   0  300 360   0  428  17   0    0    0    0   34
 1  7  0   0  360 420   0  428  17   0    0    0    0   34
 1  8  0   0  420 428   0  428  17   0    0    0    0   34
 2  1  0   1    0  46   0   46  10   0    0    0    0   22
 3  1  0   1    0  34   0   34  10   0    0   46    1   46
 4  1  0   0    0  60   0  220  10   0    0   80    2   46
 4  2  0   0   60 120   0  220  10   0    0   80    2   46
 4  3  0   0  120 180   0  220  10   0    0   80    2   46
 4  4  0   1  180 220   0  220  10   0    0   80    2   46
```

months (or 5 years) in the TDA command file *ehf5.cf*, partly shown in Box 6.5.1. Because the longest duration in a job is 428 months (see Box 2.2.5), we have to define eight intervals (accomplished with variables *V31* to *V37*) and use the split command

$$split = v31,v32,v33,v34,v35,v36,v37;$$

Finally, we use the *keep* command to select variables for the output file. Given the command

$$keep = v15,v16,v12,v20,v21,v22,v23,v10;$$

only these variables will be written into the output file, *rrdat.d60*. But note that

Box 6.5.3 Command file *ehf6.cf*

```
# ehf6.cf    estimating an exponential model with a quantitative
#            time-dependent covariate (max 60 months long subepisodes).

dfile = rrdat.d60;       data file
noc = 1021;              necessary since default noc = 1000

v1  (CASE)    = c1;      variables rrdat.d60
v2  (SPLIT)   = c2;
v3  (ORG)     = c3;
v4  (DES)     = c4;
v5  (TS)      = c5;
v6  (TF)      = c6;
v7  (TSP)     = c7;
v8  (TFP)     = c8;
v9  (EDU)     = c9;
v10 (COHO2)   = c10;
v11 (COHO3)   = c11;
v12 (LFX)     = c12;
v13 (PNOJ)    = c13;
v14 (PRES)    = c14;

# define a new variable LFX60
v15 (LFX60) = v5;

# commands to define single episode data
org =  v3;     define origin state
des =  v4;     define destination state
ts  =  v5;     define starting time
tf  =  v6;     define ending time

# command to request estimation of an exponential model
rate = 2;           model selection

# command to include covariates into model, for transition from
# origin state 0 to destination state 1.
xa (0,1) = v9,v10,v11,v12,v13,v14,v15;
```

TDA automatically adds six more variables (ID, SN, ORG, DES, TSS, and TFS) as can be seen in Box 6.5.2, where the first records of the output file are shown.

For example, for individual with *ID = 1* the original job episode with a duration 428 months is split into seven subepisodes of 60 months and an eighth subepisode of 8 months. Note again that the first seven subepisodes are right censored, that is, they have the same origin and destination states as the origin state in the original episode, that is, 0 ("being in a job"). Only the eighth split is given the same destination state as in the original episode. In this case the original episode was also censored.

Based on the new data file, *rrdat.d60*, we use command file *ehf6.cf*, shown in Box 6.5.3, to estimate an exponential model with our standard set of covariates.

Box 6.5.4   Result of command file *ehf6.cf* (Box 6.5.3)

```
Single episode data

Origin state: V3      Destination state: V4
Starting time: V5     Ending time: V6
                                      Mean
SN  Org Des   Episodes   Weighted   Duration   TS Min   TF Max
--------------------------------------------------------------
 1   0   0        563      563.00     51.62      0.00    428.00
 1   0   1        458      458.00     25.59      0.00    350.00
 1   0  Sum      1021     1021.00     39.94      0.00    428.00
--------------------------------------------------------------

Model: Exponential

Maximum likelihood estimation
Maximum of log likelihood: -2432.31

Idx SN Org Des MT Var  Label    Coeff    Error    T-Stat   Signif
-----------------------------------------------------------------
  1  1   0   1  A --   Const   -4.0138  0.2764  -14.5194  1.0000
  2  1   0   1  A V9   EDU      0.0646  0.0248    2.6051  0.9908
  3  1   0   1  A V10  COHO2    0.4073  0.1149    3.5462  0.9996
  4  1   0   1  A V11  COHO3    0.2946  0.1216    2.4224  0.9846
  5  1   0   1  A V12  LFX     -0.0039  0.0009   -4.2429  1.0000
  6  1   0   1  A V13  PNOJ     0.0647  0.0440    1.4705  0.8586
  7  1   0   1  A V14  PRES    -0.0253  0.0054   -4.6474  1.0000
  8  1   0   1  A V15  LFX60   -0.0071  0.0010   -7.1098  1.0000
```

The estimation results are shown in Box 6.5.4. This box provides estimates of two different forms of labor force experience. The parameter for the variable LFX (*V12*) is an estimate for the effect of "*general* labor force experience" and the parameter for variable LFX60 (*V15*) is an estimate for the effect of "*job-specific* labor force experience." As expected, both variables have a significantly negative effect. In other words, increases in general and job-specific labor force experience reduce the rate of job mobility. However, as can be seen in the absolute size of the coefficients, job-specific labor force experience reduces job mobility more than general labor force experience. This is in accordance with the hypotheses suggested in the literature (see chapter 4).

The approximation of job-specific labor force experience in each of the jobs is still relatively rough. We therefore reduce the maximum interval length of subepisodes from 60 months to 24 months and finally to 12 months, and then examine how the estimated coefficients for job-specific labor force experience change.[27] The results of these estimations are shown in Box 6.5.5. One can easily see that the estimates of the three models are quite similar. The estimates

---

[27] We do not show the TDA command and output files here. The files can be found on the accompanying disk. The file names are *ehf5a.cf* and *ehf6a.cf* for 24 months splits, and *ehf5b.cf* and *ehf6b.cf* for 12 months splits.

Box 6.5.5 Exponential model with episode splits (60, 24, and 12 months)

Label	60 Months Coeff	60 Months T-Stat	24 Months Coeff	24 Months T-Stat	12 Months Coeff	12 Months T-Stat
Const	-4.0138	-14.5194	-3.9498	-14.1626	-3.9187	-14.0056
EDU	0.0646	2.6051	0.0629	2.5367	0.0626	2.5264
COHO2	0.4073	3.5462	0.4060	3.5276	0.4049	3.5177
COHO3	0.2946	2.4224	0.3006	2.4641	0.2997	2.4555
LFX	-0.0039	-4.2429	-0.0039	-4.1976	-0.0039	-4.1903
PNOJ	0.0647	1.4705	0.0633	1.4359	0.0628	1.4263
PRES	-0.0253	-4.6474	-0.0249	-4.5755	-0.0248	-4.5595
LFX60	-0.0071	-7.1098				
LFX24			-0.0063	-6.9933		
LFX12					-0.0063	-7.0140

of the metric time-dependent covariate change a little when we reduce the maximum length of the subepisodes from 60 the 24 months, but they remain practically unchanged when we reduce the maximum length further from 24 to 12 months. Thus, one can conclude that, given a maximum interval length of 24 months, one achieves a relatively good approximation of the linearly changing time-dependent covariate "job-specific labor force experience." Further, one can say that, at least in substantive terms, the coefficients of the time-constant covariates are basically the same as for the exponential model in Box 4.1.5. And finally, all the coefficients (including "job-specific labor force experience") are very similar compared with the equivalent Gompertz model with covariates (see section 7.2).[28]

6.6 Application Examples

To illustrate the utility of the episode splitting method in empirical research, we refer to three investigations using this method in various ways. We concentrate on the modeling techniques used in these studies and summarize their most important findings.

Example 1: A Dynamic Approach to the Study of Life-Course, Cohort, and Period Effects in Career Mobility

Studying intragenerational mobility of German men, Blossfeld (1986) proposed introducing the changing labor market structure into event history models of career mobility in order to treat the time-dependent nature of the attainment process in an adequate manner. There are two main ways in which the changing labor market affects career opportunities. First, people start their careers in different structural labor market contexts (when this influence is

---

[28] Actually, as is demonstrated in section 7.2, we have only approximated a Gompertz model.

more or less stable over people's career, it is normally called a cohort effect; see also Blossfeld 1986), and second, the labor market structure influences the opportunities of *all* people within the labor market at each moment (this is commonly referred to as a period effect).

Any model using education (in terms of school years), labor market experience (as a life-course measure), year of entry into the labor market (as a cohort measure), and chronological year of measurement (as a period measure) implies an identification problem (Mason and Fienberg 1985) because of a linear dependency of these variables. Blossfeld, starting from a more substantive point of view, tried to find more explicit measures for the theoretically important macro effects. He suggested using 14 time series from official statistics indicating the long-term development of the labor market structure in West Germany.[29] But time series often measure similar features of a process and are highly correlated. Therefore, another identification problem invariably arises whenever several time series are included in a model simultaneously. One strategy for solving this problem is to use only one series or to choose only uncorrelated series. The problem then is that the time series chosen may only capture specific features of the labor market structural development. If time series represent aspects of an underlying regularity, it is more appropriate to look for these latent dimensions. A statistical method for doing this is factor analysis. Blossfeld's factor analysis with principal factoring and equimax rotation gave two orthogonal factors explaining 96.4 % of the variance in the 14 time series.

The first factor could be interpreted as representing the changing "level of modernization" and the second one as a measure of the changes in the labor market with regard to the business cycle, so it was called "labor market conditions." As can be seen from the plots of the scores of the two factors in Figure 6.6.1, the factor "level of modernization" shows a monotonic trend with a slightly increasing slope, while the factor "labor market conditions" shows a cyclical development with downturns around 1967 and 1973. This is in accordance with the historical development of the business cycle in Germany. Because both factors are orthogonally constructed, it is possible to include both measures simultaneously in a model estimation.

To represent the changing conditions under which cohorts enter the labor market, Blossfeld used the factor scores "level of modernization" and "labor

---

[29] These included (1) level of productivity, (2) national income per capita (deflated), (3) national income per economically active person (deflated), (4) private consumption (deflated), (5) proportion of expenditure on services in private consumption, (6) proportion of gainfully employed in public sector, (7) proportion of 13-year-old pupils attending German *Gymnasium*, (8) proportion of gainfully employed in service sector, (9) proportion of students in resident population, (10) proportion of civil servants in economically active population, (11) proportion of white-collar employees in economically active population, (12) unemployment rate, (13) proportion of gross national product invested in plant and equipment, (14) proportion of registered vacancies of all jobs, excluding self-employment.

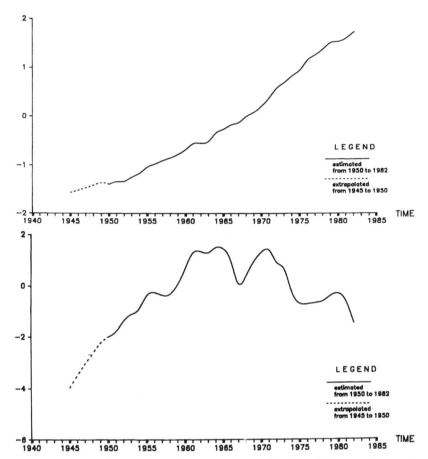

Figure 6.6.1 Development of modernization (upper figure) and labor market conditions (lower figure) in West Germany (plots of factor scores).

market conditions" *at the year persons entered the labor force.* To introduce period as a time-dependent covariate, he used the method of episode splitting described earlier. In accordance with this method, the original *job episodes were split into subepisodes every year* so that the factor scores "level of modernization" and "labor market conditions" could be updated in each job episode for all the employees every year. In the terminology of Kalbfleisch and Prentice (1980), the period measures are ancillary time-dependent covariates.

Modeling cohort and period effects this way not only provides more direct and valid measures of the explanatory concepts, but also results in the disap-

Table 6.6.1 Estimates of models for transition rates to better jobs (upward moves) for German men born 1929–31, 1939–41, and 1949–51.

Estimates for Model	Upward Moves				
	1	2	3	4	5
Log of mean rate	-6.135				
Constant		-4.241[*]	-4.288[*]	-4.943[*]	-5.585[*]
Time in labor force (life-course effect)		-0.012[*]	-0.015[*]	-0.012[*]	-0.082[*]
Education			0.187[*]	0.224[*]	0.268[*]
Prestige			-0.042[*]	-0.041[*]	-0.042[*]
Level of modernization at entry into labor market (cohort effect)				-0.294[*]	-9.664[*]
Labor market conditions at entry into labor market (cohort effect)				0.009	-1.394[*]
Level of modernization (period effect)					9.066[*]
Labor market conditions (period effect)					1.203[*]
Number of shifts	590	590	590	590	590
Subepisodes	22843	22843	22843	22843	22843
χ^2		842.21	1007.46	1024.02	2165.29
df		1	3	5	7

[*] statistically significant at 0.001 level. Rates are measured with months as units.

pearance of the problem of non-estimable parameters. It is, therefore, not necessary to impose (in substantive terms normally unjustifiable) constraints on the parameters to identify life-course, cohort, and period effects (see, e.g., Mason et al. 1973). The result of the estimation of life-course, cohort, and period effects on upward moves in an exponential model is shown in Table 6.6.1. We focus our attention on Model 5 in this table and do not give substantive interpretations of the effects of the variables "time in the labor force," "education," or "prestige" because these would be basically the same as the ones already given in section 4.1.3.

We mainly concentrate on the interpretation of the effects of changes in the labor market structure. In Model 5, the "level of modernization" at time of entry into the labor market has a negative effect on upward moves. Thus, the higher the level of modernization, the better the first job of beginners and the less likely that there will be further upward moves for them. The same is true for the negative effect of labor market conditions at entry into the labor market.

The more favorable the business cycle at entry into the labor market is for a particular cohort, the easier it is for its members to find "good jobs" at the beginning of their careers, and the harder it will be to find even better ones.

On the other hand, the period effect of "modernization" is positive on upward moves. Thus, the continuous restructuring of the economy in the process of technological and organizational modernization leads to increasing opportunities for all people to move up in the labor market. The same is true for the period effect of the labor market conditions. It is positive for upward mobility and suggests that the better the labor market conditions, the more opportunities the economy will provide.

If we take into account the effect of labor force experience (life-course effect), then this analysis supports the thesis that the career process is strongly affected by cohort, period, and life-course effects. The attainment process is time-dependent in a threefold sense. It depends on the time spent in the labor force, the historical time of entry into the labor market, and the actual historical time. Thus, analyses of standard mobility tables (e.g. Erikson and Goldthorpe 1991; Haller 1989; Handl 1988) that distinguish only structural mobility and exchange mobility on a cross-sectional basis will necessarily provide misleading pictures of the mechanisms of attainment (see also Sørensen 1986). The creation of vacancies and the loss of positions in the course of structural change count as the central mechanisms of career mobility, and affect people's mobility changes in different ways.

Example 2: Changes in the Process of Family Formation and the New Role of Women

The second example is based on an investigation by Blossfeld and Huinink (1991). They assessed the hypothesis of the "new home economics" (e.g. Becker 1981) that women's rising educational and career investments will lead to a decline in marriage and motherhood (see also Oppenheimer 1988). Because the accumulation of educational and career resources is a lifetime process, it must be modeled as a dynamic process over the life course. In West Germany in particular it is necessary to differentiate between the accumulation of general and vocational qualifications within the educational system on the one hand, and the accumulation of workplace-related labor force experience on the other.

In order to model the *accumulation of general and vocational qualifications* in the school system, the vocational training system, and the university system of the Federal Republic of Germany, Blossfeld and Huinink (1991) used the average number of years required to obtain such qualifications (see variable $V12$ (EDU) in Box 2.2.1). However, this variable was not treated as a time-constant variable, but as a time-dependent covariate. To model the changes in the accumulation of qualifications over the life course, they updated the level of education at the age when a woman obtained a particular educational rank in the hierarchy.

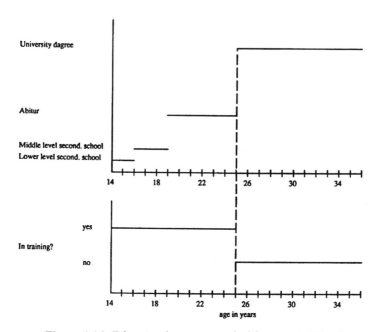

Figure 6.6.2 Educational careers over the life course in West Germany.

For example, for a woman who attains a lower school qualification at age 14, reaches the intermediate school qualification at age 16, leaves school with an *Abitur* at age 19, and finally finishes university studies at age 25, one would obtain a step function for the highest level of education over the life course as shown in the upper panel of Figure 6.6.2. The hypothesis of the "new home economics" is that such increasing levels of education raise a woman's labor-market attachment, thereby leading to greater delays in marriage and childbirth.

However, from a sociological point of view, one could also expect an effect from the fact that women are enrolled in school. When a woman is attending school, university, or a vocational training program, she is normally economically dependent on her parents. Furthermore, there are normative expectations in modern societies that young people who attend school are "not at risk" of entering marriage and parenthood. Moreover, the roles of students and mothers are sufficiently demanding, so that most women delay fertility until they have left school. Finishing one's education therefore counts as one of the important prerequisites for entering into marriage and parenthood. In order to include this influence in their model, Blossfeld and Huinink generated a time-dependent dummy variable indicating whether or not a woman is *attending the educational system* at a specific age (see the lower panel of Figure 6.6.2).

After leaving the educational system and entering into employment, women accumulate labor force experience at their workplaces. As shown earlier, economists (Mincer 1974; Becker 1975) and sociologists (Sørensen 1977; Sørensen and Tuma 1981) have often used time in the labor force as a proxy for the accumulation of labor force experience. But this procedure can be criticized on the basis of research into labor-market segmentation (see Blossfeld and Mayer 1988). First, there is a so-called secondary labor market in the economy, which offers relatively low-paying and unstable employment with poor chances of accumulating any labor force experience at all (see, e.g., Doeringer and Piore 1971; Blossfeld and Mayer 1988). Second, in some positions within so-called internal labor markets, the opportunities to accumulate labor force experience are very unequally distributed (e.g. Doeringer and Piore 1971; Doeringer 1967; Piore 1968; Blossfeld and Mayer 1988). Likewise, differences in the opportunities for acquiring labor force experience may also exist among the self-employed and people working in different kinds of professions. This means that the *speed and levels of the accumulation of labor force experience* must be modeled in dependence of the type of employment. For the dynamic modeling of job-specific investments in human capital over the life course, Blossfeld and Huinink have therefore made the following three conjectures:

Development of career resources after entry into first employment. Women who have left the educational system and entered their first job accumulate labor force experience with decreasing increments. Because on-the-job training is concentrated mainly in the earlier phases of employment, increases are large at the beginning and level off with increasing time on the job. This means that increments and final levels of labor force experience should be modeled dependent on a measure of how good the job is; for example, the prestige score, P, of jobs. A possible mathematical model of the growth rate $r(P, t)$ of career resources at age t, assuming that the first job was entered at age t_0, is therefore $(t \geq t_0)$:

$$r(P, t) = \exp\left(-\alpha\,(t - t_0)\right)$$

where

$$\alpha = \frac{P_{\max} - P_{\min}}{2}\frac{1}{P} = \frac{83.4}{P}$$

Here P is Wegener's (1985) prestige score, which is used as a proxy measure for the job quality and for the opportunity to accumulate labor force experience within a job. Given this model, the level of career resources $K(P, t)$ within a job episode at age t is then defined as

$$K(P, t) = \exp\left\{\int_{t_0}^{t} r(P, u)\, du\right\} - 1$$

Until entry into the first job, the level of career resources $K(P, t)$ is equal to zero. The maximum level of career resources $\max(K(P, t))$, within a job with the lowest prestige score (a helper with a prestige score of 20.0 on the Wegener scale), for example, is reached after nine months and has the value 0.27. For a job with the highest prestige score on the Wegener scale (a medical doctor), the maximum level of career resources is reached after about 9–10 years and has a value of 8.15.

Change of jobs. If a woman changes from a job with prestige level P_0 to a job with prestige level $P_h > P_0$ at time t_1, which is an *upward move*, her career resources will increase until the maximum career level of the new job is reached. In this case the career function for $t > t_1$ is:[30]

$$K(P_h, t) = \min \left\{ K(P_0, t_1) + K(P_h, t - t_1), \max(K(P_h, t)) \right\}$$

If a woman changes from a job with prestige level P_0 to a job with a prestige level $P_n < P_0$ at time t_2 (a *downward move*), the career resources of the preceding job decrease linearly over time and the career resources of the successive job are increased over time. However, the maximum career level of the successive job is considered to be the lower limit. Thus, with increasing time, the level of career resources decreases and will approach the maximum career level of the successive job. For $t > t_2$ the level of career resources is obtained as follows:

$$K(P_n, t) = \begin{cases} \min \left\{ (1 - (1.5/P_0)(t - t_2)) K(P_0, t_2) + K(P_n, t - t_2), \\ \qquad K(P_0, t_2) \right\} \quad \text{if} \quad t - t_2 < P_0/1.5 \\ K(P_n, t - t_2) \quad \text{otherwise} \end{cases}$$

Discontinuity of work experience. Besides continuous changes of the level of career resources as a result of upward and downward moves, one must also recognize that women tend to have several entries into and exits from the labor force after leaving school because of family events (marriage, birth of children, etc.; Mincer and Polachek 1974). Given this discontinuity of work experience, the assumption normally made for the career process of men in labor-market research (Sørensen 1977), that career resources monotonically increase with decreasing increments over the worklife, is no longer valid. If women interrupt their employment careers, then they lose career resources that have to be accumulated again after reentry into the labor force. To model the path of labor force experience of women, Blossfeld and Huinink assumed that career resources decline when women interrupt (I) their employment career at age t_3 as long as women's career resources are still positive. The speed of the decrease

---

[30] In the following formula, $\max(K(P_h, t))$ is the highest value a woman can reach in job h. The formula $K(P_h, t)$ then says that her resources equal a value that increases with time, until the maximum level, $\max(K(Pt, t))$, is reached.

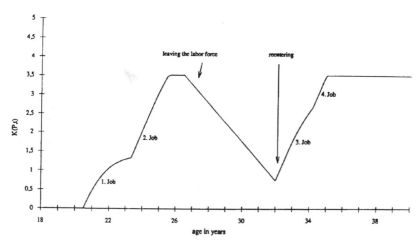

Figure 6.6.3 Career resources over the life course: an occupational career with a phase of non-employment.

is thereby dependent on the prestige level (P_0) of the job held immediately before the interruption of the career. For $t > t_3$ one gets:

$$K(I, t) = \max\left\{0, 1 - \frac{1.5}{P_0}(t - t_3) K(P_0, t_3)\right\}$$

Figure 6.6.3 shows an example for a trajectory of career resources including an upward move (from job 1 to job 2), a work interruption, and a reentry into a third job.

The goal of the transition rate analysis in this research was to specify the rates of entry into marriage or motherhood $r(t)$ as a function of time-constant (X_1) and time-dependent covariates ($X_2(t)$) in an exponential model:

$$r(t) = \exp\left(X_1 \beta_1 + X_2(t) \beta_2\right)$$

In this model, observation begins at age 15 and ends with the event of first marriage or the birth of the first child or, for right-censored cases, with the date of the interview or age 45, whichever is earlier.

A combination of two variables was used to control for the well-known non-monotonic age dependence of the marriage rate and the rate of the first birth (Coale 1971; Bloom 1982). This approach considers women at risk of entering first marriage and having a first child between the ages of 15 and 45 (i is an index for the ith one-month interval):

$$\log(D_i) = \log(\text{current age} - 15)$$
$$\log(R_i) = \log(45 - \text{current age})$$

Including these variables in the exponential model as time-dependent covariates,

$$\exp\left(\log(D_i)\,\beta' + \log(R_i)\,\beta''\right) = D_i^{\beta'}\,R_i^{\beta''}$$

the typical bell-shaped curve of the rates of entry into first marriage and first motherhood is modeled. This curve is symmetric around the age 30 for $\beta' = \beta''$, left-skewed for $\beta' < \beta''$, and right-skewed for $\beta' > \beta''$.

First marriage and first childbirth are interdependent processes and form a dynamic system. Premarital conception increases the readiness of women to enter into marriage and marriage increases the risk of childbirth. Therefore, Blossfeld and Huinink included time-dependent dummy variables for being pregnant in the marriage model and for being married in the first-birth model.

To control for cohort and period effects of historical and economic developments on family decisions, Blossfeld and Huinink introduced two different types of variables. First, they used two dummy variables for the three birth cohorts (reference group = cohort 1929-31) to measure differences among cohorts. Second, they employed a variable that reflects the continuous development of labor market conditions as a period measure (see Figure 6.6.1 in the previous example).

To include all these various time-dependent covariates in the rate equation, Blossfeld and Huinink (1991) applied the method of episode splitting, as described previously. As time-constant background variables, they incorporated father's social class, residence at age 15 (town vs. country where country is the reference category), the number of siblings, and the educational level of the partner. We cannot go into the details of this sophisticated dynamic analysis here. We only demonstrate the strength of using time-dependent covariates by reporting the most important findings of this study.

The first interesting aspect of this analysis is that the effects of the dummy variables for father's social class on entry into marriage and motherhood in Model 3 show that women from lower social classes marry earlier and have their babies sooner than women from higher social classes (see Tables 6.6.2 and 6.6.3). However, when the various time-dependent covariates for women's educational and career investments over the life course are included, this effect disappears completely. Thus, by extending education and improving career opportunities, families of higher social classes *indirectly* delay the rate of getting married and having children. In general, event history analysis provides an opportunity to study the *importance of indirect effects that operate by influencing either the timing of entry into or exit from specific states as well as with regard to variations of time-dependence within states* (see also Yamaguchi 1991).

In Model 4 (Tables 6.6.2 and 6.6.3), measures of changes in the historical background, such as cohort membership and economic development, are incorporated. There are no significant cohort effects, but one observes a significant positive effect of the economic conditions. This is to say that women

Table 6.6.2 Estimates for models of the rate of entry into marriage (women of cohorts 1929–31, 1939–41, and 1949–51).

Variables	1	2	3	Model 4	5	6	7
Intercept	-4.69*	-17.62*	-17.58*	-17.68*	- 16.28*	- 16.28*	-16.04*
Log (current age - 15)		1.76*	1.80*	1.73*	1.46*	1.47*	1.45*
Log (45 - current age)		3.20*	3.27*	3.37*	3.09*	3.09*	2.93*
Number of siblings			-0.00	0.01	0.00	0.00	-0.01
Father's social class 2			-0.13	-0.14	-0.08	-0.08	-0.04
Father's social class 3			-0.31*	-0.31*	-0.14	-0.14	-0.06
Father's social class 4			-0.61*	-0.61*	-0.33*	-0.32*	-0.25
Urban residence at age 15			-0.08	-0.11	-0.05	-0.05	-0.07
Cohort 1939–41				-0.04	-0.04	-0.03	-0.05
Cohort 1949–51				-0.09	-0.01	-0.00	0.00
Economic development				0.19*	0.21*	0.21*	0.18*
In training (dynamic measure)					-0.97*	-0.99*	-0.80*
Level of education (dynamic measure)					-0.01	-0.00	0.00
Level of career resources (dynamic measure)						-0.03	0.04
Is pregnant (dynamic measure)							2.84*
Subepisodes	85404	85404	85404	85404	85404	85404	85404
χ^2		457.80	485.55	525.01	598.39	598.47	1085.47
df		2	7	10	12	13	14

* statistically significant at 0.05 level.

enter into marriage earlier when the economic situation is favorable. In a period of economic expansion, the life-cycle prospects of young people are more predictable and it is therefore easier for women to make such long-term decisions like entering into marriage and having a baby.

After having controlled for age dependence (Model 2), social background (Model 3), and changes in the historical setting (Model 4), an answer to the question of how important the improvements in educational and career opportunities have been for women's timing of marriage can be given (Table 6.6.2).

We first look at the *dynamic effects of education* in Model 5. This model shows that attending school, vocational training programs, or university does indeed have a strong negative effect on the rate of entry into marriage. What is very interesting however is that the effect of the *level of education* is not significant. Women's timing of marriage is therefore independent of the quantity of human

Table 6.6.3 Estimates for models of the rate of entry into motherhood (women of cohorts 1929–31, 1939–41, and 1949–51).

Variables	2	3	4	Model 5	6	7	8
Intercept	-19.33*	-18.82*	-18.59*	-17.64*	-16.03*	-16.72*	-14.21*
Log (current age - 15)	2.17*	2.19*	2.08*	2.11*	1.68*	1.76*	0.08
Log (45 - current age)	3.36*	3.30*	3.33*	3.28*	2.84*	2.95*	2.24*
Number of siblings		0.04*	0.05*	0.04*	0.04*	0.04*	0.09*
Father's social class 2		-0.10	-0.10	-0.03	-0.04	-0.01	0.12
Father's social class 3		-0.34*	-0.34*	-0.21	-0.19	-0.18	-0.03
Father's social class 4		-0.45*	-0.46*	-0.13	-0.08	-0.05	0.16
Urban residence at age 15		-0.23*	-0.47*	-0.18*	-0.17*	-0.18*	-0.23*
Cohort 1939–41			-0.11	-0.03	-0.07	-0.03	-0.22
Cohort 1949–51			-0.16	-0.02	-0.05	0.03	-0.57*
Economic development			0.20*	0.19*	0.20*	0.20*	0.07
In training (dynamic measure)					-1.98*	-2.24*	-1.32*
Level of education (dynamic measure)					0.05	0.08*	0.08*
Level of career resources (dynamic measure)						-0.39*	-0.18*
Married (dynamic measure)							3.82*
Subepisodes	99506	99506	99506	99506	99506	99506	99506
χ^2	480.04	518.86	547.14	579.51	674.56	695.86	1744.10
df	2	7	10	11	13	14	15

* statistically significant at 0.05 level.

capital investments. In assessing the consequences of educational expansion on family formation, one can therefore conclude that marriage is postponed because women postpone their transition from youth to adulthood and not because women acquire greater quantities of human capital, thereby increasing their labor force attachment.

In Model 6 of Table 6.6.2, one can assess the effect of the improvement in women's career opportunities on the timing of their marriage. Again, and of great theoretical interest, this variable proves to be insignificant. Women's entry into marriage seems to be independent of their career opportunities.

Finally, in Model 7 (Table 6.6.2) a time-dependent pregnancy indicator is included. It does not change the substantive findings cited earlier, but its effect is positive and very strong. This indicates that for women experiencing premarital pregnancy the marriage rate increases sharply.

Let us now consider the estimates for first motherhood in Table 6.6.3. Again, age dependence, social background, historical period, cohort effects, and partner's educational attainment are controlled for in the first five models.

In Model 6, *women's continuously changing level of education and an indicator for their participation in school* are included to explain the rate of entry into motherhood. Again, as in the marriage model, level of education, which measures women's general human capital investments, has no significant effect on the timing of the first birth. Only attending school negatively affects the women's rate of having a first child. This means that conflicting time commitments with respect to women's roles as students and mothers exist (Rindfuss and John 1983), and that there are normative expectations that young women who attend school are not at risk of entering into motherhood.

If changes in *career resources of women* over the life course are introduced in Model 7 of Table 6.6.3, the effect of the level of education proves to be significantly positive. This is contrary to the expectations of the economic approach to the family, and means that the process of attaining successively higher levels of qualification has an augmenting, rather than a diminishing, effect on the rate of having a first child. The reason for this is that the attainment of increasing levels of education takes time and is connected with an increasing age of women (Figure 6.6.2). Women who remain in school longer and attain high qualifications are subject to pressure not only from the potential increase in medical problems connected with having children late, but also from societal age norms ("women should have their first child at least by age 30"; Menken 1985). Thus, not human capital investments, as claimed by the "new home economics," but increasing social pressure might be at work, if the level of education has an impact on the timing of the first birth.

These relationships are also illustrated in Figure 6.6.4.[31] In this figure, the estimates of the age-specific cumulative proportion of childless women (survivor function) for different levels of education are reported.[32] The longer that women are in school, the more first birth is delayed; therefore, there is a high proportion of childless women among the highly educated. After leaving the educational system, those women who have delayed having children "catch up" with their contemporaries who have less education and who got an earlier start. However, they do not only catch up. The positive effect of the educational level pushes the proportion of childless women with upper-secondary school qualifications (at about age 20) and even those with university

---

[31] Rate function coefficients and their standard errors are helpful in ascertaining how educational and career investments of women influence first motherhood and first birth, in what direction, and at what level of significance. However, the magnitude of the effects and their substantive significance are more easily assessed by examining survivor functions for typical educational and occupational careers that show the probability that a woman remains unmarried or childless until age *t*.

[32] These estimates were obtained from Model 7 of Table 6.6.3 by holding constant all other variables at the mean and assuming the women were not employed.

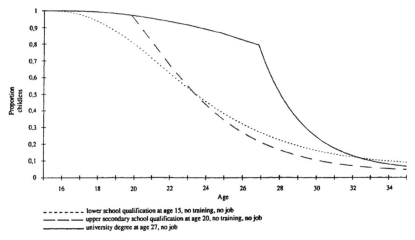

Figure 6.6.4 Estimated cumulative proportion of childless women by education (survivor function).

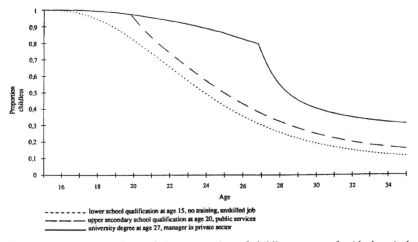

Figure 6.6.5 Estimated cumulative proportion of childless women for ideal-typical career lines (survivor function).

degrees (at about age 27) below the proportion of childless women with lower school qualifications.

A confirmation of the economic approach to the family may however be seen in the negative effect of the *level of career resources* on the rate of entry into motherhood (Model 7, Table 6.6.3). The accumulation of women's career resources conflicts with societal expectations concerning a woman's role as a mother. Women still take primary responsibility for child care and are still disadvantaged in their careers when they have to interrupt their working life because of the birth of a child. Therefore, women who have accumulated a high stock of career resources try to postpone or even avoid the birth of a first child.

Figure 6.6.5 displays examples of age-specific, cumulated proportions of childless women (survivor function) for ideal-typical career lines.[33] This exercise shows that there is a conflict between career and motherhood. An increase in career opportunities augments the proportion of childless women at any age.

Finally, in Model 8 (Table 6.6.3), Blossfeld and Huinink introduced a time-dependent dummy variable that changes its value at marriage and thus shows whether or not a woman was married before the birth of the first child. This variable increases the rate of entry into motherhood remarkably. When this variable is introduced, one can observe that the effects of "in training" and "level of career resources" become weaker. Part of their influence is therefore mediated by the marriage process (see also Blossfeld and De Rose 1992; Blossfeld and Jaenichen 1992; and for an international comparison of these models Blossfeld 1995).

In summarizing these results, it is interesting to note that empirical support for the "new home economics" has normally been claimed on the basis of cross-sectional and aggregated time-series data. However, these data do not permit a differentiation between the effect of accumulation of human capital over the life course and the effect of participation in the educational system in keeping women out of the marriage market. Therefore, it seems that such empirical support for the "new home economics" is only the result of inappropriate methods and the type of data used.

Example 3: The Effects of Pregnancy on Entry into Marriage for Couples Living in Consensual Unions

We finally report on two investigations by Blossfeld, Manting, and Rohwer (1993) and Blossfeld, Klijzing, Pohl, and Rohwer (1995). These studies are instructive because they demonstrate how sensitive the effects of time-dependent covariates can be with respect to the points in time when they are supposed to change their values.

In substantive terms, the purpose of the first study was to gain insight into the relationship between consensual unions and marriage in West Germany and the Netherlands. The study focused on the effect of fertility on the rate of entry into marriage, controlling for other important covariates in a transition rate model.

---

[33] Again these estimates are obtained from Model 7 (Table 6.6.3) by holding constant all other variables at the mean.

Table 6.6.4 Piecewise constant exponential model for transitions from consensual unions to marriage and dissolution, for West Germany (FRG) and the Netherlands (NL).

	Entry into Marriage		Dissolution	
Variable	FRG[3]	NL[4]	FRG[3]	NL[4]
Constant	-2.79**	-4.01**	-10.60**	-4.92**
Duration				
less than 2 years	0.08	-0.01	-0.49**	-0.18**
more than 2 years	-0.08	0.01	0.49**	0.18**
Birth cohort				
1950–53[1]	-0.09	0.07	0.37	-0.19
1954–58	0.01	0.16*	0.22	-0.13
1959–63	0.11	0.00	-0.68*	-0.15
1964–69[2]	-0.03	-0.23**	-0.09	0.46**
School enrolment				
at school	-0.16*	-0.36**	-0.40	0.11
not at school	0.16*	0.36**	0.40	-0.11
Educational level				
low	-0.17*	0.14*	0.03	-0.08
medium	-0.09	-0.07	0.29	0.10
high	0.26	-0.07	-0.32	-0.03
Fertility				
not pregnant	-1.19**	-0.43**	5.48**	-0.09
pregnant	1.13**	1.19**	-5.45	0.17
first child birth	1.21**	0.21	-4.75	-0.69
six months after birth	-1.15**	-0.98**	4.72*	0.61*
Sex				
men	-0.08		0.09	
women	0.08		-0.09	
Married before				
no	0.07		-0.01	
yes	-0.07		0.01	

*   statistically significant at 0.1 level. ** statistically significant at 0.05 level.
1) For West Germany the birth cohort of 1949 was also included.
2) For West Germany the birth cohort of 1969 was also included.
3) Men and women.
4) Only women.

Historically, marriage has—as a rule—preceded the birth of a child, but in recent decades, the interplay between marriage and childbirth has certainly become more complex. Some cohabiting couples wait until the woman gets pregnant and then marry. For other couples, an accidental pregnancy may lead to a marriage that otherwise might not have taken place. Pregnancy can also lead to a dissolution of the consensual union, if there is strong disagreement over the desirability of having a child. Other couples, wishing to have children in the near future, may decide to marry before the woman gets pregnant. To study these complex relationships, nationally representative longitudinal data were used. In the first analysis by Blossfeld, Manting, and Rohwer (1993), the German Socio-Economic Panel for West Germany and the Netherlands Fertility Survey were applied. Both data sets provide important information about the dynamics of consensual unions in the 1980s. In both countries, attention was limited to members of the cohorts born between 1950–1969, who started a consensual union between 1984–1989 in West Germany and between 1980–1988 in the Netherlands.[34]

However, we only want to discuss the fertility effects here. Fertility was included in the transition rate model as a series of time-dependent dummy variables (coded as centered effects)[35] with the following states: "not pregnant," "pregnant," "first childbirth," "6 months after birth." As shown in Table 6.6.4, the effects of the fertility dummy variables are significant for both countries and they basically work in the same direction. As long as women are not pregnant, a comparatively low rate of entry into marriage for people living in a consensual union is observed. But as soon as a woman becomes pregnant (and in West Germany also around the time when a woman has her child) the rate of entry into marriage increases strongly. Thus, there still seems to be a great desire among the young generations in West Germany and the Netherlands to avoid illegitimate births and to legalize the union when a child is born. However, if the couple did not get married within a certain time (around six months) after the child was born, the rate of entry into marriage again dropped to a comparatively low level in West Germany. In the Netherlands, this level is even below the "not pregnant" level.

Let us now look at the effects of fertility on the dissolution process of consensual unions, which are different in Germany and the Netherlands. In Germany, the dissolution risk is high as long as women are not pregnant. The rate drops strongly for some months when a woman is pregnant and then has her child. But six months after childbirth, the dissolution rate rises again. The strong rise six months after childbirth can also be observed in the Netherlands. Thus, in Germany and the Netherlands, women living in consensual unions with an illegitimate child not only have a comparatively low rate of entering into marriage, but also a comparatively high dissolution risk. In other words, the

---

[34] About 85 % of the entries into consensual unions between 1984 and 1989 were observed for these cohorts.

[35] Using effect coding for dummy variables, the differences between the levels of a qualitative variable are expressed as differences from a "virtual mean." The effect of the category chosen as the reference in the estimation can be computed as being the negative sum of the effects of the dummy variables included in the model.

Table 6.6.5 Exponential model for transitions from consensual unions to marriage, with a series of dummy variables, defined as lags/leads with regard to the month of childbirth.

Variable	Coefficient	p-value
Intercept	-4.4852	0.0000
Dummy: -9 months	1.4094	0.0161
Dummy: -8 months	1.9515	0.0000
Dummy: -7 months	1.7443	0.0006
Dummy: -6 months	1.4567	0.0129
Dummy: -5 months	1.0039	0.1507
Dummy: -4 months	1.3071	0.0257
Dummy: -3 months	0.2657	0.7015
Dummy: -2 months	1.8605	0.0000
Dummy: -1 months	-8.4526	0.0145
Dummy: 0 months	0.2657	0.7015
Dummy: 1 months	-8.4526	0.9114
Dummy: 2 months	0.8743	0.2208
Dummy: 3 months	-0.3593	0.0881

rise in the number of consensual unions will certainly increase the number of female-headed single-parent families in both countries.

About a year after this comparative study was conducted, Blossfeld, Klijzing, Pohl, and Rohwer (1995) wanted to examine whether these relationships could be reproduced with new data from Germany. They started to conduct some preliminary analyses and used only one dummy variable for the fertility process. However, the effect of this variable was insignificant. This was surprising because results of the earlier comparative study were convincing in theoretical terms. After checking the input data and command files, the authors noticed that the programmer had accidentally switched the time-dependent dummy variable at the time of the birth of the child and not at the time when it was clear that there was a conception (i.e. about eight to six months before birth). Thus, a shift in the switch of a time-dependent covariate by 6 months made the effect of fertility disappear. This "finding" created a lot of confusion in the research group. What happened to the fertility effect? After much discussion, one explanation seemed to unite theory and the seemingly contradictory results of the estimated models: The effect of fertility on entry into marriage must be strongly time-dependent. It must start to rise at some time shortly after conception, increase during pregnancy to a maximum, and then decrease again. Thus, when the time-dependent covariate was switched at the time of conception, the effect was strongly positive because it compared the situation before discovery of conception (cumulating a period with a low marriage rate) to the situation after discovery of conception (cumulating a high marriage rate for some months). But when the time-dependent covariate was switched at the time of childbirth, then a period with a low marriage rate up to the time of discovery of conception and a period with a high marriage rate during pregnancy was mixed (see Table 6.6.4). Thus, the average tendency to marry before the child is born more or less equals the average tendency to marry after the child is born, and the estimated coefficient for the time-dependent covariate "childbirth" is not significantly different from zero. There is, of course, a simple way to test this hypothesis. Blossfeld, Klijzing, Pohl, and Rohwer (1995) used a series of time-dependent dummy variables each indicating a month since the occurrence of conception. And in fact, as shown in Table 6.6.5, the effects of the time-dependent dummy variables at first increase, reach a maximum at about 8 months before birth of a child, and then decrease. Thus, starting with conception, there is an increasing normative pressure to avoid an illegitimate birth that increases the marriage rate, particularly for people who are already "ready for marriage." But with an increasing number of marriages, the composition of the group of still unmarried couples shifts towards couples being "less ready for marriage" or being "not ready for marriage," which, of course, decreases the fertility effect again.

This is an important result not only in substantive terms; the methodological lesson is also very revealing. One should be very careful in modeling qualitative parallel processes with only one dummy variable, particularly in situations in which it is theoretically quite open, at which point in time the value of the dummy variable must be switched.

Chapter 7
Parametric Models of Time-Dependence

In some sociological applications, substantive theory or previous empirical research suggests a *specific shape of time-dependence* for the transition rate. When this time path can be modeled in terms of a *tractable waiting time distribution*, the likelihood can be calculated by using its density $f(t)$ and survivor function $G(t)$, as has been shown for the exponential model in section 4.1. An obvious estimation strategy is then to use any computer program or software package (e.g. BMDP, GLIM, GAUSS, LIMDEP, SAS, etc.) that offers function optimization routines and to maximize the likelihood function with respect to the unknown parameters.[1] This strategy is very flexible because researchers are able to build their own parametric models, but it requires mathematical and programming skills. Our experience however shows that applied social scientists normally do not want to be bothered with writing programs and maximizing likelihood functions. TDA therefore offers the opportunity to estimate widely used parametric models with a single command. The parametric models with time-dependence can be requested with the TDA command

   rate = model_number;

where *model_number* is one of possible types shown in Box 7.1. TDA can estimate these parametric models for single and multiple episode data. In the case of multiple episodes, as shown in section 4.3, starting and ending times of the successive episodes are coded relative to first entry into the process (e.g. first entry into the labor market). Therefore, the starting and ending times of each episode determine the specific location of the successive spells within the distribution of a time-dependent model.[2] We do not demonstrate the estimation of parametric time-dependent models consisting of multiple episodes with TDA because this can be done in exactly the same way as already shown for the exponential model in section 4.3. In the examples in this chapter, we assume that the transition rate only depends on the time spent in an episode and that these durations are independently and identically distributed. In other words, we study so-called *Semi-Markov models* or *Markov renewal models* (see Tuma and Hannan 1984).

---

[1] This strategy has been demonstrated in Blossfeld, Hamerle, and Mayer (1989) using the function optimization subprogram P3R of BMDP and the P3RFUN subroutine written by Petersen (1986a, 1986b, 1988b).

[2] In many other programs only the duration of the episodes can be specified. In other words, it is assumed that all episodes begin with starting time zero. Thus, it is not possible to estimate time-dependent models across multiple episodes with such software.

Box 7.1 TDA models with a time-dependent transition rate

```
 4  Model with polynomial rates (type I).
 5  Model with polynomial rates (type II).
 6  Gompertz-Makeham model.
 7  Weibull model.
 8  Sickle model.
 9  Log-logistic model (type I).
10  Log-logistic model (type II).
11  Log-normal model (type I and II).
12  Model with a generalized Gamma distribution.
13  Model with an Inverse Gaussian distribution.
14  Model with a Box-Cox transformation.
```

Not all time-dependent models offered by TDA have the same relevance in practical empirical research. For example, the polynomial model, although quite flexible in fitting data, is normally hard to interpret in substantive terms (particularly for higher degrees). Because we prefer a theoretical approach to event history analysis in this book, we do not demonstrate the application of the polynomial model in this chapter. We also do not give any examples of models with an inverse Gaussian distribution or models with a Box-Cox transformation because they are rarely used in empirical social research.

In this chapter we begin with a discussion about the substantive meaning of time-dependence from a causal analytical point of view. Then we survey models with a monotonically decreasing or increasing transition rate, for which the Gompertz (-Makeham) and the Weibull distribution are normally applied. Finally, we demonstrate the log-logistic, the log-normal, and the sickle model that are widely used when the transition rate at first increases and then, after reaching a maximum, decreases. In our examples, these parametric models are estimated as single time-dependent rates[3] as well as models with covariates linked to various parameters of the distributions (see also Blossfeld, Hamerle, and Mayer 1989).

7.1 Interpretation of Time-Dependence

From a causal analytical point of view, it is important to realize that although the models in this chapter are called time-dependent, time itself is no causal factor. Time therefore cannot serve as an explaining variable for the observed pattern of time-dependence. Thus, what does it mean when we say that a transition rate is time-dependent?

The interpretation of time-dependence in parametric transition rate models can be approached from three different angles. First of all, observed time-dependence may be considered *spurious*, that is, it may simply be the consequence of *unobserved heterogeneity*. We discuss this perspective in detail in

---

[3] That is, a transition rate model without any covariates.

chapter 10. Second, time-dependence might be seen as the result of a *diffusion process*, reflecting the changing relationship of a set of interdependent individual units in a dynamic system over time (Diekmann 1989). And third, time-dependence can be interpreted as an *expression of a causal process* taking place in time between a continuously changing quantitative factor and the qualitative outcome variable under study (Tuma and Hannan 1984; Blossfeld, Hamerle, and Mayer 1989).

We first survey the perspective of *diffusion models* on time-dependence. These models are normally based on the idea that some sort of *contagion, infection, imitation*, or simply *social pressure* drives the process under study (Mahajan and Peterson 1985). A diffusion model, for example, has been suggested by Hernes (1972) to explain the bell-shaped transition rate of entry into marriage. In this model he posits two competing structural processes, explaining the time-dependence in the process of entry into marriage. On the one hand, with rising age t there is an increasing proportion $F(t)$ of a cohort that has already entered into first marriage, which in turn enhances the pressure to marry on those who are still unmarried. On the other hand, there is some sort of decreasing social attractiveness and, more importantly, a declining chance $s(t)$ of contact between unmarried peers with increasing time t. In particular, Diekmann (1989) has shown that the differential equation

$$\frac{dF(t)}{dt} = s(t)\, F(t)\, (1 - F(t))$$

with $s(t) = m \exp(-c(t - 1))$, corresponds to a bell-shaped transition rate, $r(t) = s(t)\, F(t)$, of entry into marriage (see also Wu 1990).

Although interpretations of time-dependence based on the idea of a diffusion process are illuminating in theoretical terms, they are still only rarely applied in the social sciences. The standard modeling strategy is to use *measures of time as proxies for time-varying causal factors*, which are difficult to observe directly (see Tuma and Hannan 1984). As discussed earlier, measures of time may serve as proxy variables, for example, for "the amount of marriage-specific investments" in divorce studies, "the stock of job-specific labor force experience" in mobility analyses, "the intensity of information flow" in organizational studies, or "the intensity of ties between a person and a locale" in migration studies. Given the difficulty of measuring such theoretically important concepts over time, time-dependent parametric models become a useful vehicle for modeling the changes in the transition rates over time.

There is a natural link between the exponential model and some time-dependent parametric models (Tuma and Hannan 1984). It can be shown, for example, that a metric causal variable increasing linearly over duration leads to a Gompertz model when it is included in an exponential model on the basis of the episode splitting method. Take the application in section 6.5 where we argued that the unobserved variable "job-specific labor force experience,"

$x_{LFX}(t)$, starts at 0 at the beginning of each new job and increases linearly over the duration t a person spends in a job. The rate equation with this latent variable $x_{LFX}(t)$, controlling for a vector of other covariates, x, would therefore be

$$r(t) = \exp(x\beta + x_{LFX}(t)\,\beta_{LFX})$$

An observable proxy variable for this latent factor is $t \simeq x_{LFX}$. Applying the method of episode splitting by measuring the proxy variable t intermittently at the beginning of arbitrarily defined subepisodes within each job leads to the following model

$$r(t) = \exp(x\beta + t\,\beta_{LFX})$$

which can be rewritten

$$r(t) = \exp(x\beta)\,\exp(t\,\beta_{LFX})$$

With $b = \exp(x\beta)$ and $c = \beta_{LFX}$, this is actually a Gompertz model

$$r(t) = b\,\exp(ct)$$

to be explained in more detail in section 7.2. Thus, if we hypothesize a causal mechanism that a linearly increasing stock of "job-specific labor force experience" leads to a monotonic decline in the job shift rate and include the time path of the duration via episode splitting in an exponential model, this is actually equivalent to *approximating* a Gompertz model.

A Weibull model, on the other hand, would be approximated if the stock of "job-specific labor force experience" is assumed to change as a *logarithmic function of duration* ($x_{LFX}(t) = \log(t)$):

$$
\begin{aligned}
r(t) &= \exp\big(x\beta + \log(x_{LFX})\beta_{LFX(t)}\big) \\
&\simeq \exp\big(x\beta + \log(t)\beta_{LFX}\big) \\
&= \exp(x\beta)\,t^{\beta_{LFX}}
\end{aligned}
$$

With $a = \exp(x\beta)$ and $b = \beta_{LFX}$ one obtains a special Weibull model, as can be seen in section 7.3.[4]

To say that the stock of "job-specific labor force experience" affects the job shift rate *logarithmically* instead of linearly with increasing job duration means that the *same* amount of job duration, t, leads to a *smaller* stock of job-specific experience, $\log(t)$. Of course, the question that arises here is which of these two causal models (Gompertz or Weibull distribution) is the correct one. Because available theory in the social sciences typically provides little or no guidance for choosing one parameterization over another, the problem normally boils down to the question of which model provides a better fit to the data. We discuss

---

[4] See Blossfeld, Hamerle, and Mayer (1989) for the various forms of the Weibull model.

some widely used methods for assessing the fit of parametric models in chapter 8.

However, given the issue of unobserved heterogeneity (chapter 10), as well as the difficulties in evaluating which of the models provides the relatively best fit, we recommend that *parametric models of time-dependence should only be applied with extreme caution*. One should always be aware of the fact that *assumed* causal factors that are (normally) *latent or unobserved* and measured only on the basis of *assumed proxies* are being dealt with. Thus, any substantive conclusion based on a time-dependent parametric model necessarily rests on a series of *untested and/or untestable assumptions*: (1) that there is indeed the supposed causal factor, (2) that this factor in fact leads to a specific shape of the transition rate (*via* an assumed causal mechanism), and (3) that the measure of time is a reasonably good proxy for the path of the unobserved factor. In summary, a strong theory is needed for these empirical applications.

In the following examples we do not pretend to have such a strong theory. Our purpose is only a didactical one. We demonstrate from a substantive point of view how different time-dependent parametric models in empirical research can be applied with TDA and how the results of the estimation are to be interpreted.

7.2   Gompertz-Makeham Models

We begin the discussion of parametric models of time-dependence with the Gompertz (-Makeham) distribution. The "Gompertz-Makeham law," which states that the transition rate decreases monotonically with time, has been successfully applied, for example, in studying the lifetime of organizations (see, e.g., Carroll and Delacroix 1982; Freeman, Carroll, and Hannan 1983; Hannan and Freeman 1989; Lomi 1995) or the durations in jobs (see, e.g., Sørensen and Tuma 1981; Blossfeld and Mayer 1988). The transition rate is given by the expression

$$r(t) = a + b \exp(c\,t) \qquad a, b \geq 0 \tag{7.1}$$

If $a = 0$, one gets the Gompertz model without a Makeham term. If $b = 0$, the model reduces to the simple exponential model. The corresponding survivor and density functions are

$$f(t) = \exp\left\{-at - \frac{b}{c}\left(\exp(c\,t) - 1\right)\right\}\left(a + b \exp(c\,t)\right)$$

$$G(t) = \exp\left\{-at - \frac{b}{c}\left(\exp(c\,t) - 1\right)\right\}$$

In the case of $c = 0$, it is assumed that these expressions reduce to the density and survivor function for a simple exponential model. Figure 7.2.1 shows

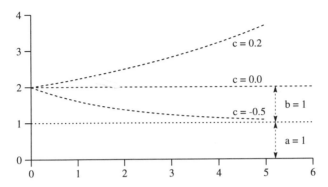

Figure 7.2.1 Gompertz-Makeham transition rate.

graphs of the transition rate function for $a = 1$, $b = 1$, and some different values of c.

The Gompertz-Makeham model has three parameters to include covariates. TDA uses exponential link functions with the A- and B-terms of the model, and a linear link function for the C-term. The model formulation for the transition rate from origin state j to destination state k is

$$r_{jk}(t) = a_{jk} + b_{jk} \exp(c_{jk} t)$$
$$a_{jk} = \exp\left\{A^{(jk)}\alpha^{(jk)}\right\}$$
$$b_{jk} = \exp\left\{B^{(jk)}\beta^{(jk)}\right\}$$
$$c_{jk} = C^{(jk)}\gamma^{(jk)}$$

It is assumed that the first component of each of the covariate (row) vectors $A^{(jk)}$, $B^{(jk)}$, and $C^{(jk)}$ is a constant equal to one. The associated coefficient vectors, $\alpha^{(jk)}$, $\beta^{(jk)}$, and $\gamma^{(jk)}$, are the model parameters to be estimated. The $A^{(jk)}$ and $B^{(jk)}$ vectors are linked exponentially to make sure that the estimated transition rate will not become negative.

Both the Gompertz and the Gompertz-Makeham model can be requested with the command

rate = 6;

Linking of covariates can be specified with the commands

xa (j,k) = list_of_A-term_variables;
xb (j,k) = list_of_B-term_variables;
xc (j,k) = list_of_C-term_variables;

If no covariates are linked to the A-term of the model, a simple Gompertz model is estimated. If at least one variable is linked to the A-term, the estimated model is of Gompertz-Makeham type. To estimate a Gompertz-Makeham model with the A-term as a single constant, one can use the command *xa(j,k)=0.*

Models without Covariates (Single Time-Dependent Rate)

In order to demonstrate the estimation and interpretation of the Gompertz model, we first specify a model without covariates:

$$r(t) = b \exp(ct), \; b = \exp(\beta_0), \; c = \gamma_0$$

We again analyze the job shift rate from "being in a job" (origin state = 0) to "having left the job" (destination state = 1) and regard duration in a job as a proxy variable for the stock of job-specific skills acquired in each new job. This implies that job-specific experience starts—as the duration itself—with each new job at $t = 0$ and then rises linearly with the time spent in a job. Because training on the job is an investment that is more or less lost when the job is changed, we hypothesize a causal mechanism that with increasing job-specific labor force experience, the transition rate declines monotonically. Given the Gompertz model, this suggests that the estimated parameter for c should be significant and negative (see Figure 7.2.1).

The TDA command file to estimate this Gompertz model, shown in Box 7.2.1, differs from the command file for an exponential model in Box 4.1.1, only in that the model selection command has been changed to *rate=6* and the command *xa(0,1)=0*, to specify a model without covariates, has been added.[5] (Furthermore, the name of the output file containing the estimated transition rate has been changed to *ehg1.prs*.)

The estimation results are shown in Box 7.2.2. A comparison of this model with the exponential model in Box 4.1.2, based on a likelihood ratio test, shows that the Gompertz model provides a significant improvement:

$$\text{LR} = 2\left((-2474.51) - (-2514.02)\right) = 79.02$$

The estimated parameters are $\hat{b} = \exp(\hat{\beta}_0) = \exp(-4.0729) = 0.017$ and $\hat{c} = \hat{\gamma}_0 = -0.0067$. Thus, as hypothesized, the estimated c is negative and significant. We therefore conclude that increasing job-specific labor force experience leads to a declining rate of moving out of the job. The estimated rate for this model is plotted in Figure 7.2.2.[6]

Some illustrations of interpreting the results should be given: If one compares, for example, an employee who has just started a new job ($\hat{r}(0) = 0.017$) with an employee who has already been working for 10 years (120 months) in the same job ($\hat{r}(120) = 0.017 \exp(-0.0067 \cdot 120) = 0.0076$), then the tendency of the second employee to change his/her job has been reduced by about 55 %, due to the accumulation of job-specific skills.

---

[5] This command is necessary because without any command to specify covariates TDA would estimate a simple exponential model.

[6] The command file used for this plot is included in the file *ehg1a.cf* on the accompanying disk.

Box 7.2.1 Command file *ehg1.cf* (Gompertz model without covariates)

```
dfile = rrdat.1;      data file

v1  (ID)    = c1 ;   ID of individual
v2  (NOJ)   = c2 ;   Serial number of the job
v3  (TStart) = c3 ;  Starting time of the job
v4  (TFin)  = c4 ;   Ending time of the job
v5  (SEX)   = c5 ;   Sex (1 men, 2 women)
v6  (TI)    = c6 ;   Date of interview
v7  (TB)    = c7 ;   Date of birth
v8  (T1)    = c8 ;   Date of entry into the labor market
v9  (TM)    = c9 ;   Date of marriage (0 if no marriage)
v10 (PRES)  = c10;   Prestige score of job i
v11 (PRESN) = c11;   Prestige score of job i + 1
v12 (EDU)   = c12;   Highest educational attainment

# Define origin and destination state. Origin state is always 0.
# Destination state is 0 if right censored, or 1.
v13 (ORG)   = 0;
v14 (DES)   = if eq(v4,v6) then 0 else 1;

# Definition of starting and ending time on a process time axis.
v15 (TSP) = 0;
v16 (TFP) = v4 - v3 + 1; one month added

# commands to define single episode data
org = v13;    define origin state
des = v14;    define destination state
ts  = v15;    define starting time
tf  = v16;    define ending time
```

```
# command to request estimation of a Gompertz model
rate = 6;          model selection
xb(0,1) = 0;       just an intercept for B-term, transition 0 -> 1

# commands to request a printout of estimated transition rate
prate = ehg1.prs;  print to output file: ehg1.prs
tab   = 0,300,10;  time axis for the table
```

Based on the survivor function of the Gompertz model

$$G(t) = \exp\left\{-\frac{b}{c}\left(\exp(ct) - 1\right)\right\}$$

it is possible to estimate the median M of the job duration, defined by $G(M) = 0.5$, as

$$G(\hat{M}) = \exp\left\{-\frac{0.017}{-0.0067}\left(\exp(-0.0067\,\hat{M}) - 1\right)\right\} = 0.5$$

Box 7.2.2 Part of TDA's standard output using *ehg1.cf* (Box 7.2.1)

```
Model: Gompertz-Makeham

Maximum likelihood estimation
Maximum of log likelihood: -2474.51
Norm of final gradient vector: 1.0e-04
Last absolute change of function value: 1.5e-09
Last relative change in parameters: 1.3e-04

Idx SN Org Des MT Var  Label    Coeff    Error     T-Stat  Signif
----------------------------------------------------------------
  1  1   0   1  B --   Const   -4.0729   0.0633   -64.3172  1.0000
  2  1   0   1  C --   Const   -0.0067   0.0009    -7.7201  1.0000
```

The estimated median is about 47.6 months. Thus the Gompertz model estimates a smaller median than the exponential model ($\hat{M} = 61.9$) in section 4.1.2.

Based on the survivor function, one can also compute the probability that an employee is still working in the same job after a period of, say, ten years:

$$G(120) = \exp\left\{ -\frac{0.017}{-0.0067}\left(\exp(-0.0067 \cdot 120) - 1 \right) \right\} \approx 0.246$$

or about 25 %. Thus, this estimate is almost the same as for the exponential model in section 4.1.2, where the estimate for this example was 26 %.

However, using this simple model without covariates assumes that there is no important heterogeneity across individuals and job episodes. This assumption is, in fact, not valid as we have already seen in discussing the exponential and piecewise constant exponential models in chapters 4 and 5. Moreover, ignoring heterogeneity in the present example is particularly problematic because a

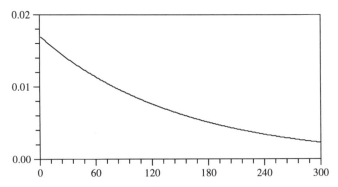

Figure 7.2.2 Gompertz transition rate estimated with command file *ehg1.cf*, (Box 7.2.1). The plot was generated with command file *ehg1a.cf*.

Box 7.2.3   Part of command file *ehg2.cf* (Gompertz model with covariates)

```
... (first part identical to first part of Box 7.2.1)

# define additional variables to include into the model
v20 (COHO2) =   ge(v7,468) . le(v7,504);    cohort 2
v21 (COHO3) =   ge(v7,588) . le(v7,624);    cohort 3
v22 (LFX)   =   v3 - v8;                     labor force experience
v23 (PNOJ)  =   v2 - 1;                      previous number of jobs

# command to request estimation of a Gompertz model
rate = 6;    model selection

# command to include covariates into model, for transition from
# origin state 0 to destination state 1.
xb (0,1)    =   v12,v20,v21,v22,v23,v10;

# command to print residuals to output file ehg2.res
pres = ehg2.res;
```

declining duration dependency can be the result of heterogeneity that is not explicitly taken into account.[7] Thus, the conclusion that the transition rate decreases due to the job-specific accumulation of skills could be wrong. It could be the consequence of unobserved heterogeneity. Therefore, in the next step, we estimate a Gompertz model controlling for a set of time-constant covariates.

Models with Covariates in the B-term

There are several options to link covariates with the parameters of the Gompertz (-Makeham) model. We demonstrate all of them. First of all, time-constant covariates can be included in the B-term of the Gompertz model, so we estimate the following model:

$$r(t) = b \exp(ct), \; b = \exp(B\beta), \; c = \gamma_0$$

The command file for this model, *ehg2.cf*, is shown in Box 7.2.3. This command file is almost identical to the command file in Box 4.1.4. There are only two differences: The selected model type has been changed to number 6, and the time-constant covariates have been linked to the B-term of the model.[8]

Results of the model estimation are shown in Box 7.2.4. The value of the log likelihood for this model is -2437.97. Thus, if this Gompertz model is

---

[7] This is discussed in chapter 10.

[8] We have also added a command to request the calculation of generalized residuals, to be written into an output file *ehg2.res*. This is discussed in chapter 8.

Box 7.2.4 Part of TDA's standard output using *ehg2.cf* (Box 7.2.3)

```
Model: Gompertz-Makeham

Maximum likelihood estimation
Maximum of log likelihood: -2437.97
Norm of final gradient vector: 9.7e-05
Last absolute change of function value: 6.7e-10
Last relative change in parameters: 1.1e-04

Idx SN Org Des MT Var  Label    Coeff    Error    T-Stat   Signif
-----------------------------------------------------------------
  1  1   0   1 B --    Const   -3.9105   0.2814  -13.8985  1.0000
  2  1   0   1 B V12   EDU      0.0634   0.0248    2.5565  0.9894
  3  1   0   1 B V20   COHO2    0.4130   0.1152    3.5849  0.9997
  4  1   0   1 B V21   COHO3    0.3119   0.1222    2.5512  0.9893
  5  1   0   1 B V22   LFX     -0.0039   0.0009   -4.1613  1.0000
  6  1   0   1 B V23   PNOJ     0.0627   0.0441    1.4241  0.8456
  7  1   0   1 B V10   PRES    -0.0250   0.0055   -4.5893  1.0000
  8  1   0   1 C --    Const   -0.0059   0.0009   -6.7272  1.0000
```

compared with a Gompertz model without covariates (Box 7.2.2), the likelihood ratio test leads to a χ^2-value of

$$LR = 2\left((-2437.97) - (-2474.51)\right) = 73.08$$

with six degrees of freedom. The model including covariates obviously provides a better fit.

In addition to this overall goodness-of-fit check, one can use the information provided in the standard errors of the estimation procedure. Assuming a large enough sample, the estimated coefficients divided by their standard errors (provided in column *T-Stat*) are approximately standard normally distributed. Using this fact, one can in particular assess the question of whether the coefficients significantly differ from zero. Box 7.2.4 provides basically the same picture as the estimation results for the simple exponential model (Box 4.1.5). With the exception of PNOJ, all variables seem to have a significant impact on the transition rate for leaving a job.

Also the estimate of c, $\hat{c} = \hat{\gamma}_0 = -0.0059$, is still significant and negative. Thus, the included time-constant factors in the B-term were not able to explain the declining transition rate completely. The c-coefficient is only a little smaller than in Box 7.2.2.

It is interesting to compare the estimates of this Gompertz model with the estimates in Box 6.5.5, where "job-specific labor force experience" in each of the jobs was approximated with the help of the method of episode splitting. The estimates for the models with the maximum subepisode length of 24 and 12 months are almost identical with the Gompertz model in Box 7.2.4. Thus, the method of episode splitting provided a quite good approximation of the Gompertz model.

Box 7.2.5 Part of command file *ehg3.cf* (Gompertz model with covariates)

```
... (first part identical to first part of Box 7.2.1)

# define additional variables to include into the model
v20 (COHO2) =   ge(v7,468) . le(v7,504);   cohort 2
v21 (COHO3) =   ge(v7,588) . le(v7,624);   cohort 3
v22 (LFX)   =   v3 - v8;                    labor force experience
v23 (PNOJ)  =   v2 - 1;                      previous number of jobs

# command to request estimation of a Gompertz model
rate = 6;      model selection

# command to include covariates into model, for transition from
# origin state 0 to destination state 1.
xb (0,1)    =   v12,v20,v21,v22,v23,v10;
xc (0,1)    =   v12,v20,v21,v22,v23,v10;

# command to print residuals to output file ehg3.res
pres = ehg3.res;
```

Models with Covariates in the B- and C-Terms

In surveying the exponential model with period-specific effects in section 5.4, we have already seen that the effect of time-constant covariates varies over duration. The hypothesis is that the effects of some of the time-constant covariates serving as signals decline with job duration (Arrow 1973; Spence 1973, 1974). This hypothesis has been empirically supported in Box 5.4.2. A similar test, making the parameter c of the Gompertz model dependent on time-constant covariates, can now be conducted with the Gompertz model. The model to be used is

$$r(t) = b \exp(c\,t)\,, \quad b = \exp(B\beta)\,, \quad c = C\gamma$$

As shown in Box 7.2.5, this model can be estimated by simply adding a command to also include a set of covariates in the C-term of the model. The estimation results are shown in Box 7.2.6.

Looking at the log likelihood value in Box 7.2.6, which is -2433.39, it becomes clear that this model provides only a slight improvement over the model in Box 7.2.4. Thus, if this model is compared with the Gompertz model with covariates only in the B-term (Box 7.2.4), the likelihood ratio test statistic is not significant with

$$LR = 2\left((-2433.39) - (-2437.97)\right) = 9.16$$

and six degrees of freedom. However, we briefly want to discuss the results for the C-term. An inspection of the single estimated coefficients of the C-term shows that only the effect of PNOJ ("number of previously held jobs") is

Box 7.2.6 Part of TDA's standard output using *ehg3.cf* (Box 7.2.5)

```
Model: Gompertz-Makeham

Maximum likelihood estimation
Maximum of log likelihood: -2433.39
Norm of final gradient vector: 1.3e-07
Last absolute change of function value: 3.6e-16
Last relative change in parameters: 9.8e-07

Idx SN Org Des MT Var  Label   Coeff    Error    T-Stat   Signif
-----------------------------------------------------------------
  1  1   0   1  B --   Const  -4.0167   0.3663  -10.9652  1.0000
  2  1   0   1  B V12  EDU     0.0918   0.0318    2.8843  0.9961
  3  1   0   1  B V20  COHO2   0.5074   0.1547    3.2789  0.9990
  4  1   0   1  B V21  COHO3   0.2069   0.1687    1.2269  0.7801
  5  1   0   1  B V22  LFX    -0.0051   0.0013   -3.9165  0.9999
  6  1   0   1  B V23  PNOJ    0.1513   0.0604    2.5060  0.9878
  7  1   0   1  B V10  PRES   -0.0323   0.0071   -4.5315  1.0000
  8  1   0   1  C --   Const  -0.0054   0.0057   -0.9497  0.6577
  9  1   0   1  C V12  EDU    -0.0005   0.0005   -1.1416  0.7464
 10  1   0   1  C V20  COHO2  -0.0019   0.0022   -0.8685  0.6149
 11  1   0   1  C V21  COHO3   0.0030   0.0028    1.0626  0.7120
 12  1   0   1  C V22  LFX     0.0000   0.0000    1.3730  0.8303
 13  1   0   1  C V23  PNOJ   -0.0019   0.0010   -2.0254  0.9572
 14  1   0   1  C V10  PRES    0.0002   0.0001    1.6056  0.8916
```

significant. Its effect has a declining relevance over job duration. However, in contradiction to the signal or filter theory, the effects of prestige (PRES), educational attainment (EDU), and general labor force experience at the beginning of each job (LFX) have no effect on the "shape parameter" c. Thus, the result of this model contradicts the result of the exponential model with period-specific effects in section 5.4. This suggests that caution is required in dealing with highly sophisticated parametric models linking many covariates to various parameters.

On the other hand, a comparison with the results of the exponential model with period-specific effects in Box 5.4.2 also shows that the parameters for the first period from 0 to 24 months are indeed very similar to the coefficients for the B-term in Box 7.2.6. Thus, the B-term effects of the covariates in the Gompertz model seem to do a good job in describing the effects of the covariates at a starting phase of each new job.

Models with Covariates in the A-, B-, and C-Terms

In the Gompertz model, the transition rate asymptotically approaches the value zero if the parameter c is negative and duration becomes large ($t \rightarrow \infty$). In the case of our job change example, this implies that there would be basically no job shift for large job durations. This is an unrealistic assumption. Thus,

Box 7.2.7   Part of command file *ehg4.cf* (Gompertz model with covariates)

```
   ... (first part identical to first part of Box 7.2.1)

   # define additional variables to include into the model
   v20 (COHO2) =   ge(v7,468) . le(v7,504);    cohort 2
   v21 (COHO3) =   ge(v7,588) . le(v7,624);    cohort 3
   v22 (LFX)   =   v3 - v8;                     labor force experience
   v23 (PNOJ)  =   v2 - 1;                      previous number of jobs

   # command to request estimation of a Gompertz model
   rate = 6;       model selection

   # command to include covariates into model, for transition from
   # origin state 0 to destination state 1.
   xa (0,1)    =   v12,v20,v21,v22,v23,v10;
   xb (0,1)    =   v12,v20,v21,v22,v23,v10;
   xc (0,1)    =   v12,v20,v21,v22,v23,v10;

   # command to print residuals to output file ehg3.res
   pres = ehg4.res;
```

what we need is a modification of the Gompertz model, allowing job shifts to also occur at rather large job durations. This model is called the *Gompertz-Makeham model*. It alleviates the problem by adding a positive constant, a, to the Gompertz model. For large durations, the rate of change no longer declines towards zero, but towards the value of the parameter a (see Figure 7.2.1). Of course, one can also link a vector of covariates to the a parameter of the model, as shown in the following specification

$$r(t) = a + b \exp(c\,t)\,, \quad a = \exp(A\alpha)\,, \quad b = \exp(B\beta)\,, \quad c = C\,\gamma$$

In our example, the estimated parameters of the covariates in the A-term reflect the importance and direction of the influence on the job shift behavior on a job "in the long run" (for very long durations). Thus, according to signaling theory, filter variables such as level of education, prestige, or general labor force experience measured at the beginning of each job should not be significant in the A-term. An influence upon job change behavior for long durations would be more likely to occur with regard to relatively stable personality variables. Unfortunately, in the GLHS no psychological indicators are available to classify an individual as "stable" or "mobile." However, the variable PNOJ ("number of previously held jobs") might serve as a proxy variable for the tendency of individuals to change their jobs. The greater the value of PNOJ, the greater the likelihood that the individual has an unstable relationship to his/her job(s). In order to examine the thesis (as suggested by the signaling theory), we estimate a Gompertz-Makeham model with the same covariates in the A-, B-, and C-terms with command file *ehg4.cf* shown in Box 7.2.7. The command file is

Box 7.2.8 Part of TDA's standard output using *ehg4.cf* (Box 7.2.7)

```
Model: Gompertz-Makeham

Maximum likelihood estimation
Maximum of log likelihood: -2423.85
Norm of final gradient vector: 4.8e-05
Last absolute change of function value: 2.9e-13
Last relative change in parameters: 1.5e-04
```

Idx	SN	Org	Des	MT	Var	Label	Coeff	Error	T-Stat	Signif
1	1	0	1	A	--	Const	-14.9029	3.6611	-4.0706	1.0000
2	1	0	1	A	V12	EDU	-0.1348	0.2272	-0.5932	0.4470
3	1	0	1	A	V20	COHO2	2.2350	1.7415	1.2834	0.8006
4	1	0	1	A	V21	COHO3	-3.4706	14.2396	-0.2437	0.1926
5	1	0	1	A	V22	LFX	0.0162	0.0082	1.9770	0.9520
6	1	0	1	A	V23	PNOJ	-2.9917	0.8958	-3.3397	0.9992
7	1	0	1	A	V10	PRES	0.2087	0.0601	3.4714	0.9995
8	1	0	1	B	--	Const	-3.8740	0.3855	-10.0491	1.0000
9	1	0	1	B	V12	EDU	0.0988	0.0334	2.9581	0.9969
10	1	0	1	B	V20	COHO2	0.4783	0.1673	2.8581	0.9957
11	1	0	1	B	V21	COHO3	0.2640	0.1741	1.5164	0.8706
12	1	0	1	B	V22	LFX	-0.0057	0.0014	-3.9031	0.9999
13	1	0	1	B	V23	PNOJ	0.1898	0.0624	3.0432	0.9977
14	1	0	1	B	V10	PRES	-0.0407	0.0080	-5.1086	1.0000
15	1	0	1	C	--	Const	-0.0045	0.0064	-0.7146	0.5251
16	1	0	1	C	V12	EDU	-0.0005	0.0005	-1.0523	0.7073
17	1	0	1	C	V20	COHO2	-0.0024	0.0024	-0.9801	0.6729
18	1	0	1	C	V21	COHO3	0.0031	0.0029	1.0850	0.7221
19	1	0	1	C	V22	LFX	0.0000	0.0000	1.4054	0.8401
20	1	0	1	C	V23	PNOJ	-0.0018	0.0010	-1.8275	0.9324
21	1	0	1	C	V10	PRES	0.0002	0.0001	1.2268	0.7801

basically the same as *ehg3.cf* shown in Box 7.2.5; only one command is added to also include covariates in the A-term of the model.

The estimation results in Box 7.2.8 show that there is some improvement in the fit of the model. The log likelihood is -2423.85. Thus, if this model is compared with the Gompertz model with covariates only in the B- and C-terms in Box 7.2.6, the likelihood ratio statistics has a value of 19.08 with six degrees of freedom.

The effects of this model are, however, mixed and generally do not support our hypotheses. First, the statistically significant *negative* effect of PNOJ in the A-term contradicts our hypothesis. An increasing number of previously held jobs decreases the inclination of a worker to change jobs in the long run instead of increasing it. The effect of prestige (PRES) is in contradiction with the signaling theory. Its influence is significant and positive. This means that for large durations, the prestige level of the job is a stimulating effect on the mobility process. On the other hand, the effects of the variable educational attainment (EDU), general labor force experience at the beginning of each job (LFX), and prestige (PRES) in the B-term make sense from the perspective of the signaling theory because these variables turn out to be particularly important at the beginning of each new job. Finally, none of the covariates has a significant effect on the parameter c, which is responsible for the shape of the time-dependence. However, this could also be a consequence of the small number of events in our data set.

7.3 Weibull Models

This section describes the Weibull model. In the single transition case, it is derived by assuming a Weibull distribution for the episode durations. Density function, survivor function, and the transition rate are given, respectively, by

$$
\begin{aligned}
f(t) &= b\,a^{b}\,t^{b-1}\exp\left\{-(at)^{b}\right\} \qquad a,b>0 \\
G(t) &= \exp\left\{-(at)^{b}\right\} \\
r(t) &= b\,a^{b}\,t^{b-1}
\end{aligned}
$$

Figure 7.3.1 shows graphs of the transition rate for $a = 1$ and different values of b.

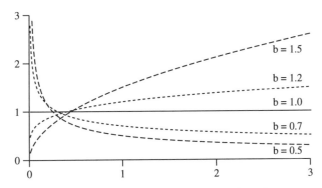

Figure 7.3.1 Weibull transition rates $(a = 1)$.

The Weibull model is also flexible and appropriate for a wide variety of situations. Like the Gompertz model, the Weibull model can also be used to model a monotonically falling $(0 < b < 1)$ or monotonically increasing rate $(b > 1)$; see Figure 7.3.1. For the special case of $b = 1$, one obtains the exponential model. It is therefore possible to test the hypothesis of a constant risk against the alternative of $b \neq 1$.

Box 7.3.1   Part of command file *ehg5.cf* (Weibull model without covariates)

```
... (first part equal to first part of Box 7.2.1)

# command to request estimation of a Weibull model
rate = 7;         model selection

# commands to request a printout of estimated transition rate
prate = ehg5.prs;  print to output file: ehg5.prs
tab   = 0,300,1 ;  time axis for the table
```

The Weibull model has two parameters, so one has two possibilities to include covariates. Using standard exponential link functions, TDA's model formulation for the transition rate from origin state j to destination state k is

$$r_{jk}(t) = b_{jk} a_{jk}^{b_{jk}} t^{b_{jk}-1}, \ a_{jk} = \exp\left\{A^{(jk)}\alpha^{(jk)}\right\}, \ b_{jk} = \exp\left\{B^{(jk)}\beta^{(jk)}\right\}$$

It is assumed that the first component of each of the covariate (row) vectors $A^{(jk)}$ and $B^{(jk)}$ is a constant equal to one. The associated coefficient vectors, $\alpha^{(jk)}$ and $\beta^{(jk)}$, are the model parameters to be estimated. The TDA command to request estimation of a Weibull model is *rate=7*.

Models without Covariates (Single Time-Dependent Rate)

In order to demonstrate the estimation and interpretation of the Weibull model, we first specify a model without covariates:

$$r(t) = b\, a^b\, t^{b-1}, \ a = \exp(\alpha_0), \ b = \exp(\beta_0),$$

Again, we use the job shift example of movement from "being in a job" (origin state = 0) to "having left the job" (destination state = 1), but now assume that the *logarithm* of the duration in a job is a proxy variable for the change in the stock of job-specific skills acquired in each new job. This means that job-specific experience starts—as the duration itself—in each new job and then rises as a logarithmic function of the time spent in the job. Again, we hypothesize that with increasing job-specific labor force experience the transition rate declines monotonically. Given the Weibull model, this suggests that the estimated parameter b is significant and its size is between 0 and 1 (see Figure 7.3.1).

The TDA command file (*ehg5.cf*) to estimate this Weibull model, shown in Box 7.3.1, differs from the command file for the Gompertz model in Box 7.2.1 only in that now the model type number has been changed to 7 and that an assignment for the B-term is unnecessary here.

The estimation results are shown in Box 7.3.2. A comparison with the exponential model in Box 4.1.2 leads to a highly significant likelihood ratio test statistic: 18.24 with one degree of freedom. However, there is little improvement compared to the Gompertz model (see Box 7.2.2). Thus, the Gompertz

Box 7.3.2 Part of TDA's standard output using *ehg5.cf* (Box 7.3.1)

```
Model: Weibull

Maximum likelihood estimation
Maximum of log likelihood: -2504.9
Norm of final gradient vector: 1.0e-04
Last absolute change of function value: 1.4e-08
Last relative change in parameters: 1.6e-03

Idx SN Org Des MT Var  Label   Coeff    Error    T-Stat  Signif
--------------------------------------------------------------------
  1  1   0   1  A --   Const  -4.4616   0.0544  -82.0244  1.0000
  2  1   0   1  B --   Const  -0.1477   0.0360   -4.1025  1.0000
```

model seems to provide a better fit of the observed data. This highlights an advantage of a linear over a log-linear specification of the accumulation of job-specific labor force experience over duration. In the A-term, the estimated parameter is

$$\hat{a} = \exp(\hat{\alpha}_0) = \exp(-4.4616) = 0.0115$$

In the B-term the estimated parameter is

$$\hat{b} = \exp(\hat{\beta}_0) = \exp(-0.1477) = 0.8627$$

As expected, the estimate of b is significant, positive, and smaller than 1. Thus, the Weibull model also predicts a decreasing rate to move out of the job with increasing job-specific labor force experience.

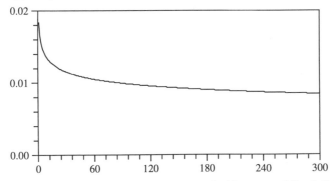

Figure 7.3.2 Weibull transition rate estimated with command file *ehg5.cf*, (Box 7.3.1). The plot was generated with command file *ehg5a.cf*.

The estimated rate for this model is plotted in Figure 7.3.2.[9] Compared to the Gompertz rate in Figure 7.2.2, the Weibull rate is flat and bears a closer

---

[9] The command file to plot this rate is included in the file *ehg5a.cf* on the accompanying disk.

resemblance to the exponential model. This could be why the likelihood ratio test statistic is so small for the Weibull model, as compared to the Gompertz model likelihood ratio test statistic.

If we again compare an employee who has just started a new job:

$$\hat{r}(0) = 0.8627 \cdot 0.0115^{0.8627} = 0.018$$

with an employee who has already been working for 10 years (or 120 months), in the same job:

$$\hat{r}(120) = 0.8627 \cdot 0.0115^{0.8627} \cdot 120^{0.8627-1} = 0.0095$$

then the tendency of the second employee to change his/her job has been reduced, through the accumulation of job-specific skills, by about 48 %.

Based on the survivor function of the Weibull model, that is

$$G(t) = \exp\left(-(at)^b\right)$$

it is again possible to estimate the median, $\hat{M}$, of the job duration by

$$G(\hat{M}) = \exp\left(-(0.0115\,M)^{0.8627}\right) = 0.5$$

resulting in $\hat{M} = 56.9$ months. Thus, the median estimated with the Weibull model is greater than that estimated with the Gompertz model ($\hat{M} = 47.7$, see section 7.2) and smaller than the estimate resulting from an exponential model ($\hat{M} = 61.9$, see section 4.1.2).

In the next step, we estimate the Weibull model and include our well-known set of time-constant covariates.

Models with Covariates in the A-Term

The Weibull distribution also offers several parameters to include covariates. In the first step, we include the time-constant covariates only into the A-term of the Weibull model and estimate the following model

$$r(t) = b\,a^b\,t^{b-1}, \quad a = \exp\left(A\alpha\right), \quad b = \exp\left(\beta_0\right)$$

The TDA command file for this model, *ehg6.cf*, is shown in Box 7.3.3. This command file differs from the command file for the Gompertz model in Box 7.2.3 only by the model selection number, which is now 7, and the command to include covariates, which are now included in the A-term instead of the B-term.

Part of the estimation results are presented in Box 7.3.4. As can be seen in that box, the value of the log likelihood function for this model is -2462.76. Thus, if this model is compared with the Weibull model without covariates, one gets a significant likelihood ratio statistic of 84.28 with six degrees of freedom.

Box 7.3.3   Part of command file *ehg6.cf* (Weibull model with covariates)

```
   ... (first part identical to first part of Box 7.2.1.)

   # define additional variables to include into the model
   v20 (COHO2) =   ge(v7,468) . le(v7,504);    cohort 2
   v21 (COHO3) =   ge(v7,588) . le(v7,624);    cohort 3
   v22 (LFX)   =   v3 - v8;                     labor force experience
   v23 (PNOJ)  =   v2 - 1;                      previous number of jobs

   # command to request estimation of a Weibull model
   rate = 7;      model selection

   # command to include covariates into A-term of model, for transition
   # from origin state 0 to destination state 1.
   xa (0,1)    =   v12,v20,v21,v22,v23,v10;

   # command to print residuals to output file ehg6.res
   pres = ehg6.res;
```

Box 7.3.4   Part of TDA's standard output using *ehg6.cf* (Box 7.3.3)

```
   Model: Weibull

   Maximum likelihood estimation
   Maximum of log likelihood: -2462.76

   Idx SN Org Des MT Var  Label   Coeff    Error     T-Stat  Signif
   ------------------------------------------------------------------
     1  1   0   1  A --   Const  -4.4063   0.3060  -14.3996  1.0000
     2  1   0   1  A V12  EDU     0.0779   0.0270    2.8848  0.9961
     3  1   0   1  A V20  COHO2   0.6062   0.1242    4.8821  1.0000
     4  1   0   1  A V21  COHO3   0.5777   0.1303    4.4318  1.0000
     5  1   0   1  A V22  LFX    -0.0036   0.0010   -3.5040  0.9995
     6  1   0   1  A V23  PNOJ    0.0637   0.0484    1.3184  0.8126
     7  1   0   1  A V10  PRES   -0.0292   0.0060   -4.8396  1.0000
     8  1   0   1  B --   Const  -0.0903   0.0364   -2.4830  0.9870
```

So the covariates seem to have an important impact on job duration. This is confirmed by looking at the estimated standard errors. In particular, the estimate of b, $\hat{b} = \exp(-0.0903) = 0.9137$, is still significant, positive, and less than 1. Again, the included time-constant variables cannot explain the declining transition rate.

Models with Covariates in the A- and B-Terms

Finally, we link the b parameter of the Weibull model with a vector of covariates to see the effects of covariates on the time-dependence. Thus, this Weibull

Box 7.3.5 Part of command file *ehg7.cf* (Weibull model with covariates)

```
    ... (first part identical to first part of Box 7.2.1)

    # define additional variables to include into the model
    v20 (COHO2) =   ge(v7,468) . le(v7,504);    cohort 2
    v21 (COHO3) =   ge(v7,588) . le(v7,624);    cohort 3
    v22 (LFX)   =   v3 - v8;                     labor force experience
    v23 (PNOJ)  =   v2 - 1;                      previous number of jobs

    # command to request estimation of a Weibull model
    rate = 7;    model selection

    # commands to include covariates into A- and B-term of model,
    # for transition from origin state 0 to destination state 1.

    xa (0,1)   =   v12,v20,v21,v22,v23,v10;
    xb (0,1)   =   v12,v20,v21,v22,v23,v10;

    # command to print residuals to output file ehg7.res
    pres = ehg7.res;
```

Box 7.3.6 Part of TDA's standard output using *ehg7.cf* (Box 7.3.5)

```
    Model: Weibull

    Maximum likelihood estimation
    Maximum of log likelihood: -2459.6
    Norm of final gradient vector: 7.9e-09
    Last absolute change of function value: 2.2e-14
    Last relative change in parameters: 3.3e-06

    Idx SN Org Des MT Var  Label   Coeff    Error    T-Stat  Signif
    ----------------------------------------------------------------
      1  1   0   1  A --   Const  -4.4951   0.3073  -14.6293  1.0000
      2  1   0   1  A V12  EDU     0.0858   0.0274    3.1351  0.9983
      3  1   0   1  A V20  COHO2   0.5985   0.1285    4.6586  1.0000
      4  1   0   1  A V21  COHO3   0.5582   0.1297    4.3040  1.0000
      5  1   0   1  A V22  LFX    -0.0032   0.0011   -2.9481  0.9968
      6  1   0   1  A V23  PNOJ    0.0571   0.0496    1.1512  0.7503
      7  1   0   1  A V10  PRES   -0.0290   0.0061   -4.7176  1.0000
      8  1   0   1  B --   Const  -0.1613   0.2224   -0.7252  0.5317
      9  1   0   1  B V12  EDU    -0.0027   0.0188   -0.1441  0.1146
     10  1   0   1  B V20  COHO2   0.0835   0.0856    0.9751  0.6705
     11  1   0   1  B V21  COHO3   0.2017   0.0914    2.2051  0.9726
     12  1   0   1  B V22  LFX     0.0010   0.0007    1.4443  0.8513
     13  1   0   1  B V23  PNOJ   -0.0385   0.0363   -1.0614  0.7115
     14  1   0   1  B V10  PRES    0.0005   0.0041    0.1249  0.0994
```

model is an equivalent to the Gompertz model with covariates in its *B*- and *C*-terms. The model specification now becomes

$$r(t) = b\,a^b\,t^{b-1}, \quad a = \exp(A\alpha), \quad b = \exp(B\beta)$$

As shown in Box 7.3.5, this model can be estimated by simply adding a command to include covariates into the B-term of the model. Using the modified command file (*ehg7.cf*), part of the estimation results is shown in Box 7.3.6.

The log likelihood value is -2459.6 and is only slightly better than that for the model with a single constant in the B-term (Box 7.3.4). The likelihood ratio test statistic to compare the two models is 5.72 with six degrees of freedom and does not show a significant improvement in model fit. If we look at the estimated coefficients of the B-term, then only the effect of the cohort dummy variable COHO3 is significant. Its effect has an increasing relevance over the job duration. Again, the result that so few parameters are not significant might also be a consequence of the small number of events in the example data set.

7.4   Log-Logistic Models

The log-logistic model is even more flexible than the Gompertz and Weibull distributions. As Figure 7.4.1 shows, for $b \leq 1$ one obtains a monotonically declining transition rate, and for $b > 1$ the transition rate at first rises monotonically up to a maximum and then falls monotonically. Thus, this model can be used to test a monotonically declining time-dependence against a non-monotonic pattern. In the literature, the log-logistic model along with the log-normal and the sickle distributions are the most commonly recommended models if the transition rate is somehow bell-shaped.[10] This is often the case in divorce, marriage, or childbirth studies (see Diekmann 1989; Blossfeld 1995).

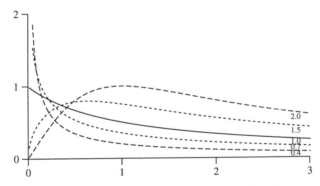

Figure 7.4.1 Log-logistic transition rates ($a = 1$).

This section first describes the standard log-logistic model and an extension. In the single transition case the standard log-logistic model is based on the assumption that the duration of episodes follows a log-logistic distribution.

---

[10] As demonstrated in the application example 2 of section 6.6, another flexible strategy to model bell-shaped transition rates is to use a combination of two time-dependent variables.

The density, survivor, and rate functions for this distribution are

$$f(t) = \frac{b\,a^b\,t^{b-1}}{[1+(at)^b]^2} \qquad a, b > 0$$

$$G(t) = \frac{1}{1+(at)^b}$$

$$r(t) = \frac{b\,a^b\,t^{b-1}}{1+(at)^b}$$

Figure 7.4.1 shows graphs of the rate function for $a = 1$ and different values of b. The time t_{max} when the rate reaches its maximum, r_{max}, is given by

$$t_{max} = \frac{1}{a}(b-1)^{\frac{1}{b}} \qquad r_{max} = a\,(b-1)^{1-\frac{1}{b}}$$

A sometimes useful extension of the standard log-logistic model was proposed by Brüderl (1991b; see also Brüderl and Diekmann 1994). The idea is to include a third parameter to allow for varying levels of the transition rate. The model definition is

$$r(t) = c\,\frac{b\,(a\,t)^{b-1}}{1+(at)^b} \qquad a, b, c > 0$$

The associated density and survivor functions are

$$f(t) = c\,\frac{b\,(a\,t)^{b-1}}{[1+(at)^b]^{\frac{c}{a}+1}}$$

$$G(t) = \frac{1}{[1+(at)^b]^{\frac{c}{a}}}$$

Both versions of the log-logistic transition rate model can be estimated by TDA. The model selection commands are

> rate = 9; to estimate a log-logistic model type I
> rate = 10; to estimate a log-logistic model type II

The *standard* log-logistic model has two parameters, so there are two possibilities to include covariates. TDA uses exponential link functions, so one gets the following model formulation for the transition rate from origin state j to destination state k.

$$r_{jk}(t) = \frac{b_{jk}\,a_{jk}^{b_{jk}}\,t^{b_{jk}-1}}{1+(a_{jk}t)^{b_{jk}}}, \quad a_{jk} = \exp\left\{A^{(jk)}\alpha^{(jk)}\right\}, \quad b_{jk} = \exp\left\{B^{(jk)}\beta^{(jk)}\right\}$$

The *extended* log-logistic model has three parameters, providing three possibilities to include covariates. Using standard exponential link functions, one gets

Box 7.4.1 Part of command file *ehg8.cf* (Log-logistic model without covariates)

```
... (first part equal to first part in Box 7.2.1)

# define additional variables to include into the model
v20 (COHO2) =   ge(v7,468) . le(v7,504);    cohort 2
v21 (COHO3) =   ge(v7,588) . le(v7,624);    cohort 3
v22 (LFX)   =   v3 - v8;                     labor force experience
v23 (PNOJ)  =   v2 - 1;                      previous number of jobs

# command to request estimation of a log-logistic model, type I
rate = 9;         model selection

# commands to request a printout of estimated transition rate
prate = ehg8.prs;  print to output file: ehg8.prs
tab   = 0,300,1 ;  time axis for the table
```

the following model formulation for the transition rate from origin state j to destination state k.

$$r_{jk}(t) = c_{jk} \frac{b_{jk}(a_{jk}t)^{b_{jk}-1}}{1+(a_{jk}t)^{b_{jk}}}$$

$$a_{jk} = \exp\left\{A^{(jk)}\alpha^{(jk)}\right\}, \; b_{jk} = \exp\left\{B^{(jk)}\beta^{(jk)}\right\}, \; c_{jk} = \exp\left\{C^{(jk)}\gamma^{(jk)}\right\}$$

Again, it is assumed that the first component of each of the covariate vectors $A^{(jk)}$, $B^{(jk)}$, and $C^{(jk)}$ is a constant equal to one. The coefficients $\alpha^{(jk)}$, $\beta^{(jk)}$, and $\gamma^{(jk)}$ are the model parameters to be estimated.

Models without Covariates (Single Time-Dependent Rate)

Illustrating the application of the log-logistic distribution, we begin with a model without covariates:

$$r(t) = \frac{b\,a^b\,t^{b-1}}{1+(at)^b}, \; a = \exp(\alpha_0), \; b = \exp(\beta_0)$$

Using the job shift example again, we can examine whether the rate from "being in a job" (origin state = 0) to "having left the job" (destination state = 1) monotonically declines ($b \leq 1$) or is bell-shaped ($b > 1$) over the duration in a job. As discussed in section 5.2, a bell-shaped transition rate is quite plausible in theoretical terms. It could be the result of an interplay of two contradictory causal forces (increases in job-specific investments and decreases in the need to resolve mismatches) that cannot easily be measured, so that the duration in a job has to serve as a proxy variable for them. Empirical evidence for this thesis has already been provided in Figure 5.2.1.

A TDA command file to estimate this standard log-logistic model is given in Box 7.4.1. The model selection command is now *rate=9*. Estimation results are shown in Box 7.4.2. The estimated parameters are $\hat{a} = \exp(-3.8434) = 0.0214$

Box 7.4.2 Part of TDA's standard output using *ehg8.cf* (Box 7.4.1)

```
Model: Log-logistic (I)

Maximum likelihood estimation
Maximum of log likelihood: -2460.49
Norm of final gradient vector: 2.1e-05
Last absolute change of function value: 4.6e-09
Last relative change in parameters: 4.3e-04

Idx SN Org Des MT Var  Label   Coeff    Error    T-Stat  Signif
---------------------------------------------------------------
  1  1   0   1  A --   Const  -3.8434  0.0549  -70.0613  1.0000
  2  1   0   1  B --   Const   0.2918  0.0385    7.5742  1.0000
```

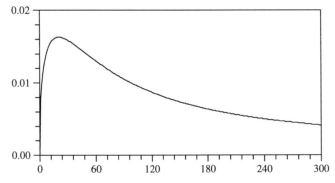

Figure 7.4.2 Log-logistic transition rate estimated with command file
ehg8.cf, Box 7.4.1. The plot was generated with command file *ehg8a.cf*.

and $\hat{b}$ = exp(0.2918) = 1.34. As expected on the basis of the results of
the piecewise constant exponential model in section 5.2, our estimate of b is
greater than 1. Thus, we conclude that increasing job-specific labor force
experience leads to an increasing and then decreasing rate of job shifts. This
result demonstrates that *the Gompertz and the Weibull model are not able to reflect
the increasing rate at the beginning of each job.* They can only catch a monotonic
decline or a monotonic increase over time. Because the job shift rate only
increases for some few months at the beginning of each job and then strongly
decreases, both fit a model with a decreasing rate to the data. Thus, after
"the first job phase," the log-logistic model arrives at the same substantive
interpretation as the Gompertz and the Weibull model. However, the log-
logistic model offers a more appropriate modeling in the first phase, which is
demonstrated in the comparatively high LR test statistics.

Box 7.4.3 Part of command file *ehg9.cf* (Log-logistic model with covariates)

```
... (first part identical to first part of Box 7.2.1)

# define additional variables to include into the model
v20 (COHO2) =    ge(v7,468) . le(v7,504);    cohort 2
v21 (COHO3) =    ge(v7,588) . le(v7,624);    cohort 3
v22 (LFX)   =    v3 - v8;                     labor force experience
v23 (PNOJ)  =    v2 - 1;                      previous number of jobs

# command to request estimation of a log-logistic model, type I
rate = 9;     model selection

# command to include covariates into A-term of model, for transition
# from origin state 0 to destination state 1.
xa (0,1)    =    v12,v20,v21,v22,v23,v10;

# command to print residuals to output file ehg9.res
pres = ehg9.res;
```

The maximum of the log-logistic distribution is reached after a duration of about 21 months:

$$\frac{1}{0.0214} (1.34 - 1)^{1/1.34} = 20.89$$

Thus, there seems to be an adjustment process leading to a rising rate up to this job duration. However, after this point in time, further increases in job-specific investments will more and more outweigh the force of resolving mismatches, so that the job shift rate declines with increasing duration. The estimated rate for this model is plotted in Figure 7.4.2.[11] With the exception of the first part, this plot is very similar to the Gompertz model plot in Figure 7.2.2.

Models with Covariates in the A-Term

Also in the log-logistic distribution are several parameters to which covariates can be linked. We include covariates only in the A-term of the log-logistic model. Thus, we estimate the following model

$$r(t) = \frac{b\, a^b\, t^{b-1}}{1 + (at)^b}, \quad a = \exp{(A\alpha)}, \quad b = \exp{(\beta_0)}$$

A command file to estimate this model is presented in Box 7.4.3. It is very much the same as previously used command files, except the model selection command that had been changed to *rate=9*.

The estimation results are shown in Box 7.4.4. The value of the likelihood ratio statistic for comparison with a model without covariates is 83.18 with six

---

[11] The TDA command file, *ehg8a.cf*, used to generate this plot, is provided on the accompanying disk.

Box 7.4.4   Part of TDA's standard output using *ehg9.cf* (Box 7.4.3)

```
Model: Log-logistic (I)

Maximum likelihood estimation
Maximum of log likelihood: -2418.9
Norm of final gradient vector: 7.2e-04
Last absolute change of function value: 1.9e-09
Last relative change in parameters: 3.0e-04

Idx SN Org Des MT Var  Label     Coeff    Error    T-Stat  Signif
-----------------------------------------------------------------
  1  1   0   1  A --   Const   -3.7785   0.2926  -12.9144  1.0000
  2  1   0   1  A V12  EDU      0.0819   0.0269    3.0485  0.9977
  3  1   0   1  A V20  COHO2    0.5338   0.1249    4.2726  1.0000
  4  1   0   1  A V21  COHO3    0.4005   0.1318    3.0382  0.9976
  5  1   0   1  A V22  LFX     -0.0043   0.0009   -4.6566  1.0000
  6  1   0   1  A V23  PNOJ     0.0970   0.0476    2.0368  0.9583
  7  1   0   1  A V10  PRES    -0.0297   0.0056   -5.2900  1.0000
  8  1   0   1  B --   Const    0.3615   0.0386    9.3736  1.0000
```

degrees of freedom. So the model fit has been highly improved by including the covariates. Again, all single coefficients are significant and are quite similar to the parameter estimates for the exponential model. There is only one difference: The effect of PNOJ, the number of previously held jobs, is now also significant.

Also the estimated shape parameter, $\hat{b} = \exp(0.3615) = 1.44$, is still significant and greater than 1. However, the included time-constant variables in the A-term made the b value even greater and therefore the non-monotonic pattern steeper and more skewed to the left.

It would also be possible to link the B-term with the time-constant covariates, too, but this model provides basically the same result. In the A-term the parameter estimates are about the same and in the B-term the parameters are all not significant. We are therefore not presenting this model here.

7.5   Log-Normal Models

Like the log-logistic model, the log-normal model is a widely used model of time-dependence that implies a non-monotonic relationship between the transition rate and duration: The transition rate initially increases to a maximum and then decreases (see Figure 7.5.1).

This section describes two versions of the log-normal model: a standard log-normal model and a model with an additional shift parameter. The models correspond to the two-parameter and three-parameter log-normal distributions as described, for instance, by Aitchison and Brown (1973). Descriptions of log-normal rate models are given by Lawless (1982, p. 313) and Lancaster (1990, p. 47).

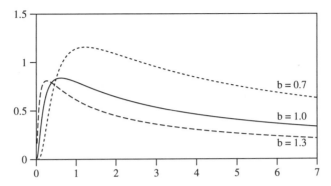

Figure 7.5.1 Log-normal transition rates ($a = 0$).

In the single transition case, the standard (two-parameter) log-normal model is derived by assuming that the logarithm of the episode durations follows a normal distribution or, equivalently, that the durations follow a log-normal distribution with density function

$$f(t) = \frac{1}{bt} \, \phi \left(\frac{\log(t) - a}{b} \right) \qquad b > 0$$

ϕ and Φ are used, respectively, to denote the standard normal density and distribution functions:

$$\phi(t) = \frac{1}{\sqrt{2\pi}} \exp \left(-\frac{t^2}{2} \right) \quad \text{and} \quad \Phi(t) = \int_0^t \phi(\tau) \, d\tau$$

The survivor function is

$$G(t) = 1 - \Phi \left(\frac{\log(t) - a}{b} \right)$$

and the transition rate can be written as

$$r(t) = \frac{1}{bt} \frac{\phi(z_t)}{1 - \Phi(z_t)} \quad \text{with} \quad z_t = \frac{\log(t) - a}{b}$$

Figure 7.5.1 shows graphs of the rate function for $a = 0$ and some different values of b. As can be seen, the graphs are very similar for the log-normal and the log-logistic model, provided that $b > 1$ in the latter case.

A simple, sometimes useful extension of the standard log-normal model is derived by adding a shift parameter $c > 0$. The assumption then is that it is not the episode duration T, but $T - c$, that follows a log-normal distribution. Of course, this assumption implies that no episode ends before c, meaning that c can be thought of as a basic waiting time until the risk of leaving the origin state becomes positive.

The resulting model formulation is very similar to the standard log-normal model. The density, survivor, and rate functions have the same expressions as given earlier for the standard case, only $t - c$ must be substituted for t. The result is a simple shift of the functions to the right by an amount of c.

The standard log-normal model has two parameters, so there are two possibilities to include covariates. Following Lawless (1982, p. 313), TDA uses a linear link function for a, but additionally provides the possibility to link covariates to the dispersion parameter, b, via an exponential link function. So one gets the following model formulation for the transition rate from origin state j to destination state k:

$$r_{jk}(t) = \frac{1}{b_{jk}\,t}\,\frac{\phi\left(z_t^{(jk)}\right)}{1 - \Phi\left(z_t^{(jk)}\right)}$$

$$z_t^{(jk)} = \frac{\log(t) - a_{jk}}{b_{jk}}\,, \quad a_{jk} = A^{(jk)}\alpha^{(jk)}\,, \quad b_{jk} = \exp\left(B^{(jk)}\beta^{(jk)}\right)$$

The extended three-parameter model is defined analogously by substituting $t - c_{jk}$ for t, on the right-hand side, and adding the parameterization

$$c_{jk} = \exp\left\{C^{(jk)}\gamma^{(jk)}\right\}$$

In both cases it is assumed that the first component of each of the covariate (row) vectors $A^{(jk)}$, $B^{(jk)}$, and $C^{(jk)}$ in the extended model is a constant equal to one. The associated coefficient vectors $\alpha^{(jk)}$, $\beta^{(jk)}$, and $\gamma^{(jk)}$ are the model parameters to be estimated.

Notice that in the TDA implementation the two versions of the log-normal model have no different model type numbers. Both versions are requested with the command *rate=12*. The two model types are distinguished by the definition of a C-term of the model. If this term is defined, TDA estimates an extended model; otherwise a standard log-normal model is applied. To request estimation of a log-normal model of type II with a single constant in the C-term, one can use the command *xc(j,k)=0*, meaning that only a constant is linked to the C-term of the model.

Models without Covariates (Single Time-Dependent Rate)

To demonstrate the application of the log-normal distribution, we first estimate a model without covariates:

$$r(t) = \frac{1}{b\,t}\,\frac{\phi\,(z_t)}{1 - \Phi\,(z_t)}\,, \quad z_t = \frac{\log(t) - a}{b}\,, \quad a = \alpha_0\,, \quad b = \exp\,(\beta_0)$$

Using the job shift example, we can examine whether the rate from "being in a job" (origin state = 0) to "having left the job" (destination state = 1) is

Box 7.5.1 Part of command file *ehg10.cf* (Log-normal model without covariates)

```
... (first part equal to first part of Box 7.2.1)

# command to request estimation of a log-normal model, type I
rate = 12;       model selection

# commands to request a printout of estimated transition rate
prate = ehg10.prs;   print to output file: ehg10.prs
tab   = 0,300,1;     time axis for the table
```

Box 7.5.2 Part of TDA's standard output using *ehg10.cf* (Box 7.5.1)

```
Model: Log-normal

Maximum likelihood estimation
Maximum of log likelihood: -2456.14
Norm of final gradient vector: 2.9e-09
Last absolute change of function value: 5.6e-13
Last relative change in parameters: 7.0e-06

Idx SN Org Des MT Var  Label    Coeff    Error    T-Stat  Signif
----------------------------------------------------------------
  1  1   0   1 A --   Const    3.8852   0.0548   70.8561  1.0000
  2  1   0   1 B --   Const    0.2436   0.0342    7.1252  1.0000
```

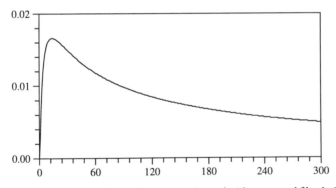

Figure 7.5.2 Log-normal transition rate estimated with command file *ehg10.cf*, Box 7.5.1. The plot was generated with command file *ehg10a.cf*.

bell-shaped over the duration in a job. The substantive interpretation is the same as for the log-logistic model in the previous section.

The TDA command file to estimate this standard log-normal model is shown in Box 7.5.1. Part of the estimation results are shown in Box 7.5.2. The estimated parameters are $\hat{a} = 3.8852$ and $\hat{b} = \exp(0.2436) = 1.28$. The

Box 7.5.3 Part of command file *ehg11.cf* (Log-normal model with covariates)

```
    ... (first part identical to first part of Box 7.2.1)

    # define additional variables to include into the model
    v20 (COHO2) =   ge(v7,468) . le(v7,504);    cohort 2
    v21 (COHO3) =   ge(v7,588) . le(v7,624);    cohort 3
    v22 (LFX)   =   v3 - v8;                     labor force experience
    v23 (PNOJ)  =   v2 - 1;                      previous number of jobs

    # command to request estimation of a log-normal model
    rate = 12;     model selection

    # command to include covariates into A-term of model, for transition
    # from origin state 0 to destination state 1.
    xa (0,1)    =   v12,v20,v21,v22,v23,v10;

    # command to print residuals to output file ehg11.res
    pres = ehg11.res;
```

Box 7.5.4 Part of TDA's standard output using *ehg11.cf* (Box 7.5.3)

```
    Model: Log-normal

    Maximum likelihood estimation
    Maximum of log likelihood: -2415.88
    Norm of final gradient vector: 9.8e-04
    Last absolute change of function value: 7.6e-09
    Last relative change in parameters: 8.4e-04

    Idx SN Org Des MT Var  Label    Coeff    Error    T-Stat  Signif
    ----------------------------------------------------------------
     1  1   0   1  A  --   Const    3.8567   0.2916   13.2280  1.0000
     2  1   0   1  A  V12  EDU     -0.0813   0.0270   -3.0127  0.9974
     3  1   0   1  A  V20  COHO2   -0.5164   0.1247   -4.1422  1.0000
     4  1   0   1  A  V21  COHO3   -0.4514   0.1295   -3.4868  0.9995
     5  1   0   1  A  V22  LFX      0.0039   0.0009    4.4413  1.0000
     6  1   0   1  A  V23  PNOJ    -0.0849   0.0464   -1.8296  0.9327
     7  1   0   1  A  V10  PRES     0.0287   0.0056    5.1330  1.0000
     8  1   0   1  B  --   Const    0.1794   0.0342    5.2437  1.0000
```

estimated rate for this model is plotted in Figure 7.5.2.[12] The shape of this plot is very similar to the shape of the log-logistic model in section 7.4 (see Figure 7.4.2). Thus, the interpretation for this model is basically identical with the interpretation of the log-logistic model. In the next step we again include our set of time-constant covariates.

---

[12] The command file for this plot is included on the accompanying disk as *ehg10a.cf*.

Models with Covariates in the A-term

We include covariates in the A-term of the log-normal model and estimate the following model:

$$r(t) = \frac{1}{b\,t}\,\frac{\phi\,(z_t)}{1 - \Phi\,(z_t)}\,,\ z_t = \frac{\log(t) - a}{b}\,,\ a = A\alpha\,,\ b = \exp\,(\beta_0)$$

The TDA command file for this model is presented in Box 7.5.3. Part of the estimation results are shown in Box 7.5.4. The likelihood ratio test statistics for comparison with a log-normal model without covariates (Box 7.5.2) is 80.52 with six degrees of freedom, again showing a significant improvement of the model fit. In terms of the statistical significance and influence direction of covariates, the result for the log-normal model is basically the same as the result for an exponential model.[13] With regard to the log-logistic model, there is however one difference: The effect of the number of previously held jobs (PNOJ) is not significant.

The estimated coefficient $\hat{b} = \exp(0.1794) = 1.20$ is still significant and greater than 1. In fact, the included time-constant variables in the A-term of the log-normal model make the non-monotonic pattern even steeper and more skewed to the left than was the case for the log-logistic model

Again, it would be possible in the next step to also link the B-term with the time-constant covariates, but this model does not provide a different result. In the A-term the parameter estimates stay about the same, and in the B-term all of the parameters are not significant. We therefore do not present this model here.

7.6   Sickle Models

Another model that is appropriate for a non-monotonic, bell-shaped transition rate is the *sickle model* proposed by Diekmann and Mitter (1983, 1984). The implied distribution for waiting times is defective, meaning that there is a certain proportion of individuals who will never experience an event.[14] For example, in marriage and divorce studies there is always a certain proportion of people who never marry or are never divorced (these are also often called "stayers"; see Blumen, Kogan, and McCarthy 1955).

---

[13] Note however that when we use the TDA parameterization, the signs of the estimated parameters must be multiplied by -1 to get coefficients comparable to the other models estimated in this book.

[14] This is sometimes seen as an advantage of the sickle model. One should however not forget that a truncated version of a transition rate model with an implied defective distribution can always be constructed. With right censored data, the proportion of individuals who will stay in the origin state "forever" (until death) cannot be identified, regardless of whether the distribution used for model estimation is defective or not.

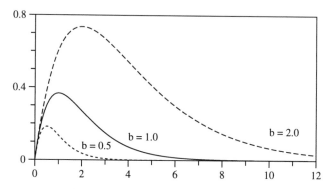

Figure 7.6.1 Sickle transition rates ($a = 1$).

This section describes the sickle model that is formulated for the single transition case first. It starts with the assumption of a transition rate given by the expression

$$r(t) = a\,t\,\exp\left\{-\frac{t}{b}\right\} \qquad a, b > 0$$

The corresponding survivor and density functions are

$$f(t) = \exp\left\{-a\,b\,[\,b - (t+b)\exp(-\frac{t}{b})]\right\}\,a\,t\,\exp\left\{-\frac{t}{b}\right\}$$

$$G(t) = \exp\left\{-a\,b\,[\,b - (t+b)\exp(-\frac{t}{b})]\right\}$$

As is easily seen, this distribution is defective. The survivor function does not tend to zero if $t \to \infty$; instead one finds that

$$\lim_{t \to \infty} G(t) = \exp(-a\,b^2)$$

Figure 7.6.1 shows graphs of the rate function for $a = 1$ and some values of b. It looks like a sickle, after which the model has been named.

The sickle model has two parameters, so there are two possibilities of including covariates. Because both of the parameters must be positive, TDA uses standard exponential link functions. One then gets the following model formulation for the transition rate from origin state j to destination state k:

$$r_{jk}(t) = a_{jk}\,t\,\exp\left\{-\frac{t}{b_{jk}}\right\}$$

$$a_{jk} = \exp\left(A^{(jk)}\alpha^{(jk)}\right), \quad b_{jk} = \exp\left(B^{(jk)}\beta^{(jk)}\right)$$

It is assumed that the first component of each of the covariate (row) vectors $A^{(jk)}$ and $B^{(jk)}$ is a constant equal to one. The associated coefficient vectors

Box 7.6.1 Part of command file *ehg12.cf* (Sickle model without covariates)

```
... (first part equal to first part in Box 7.2.1)

# command to request estimation of a Sickle model
rate = 8;        model selection

# commands to request a printout of estimated transition rate
prate = ehg12.prs;   print to output file: ehg12.prs
tab   = 0,300,1 ;   time axis for the table
```

Box 7.6.2 Part of TDA's standard output using *ehg12.cf* (Box 7.6.1)

```
Model: Sickle

Maximum likelihood estimation
Maximum of log likelihood: -2486.37
Norm of final gradient vector: 2.4e-07
Last absolute change of function value: 4.9e-11
Last relative change in parameters: 6.3e-06

Idx SN Org Des MT Var  Label   Coeff   Error    T-Stat  Signif
--------------------------------------------------------------
  1  1   0   1    A --  Const  -6.5843  0.0775  -84.9960  1.0000
  2  1   0   1    B --  Const   3.6467  0.0481   75.8802  1.0000
```

$\alpha^{(jk)}$ and $\beta^{(jk)}$ are the model parameters to be estimated. The TDA command to request estimation of a sickle model is *rate=8*.

Models without Covariates (Single Time-Dependent Rate)

To illustrate the application of the sickle distribution, we begin with a model without covariates:

$$r(t) = a\,t\,\exp\left\{-\frac{t}{b}\right\}\ ,\ a = \exp(\alpha_0)\ ,\ b = \exp(\beta_0)$$

Again, we use the job shift example and examine how large the shape parameter b is for the transition rate from "being in a job" (origin state = 0) to "having left the job" (destination state = 1).

A command file for model estimation, *ehg12.cf*, is shown in Box 7.6.1. Part of the estimation results is shown in Box 7.6.2. The estimated parameters of the sickle distribution are

$$\hat{a} = \exp(\hat{\alpha}_0) = \exp(-6.5843) = 0.0014\,,\ \text{and}$$
$$\hat{b} = \exp(\hat{\beta}_0) = \exp(3.6467) = 38.35$$

respectively. Both effects are significant. Thus, we conclude that increasing job-specific labor force experience leads to an increasing and then decreasing job shift rate.

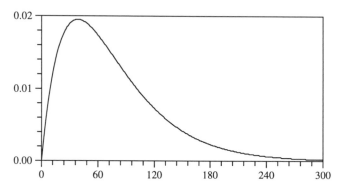

Figure 7.6.2 Sickle transition rate estimated with command file *ehg12.cf*, Box 7.5.1. The plot was generated with command file *ehg12a.cf*.

The estimated rate for the sickle model is plotted in Figure 7.6.2.[15] It is characteristic that the sickle rate approaches zero. Thus, there will be no further job change for long durations. Of course, before drawing further conclusions, we should include our standard covariates.

Models with Covariates in the A-Term

The sickle model offers two parameters to which covariates might be linked. In our example, we include covariates only in the A-term. Thus, we estimate the following model:

$$r(t) = a\, t\, \exp\left\{-\frac{t}{b}\right\} \ , \quad a = \exp(A\alpha) \ , \quad b = \exp(\beta_0)$$

The TDA command file for this sickle model is presented in Box 7.6.3, and part of the estimation results are shown in Box 7.6.4. Comparing the estimation results with a model without covariates gives a likelihood ratio test statistic of 84.86 with six degrees of freedom, showing a significant improvement in the model fit. The estimated coefficient $\hat{b} = \exp(3.6897) = 40.03$ is still highly significant and even greater than in Box 7.6.2.

Conclusion. As shown in the present chapter, TDA can be used to estimate a variety of transition rate models with a time-dependent transition rate. It is easy to select different model types and to specify different ways of including covariates. However, we have already remarked that using parametric transition rate models with only limited capabilities to adapt to a given set of data can lead to misleading results; for instance when using a Weibull model whose transition

---

[15] The command file, *ehg12a.cf*, which has been used to generate the plot, is supplied on the accompanying disk.

Box 7.6.3 Part of command file *ehg13.cf* (Sickle model with covariates)

```
    ... (first part identical to first part of Box 7.2.1)

    # define additional variables to include into the model
    v20 (COHO2) =   ge(v7,468) . le(v7,504);     cohort 2
    v21 (COHO3) =   ge(v7,588) . le(v7,624);     cohort 3
    v22 (LFX)   =   v3 - v8;                      labor force experience
    v23 (PNOJ)  =   v2 - 1;                       previous number of jobs

    # command to request estimation of a Sickle model
    rate = 8;     model selection

    # command to include covariates into A-term of model, for transition
    # from origin state 0 to destination state 1.
    xa (0,1)    =   v12,v20,v21,v22,v23,v10;

    # command to print residuals to output file ehg13.res
    pres = ehg13.res;
```

Box 7.6.4 Part of TDA's standard output using *ehg13.cf* (Box 7.6.3)

```
    Model: Sickle

    Maximum likelihood estimation
    Maximum of log likelihood: -2443.94
    Norm of final gradient vector: 1.7e-06
    Last absolute change of function value: 1.3e-11
    Last relative change in parameters: 6.9e-05
    Numerical problems: 1,4

    Idx SN Org Des MT Var  Label    Coeff    Error     T-Stat  Signif
    ----------------------------------------------------------------
      1  1   0   1  A --   Const   -6.4245   0.2831  -22.6909  1.0000
      2  1   0   1  A V12  EDU      0.0767   0.0250    3.0711  0.9979
      3  1   0   1  A V20  COHO2    0.4259   0.1149    3.7073  0.9998
      4  1   0   1  A V21  COHO3    0.2785   0.1206    2.3095  0.9791
      5  1   0   1  A V22  LFX     -0.0043   0.0009   -4.5725  1.0000
      6  1   0   1  A V23  PNOJ     0.0782   0.0438    1.7867  0.9260
      7  1   0   1  A V10  PRES    -0.0288   0.0055   -5.1914  1.0000
      8  1   0   1  B --   Const    3.6897   0.0502   73.4793  1.0000
```

rate is, in fact, bell-shaped. One provision against this danger is to estimate
a variety of different models and see whether the estimation results—for the
most interesting covariates—are robust. We come back to this topic at the end
of chapter 10.

Chapter 8
Methods to Check Parametric Assumptions

As discussed in the previous chapter, the standard strategy in using parametric models of time-dependence is to consider measures of time as proxies for time-varying causal factors that are difficult to observe directly. However, available theory in the social sciences normally provides little or no guidance for choosing one parametric model over another. For example, as shown in the previous chapter, whether job-specific labor force experience changes linearly (Gompertz model) or log-linearly (Weibull model) over time can hardly be decided on a theoretical basis. Thus, it is important to empirically check the adequacy of models upon which inferences are based. One way of doing this was demonstrated in the previous chapter by using likelihood ratio tests as a tool for comparing the improvement in the goodness-of-fit of alternative models. This method is, however, limited to nested models.

In this chapter, we consider two different approaches to checking the suitability of parametric models. First, we survey an informal method for evaluating the fit of parametric models by comparing *transformations of nonparametric estimates of survivor functions* with the predictions from parametric models. And second, we demonstrate how *pseudoresiduals*, also often called *generalized residuals*, can be calculated and used in evaluating distributional assumptions. Although both approaches might give some hints in empirical applications, they still only have the character of *heuristic tools*, as we demonstrate in this chapter.

8.1 Simple Graphical Methods

Several authors have proposed simple graphical methods for identifying systematic departures of parametric models from the data.[1] The basic idea is to produce plots that should be roughly linear, if the assumed family of models is appropriate because departures from linearity can be readily recognized by eye. Most of these approaches begin with a nonparametric estimation of a survivor function using the life table method or, preferably, the product limit (Kaplan-Meier) estimator. Then, given a parametric assumption about the distribution of waiting times, one tries to find a suitable transformation of the survivor function so that the result becomes a linear function ($y = a + bx$) that

---

[1] See, among others, Lawless (1982), Wu (1989, 1990), and Wu and Tuma (1990).

can be plotted for visual inspection. In addition, this approach often provides the first estimates for the parameters of the assumed distribution, which can then be used as starting values for fitting the model via maximum likelihood.[2]

We demonstrate this method by testing the fit of four parametric distributions: the exponential, the Weibull, the log-logistic, and the log-normal model.

Exponential model. This model was discussed in chapter 4. The survivor function for the basic exponential distribution is

$$G(t) = \exp(-rt)$$

Taking the logarithm, we get a straight line

$$\log(G(t)) = -r\,t$$

Thus, if the exponential model holds, a plot of $\log(\hat{G}(t))$ versus t, using the estimated survivor function $\hat{G}(t)$, should provide a roughly linear graph passing through the origin. The negative slope of this line is an estimate of the transition rate r.

Weibull model. This model was discussed in section 7.3. The survivor function of the Weibull model is

$$G(t) = \exp\left(-(at)^b\right)$$

Taking the logarithm, we get

$$\log(G(t)) = -(at)^b$$

and taking the logarithm again results in the linear function

$$\log\left(\log(-G(t))\right) = b\log(a) + b\log(t)$$

Thus, if the Weibull model holds, a plot of $\log(\log(-\hat{G}(t)))$ versus $\log(t)$ should be approximately linear. The slope of this line is an estimate of b.

Log-logistic model. This model was discussed in section 7.4. The survivor function for the basic (type I) version of the log-logistic model is

$$G(t) = \frac{1}{1 + (at)^b}$$

This can be transformed in the following way. First, we get

$$1 - G(t) = \frac{(at)^b}{1 + (at)^b}$$

---

[2] Blossfeld, Hamerle, and Mayer (1989) suggested complementing the visual inspection of transformed survivor curves by fitting an ordinary least squares regression line. However, using OLS can also only be considered a heuristic approach in this case because the data are heteroscedastic and the residuals are highly correlated.

Box 8.1.1 Command file *ehh1.cf* (graphical check of exponential distribution)

```
dfile = ehc5.ple;                  data file

# select suitable range of time and survivor function
dsel = gt(c3,0) . gt(c7,0) . lt(c7,1);

v1(Time)     = c3;                 time axis
v2(Survivor) = c7;                 survivor function
v3(Log-Surv) = log(v2);            log of survivor function

lsreg = 1;                         request OLS regression
y = v3;
x = v1;

postscript = ehh1.ps;              PostScript output file

plabel = 'Graphical Test (Exponential)';

pxlen = 80;                        physical width (in mm)
pylen = 40;                        physical height (in mm)
pxa(60,5) = 0,300;                 user coordinates on X axis
pya(1,10) = -3,0;                  user coordinates on Y axis

plot = v1,v3;                      plot v1 vs v3
plotp = 0, -0.3527, 300, -2.6027; plot regression line
```

and, dividing by $G(t)$, we get

$$\frac{1 - G(t)}{G(t)} = (at)^b$$

Then, taking logarithms results in the linear function

$$\log\left(\frac{1 - G(t)}{G(t)}\right) = b\log(a) + b\log(t)$$

Therefore, if the log-logistic model holds, a plot of $\log((1 - \hat{G}(t))/\hat{G}(t))$ versus $\log(t)$ should be approximately linear. The slope of this line is an estimate of b.

Log-normal model. This model was discussed in section 7.5. The survivor function for the basic log-normal model is

$$G(t) = 1 - \Phi\left(\frac{\log(t) - a}{b}\right)$$

with Φ used to denote the standard normal distribution function. Using Φ^{-1} to denote the inverse of this function, one gets the linear function

$$\Phi^{-1}(1 - G(t)) = -\frac{a}{b} + \frac{1}{b}\log(t)$$

Box 8.1.2 Part of TDA's standard output using command file *ehh1.cf* (Box 8.1.1)

```
Least squares regression (intercept included)

Sum of squared residuals          5.3213
Variance of residuals             0.0416
Squared multiple correlation      0.8809
R-Square adjusted                 0.8800

Idx  Term  Label        Coeff     Error     t-Stat   Signif
-----------------------------------------------------------
  1   I    Intercept   -0.3527   0.0280   -12.6000   1.0000
  2   X1   V1          -0.0075   0.0002   -30.7721   1.0000
```

Therefore, if the log-normal model holds, a plot of $\Phi^{-1}(1 - \hat{G}(t))$ versus $\log(t)$ should be approximately linear.

In order to demonstrate the application of these graphical tests with TDA, we use our standard example data (*rrdat.1*). How to get a product limit estimation of the survivor function has already been shown in command file *ehc5.cf* (Box 3.2.1). The output file containing the estimated survivor function is *ehc5.ple*, part of which is shown in Box 3.2.2.

We only describe the procedure for the exponential model because the technical steps are the same for all four distributions. The respective TDA command files to plot the graphs and to compute OLS regressions are: *ehh1.cf* for the exponential model, *ehh2.cf* for the Weibull model, *ehh3.cf* for the log-logistic model, and *ehh4.cf* for the log-normal model.

Given an exponential model, the graphical test requires that we take the logarithm of the estimated survivor function, $\log(\hat{G}(t))$, and then plot this function against t. This is achieved with command file *ehh1.cf* shown in Box 8.1.1. The file *ehc5.ple*, containing the estimated survivor function, is used as an input data file. In addition to the plot commands, the command file contains the commands

$$lsreg = 1;$$
$$y = v3;$$
$$x = v1;$$

to perform an OLS regression of variable *V3* on *V1*. The results, shown in Box 8.1.2, are used to specify the command to plot the regression line.

The resulting plot is shown in Figure 8.1.1. As can be seen in this figure, the exponential model only appears to provide a moderate fit of the data because the transformed survivor curve exhibits sharp departures from a straight line over the whole duration. At the beginning it is above the estimated regression line, for durations between 30 and 200 months it drops below the estimated regression line, and at the end—for large durations—it exceeds the regression line again. The accuracy of the fit can be evaluated with the R^2 measure,

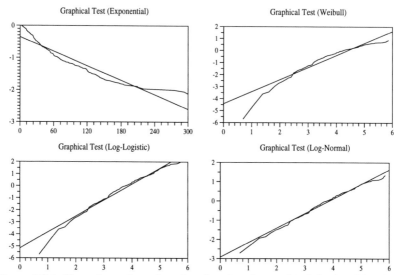

Figure 8.1.1 Plots of transformed survivor functions for graphical checks of distributional assumptions. The plots have been generated with the command files *ehh1.cf*, *ehh2.cf*, *ehh3.cf*, and *ehh4.cf*.

provided by the regression. For the exponential model we get $R^2 = 0.88$ (see Box 8.1.2).

Box 8.1.3 shows the regression results for all four models. These results provide some kind of nonparametric estimation of the parameters of the various distributions. In the case of the exponential model, the negative slope of the regression line is an estimate of the rate. Thus, our estimate is $\hat{r} = 0.0075$. Notice that this estimate is much smaller than the maximum likelihood estimate in Box 4.1.2 (i.e. $\hat{r} = \exp(-4.4891) = 0.0112$).

The Weibull model seems to offer a better fit than the exponential, although the departure at the beginning of the duration for this distribution is still large (see Figure 8.1.1). The improvement of the fit is reflected in a higher $R^2 = 0.92$ in Box 8.1.3. In the case of the Weibull model, the slope of the regression line can be considered as an estimate of b, and the intercept on the x axis is an estimate of $b \log(a)$. Thus, the nonparametric estimates for the Weibull parameters are $\hat{b} = 1.008$ and $\hat{a} = 0.0124$. The maximum likelihood estimates were $\hat{b} = 0.8627$ and $\hat{a} = 0.0115$ (see section 7.3).

Somewhat better than for the Weibull model is the fit for the log-logistic model (see Figure 8.1.1). This is again reflected in a higher $R^2 = 0.98$ in Box 8.1.3. For the log-logistic model the slope of the regression line is an estimate of $\hat{b} = 1.33$, and the intercept on the x axis is an estimate of $b \log(a)$. Thus, we

Box 8.1.3 Regression results for graphical checks

```
Least squares regression: exponential model

Squared multiple correlation      0.8809
R-Square adjusted                 0.8800

Idx  Term  Label        Coeff     Error    t-Stat  Signif
----------------------------------------------------------
 1   I     Intercept   -0.3527   0.0280  -12.6000  1.0000
 2   X1    V1          -0.0075   0.0002  -30.7721  1.0000

Least squares regression: Weibull model

Squared multiple correlation      0.9159
R-Square adjusted                 0.9153

Idx  Term  Label        Coeff     Error    t-Stat  Signif
----------------------------------------------------------
 1   I     Intercept   -4.4238   0.1135  -38.9803  1.0000
 2   X1    V3           1.0080   0.0270   37.3474  1.0000

Least squares regression: log-logistic model

Squared multiple correlation      0.9761
R-Square adjusted                 0.9760

Idx  Term  Label        Coeff     Error    t-Stat  Signif
----------------------------------------------------------
 1   I     Intercept   -5.1604   0.0771  -66.9337  1.0000
 2   X1    V3           1.3268   0.0183   72.3628  1.0000

Least squares regression: log-normal model

Squared multiple correlation      0.9887
R-Square adjusted                 0.9886

Idx  Term  Label        Coeff     Error    t-Stat  Signif
----------------------------------------------------------
 1   I     Intercept   -2.9220   0.0301  -97.2089  1.0000
 2   X1    V3           0.7578   0.0071  105.9948  1.0000
```

get $\hat{a} = 0.020$ The respective maximum likelihood estimates were $\hat{a} = 0.021$ and $\hat{b} = 1.34$, quite similar in this case.

Finally, the log-normal model seems to yield the best fit among the four distributions (see Figure 8.1.1). This is also reflected in the highest $R^2 = 0.99$ (Box 8.1.3). The OLS estimates of the parameters are $\hat{a} = 3.86$ and $\hat{b} = 1.32$. The respective maximum likelihood estimates were $\hat{a} = 3.88$ and $\hat{b} = 1.28$ (see section 7.5).

What do we conclude based on the visual inspection of the transformed sur-

vivor functions in Figure 8.1.1 and the results of the OLS regressions in Box
8.1.3? Figure 8.1.1 suggests that all four models exhibit some departures from
the data. However, the log-normal model seems to provide the best fit. Both
the Weibull and the log-logistic model fit the data less well and the poorest
performance was provided by the exponential model. Thus, based on this
comparison the decision seems to be clear. The log-normal model should be
recommended. However, this should only be done if there is also a convincing
substantive interpretation of this type of parametric model because the time-
dependency is a proxy for the effect of an unmeasured causal factor. In our job
mobility example the interpretation is straightforward, as discussed in the previous chapter. There is, however, a more serious problem with this method. It
is that these checks have not explicitly controlled for sources of heterogeneity.
As discussed in chapter 3, interpretations of survivor functions (and their transformations) are only sensible if a homogeneous population can be assumed.
But we have already learned that including a set of covariates can significantly
improve the model fit. Also, as is shown in chapter 10, neglected heterogeneity
between observation units and/or successive episodes can have an important
impact on the estimated shape of the transition rate. One should therefore be
extremely cautious when drawing conclusions from statistical checks that do
not explicitly account for heterogeneity (covariates). We therefore conclude
that graphical checks of parametric assumptions should only be considered as
heuristic tools, which are useful, at best, in supporting first steps in model
selection.

8.2   Pseudoresiduals

Additional information for model selection can be gained by using *pseudoresiduals*, also called *generalized residuals*. In OLS regression analysis, the traditional
and perhaps best way to evaluate possible violations of the underlying model assumptions is through a direct examination of residuals. Residuals are deviations
of the *observed* values of the dependent variable from the values *estimated* under
the assumptions of a specific model. In transition rate models the "dependent
variable" is the transition rate, which is, however, *not observable*. Thus, it is not
possible to compute residuals by comparing observed vs. predicted transition
rates for each unit or episode.

   Nonetheless, there is a similar approach that can be used with transition
rate models. This approach is based on *pseudoresiduals* (generalized residuals)
suggested by Cox and Snell (1968). For applying this method to transition rate
models, see, for instance, Blossfeld, Hamerle, and Mayer (1989, p. 82), and
Lancaster (1985).

   The definition is as follows. Let $\hat{r}(t; x)$ denote the estimated rate, depending
on time t and on a vector of covariates, x. The estimation is based on a random
sample of individuals $i = 1, \ldots, N$, with duration t_i and covariate vectors x_i.

Box 8.2.1 Variables in TDA's output files for pseudoresiduals

```
C1   Case (episode) number.
C2   Origin state of the episode.
C3   Destination state of the episode.
C4   Starting time of the episode.
C5   Ending time of the episode.
C6   Estimated transition rate, evaluated at the ending time of
     the episode. (Note: The calculation is independent of whether
     the episode is right censored or not. The information about
     origin and destination states can be used to select censored
     and uncensored cases.)
C7   Estimated survivor function, evaluated at the ending time
     of the episode.
C8   Residual.
C9   Case weight.
```

Pseudoresiduals are then defined as cumulative transition rates, evaluated for the given sample observations, that is,

$$\hat{e}_i = \int_0^{t_i} \hat{r}(\tau; x_i) \, d\tau \qquad i = 1, \ldots, N$$

The reasoning behind this definition is that, if the model is appropriate, and if there were no censored observations, the set of residuals should approximately behave like a sample from a standard exponential distribution. If some of the observations are censored, the residuals may be regarded as a censored sample from a standard exponential distribution. In any case, one can calculate a product-limit estimate of the survivor function of the residuals, say $G_{\hat{e}}(e)$, and a plot of $-\log(G_{\hat{e}}(\hat{e}_i))$ versus $\hat{e}_i$ can be used to check whether the residuals actually follow a standard exponential distribution.

For most continuous time transition rate models, which can be estimated by TDA, a table of residuals can be requested with the command

       pres = name_of_an_output_file

Based on the estimated model, the residuals are calculated and written into the specified output file. The output file conforms to TDA's definition of free-format data files and can, therefore, be used as an input data file in subsequent runs of the program. The number of data records in the output file is equal to the number of cases (episodes) used to estimate the model. The variables (columns) in the output file are shown in Box 8.2.1.

One should note that the calculations in TDA are conditional on given starting times, which may be greater than zero. Pseudoresiduals are calculated according to

$$\hat{e}_i = \int_{s_i}^{t_i} \hat{r}(\tau; x_i) \, d\tau \qquad i = 1, \ldots, N$$

with s_i and t_i denoting the starting and ending times of the episode, respectively.

Box 8.2.2 Calculation of pseudoresiduals in TDA

Exponential model

$$\hat{r}(t_i) = a_i \qquad a_i = \exp(A_i\alpha)$$
$$\hat{G}(t_i \mid s_i) = \exp\{-(t_i - s_i)\,a_i\}$$

Piecewise constant exponential model (proportional effects)

$$\hat{r}(t_i) = \exp\{\bar{\alpha}_l + A_i\alpha\} \quad \text{if} \quad t_i \in I_l$$
$$\hat{G}(t_i \mid s_i) = \exp\left\{-\sum_{l=1}^{m} \Delta[s_i, t_i, l] \,\exp(\bar{\alpha}_l + A_i\alpha)\right\}$$

Piecewise constant exponential model (period-specific effects)

$$\hat{r}(t_i) = \exp\{\bar{\alpha}_l + A_i\alpha_l\} \quad \text{if} \quad t_i \in I_l$$
$$\hat{G}(t_i \mid s_i) = \exp\left\{-\sum_{l=1}^{m} \Delta[s_i, t_i, l] \,\exp(\bar{\alpha}_l + A_i\alpha_l)\right\}$$

Gompertz-Makeham model

$$\hat{r}(t_i) = a_i + b_i \exp(c_i\, t_i) \qquad a_i = \exp(A_i\alpha),\ b_i = \exp(B_i\beta),\ c_i = C_i\gamma$$
$$\hat{G}(t_i \mid s_i) = \exp\left\{a_i\,(s_i - t_i) + \frac{b_i}{c_i}\left[\exp(c_i s_i) - \exp(c_i t_i)\right]\right\}$$

Weibull model

$$\hat{r}(t_i) = b_i\, a_i^{b_i}\, t_i^{b_i - 1} \qquad a_i = \exp(A_i\alpha),\ b_i = \exp(B_i\beta)$$
$$\hat{G}(t_i \mid s_i) = \exp\left\{(a_i s_i)^{b_i} - (a_i t_i)^{b_i}\right\}$$

Sickle model

$$\hat{r}(t_i) = a_i\, t_i\, \exp\left\{-\frac{t_i}{b_i}\right\} \qquad a_i = \exp(A_i\alpha),\ b_i = \exp(B_i\beta)$$
$$\hat{G}(t_i \mid s_i) = \exp\left\{a_i b_i \left[(t_i + b_i)\exp\left(-\frac{t_i}{b_i}\right) - (s_i + b_i)\exp\left(-\frac{s_i}{b_i}\right)\right]\right\}$$

Also the survivor functions printed into the output file are conditional on starting times, meaning that the program calculates and prints

$$\hat{G}(t_i \mid s_i; x_i) = \exp\left\{-\int_{s_i}^{t_i} \hat{r}(\tau; x_i)\, d\tau\right\} \qquad i = 1, \ldots, N$$

Box 8.2.2 (continued)   Calculation of pseudoresiduals in TDA

Log-logistic model (type I)

$$\hat{r}(t_i) = \frac{b_i \, a_i^{b_i} \, t_i^{b_i-1}}{1 + (a_i t_i)^{b_i}} \qquad a_i = \exp(A_i\alpha), \; b_i = \exp(B_i\beta)$$

$$\hat{G}(t_i \mid s_i) = \frac{1 + (a_i s_i)^{b_i}}{1 + (a_i t_i)^{b_i}}$$

Log-normal model

$$\hat{r}(t_i) = \frac{1}{b_i \, t_i} \frac{\phi\left(z_{t_i}\right)}{1 - \Phi\left(z_{t_i}\right)} \qquad z_t = \frac{\log(t) - a_i}{b_i}$$

$$\hat{G}(t_i \mid s_i) = \frac{1 - \Phi\left(z_{t_i}\right)}{1 - \Phi\left(z_{s_i}\right)} \qquad a_i = A_i\alpha, \; b_i = \exp(B_i\beta)$$

Therefore, if the starting times are not zero, in particular if the *method of episode splitting* is applied, the *output file will not already contain proper information about residuals.*

Box 8.2.2 shows how TDA calculates pseudoresiduals for the parametric transition rate models discussed in previous chapters. One should note that the calculations in TDA are actually done separately for each transition found in the input data. However, to ease notation, only formulas are given for the single transition case.[3]

Our demonstration of how to generate and use pseudoresiduals for checking model assumptions is only based on the exponential model because the procedure is basically the same for all models. There are three steps.

Step 1. In the first step, when estimating the model with command file *ehd2.cf* (Box 4.1.4), the pseudoresiduals are written into the output file *ehd2.res*.[4] Part of this output file is shown in Box 8.2.3. In this file, the estimated rate (column 6) and the pseudoresiduals (column 8) are presented for each episode (column *Case*). For example, for job episode 1, the covariates have the following values (see Box 2.2.2): LFX = 0, PNOJ = 0, PRES = 34, COHO2 = 0, COHO3 = 0, and

---

[3] The notation closely follows the definition of models given in chapters 4, 5, and 7. To avoid redundancy, no additional explanations are given here. Also, because the calculation of residuals is always done according to

$$\hat{e}_i = -\log\left\{\hat{G}(t_i \mid s_i)\right\}$$

only formulas for the calculation of estimated rates and conditional survivor functions are given.

[4] The required additional command, already part of *ehd2.cf* but not shown in Box 4.1.4, is *pres=ehd2.res*.

Box 8.2.3 Part of *ehd2.res* (Pseudoresiduals for exponential model)

```
Generalized residuals
Model: Exponential
                                          Survivor
Case Org Des    TS       TF      Rate  Function Residual  Weight
-------------------------------------------------------------------
   1  0   0  0.0000 428.0000  0.0161  0.0010   6.9004   1.0000
   2  0   1  0.0000  46.0000  0.0131  0.5465   0.6042   1.0000
   3  0   1  0.0000  34.0000  0.0061  0.8113   0.2091   1.0000
   4  0   1  0.0000 220.0000  0.0059  0.2756   1.2890   1.0000
   5  0   1  0.0000  12.0000  0.0153  0.8322   0.1837   1.0000
   6  0   1  0.0000  30.0000  0.0156  0.6255   0.4692   1.0000
   7  0   1  0.0000  12.0000  0.0139  0.8466   0.1665   1.0000
   8  0   1  0.0000  75.0000  0.0142  0.3453   1.0633   1.0000
   9  0   1  0.0000  12.0000  0.0119  0.8674   0.1423   1.0000
  10  0   1  0.0000  55.0000  0.0121  0.5139   0.6658   1.0000
................................................................
 590  0   0  0.0000  30.0000  0.0126  0.6843   0.3794   1.0000
 591  0   1  0.0000  28.0000  0.0095  0.7670   0.2652   1.0000
 592  0   0  0.0000 119.0000  0.0092  0.3347   1.0945   1.0000
 593  0   1  0.0000  35.0000  0.0104  0.6942   0.3649   1.0000
 594  0   1  0.0000  34.0000  0.0102  0.7073   0.3462   1.0000
 595  0   1  0.0000 119.0000  0.0081  0.3821   0.9620   1.0000
 596  0   1  0.0000  66.0000  0.0054  0.7000   0.3567   1.0000
 597  0   0  0.0000 112.0000  0.0051  0.5675   0.5665   1.0000
 598  0   0  0.0000 103.0000  0.0171  0.1726   1.7567   1.0000
 599  0   1  0.0000  22.0000  0.0197  0.6483   0.4333   1.0000
 600  0   1  0.0000  13.0000  0.0191  0.7799   0.2486   1.0000
```

EDU = 17. Thus, the estimated rate for this job episode, based on the estimates for the exponential model in Box 4.1.5, is

$$\hat{r}(t \mid x) = \exp\left(-4.4894 + 0.0773 \cdot 17 - 0.0280 \cdot 34\right) = 0.0161$$

This estimate is printed in the column *Rate* in Box 8.2.3. The corresponding pseudoresidual, for the first episode with duration 428 months, is calculated as follows:

$$\hat{e} = -\log\left(\hat{G}(t \mid x)\right) = -\log\left(\exp(-0.0161 \cdot 428)\right) = 6.9004$$

Step 2. Given censored data, one must estimate the survivor function for the pseudoresiduals $(\hat{G}(t \mid x) = \exp(-\hat{e}))$ with the help of the product-limit estimator in the second step (see section 3.2). This is done with command file *ehd2s.cf*, shown in Box 8.2.4, where the file *ehd2.res*, shown in Box 8.2.3, is used as an input data file. Each of the pseudoresiduals is used as if it were the duration of an episode, with origin and destination state corresponding to the original episode. Part of the resulting product-limit estimate of the survivor function for the residuals is shown in Box 8.2.5.

Box 8.2.4 Command file *ehd2s.cf* (product-limit estimation for residuals)

```
dfile = ehd2.res;       data file with residuals
v1 (NULL) = 0;
v2 (RES)  = c8;         column 8 with residuals
v3 (ORG)  = c2;         origin state
v4 (DES)  = c3;         destination state

# define episode data
ts  = v1;
tf  = v2;
org = v3;
des = v4;

# request product limit estimation
ple = ehd2s.ple;
```

Box 8.2.5 Part of *ehd2s.ple* (Box 8.2.4)

```
SN 1. Transition: 0,1 - Product-Limit Estimation

                  Number  Number   Exposed  Survivor   Std.      Cum.
ID Index  Time    Events  Censored to Risk  Function   Error     Rate
 0     0  0.00       0       0        600    1.00000  0.00000  0.00000
 0     1  0.02       1       1        599    0.99833  0.00167  0.00167
 0     2  0.02       1       0        598    0.99666  0.00236  0.00334
 0     3  0.04       1       2        595    0.99499  0.00289  0.00503
 0     4  0.04       1       0        594    0.99331  0.00333  0.00671
 0     5  0.04       1       1        592    0.99163  0.00373  0.00840
 0     6  0.04       1       0        591    0.98996  0.00408  0.01010
 0     7  0.04       1       0        590    0.98828  0.00440  0.01179
 ...........................................................................
 0   441  2.90       1       2         24    0.10603  0.01661  2.24408
 0   442  2.98       1       0         23    0.10142  0.01652  2.28853
 0   443  3.05       1       2         20    0.09634  0.01645  2.33982
 0   444  3.22       1       4         15    0.08992  0.01656  2.40882
 0   445  3.32       1       1         13    0.08300  0.01667  2.48886
 0   446  3.60       1       2         10    0.07470  0.01694  2.59422
 0   447  6.90       0       9
Median Duration: 0.51
Duration times limited to: 3.5951
Cases: 600  weighted: 600
```

Step 3. Finally, we perform a graphical check of the distribution of the pseudoresiduals. As explained previously, if the model is appropriate, the residuals should follow approximately a standard exponential distribution. We already have a survivor function for the residuals, so we can apply the graphical check described in section 8.1. A plot of the logarithm of the survivor function against the residuals should be approximately a straight line that passes through the origin. To create this plot we use command file *ehd2p.cf* shown in Box 8.2.6.

Box 8.2.6 Command file *ehd2p.cf* (graphical check of pseudoresiduals)

```
dfile = ehd2s.ple;              data file

# select suitable range of time and survivor function
dsel = gt(c3,0) . gt(c7,0) . lt(c7,1);

v1(Time)     = c3;              time axis
v2(Survivor) = c7;              survivor function
v3(Log-Surv) = log(v2);         log of survivor function

postscript = ehd2p.ps;          PostScript output file
pltext(1.5,-0.7) = 'Exponential Model';

pxlen = 80;                     physical width (in mm)
pylen = 40;                     physical height (in mm)
pxa(1,0) = 0,4;                 user coordinates on X axis
pya(1,0) = -3,0;                user coordinates on Y axis

plot = v1,v3;                   plot v1 vs v3
plotp = 0,0,3,-3;               plot line
```

The same procedure, following the three steps outlined earlier, can be followed for all other transition rate models. The necessary command files are supplied on the accompanying disk.[5]

Figure 8.2.1 shows the plots for eight different models that were discussed in chapters 4, 5, and 7. As can be seen in this figure, the plot for the exponential model has the poorest fit with respect to a straight line with slope of -1. Also the plot for the Weibull distribution departs strongly from linearity. The Gompertz, the log-logistic, the log-normal, and the sickle models, on the other hand, provide better fits. But which one fits best? The log-logistic, log-normal, and piecewise constant exponential models resemble each other closely. Also the estimated shapes of the transition rates for these four models are almost identical. All four models estimate a non-monotonic hazard rate. Thus, in substantive terms it would not matter which one of them we choose. There is, however, a big difference with regard to the Gompertz model, which, although providing a similarly good fit, predicts only a monotonically declining rate. Thus, this example demonstrates that graphical checks of pseudoresiduals should not be understood as goodness-of-fit *tests*. They only provide some hints

---

[5] We have prepared command files for the exponential model (*ehd2.cf*), the piecewise constant exponential model, typ I and II (*ehe2.cf* and *ehe3.cf*), the Gompertz model (*ehg2.cf*), the Weibull model (*ehg6.cf* and *ehg7.cf*), the log-logistic model (*ehg9.cf*), the log-normal model (*ehg11.cf*), and the sickle model (*ehg13.cf*). The command and output files are named as follows: if *xyz.cf* is the command file to estimate a model, then the output file containing the pseudoresiduals is called *xyz.res*, the command file to perform product-limit estimations is called *xyzs.cf*, the resulting table of product-limit estimates is called *xyzs.ple*, and the command file to generate the plots is called *xyzp.cf*.

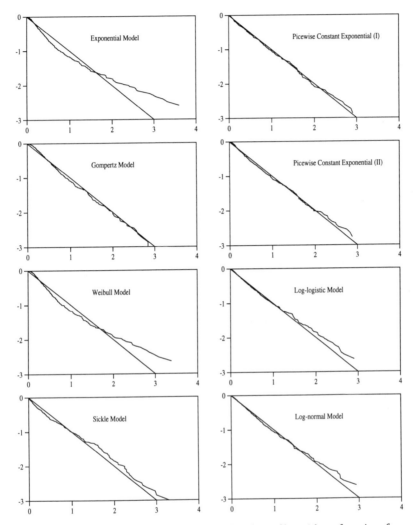

Figure 8.2.1 Graphical check of pseudoresiduals. Plots of logarithm of survivor functions (of residuals) vs. residuals.

for model selection; and the final selection should also be based on theoretical considerations. In any case, the piecewise constant exponential models in this example clearly provide the best fit, and because they only rely on very weak distributional assumptions, they are often a good choice in model selection.

Chapter 9
Semi-Parametric Transition Rate Models

Models with a time-dependent transition rate, as surveyed in chapter 7, are based on specific parametric assumptions about the distribution of durations and allow for straightforward maximum likelihood estimations. As demonstrated in detail, time in these models normally serves as a proxy variable for a latent causal factor that is difficult to measure directly. The problem in substantive applications is that theories in the social sciences, at least at their current level of development, rarely offer strong arguments for a specific parametric model. We therefore suggested in chapter 7 to use these models with extreme caution. Estimating a variety of model specifications and comparing the outcomes seems to be an appropriate strategy. However, this leads to another problem: the adequacy of alternative parametric models of time-dependence can only be evaluated with heuristic tools, as demonstrated in chapter 8. Although these goodness-of-fit checks may provide some rough hints as to which classes of models may be preferable, they cannot serve as strict tests to support a specific parametric model. Therefore, an interesting alternative strategy is to specify only a functional form for the influence of covariates, but leave the shape of the transition rate as unspecified as possible. Such models are known as semi-parametric models.

The most widely applied semi-parametric model is the proportional hazards model proposed by Cox (1972). We call this model the *Cox model*, as stated in the literature. It may be written as

$$r(t) = h(t) \exp\left(A(t)\alpha\right) \tag{9.1}$$

The transition rate, $r(t)$, is the product of an unspecified *baseline rate*, $h(t)$, and a second term specifying the possible influences of a covariate vector $A(t)$ on the transition rate.[1]

Model (9.1) is a special case of so-called *proportional* transition rate models because the effects of covariates can only induce proportional shifts in the transition rate but cannot change its shape. Therefore, the Cox model should only be used if this proportionality assumption is justified.

The Cox model has been widely used, although the proportionality assumption restricts the range of possible empirical applications. It is particularly

---

[1] The linear combination of a row vector of possible time-dependent covariates, $A(t)$, and a column vector of associated coefficients, α, cannot contain an intercept because this is absorbed in the baseline rate, $h(t)$.

attractive when the researcher (1) has no clear idea about the shape of time-dependence, or (2) has only a weak theory supporting a specific parametric model, or (3) knows the time path of the process, but is not adequately able to model its fluctuations with a tractable waiting time distribution, or (4) is only interested in the magnitude and direction of the effects of observed covariates, controlling for time-dependence.

The Cox model (9.1) can be extended for multiple origin and destination states, and also for multi-episode data. This chapter describes how to estimate such models with TDA. First, we explain the partial likelihood estimation of the model and present an example. Second, we discuss the use of time-dependent covariates based on partial likelihood estimation, in particular, how to use the method of episode splitting with Cox models. Third, we describe some methods for testing the proportionality assumption that is required in Cox models. In particular, we show how to estimate stratified Cox models to cope with the proportionality requirement. Fourth, we describe how to estimate rate and survivor functions for the Cox model. Finally, we give some application examples.

9.1   Partial Likelihood Estimation

The implementation of the Cox model in TDA is based on the following model formulation

$$r_{jk}(t) = h_{jk}(t) \, \exp\left\{ A^{(jk)}(t) \, \alpha^{(jk)} \right\}$$

$r_{jk}(t)$ is the transition rate at time t for the transition from origin state j to destination state k. $h_{jk}(t)$ is the unspecified baseline rate for the same transition.[2] $A^{(jk)}(t)$ is a (row) vector of covariates, specified for the transition (j, k), and $\alpha^{(jk)}$ is a vector of associated coefficients. The covariates may have time-dependent values; examples are given in section 9.2.

Furthermore, it is possible to explain each transition by a specific set of covariates. One should note, however, that model estimation requires that *all* covariates be defined for all members of a sample of episodes. This is necessary to calculate the risks for all transitions, regardless of the transition that actually happens at the end of an episode. One should also note that it is necessary to include at least one covariate for each transition because Cox models do not contain any intercept terms; all constant effects are included in the baseline rates.

Model estimation is based on the method of partial likelihood (Cox 1972, 1975). To explain this method, we first consider the case of a single transition (j, k) from origin state j to destination state k. Indices referring to transitions

---

[2] The formulation implies that the baseline rates are allowed to vary between different transitions. A special type of Cox model arises if the baseline rates are constrained to be identical for all transitions; see Kalbfleisch and Prentice (1980, p. 170).

are dropped to simplify notation. With the assumption of no ties (i.e. all ending times in the sample are different), the partial likelihood, L^p, may be written as

$$L^p = \prod_{i \in \mathcal{E}} \frac{\exp(A_i(t_i)\,\alpha)}{\sum_{l \in \mathcal{R}(t_i)} \exp(A_l(t_i)\,\alpha)} \qquad (9.2)$$

$\mathcal{E}$ denotes the set of all not censored episodes belonging to the (single) transition (j, k) (i.e. having an event at their ending time). $\mathcal{R}(t_i)$ is the risk set at the ending time, say t_i, of the ith episode contained in $\mathcal{E}$. The definition of the risk set is exactly the same as was given for the product-limit estimator: the set of all episodes, exiting with an event or being censored, with starting time less than t_i and ending time equal to or greater than t_i. $A_i(t_i)$ is the (row) vector of covariates for the ith episode (evaluated at t_i), and α is the vector of associated coefficients to be estimated.

Given this notation, the calculation of the partial likelihood is easily understood: One looks at the ending times of episodes ending with an event; then, for each of these points in time, the risk set is created; and finally the expression on the right-hand side of (9.2) is evaluated. This expression may be interpreted as the probability that it is just the ith individual to have an event at this point in time, given the risk set containing all individuals who could have an event. Note that in the calculation of these probabilities time-dependent covariates can be accounted for in a simple way: At each successive point in time, the actual covariate values can be used.

As was shown by Cox and other authors, the partial likelihood defined in (9.2) may be treated as if it were a standard likelihood. Estimates of model coefficients reached by maximizing the partial likelihood have properties similar to those of standard maximum likelihood estimates.

Difficulties only arise if there are tied ending times. Then it is complicated to calculate the partial likelihood exactly. Therefore, several simplifying approximations have been proposed. As computed by BMDP and SAS, the TDA algorithm for the partial likelihood calculation uses an approximation proposed by Breslow (1974).[3]

Assume there are d_i episodes, with indices contained in a set D_i, all having the same ending time, t_i. The partial likelihood factor for this point in time is then approximated by

$$\frac{\exp(S_i(t_i)\,\alpha)}{\left[\sum_{l \in \mathcal{R}(t_i)} \exp(A_l(t_i)\,\alpha)\right]^{d_i}} = \prod_{j \in D_i} \frac{\exp(A_j(t_i)\,\alpha)}{\sum_{l \in \mathcal{R}(t_i)} \exp(A_l(t_i)\,\alpha)}$$

with $S_i(t_i)$ defined as the sum of the covariate vectors for the d_i episodes with events at t_i (evaluated at t_i). As can easily be seen, the use of this approximation is already accounted for in the formulation of the partial likelihood in (9.2),

---

[3] We are following the formulation given by Lawless (1982, p. 346). An introduction to Breslow's approximation may also be found in Namboodiri and Suchindran (1987, p. 213).

Box 9.1.1 Partial likelihood algorithm in TDA

For all transitions: TRAN = 1,...,NT {
    ORG = origin state of transition TRAN
    DES = destination state of transition TRAN
    For all groups: G = 1,...,NG {
        TIME = 0
        For all episodes: EP = 1,...,NE (according to their ending times) {
            ORGI = origin state of episode EP
            DESI = destination state of episode EP
            TF = ending time of episode EP
            If (ORGI = ORG and DESI = DES and EP belongs to group G) {
                If (no time-dependent covariates) {
                    Add to the risk set all episodes which belong to group G,
                    have origin state org, and starting time less than TF.
                }
                If (TF greater than TIME) {
                    If (no time-dependent covariates) {
                        Eliminate from the risk set all episodes which
                        belong to group G, have origin state ORG,
                        and have ending time less than TF.
                    }
                    If (time-dependent covariates) {
                        Create a new risk set: all episodes that belong to
                        group G, have origin state ORG, starting time less
                        than TF and ending time greater or equal to TF.
                        While creating this new risk set, use the values
                        of time-dependent covariates at TF.
                    }
                    TIME = TF
                }
                Update partial likelihood (and derivatives) with episode EP.
            }
        }
    }
}

Note: If no groups (strata) are defined, this algorithm assumes that there is exactly one group containing all episodes.

because in this formulation the product goes over all episodes, tied or not, contained in $\mathcal{E}$.

As is generally assumed, this approximation is sufficient if there are only "relatively few" ties in a sample of episode data. If there are "too many" ties, it seems preferable to use a discrete time model.[4]

---

[4] Some discrete time transition rate models can be estimated with TDA, see Rohwer (1994, TDA-WP 5-6).

Box 9.1.2   Part of command file *ehi1.cf* (Cox model)

```
dfile = rrdat.1;      data file

v1  (ID)    = c1 ;    ID of individual
v2  (NOJ)   = c2 ;    Serial number of the job
v3  (TStart) = c3 ;   Starting time of the job
v4  (TFin)  = c4 ;    Ending time of the job
v5  (SEX)   = c5 ;    Sex (1 men, 2 women)
v6  (TI)    = c6 ;    Date of interview
v7  (TB)    = c7 ;    Date of birth
v8  (T1)    = c8 ;    Date of entry into the labor market
v9  (TM)    = c9 ;    Date of marriage (0 if no marriage)
v10 (PRES)  = c10;    Prestige score of job i
v11 (PRESN) = c11;    Prestige score of job i + 1
v12 (EDU)   = c12;    Highest educational attainment

# Define origin and destination state. Origin state is always 0.
# Destination state is 0 if right censored, or 1.
v13 (ORG)   = 0;
v14 (DES)   = if eq(v4,v6) then 0 else 1;

# Definition of starting and ending time on a process time axis.
v15 (TSP) = 0;
v16 (TFP) = v4 - v3 + 1; one month added

# define additional variables to include into the model
v20 (COHO2) =   ge(v7,468) . le(v7,504);   cohort 2
v21 (COHO3) =   ge(v7,588) . le(v7,624);   cohort 3
v22 (LFX)   =   v3 - v8;                    labor force experience
v23 (PNOJ)  =   v2 - 1;                     previous number of jobs

# commands to define single episode data
org = v13;    define origin state
des = v14;    define destination state
ts  = v15;    define starting time
tf  = v16;    define ending time
```

```
# command to request estimation of a Cox model
rate = 1;    model selection

# command to include covariates into model, for transition from
# origin state 0 to destination state 1.
xa (0,1)   =   v12,v20,v21,v22,v23,v10;
```

Box 9.1.1 shows how the partial likelihood calculation is done with TDA. The algorithm includes the possibility of applying stratification variables and time-dependent covariates explained later on.

An example of a partial likelihood estimation of the Cox model with TDA is shown in Box 9.1.2. The command file, *ehi1.cf*, is almost identical to the

Box 9.1.3 Estimation results using command file *ehi1.cf* (Box 9.1.2)

```
Model: Cox (partial likelihood)

Maximum of log likelihood: -2546.78
Norm of final gradient vector: 3.7e-05
Last absolute change of function value: 1.0e-10
Last relative change in parameters: 2.2e-04

Idx SN Org Des MT Var  Label   Coeff   Error    T-Stat  Signif
--------------------------------------------------------------
  1  1   0   1  A V12  EDU    0.0669  0.0249    2.6835  0.9927
  2  1   0   1  A V20  COHO2  0.4113  0.1153    3.5658  0.9996
  3  1   0   1  A V21  COHO3  0.3053  0.1220    2.5024  0.9877
  4  1   0   1  A V22  LFX   -0.0040  0.0009   -4.2781  1.0000
  5  1   0   1  A V23  PNOJ   0.0686  0.0442    1.5529  0.8796
  6  1   0   1  A V10  PRES  -0.0262  0.0055   -4.7574  1.0000
```

command file for the exponential model in Box 4.1.4. Only the model selection command has been changed to

  rate = 1; to select estimation of a Cox model

and the *pres* command has been dropped because there is no direct way to calculate generalized residuals with the Cox model.

Part of the estimation results are shown in Box 9.1.3. The estimated coefficients surprisingly resemble the results obtained for the exponential model in Box 4.1.5. Thus, about the same substantive conclusions must be drawn (at least in terms of direction of influence and statistical significance of effects) with regard to the covariates included. It should be noted that in Box 9.1.3 there is no estimate for the constant anymore. It cannot be identified in the Cox model because all members of a risk set have the same value for each event time, causing it to be canceled from the numerator and denominator of every term in the partial likelihood. Thus, the constant becomes part of the baseline hazard rate in the Cox model.

Multiple Origin and Destination States

To extend the Cox model to the case of multiple origin and destination states (see, e.g., Blossfeld and Hamerle 1989a), we follow the general remarks in 4.3. First, it should be restated that in the context of duration analysis all estimations performed are conditional on given origin states. Therefore, with two or more origin states, the (partial) likelihood may be constructed separately for all of them; each single term may be maximized separately, or the product of all origin-specific terms can be taken and maximized simultaneously.[5]

---

[5] The algorithm in TDA maximizes the partial likelihood simultaneously for all transitions to provide for the possibility of constraints on model parameters across transitions. In this case, the

The case of two or more transitions from a given origin state is also simple.[6] One only needs an appropriate definition of the risk set. The risk set is now conditional on a given origin state, so we write $\mathcal{R}_j(t)$ with j to indicate the origin state; but one must include all the episodes with the given origin state j that are at risk for a transition to state k at time t, regardless of which destination state they will actually reach at some later point in time. Therefore, the risk set $\mathcal{R}_j(t)$ is defined as the set of *all* episodes with origin state j, provided that their starting time is less than t and their ending time is equal to or greater than t.

The partial likelihood in the case of possibly more than one origin and/or destination state may then be written as

$$L^p = \prod_{j \in \mathcal{O}} \prod_{k \in \mathcal{D}_j} \prod_{i \in \mathcal{E}_{jk}} \frac{\exp\left(A^{(jk)}(t_i)\,\alpha^{(jk)}\right)}{\sum_{l \in \mathcal{R}_j(t_i)} \exp\left(A^{(jk)}(t_l)\,\alpha^{(jk)}\right)}$$

Box 9.1.1 shows the implementation of this partial likelihood calculation in TDA. Should there be only one transition, it is reduced to the partial likelihood given in (9.2). Also the approximation is the same as in the single transition case if there are tied ending times.

9.2 Time-Dependent Covariates

Cox models offer an easy way to include time-dependent covariates. The standard method is based on the fact that the partial likelihood calculation gradually goes through all points in time where at least one of the uncensored episodes has an event. Consequently, it is possible to re-evaluate the values of time-dependent covariates at these points in time. This is already provided for in the partial likelihood formula (9.2). As can be seen from the algorithm in Box 9.1.1, the risk set is re-calculated at every new point in time. Of course, this is a very time-consuming process.

To define time-dependent covariates, TDA provides a special operator called *TIME*. It is, at any step in the partial likelihood calculation, the actual value of the process time; and it is a discrete variable, taking different values only at points in time when some event occurs (i.e. at the ending times of the not-censored episodes).

To illustrate the inclusion of a time-dependent covariate in a Cox model, we again examine whether first marriage has an effect on the job exit rate (see section 6.4). Thus, we must create a time-dependent dummy variable MARR ("marriage"). Command file *ehi2.cf* (Box 9.2.1) shows how this can be accomplished. First, as described for the exponential model in Box 6.4.5, a variable MDATE ($V25$) is created that expresses the marriage date relative to

---

transition-specific terms of the likelihood are no longer independent, and the maximization must be done simultaneously.

[6] See Kalbfleisch and Prentice (1980, p. 169).

Box 9.2.1   Part of command file *ehi2.cf* (time-dependent covariates)

```
... (first part identical to first part of Box 9.1.2)

# define marriage date (MDATE) and a dummy variable (MARR), taking
# the value 1 if a person is married.
v25 (MDATE) = if le(v9,0) then 10000 else v9 - v3;
v26 (MARR)  = gt (TIME,v25);

# command to request estimation of a Cox model
rate = 1;    model selection

# command to include covariates into model, for transition from
# origin state 0 to destination state 1.
xa (0,1)    =   v12,v20,v21,v22,v23,v10,v26;
```

Box 9.2.2   Estimation results of command file *ehi2.cf* (Box 9.2.1)

```
Model: Cox (partial likelihood)

Maximum of log likelihood: -2546.62
Norm of final gradient vector: 4.4e-05
Last absolute change of function value: 1.2e-10
Last relative change in parameters: 2.4e-04

Idx SN Org Des MT Var  Label    Coeff     Error    T-Stat  Signif
-----------------------------------------------------------------
  1  1   0   1  A V12  EDU     0.0665    0.0249    2.6647  0.9923
  2  1   0   1  A V20  COHO2   0.4056    0.1158    3.5038  0.9995
  3  1   0   1  A V21  COHO3   0.2901    0.1249    2.3225  0.9798
  4  1   0   1  A V22  LFX    -0.0042    0.0010   -4.1789  1.0000
  5  1   0   1  A V23  PNOJ    0.0674    0.0443    1.5220  0.8720
  6  1   0   1  A V10  PRES   -0.0263    0.0055   -4.7804  1.0000
  7  1   0   1  A V26  MARR    0.0660    0.1192    0.5541  0.4205
```

the beginning time of each of the jobs in an occupational career. The variable is given the value 10000 months, a value that can never be reached in any of the job episodes, if the individual was still unmarried at the time of the interview; it is negative when the marriage took place before the individual entered into the respective job; it is zero if the marriage took place in the month when the individual entered into the respective job; and it is positive if the marriage occurs after the individual entered the respective job. Second, variable MDATE is compared with the special operator *TIME*. If MDATE is greater than the actual value of *TIME* (process time), then the time-dependent dummy variable MARR is switched from 0 (unmarried) to 1 (married).[7]

---

[7] Note that because partial likelihood estimation is based on the order of events and censored times, estimation results of the Cox model can differ depending on whether the *greater* (*gt*) or *greater/equal* (*ge*) operator is used to define a time-dependent covariate. The decision on a proper

The estimation results of using command file *ehi2.cf* are presented in Box 9.2.2. The time-dependent covariate "marriage" does not seem to be significant, and entry into marriage also does not seem to affect the job exit rate in the Cox model. This conclusion is in sharp contrast to the one reached for the equivalent exponential in Box 6.4.6, where the variable MARR ("marriage") was found to be significant. Thus, controlling for an unspecified baseline hazard rate in the Cox model seems to strongly affect the coefficient of this time-dependent covariate.[8] However, we already know that the effect of marriage is different for men and for women, so we should take this into account in a proper model specification. Before doing this, we discuss another, more efficient method to include time-dependent covariates into Cox models.

Episode Splitting

A disadvantage of the standard method for including time-dependent variables into a Cox model is that the partial likelihood calculation becomes very time-consuming (see Blossfeld, Hamerle, and Mayer 1989). The reason for this is that the risk set must be re-calculated, and the values of the covariates must be re-evaluated (including comparisons with the process time), for every point in time that has at least one event.

If the time-dependent covariates change their values only at some discrete points in time, the method of episode splitting can be used instead. The original episodes are split at every point in time where one of the time-dependent covariates changes its value. Each of the original episodes is replaced by a contiguous set of subepisodes (splits) with appropriate values of the covariates. The last of these splits has the same exit status as the original episode; all other splits are regarded as right censored.[9]

To use this method with partial likelihood maximization, it is only necessary to be precise in the definition of the risk set. At every point in time, *t*, the risk set should contain all episodes, or splits, that have a starting time less than *t* and ending time greater than or equal to *t*, regardless of their exit status. Consequently, the risk set at every point in time only contains a single split, associated with appropriate values of the time-dependent covariates for each of the original episodes. Clearly, it is necessary for the partial likelihood algorithm to take into account both the different ending *and* starting times of

---

definition of time-dependent covariates should be based on substantive considerations, taking into account that, for a causal interpretation, the cause should precede its possible effect.

[8] Our experience with various event history models in social research suggests that changes in the specification of time-dependence may often strongly affect the coefficients of other time-dependent covariates, but they normally have almost no effect on the coefficients of time-constant covariates.

[9] See the discussion of the episode splitting method in section 6.4.

Box 9.2.3 Command file *ehi3.cf* (Cox model with episode splitting)

```
dfile = rrdat.s1;        data file with episode splits
noc = 761;

v1  (CASE)    = c1;
v2  (SPLIT)   = c2;
v3  (ORG)     = c3;
v4  (DES)     = c4;
v5  (TS)      = c5;
v6  (TF)      = c6;
v7  (TSP)     = c7;
v8  (TFP)     = c8;
v9  (EDU)     = c9;
v10 (COHO2)   = c10;
v11 (COHO3)   = c11;
v12 (LFX)     = c12;
v13 (PNOJ)    = c13;
v14 (PRES)    = c14;
v15 (MarrDate) = c15;
v16 (Sex)     = c16;

# commands to define single episode data

org =  v3;   define origin state
des =  v4;   define destination state
ts  =  v5;   define starting time
tf  =  v6;   define ending time

# command to request estimation of a Cox model

rate = 1;    model selection

# command to include covariates into model, for transition from
# origin state 0 to destination state 1.

xa (0,1)    =   v9,v10,v11,v12,v13,v14;
```

the episodes (splits). As shown in Box 9.1.1, this is a general feature of TDA's partial likelihood algorithm.[10]

Unfortunately, TDA's method of *internal* episode splitting cannot be used with the partial likelihood algorithm (see section 6.4). This is because episode splits are only virtually created to save storage space. However, to be sorted according to starting and ending times simultaneously, they must be present in the program's data matrix. Consequently, if one wishes to use the method of episode splitting to estimate Cox models, or analogously for product-limit estimates, only the method of *external* episode splitting can be applied. There are two steps.

---

[10] The method has been inspired by the program RATE (Tuma 1980), which we assume was the first program that used starting and ending times for updating the risk set simultaneously.

Box 9.2.4 Part of command file *ehi4.cf* (Cox model with time-dependent covariate)

```
... (first part identical to first part in Box 9.2.3)

# define a time-dependent covariate MARR
v17 (MARR) = le(v15,ts);

# command to request estimation of a Cox model
rate = 1;     model selection

# command to include covariates into model, for transition from
# origin state 0 to destination state 1.
xa (0,1)   =   v9,v10,v11,v12,v13,v14,v17;
```

1. The first step is to create a new data file with split episodes. This can be done by using TDA's *split* command and then creating a new data file with the *pdate* command (see Box 6.4.1).

2. In the second step, the data file containing the episode splits can be used as if it were a set of "original" episodes. Based on these input data, one can estimate Cox models with time-dependent covariates. It is also possible to request product-limit estimates based on a set of episode splits; one should get exactly the same results as if the original episodes were used.

In demonstrating the method of episode splitting for the Cox model, it is helpful in a first step to show that using a data file with episode splits does not change the estimated results. This is done with the command file *ehi3.cf* shown in Box 9.2.3. The input data file with the splits is *rrdat.s1*, created with the command file *ehf1.cf* (see Box 6.4.1). Note that we now simply use the origin (*V3*) and destination states (*V4*) as well as the starting (*V5*) and ending times (*V6*) of the splits to define the episode data. We do not define a time-dependent covariate in this example, but only include the same covariates into the model as for the model in Box 9.1.2. Using this command file with TDA yields the same estimation results as with command file *ehi1.cf* (see Box 9.1.3), so the results are not shown again.

In a second step, we now define a time-dependent covariable, MARR (*V17*), and include it into the model specification with command file *ehi4.cf* (Box 9.2.4). Using this command file, we get the exact same results as with command file *ehi2.cf* (Box 9.2.1), that is, the standard method to define time-dependent covariates.[11] However, using *ehi4.cf* instead of *ehi2.cf* drastically reduces the computing time. In fact, it turns out that the method of episode splitting is much more efficient than the standard method of using time-dependent covariates with the Cox model.

Finally, we add the time-dependent interaction variable MARR.MEN to capture possible interaction effects of marriage and sex. It is basically the same

---

[11] Because the estimation results are identical to Box 9.2.2, we do not show a separate table.

Box 9.2.5 Part of command file *ehi5.cf* (Cox model with time-dependent covariates)

```
... (first part identical to first part in Box 9.2.3)

# define a time-dependent covariate MARR
v17 (MARR) = le(v15,ts);

# define a time-dependent interaction of MARR and dummy for men
v18 (MARR.MEN) = le(v15,ts) . v16[1];

# command to request estimation of a Cox model
rate = 1;    model selection

# command to include covariates into model, for transition from
# origin state 0 to destination state 1.
xa (0,1)    =    v9,v10,v11,v12,v13,v14,v17,v18;
```

Box 9.2.6 Estimation results with command file *ehi5.cf* (Box 9.2.5)

```
Model: Cox (partial likelihood)

Maximum of log likelihood: -2528.45
Norm of final gradient vector: 2.7e-04
Last absolute change of function value: 7.5e-10
Last relative change in parameters: 4.1e-04

Idx SN Org Des MT Var  Label     Coeff   Error   T-Stat  Signif
--------------------------------------------------------------
  1  1   0   1  A V9   EDU       0.0792  0.0241   3.2867  0.9990
  2  1   0   1  A V10  COHO2     0.3767  0.1158   3.2537  0.9989
  3  1   0   1  A V11  COHO3     0.2928  0.1243   2.3556  0.9815
  4  1   0   1  A V12  LFX      -0.0045  0.0010  -4.4408  1.0000
  5  1   0   1  A V13  PNOJ      0.1012  0.0449   2.2524  0.9757
  6  1   0   1  A V14  PRES     -0.0252  0.0054  -4.6858  1.0000
  7  1   0   1  A V17  MARR      0.5046  0.1303   3.8733  0.9999
  8  1   0   1  A V18  MARR.MEN -0.8608  0.1420  -6.0624  1.0000
```

approach as already demonstrated in section 6.4 (see command file *ehf4.cf* in Box 6.4.7). The command file now is *ehi5.cf*, shown in Box 9.2.5. The estimated parameters in Box 9.2.6 are again in accordance with our expectations and basically in agreement with the results of the exponential model in Box 6.4.8. The coefficient of marriage on the rate of moving out of the job is still positive for women. This effect is however greater than in the exponential model. In the Cox model marriage *increases* the job exit rate for women by about 66 %;[12] in the exponential model it is only 31 %. For men the effect of marriage on the job change rate is negative. Marriage *decreases* the rate of

---

[12] $(\exp(0.5046) - 1) \cdot 100\% \approx 65.6$.

Box 9.3.1 Part of command file *ehi6.cf* (graphical proportionality check)

```
dfile = ehc7.ple;                    data file
dsel = gt(c7,0) . lt(c7,1);          selection of admissible values

v1(Sel_Men)    = c1[0];              variable to select men
v2(Sel_Women)  = c1[1];              variable to select women
v3(Time)       = c3;                 time axis
v4(Survivor)   = log (-log (c7));    survivor function

postscript = ehi6.ps;                PostScript output file
pxlen = 80;                          physical width (in mm)
pylen = 40;                          physical height (in mm)
pxa(24,0) = 0,240 ;                  user coordinates on X axis
pya(1,0)  = -5, 1 ;                  user coordinates on Y axis

plot = v3,v4, sel = v1;              plot variable 3 vs 4, select men
plot = v3,v4, sel = v2;              plot variable 3 vs 4, select women

pltext(192,0.6) = Women;             labels
pltext(216,0.1) = Men;
```

moving out of the job by about 30 %;[13] in the exponential model it was 52 %. Thus, marriage does indeed make men less mobile. In summary, the exponential as compared to the Cox model underestimated the impact of marriage on women and overestimated it for men.[14]

9.3 The Proportionality Assumption

A basic feature of the Cox model is that transition rates for different values of covariates are proportional. If, for instance, the transition rates, $r(t)$ and $r'(t)$, corresponding with the values of the ith covariate, A_i and A_i', are compared, then

$$\frac{r(t)}{r'(t)} = \exp\left\{(A_i - A_i')\alpha_i\right\}$$

Models with this feature are called *proportional transition rate models*. This feature is not specific to the Cox model, but implied in at least some of the many parametric models shown in chapters 4, 5, 6, and 7. This section discusses methods of checking whether a sample of episode data satisfies the proportionality assumption.

---

[13] $(\exp(0.5046 - 0.8608) - 1) \cdot 100\% \approx 30\%$.

[14] One has to be careful here because in this example we did not take into account that the covariate effects are not proportional for men and women, see section 9.3.

Graphical Methods

If there are only a few categorical covariates in a model, it is possible to perform simple graphical checks to examine the proportionality assumption. Let
us assume that this is the case, and that A and A' are two different vectors of
covariate values. The sample can then be split into two groups, and nonparametric, Kaplan-Meier estimates of the survivor function, say $G(t)$ and $G'(t)$,
can be calculated for both of these groups. The proportionality assumption
implies that

$$\frac{\log(G(t))}{\log(G'(t))} = \exp\left\{(A - A')\alpha\right\}$$

Or, taking logarithms once more, this becomes

$$\log\left\{-\log(G(t))\right\} = \log\left\{-\log(G'(t))\right\} + (A - A')\alpha$$

Therefore, a plot of the transformed survivor functions may be used to check
whether the proportionality assumption is (nearly) correct.

We use the product-limit estimate of the survivor functions for men and
women generated with command file $ehc7.cf$ (Box 3.3.1) to give an illustration
of a graphical check of the proportionality assumption. The estimated survivor
functions have been written into the file $ehc7.ple$, which is now used as an input
data file in command file $ehi6.cf$ shown in Box 9.3.1. This command file creates
a plot of $\log(-\log(C7))$ (where $C7$ is the value of the survivor function) versus
time, for both men and women.

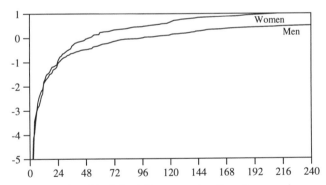

Figure 9.3.1 Graphical check for proportionality of men and women.
Plot of $\log(-\log(\hat{G}(t)))$ against t (in months).

The resulting plots for men and women are presented in Figure 9.3.1. It
is easy to see that, after about 24 months (or 2 years), there is a growing gap
between the transformed survivor functions. The difference between the curves
for men and women is however not too large. Thus, the question of whether the

Box 9.3.2 Part of command file *ehi7.cf* (test of proportionality)

```
... (first part identical to first part of Box 9.2.2)

# define a dummy variable for women and an interaction variable with
# the process time.
v25 (Women) = v5[2];
v26 (WTEST) = v25 * (log(TIME) - 4.73);

# command to request estimation of a Cox model
rate = 1;     model selection

# command to include covariates into model, for transition from
# origin state 0 to destination state 1.
xa (0,1)    =    v12,v20,v21,v22,v23,v10,v25,v26;
```

difference is sufficiently large to violate the proportionality assumption arises. A visual inspection of the plotted curves hardly can answer this question. Thus, it is more appropriate to apply a statistical test.

Testing Time-Dependence

This test is based on the idea that if the proportionality assumption is correct, there should be no interaction effect between the covariates and process time. Assuming that the ith component of the covariate vector A is to be tested, a model like the following could be set up and estimated:

$$r(t) = h(t) \exp \left\{ A \alpha + A_i \left(\log(TIME) - M \right) \alpha_i' \right\} \tag{9.3}$$

The constant M is added to facilitate the estimation. It should be the logarithm of the mean (or median) duration of the sample episodes used for the estimation. If the added interaction variable gives a significant coefficient (i.e. if there is a significant interaction effect), the proportionality assumption for this covariate is probably not valid.

As an illustration of this test we again examine whether men and women have proportional transition rates. The command file is *ehi7.cf* shown in Box 9.3.2. The additional variable is WTEST, constructed according to (9.3). The estimation results of this model specification are shown in Box 9.3.3. WTEST is obviously significant. In other words, the assumption that men and women have proportional job exit risks is not justified.

What is the consequence of this result? There are at least two possible reactions: First, the researcher can estimate a stratified Cox model with *group-specific baseline transition rates* for men and women (see below); or he/she can simply use a *nonproportional* Cox model (i.e. the model just estimated), which includes the interaction effect and automatically corrects the violation of the proportionality assumption.

Box 9.3.3 Estimation results using command file *ehi7.cf* (Box 9.3.2)

```
Model: Cox (partial likelihood)

Maximum of log likelihood: -2536.27
Norm of final gradient vector: 4.8e-05
Last absolute change of function value: 1.3e-10
Last relative change in parameters: 2.0e-04

Idx SN Org Des MT Var  Label    Coeff    Error     T-Stat  Signif
-----------------------------------------------------------------
 1   1   0   1  A V12  EDU      0.0803   0.0247    3.2566  0.9989
 2   1   0   1  A V20  COHO2    0.3937   0.1155    3.4097  0.9993
 3   1   0   1  A V21  COHO3    0.2716   0.1222    2.2231  0.9738
 4   1   0   1  A V22  LFX     -0.0041   0.0009   -4.3657  1.0000
 5   1   0   1  A V23  PNOJ     0.0888   0.0447    1.9872  0.9531
 6   1   0   1  A V10  PRES    -0.0259   0.0054   -4.7654  1.0000
 7   1   0   1  A V25  Women    0.7111   0.1607    4.4244  1.0000
 8   1   0   1  A V26  WTEST    0.2587   0.0987    2.6211  0.9912
```

A Goodness-of-Fit Test

The idea of checking for interactions between covariates and the process time may be generalized for a global goodness-of-fit test for the Cox model. This was proposed by Moreau et al. (1985). In the following, we describe their test statistics as well as their implementation in TDA.

Is is assumed that all episodes start at the origin of the process time (i.e. have starting times zero). The process time axis is divided into intervals according to

$$0 = \tau_1 < \tau_2 < \ldots < \tau_q, \quad \tau_{q+1} = \infty$$

The lth time interval is defined as

$$I_l = \{t \mid \tau_l \le t < \tau_{l+1}\} \quad l = 1, \ldots, q$$

Moreau et al. (1985) proposed looking at a general model formulation that provides for possibly different covariate effects in the different time intervals. In the single transition case, the model may be formulated as

$$r(t) = h(t) \, \exp\{A(\alpha + \gamma_l)\} \quad \text{if} \quad t \in I_l \tag{9.4}$$

In the lth time interval the coefficients associated with the covariate vector A are given by $\alpha + \gamma_l$. If the proportionality assumption holds, then all γ_l vectors should be zero. Because one of these vectors is obviously redundant, we set $\gamma_1 = 0$, and the null hypothesis becomes

$$\gamma_2 = \gamma_3 = \ldots = \gamma_q = 0 \tag{9.5}$$

Box 9.3.4 Part of command file *ehi8.cf* (test of proportionality)

```
... (first part identical to first part of Box 9.2.2)

# define a dummy variable for women
v25 (Women) = v5[2];

# define time periods for test statistics
tp = 0 (12) 96;

# command to request estimation of a Cox model
rate = 1;      model selection

# command to include covariates into model, for transition from
# origin state 0 to destination state 1.
xa (0,1)    =   v12,v20,v21,v22,v23,v10,v25;
```

To test this null hypothesis, Moreau et al. (1985) proposed a score test. The test statistic, say S, is defined by

$$S = U' V^{-1} U \qquad\qquad (9.6)$$

where U is a vector of first derivatives of the log likelihood of model (9.4), evaluated with hypothesis (9.5) and with maximum partial likelihood estimates of the vector α. And V is the observed information matrix, that is, minus the matrix of second derivatives of the log likelihood of (9.4), evaluated the same way. Given the null hypothesis, the statistic S asymptotically follows a χ^2 distribution whose degrees of freedom are equal to the number of parameters of model (9.4), that is, $(q - 1) p$ where p is the dimension of α.[15]

A generalization to the case of multiple transitions is simple because the log likelihood factors into separate components for each transition. Therefore, separate test statistics can be calculated for each transition, say (j, k), taking into account all episodes with the origin state j, and regarding all episodes that do not end with the destination state k as censored.

To request a calculation of the Moreau et al. test statistics, one can simply add a definition of time periods to the specification of a Cox model. The test statistics are then printed into the standard output of the program. In addition to the test statistics and associated degrees of freedom, TDA prints the corresponding value of the χ^2 distribution function.

To illustrate the calculation of this test statistic, we use command file *ehi8.cf* shown in Box 9.3.4. It is basically identical to command file *ehi7.cf*; the only differences are that we have *not* included the variable WTEST in the model specification and have added a command to define time periods (the same time periods as were used in chapter 5 for the piecewise constant exponential

---

[15] As shown by Moreau et al. (1985), the calculation of S can be greatly simplified. See Rohwer (1994, TDA-WP 5-4) for details.

Box 9.3.5 Estimation results using command file *ebi8.cf* (Box 9.3.4)

```
Model: Cox (partial likelihood)

Maximum of log likelihood: -2539.68
Norm of final gradient vector: 5.0e-05
Last absolute change of function value: 1.4e-10
Last relative change in parameters: 2.0e-04

Idx SN Org Des MT Var  Label    Coeff    Error    T-Stat  Signif
----------------------------------------------------------------
  1  1   0   1  A V12  EDU     0.0763   0.0247    3.0944  0.9980
  2  1   0   1  A V20  COHO2   0.3860   0.1154    3.3457  0.9992
  3  1   0   1  A V21  COHO3   0.2959   0.1220    2.4252  0.9847
  4  1   0   1  A V22  LFX    -0.0041   0.0009   -4.3800  1.0000
  5  1   0   1  A V23  PNOJ    0.0903   0.0448    2.0145  0.9560
  6  1   0   1  A V10  PRES   -0.0249   0.0054   -4.5969  1.0000
  7  1   0   1  A V25  Women   0.3699   0.0976    3.7884  0.9998

Global Goodness-of-Fit
SN Org Des      TStat    DF   Signif
------------------------------------
  1   0   1   62.9201    56   0.7553
```

model). The estimation results are shown in Box 9.3.5. Because the resulting test statistic is not significant, the model can reasonably be assumed to conform with the proportionality assumption.

Stratification

If, for some covariates, the proportionality assumption is not acceptable, it is sometimes sensible to estimate a stratified model. This is possible if the covariates are categorical.[16] The whole sample can then be split into groups (strata), and there is one group for each of the possible combinations of categories. In the simplest case, with only a single dummy variable, there will only be two groups. Let $\mathcal{G}$ denote the set of groups. The model should then be specified so that the baseline rate can be different for each group. There are two possibilities. The first is to define a different model for each group. Then not only the baseline rates but also the covariate effects can vary across all groups.

This approach is, of course, limited to fairly large sets of episode data. When data sets are relatively small, or when there are no significant interaction effects, it may be sensible to build on the assumption that covariate effects are the same

---

[16] Metric covariates could be used by grouping the individual data into appropriate classes.

Box 9.3.6 Part of command file *ehi9.cf* (stratification)

```
... (first part identical to first part of Box 9.2.2)

# define two indicator variables for men and women, and define groups.
v25 (Men)   = v5[1];
v26 (Women) = v5[2];
grp         = v25,v26;

# command to request estimation of a Cox model
rate = 1;    model selection

# command to include covariates into model, for transition from
# origin state 0 to destination state 1.
xa (0,1)    =   v12,v20,v21,v22,v23,v10;
```

Box 9.3.7 Estimation results using command file *ehi9.cf* (Box 9.3.6)

```
Model: Cox (partial likelihood)

Maximum of log likelihood: -2224.63
Norm of final gradient vector: 2.1e-05
Last absolute change of function value: 6.5e-11
Last relative change in parameters: 1.3e-04

Idx SN Org Des MT Var  Label    Coeff    Error    T-Stat  Signif
----------------------------------------------------------------
 1  1   0   1  A V12   EDU     0.0793   0.0248    3.2013  0.9986
 2  1   0   1  A V20   COHO2   0.3975   0.1156    3.4391  0.9994
 3  1   0   1  A V21   COHO3   0.2801   0.1226    2.2848  0.9777
 4  1   0   1  A V22   LFX    -0.0040   0.0009   -4.3158  1.0000
 5  1   0   1  A V23   PNOJ    0.0889   0.0448    1.9856  0.9529
 6  1   0   1  A V10   PRES   -0.0258   0.0054   -4.7261  1.0000
```

in all groups.[17] Based on this assumption, a model for the single transition case can be written as

$$r_g(t) = h_g(t) \exp(A\,\alpha) \qquad g \in \mathcal{G}$$

This model must be estimated for all groups simultaneously. Consequently, the partial likelihood approach given in (9.2) needs a small modification; the partial likelihood must be calculated as being the product of the group-specific likelihoods. For the multiple transition case, this may be written as

$$L^p = \prod_{j \in \mathcal{O}} \prod_{k \in \mathcal{D}_j} \prod_{g \in \mathcal{G}_j} \prod_{i \in \mathcal{E}_{jk,g}} \frac{\exp\left(A^{(jk)}(t_i)\,\alpha^{(jk)}\right)}{\sum_{l \in \mathcal{R}_{j,g}(t_i)} \exp\left(A^{(jk)}(t_l)\,\alpha^{(jk)}\right)} \qquad (9.7)$$

---

[17] See Kalbfleisch and Prentice (1980, p. 87), Lawless (1982, p. 365), and Blossfeld, Hamerle, and Mayer (1989).

with $\mathcal{G}_j$ denoting the set of groups of episodes with origin state j. $\mathcal{E}_{jk,g}$ is the set of all not censored episodes having origin state j and destination state k *and* belonging to group g. Accordingly, $\mathcal{R}_{j,g}(t)$ is the risk set at time t containing all episodes with origin state j, starting time less than t, ending time equal to or greater than t, and belonging to group g. In fact, TDA used the partial likelihood defined in (9.7) as is already reflected in the algorithm in Box 9.1.1.

To illustrate the estimation of a stratified Cox model, we use our standard example. The command file is *ehi9.cf* (Box 9.3.6). The sample is stratified according to sex (there are two groups, men and women). The estimation results are shown in Box 9.3.7. They are fairly similar to the estimation results shown in Box 9.1.3, where the same model without stratification according to sex was estimated.

9.4 Baseline Rates and Survivor Functions

The partial likelihood method gives estimates of the parameters of a Cox model but no direct estimate of the underlying baseline rate. Clearly, it would be useful to have such estimates, as they could give some information about the type of time-dependence in a set of episode data, and this could give us some insight as to whether a fully parametrical model would be appropriate.

There are different proposals for estimating the baseline rate. TDA's approach is based on a proposal made be Breslow (1974), also discussed in Blossfeld et al. (1989). To explain this method, we begin by assuming a single transition and that all episodes have the starting time zero. Then, in the usual notation, $\mathcal{E}$ denotes the set of, say, q, not censored episodes, and the ordered ending times may be given by

$$\tau_1 < \tau_2 < \ldots < \tau_q$$

Let E_i be the number of events at τ_i and let $\mathcal{R}_i$ be the risk set at τ_i. Furthermore, let $\hat{\alpha}$ be the partial likelihood estimate of the model parameters. Then, defining $\tau_0 = 0$, we can consider

$$\hat{h}_i^b = \frac{E_i}{(\tau_i - \tau_{i-1}) \sum_{l \in \mathcal{R}_i} \exp(A_l \, \hat{\alpha})} \qquad i = 1, \ldots, q$$

to be an estimate of the baseline rate of the model. It is a constant during each interval $(\tau_{i-1}, \tau_i]$, resulting in a step function with steps at the points in time where at least one event occurs. This step function can now be integrated to provide an estimate of the cumulative baseline rate:

$$\hat{H}^b(t) = \sum_{l=1}^{i} (\tau_l - \tau_{l-1}) \, \hat{h}_l + (t - \tau_i) \, \hat{h}_{i+1} \qquad \tau_i < t \le \tau_{i+1}$$

An estimate of the baseline survivor function may then be calculated by

$$\hat{G}^b(t) = \exp\left\{ -\hat{H}^b(t) \right\}$$

Box 9.4.1 Part of command file *ehi10.cf* (baseline rate calculation)

```
... (first part identical to first part of Box 9.2.2)

# command to request estimation of a Cox model
rate = 1;     model selection

# command to include covariates into model, for transition from
# origin state 0 to destination state 1.
xa (0,1)    =   v12,v20,v21,v22,v23,v10;

# commands to request baseline rate calculation for two types
# of covariate constellations
prate = ehi10.bl;   output file
ev12 = 13,13;       education
ev20 =  0, 0;       coho2 = 0
ev21 =  0, 1;       coho3 = 0 or 1
ev22 =  5, 5;       labor force experience
ev23 =  1, 1;       one previous job
ev10 = 30,30;       mean prestige value
```

Box 9.4.2 Part of output file *ehi10.bl* (Box 9.4.1)

```
Cox Model. Baseline Rate Calculation

Idx SN Org Des MT Var  Label         Coeff    Cov-1      Cov-2
-----------------------------------------------------------------
  1  1   0   1  A V12  EDU           0.0669  13.0000    13.0000
  2  1   0   1  A V20  COHO2         0.4113   0.0000     0.0000
  3  1   0   1  A V21  COHO3         0.3053   0.0000     1.0000
  4  1   0   1  A V22  LFX          -0.0040   5.0000     5.0000
  5  1   0   1  A V23  PNOJ          0.0686   1.0000     1.0000
  6  1   0   1  A V10  PRES         -0.0262  30.0000    30.0000

                            Risk        Cov-1            Cov-2
 ID    Time Events Censored  Set   Surv.F  C.Rate    Surv.F  C.Rate
-----------------------------------------------------------------
  0    0.00    0.0      0.0 600.0 1.00000 0.00000   1.00000 0.00000
  0    2.00    2.0      0.0 600.0 0.99568 0.00432   0.99415 0.00587
  0    3.00    5.0      1.0 597.0 0.98491 0.01520   0.97958 0.02063
  0    4.00    9.0      2.0 590.0 0.96561 0.03499   0.95363 0.04748
  .........................................................
  0  312.00    1.0      3.0  16.0 0.04611 3.07675   0.01537 4.17504
  0  326.00    1.0      1.0  14.0 0.04174 3.17627   0.01343 4.31009
  0  332.00    1.0      2.0  11.0 0.03694 3.29835   0.01138 4.47575
  0  350.00    1.0      1.0   9.0 0.03194 3.44391   0.00934 4.67327
```

Finally, due to the assumption of proportional effects, the cumulative transition rate for an arbitrary covariate vector A can be estimated by

$$\hat{H}(t) = \hat{H}^b(t) \exp\left(A\hat{\alpha}\right) \tag{9.8}$$

and the corresponding survivor function estimate is

$$\hat{G}(t) = \exp\left\{-\hat{H}^b(t) \exp\left(A\hat{\alpha}\right)\right\} = \hat{G}^b(t)^{\exp(A\hat{\alpha})} \qquad (9.9)$$

TDA uses these formulas to provide estimates of the cumulative baseline transition rate and the corresponding baseline survivor function. A generalization to the case of multiple origin and destination states can be done analogously: Each transition is treated separately. For instance, with respect to the transition (j, k), the procedure outlined previously is applied to all episodes with the origin state j; all episodes not ending in the destination state k are regarded as censored. The resulting estimates are then pseudosurvivor functions and transition-specific cumulative rates, respectively.

To illustrate the calculation of cumulative baseline rates and survivor functions, we again use our standard example data. The command file is *ehi10.cf* (Box 9.4.1) and it is basically identical to command file *ehi1.cf* shown in Box 9.1.2. We just have added the command

   prate = ehi10.bl;

to request the baseline rate calculation. In this example, the resulting table is written into the output file *ehi10.bl*. Furthermore, we have used the commands

   ev12 = 13,13;   education
   ev20 = 0, 0;   coho2 = 0
   ev21 = 0, 1;   coho3 = 0 or 1
   ev22 = 5, 5;   labor force experience
   ev23 = 1, 1;   one previous job
   ev10 = 30,30;   mean prestige value

to define two covariate constellations (i.e. we have assigned different values to the covariates in the model). In our example, one of these covariate constellations is for birth cohort 1, the other one is for birth cohort 3.

Box 9.4.2 shows part of the output file *ehi10.bl*. The header shows which covariate constellations have been used for the calculations. The main table has one line for each point in time when at least one event takes place (an uncensored ending time). There are two columns for each covariate constellation: *Surv.F*, containing an estimate of the survivor function according to (9.9), and *C.Rate*, containing an estimate of the cumulative transition rate according to (9.8).

Figure 9.4.1 shows a plot of the cumulative baseline rates for birth cohorts 1 and 3 as contained in the output file *ehi10.bl*. It would be helpful for interpretation to see a plot of the baseline rate, instead of the *cumulative* baseline rate. Therefore, what we need is the first derivative of the cumulative rate. To calculate this derivative, one can use numerical differentiation. Differentiation of the cumulative rate would however result in strong fluctuations. It is therefore useful to first smooth the cumulative rate. One possibility is to apply a smoothing spline function. An algorithm offered by TDA is based on Dierckx (1975). A command file, *ehi12.cf*, to generate the smoothed estimates

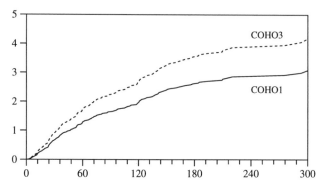

Figure 9.4.1 Cumulative baseline rates for birth cohorts 1 and 3, generated with *ehi10.cf*. The plot was generated with command file *ehi11.cf*.

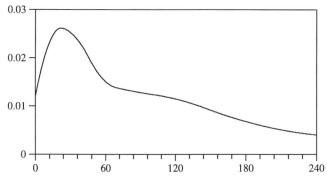

Figure 9.4.2 Smoothed baseline rate, for birth cohort 1, calculated by numerical differentiation based on smoothing of column $C7$ in *ehi10.bl* with a smoothing spline of degree 3.

of the cumulative baseline rate for birth cohort 1 and its first derivative, and a command file to generate a plot of the derivatives, *ehi13.cf*, can be found on the accompanying disk. Figure 9.4.2 shows the plot.

9.5 Application Example

Finally, we want to give at least one application example for the Cox model. For this purpose we use a demographic study of divorce rates (Blossfeld, De Rose, Hoem, and Rohwer 1993). From a methodological point of view, this example is particularly instructive because it compares a piecewise constant exponential model (see chapter 5) with a Cox model. Both models are proportional hazards models. The Cox model leaves the baseline hazard rate completely unspecified, whereas the piecewise constant exponential model tries to approximate the baseline rate with a series of period-specific constants. In other words, with sufficiently small time periods, a piecewise constant exponential model basically becomes a Cox model providing a direct estimation of the baseline hazard rate.

The application example stems from an international collaborative research project, conducted by Alessandra De Rose (Italy) and Jan M. Hoem (Sweden) together with the authors of this book, on the relationship between changes in women's educational attainment and the development of marriage disruption risks in modern societies.

The study focused mainly on two hypotheses. The first is that an increasing educational level raises the risk of marital disruption. This was expected because women with higher educational attainment normally have higher abilities and are more willing to violate social norms by dissolving unhappy marriages. They are also better able to cope with the consequences due to being in a better position to deal with any social or religious stigma produced by a divorce. The second hypothesis is that the importance of women's educational attainment on disruption risks is not constant over historical time. In particular, it changes as family systems are transformed. Because the three countries under study (Italy, West Germany, and Sweden) represent quite different stages in the development and differentiation of socially accepted living arrangements and levels of divorce risks, a comparison of the gradient in the effects of women's educational level on divorce risks in these countries should show that the "liberating" impact of a woman's higher educational attainment declines strongly as the family system becomes less "traditional" and as divorce customs get more permissive for all women. Specifically, it was expected that the effect of women's education on divorce is stronger in Italy than in West Germany, and stronger there than in Sweden.

Using event history data from Italy, West Germany, and Sweden, the authors specified women's divorce rate as a function of time-constant and time-dependent covariates with the help of two models: an exponential model with marriage-duration specific piecewise constant baseline rates, and a proportional hazards model that did not specify the baseline hazard rate at all.

Observation started with the time of first birth within the first marriage and ended with the event of the first date of *de facto* separation or, for right censored cases, with the date of the interview, with a marriage duration of 15 years, with the date of birth of the fourth child, or with some other very specific life events (such as the death of the husband, the birth of twins, etc.) whichever occurred first. The reason we did not go beyond a marriage duration of 15 years and did not include women with more than three children was a methodological one: These marriages took place under more specific conditions with very specific divorce risks.

Although the transition rate analysis focused on the effect of women's educational attainment, the authors included a series of covariables to avoid compositional effects and to clearly bring out the direct (or partial) effect of educational

Table 9.5.1 Estimation results for a Cox model and a piecewise constant exponential model for divorce rates. Results taken from Blossfeld et al. (1993).

	Cox Model			Piecewise Constant		
Variable	Italy	Germany	Sweden	Italy	Germany	Sweden
Period 0– 24				-9.68	-9.58	-7.18
Period 24– 48				-9.37	-7.41	-6.52
Period 48– 72				-9.03	-7.48	-6.30
Period 72– 96				-8.68	-7.31	-6.60
Period 96–120				-8.26	-7.07	-6.37
Period 120–144				-8.42	-7.33	-5.94
Period 144–168				-8.49	-6.65	-6.15
Period 168–				-8.66	-7.42	-5.80
Cohort 1939–43	0.36	-0.52	0.16	0.36	-0.52	0.16
	1.36	1.54	0.69	1.36	1.55	0.71
Cohort 1944–48	0.37	-0.10	0.49	0.38	-0.09	0.49
	1.38	0.31	2.19	1.40	0.28	2.22
Cohort 1949–53	0.21	0.29	0.37	0.21	0.33	0.38
	0.69	0.88	1.38	0.70	0.99	1.41
Cohort 1954–58	0.38	1.01	1.05	0.38	1.07	1.04
	1.08	2.71	2.79	1.08	2.87	2.75
Age at marriage	-0.83	-0.30	-0.56	-0.84	-0.30	-0.56
20–22	3.82	1.22	3.55	3.82	1.21	3.55
Age at marriage	-0.71	-0.65	-0.74	-0.71	-0.64	-0.74
23–25	3.11	1.81	3.58	3.10	1.79	3.58
Age at marriage	-1.21	-0.67	-0.65	-1.21	-0.66	-0.65
26–28	3.44	1.18	2.10	3.44	1.17	2.10
Age at marriage	-1.04	-1.49	-1.27	-1.03	-1.46	-1.27
28–	2.39	1.43	2.11	2.38	1.40	2.11
Second child	-1.04	-0.40	-0.75	-1.04	-0.42	-0.76
	5.32	1.74	4.52	5.35	1.81	4.63
Third child	-1.31	-0.66	-0.72	-1.31	-0.65	-0.74
	4.02	1.64	2.96	4.02	1.63	3.06
Education	0.77	0.42	0.30	0.77	0.42	0.30
middle level	4.24	1.70	1.98	4.24	1.73	1.98
Education	1.74	1.22	0.53	1.74	1.24	0.54
high level	5.79	2.66	2.77	5.78	2.70	2.78
Pregnant	0.76	0.87	0.38	0.76	0.88	0.38
at marriage	4.12	4.11	2.78	4.13	4.13	2.77
Log likelihood	-1325.3	-614.4	-1698.2	-1495.8	-759.0	-1849.5
χ^2	117.8	58.4	71.9	118.4	60.3	73.1
df	13	13	13	20	20	20

Coefficients divided by their estimated standard errors are shown in cursive.

level on the disruption risk. Most effect patterns for the controls were as expected and do not get any further attention here.

In the piecewise constant model shown in Table 9.5.1, a set of eight different periods for marriage duration was applied. It is easy to see that over the whole duration of marriage the divorce rate is continuously lower in Italy than in Germany, and continuously lower in Germany than in Sweden. Thus, there are persistent differences in divorce risks across duration in each country. In all three countries, the divorce rate slightly increases with marriage duration, up to a duration of about 10 years. Then, in Sweden and Germany, the divorce rates become more or less stable, while in Italy we observe some kind of trend reversal: Long-term marriages become increasingly stable. The amount of this marriage duration effect that may be due to selective attrition through divorce, and the amount that may be due to actual changes in propensity to divorce with duration, cannot be discussed here. Neither can we give an answer to the question of whether the reasons for divorce change with duration. Controlling for marriage duration patterns in the piecewise constant and in the Cox model at least shows that the piecewise constant model provides almost identical estimates for the observed variables (cohort membership, age at marriage, children, educational level, and pregnancy at marriage) for all three countries. Thus, the results are relatively robust against the model specification. The eight period dummies in the piecewise constant model seem to yield a reasonably good approximation of the baseline hazard rate. This model, of course, has an additional advantage over the Cox model, in that it offers direct estimates of the baseline rate.

After having controlled for important covariables on the rate of divorce, it is possible to evaluate the hypothesis described earlier. Women's educational attainment was included in the form of three levels (reference category: "low educational level"). Table 9.5.1 shows that an increasing level of educational attainment does indeed have a positive effect on the rate of divorce in all three countries. In addition, there is in fact the expected order of these effects between the three countries. Compared to women with a lower secondary qualification, the inclination to divorce of women with an upper secondary qualification is in Italy about 470 %, in West Germany about 239 %, and in Sweden about 70 %. This result means that in all three countries women's educational attainment can in fact be considered at least part of the explanation for high divorce rates. This is especially true in Italy where all significant cohort effects on the divorce rate could be explained by women's increasing educational attainment. In this perspective, the initially accelerating divorce risks from the mid-1960s to the mid-1980s and the following leveling off and stabilization of these risks in countries that have already reached relatively high levels of divorce rates can be understood as a manifestation of a first increasing and then decreasing lack of equilibrium among elements in the macrostructure of society (educational expansion and structure of the family system), as well as in the respective roles and expectations of the microstructure in intimate relationships.

Chapter 10

Problems of Model Specification

Previously, we stressed that time-dependence can be interpreted from various angles. In chapter 7, we discussed time-dependence from a substantive perspective, where it was derived from a theoretically supposed underlying diffusion process, or as an expression of a theoretically important latent causal factor operating in time. In this chapter we approach time-dependence from a methodological point of view and consider it to be a consequence of unobserved heterogeneity. We see that such a switch in perspective means that scientists can investigate the same data using different assumptions and logically reach valid but perhaps contradictory substantive conclusions (Manski 1993). Thus, distinguishing between competing (substantive and methodological) interpretations of the same data can be considered one of the most challenging problems in causal analysis. Therefore, it is not surprising that the estimation of event history models in the presence of omitted variables has become a prime focus of much technical work in recent years.

In Section 10.1 we discuss the issue of unobserved heterogeneity in general terms and provide some illustrative examples. Some researchers have proposed using so-called mixture models to account for unobserved heterogeneity. These approaches are demonstrated in Section 10.2. In particular, we show how to estimate transition rate models, in which it is assumed that the unobserved heterogeneity follows a gamma distribution. However, our discussion is mainly critical of the usefulness of these approaches because there is, in general, no way to make reliable assumptions about what has *not* been observed. Section 10.3 summarizes the discussion and stresses the fact that unobserved heterogeneity is just *one* aspect of a broad variety of model specification problems.

10.1 Unobserved Heterogeneity

Using transition rate models, we try to find empirical evidence about how the transition rates, describing the movements of individuals (or other units of analysis) in a given state space, depend on a set of covariates. Unfortunately, we are not always able to include all important factors. One reason is the limitation of available data; we would like to include some important variables but we simply do not have the information. Furthermore, we often do not know what is important. So what are the consequences of this situation? Basically, there are two aspects to be taken into consideration.

The first one is well known from traditional regression models. Because our covariates are normally correlated, the parameter estimates depend on the specific set of covariates included in the model. Every change in this set is likely to change the parameter estimates of the variables already included in previous models. Thus, in practice, the only way to proceed is to estimate a series of models with different specifications and then to check whether the estimation results are stable or not. However, this sequential model specification and estimation can also be seen as a resource for theoretical development. This procedure can provide additional insights into what may be called context sensitivity of causal effects in the social world.

Second, changing the set of covariates in a transition rate model will very often also lead to changes in the time-dependent shape of the transition rate. A similar effect occurs in traditional regression models: Depending on the set of covariates, the empirical distribution of the residuals changes. But, as opposed to regression models, where the residuals are normally only used for checking model assumptions, in transition rate models the residuals become the focus of modeling. In fact, if transition rate models are reformulated as regression models, the transition rate becomes a description of the residuals, and any change in the distribution of the residuals becomes a change in the time-dependent shape of the transition rate. Consequently, the empirical insight that a transition rate model provides for the time-dependent shape of the transition rate more or less depends on the set of covariates used to estimate the model.[1] So the question is whether a transition rate model can provide at least some reliable insights into a time-dependent transition rate.

Before discussing this question, some examples to illustrate possible consequences of "unobserved heterogeneity" are in order (see   also Blossfeld and Hamerle 1992; Vaupel and Yashin 1985). Let us assume a single transition from only one origin state to only one destination state so that the episodes can be described by a single random variable T for the duration in the origin state. The distribution of T can be represented by a density function $f(t)$, a survivor function $G(t)$, or by a transition rate $r(t) = f(t)/G(t)$.

Now let us assume that the population consists of two groups to be distinguished by a variable x, with $x = 1$ for group 1 and $x = 2$ for group 2. Then we can define duration variables T_1 and T_2 separately for these two groups. And, like T, these duration variables can be described separately by density, survivor, and transition rate functions:

$$T_1 \sim f_1(t), \ G_1(t), \ r_1(t) = f_1(t)/G_1(t)$$
$$T_2 \sim f_2(t), \ G_2(t), \ r_2(t) = f_2(t)/G_2(t)$$

The transition behavior in both groups can be quite different. If we are able to separate both groups we can gain some insight into these differences by

---

[1] And it also depends on the type of model. As shown in chapter 7, all parametric models are only able to fit a limited range of shapes of a time-dependent transition rate.

estimating $f_i(t)$, $G_i(t)$, and $r_i(t)$ separately for both groups ($i = 1, 2$). If, however, we do not have information about group membership, we can only estimate the transition behavior in both groups together, that is, we can only estimate $f(t)$, $G(t)$, and $r(t)$.

The important point is that the distribution describing T can be quite different from the distributions describing T_1 and T_2, or put in more substantive terms: The transition behavior in the population as a whole can be quite different from the transition behavior in the two subpopulations (groups). To describe this more formally, one can proceed as follows. First, let π_1 and π_2 denote the proportions of the two groups at the beginning of the process ($\pi_1 + \pi_2 = 1$). Then we find that

$$f(t) = \pi_1 f_1(t) + \pi_2 f_2(t) \quad \text{and}$$
$$G(t) = \pi_1 G_1(t) + \pi_2 G_2(t)$$

Using the general formula $r(t) = f(t)/G(t)$, we can now derive the following expression for the transition rate in the population:

$$r(t) = r_1(t) \pi_1 \frac{G_1(t)}{G(t)} + r_2(t) \pi_2 \frac{G_2(t)}{G(t)} \tag{10.1}$$

The transition rate $r(t)$ in the population is a weighted average of the transition rates in the two groups, $r_1(t)$ and $r_2(t)$. But the weights change during the process. In fact, the weights are just the proportions of the two groups in the "risk set" at every point in time.[2] Let us give three examples.

Example 1: Suppose a sample of employees is divided into two subpopulations, denoted by $x = 1$ (men) and $x = 2$ (women). The job exit rates for these two groups are supposed to be constant:[3]

$$r_1(t) = 0.01$$
$$r_2(t) = 0.04$$

and the proportions of the two groups in the population are assumed to be $\pi_1 = 0.5$ and $\pi_2 = 0.5$. The survivor functions are then

$$G_1(t) = \exp(-0.01 t)$$
$$G_2(t) = \exp(-0.04 t)$$
$$G(t) = 0.5 \exp(-0.01 t) + 0.5 \exp(-0.04 t)$$

and, using (10.1), we find the transition rate

$$r(t) = \frac{0.01 \exp(-0.01 t) + 0.04 \exp(-0.04 t)}{\exp(-0.01 t) + \exp(-0.04 t)}$$

---

[2] The "risk set" at time t is the set of individuals who did not have a transition before t, so it is the number of individuals at $t = 0$ multiplied by the survivor function $G(t)$.

[3] That is, we assume an exponential model for both groups; see chapter 4.

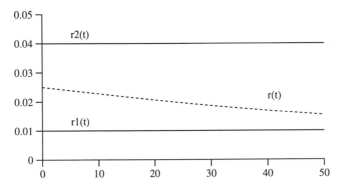

Figure 10.1.1 Mixture of two exponential transition rates.

Figure 10.1.1 illustrates the transition rates. Obviously, the transition rate in the population $r(t)$ declines, although there is a constant transition rate in both subpopulations. The reason is that the proportion of both groups in the risk set continuously changes. For instance, at the beginning of the process there are 50 % men and 50 % women. But women, in this example, leave their jobs faster than men, which is shown by their greater transition rate. Therefore, after (say) 36 months we find

$$G_1(t) = \exp(-0.01 \cdot 36) = 0.698$$
$$G_2(t) = \exp(-0.04 \cdot 36) = 0.237$$
$$G(t) = 0.5 \exp(-0.01 \cdot 36) + 0.5 \exp(-0.04 \cdot 36) = 0.468$$

This means that only 30.2 % of the men, but already 76.3 % of the women have left their job. So the risk set at $t = 36$ consists of $0.5 \cdot 0.698/0.468 = 74.6\%$ men and $0.5 \cdot 0.237/0.468 = 25.3\%$ women.

Example 2: Now assume the same setup as in Example 1, but the transition rate in group 1 is of the Weibull type, for instance (with $a = 0.01$ and $b = 1.5$):[4]

$$r_1(t) = 1.5 \cdot 0.01^{1.5} \cdot t^{0.5}$$
$$r_2(t) = 0.04$$

The survivor functions are then

$$G_1(t) = \exp\left(-(0.01\,t)^{1.5}\right)$$
$$G_2(t) = \exp\left(-0.04\,t\right)$$
$$G(t) = 0.5 \exp\left(-(0.01\,t)^{1.5}\right) + 0.5 \exp\left(-0.04\,t\right)$$

---

[4] See Section 7.3 for a definition of the Weibull model.

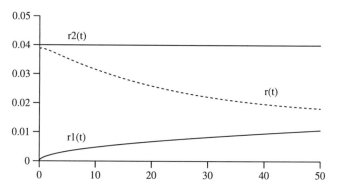

Figure 10.1.2 Mixture of an exponential and a Weibull transition rate.

and, using (10.1), we find the transition rate

$$r(t) = \frac{1.5 \cdot 0.01^{1.5} \cdot t^{0.5} \exp\left(-(0.01\,t)^{1.5}\right) + 0.04 \exp\left(-0.04\,t\right)}{\exp\left(-(0.01\,t)^{1.5}\right) + \exp\left(-0.04\,t\right)}$$

Figure 10.1.2 illustrates the transition rates for this example. While the transition rate is increasing in group 1 and constant in group 2, the resulting transition rate for the population is *decreasing*.

Example 3: Finally, suppose that both groups follow a Weibull transition rate, for instance

$$r_1(t) = 1.5 \cdot 0.01^{1.5} \cdot t^{0.5}$$
$$r_2(t) = 1.2 \cdot 0.04^{1.2} \cdot t^{0.2}$$

The survivor functions are then

$$G_1(t) = \exp\left(-(0.01\,t)^{1.5}\right)$$
$$G_2(t) = \exp\left(-(0.04\,t)^{1.2}\right)$$
$$G(t) = 0.5 \exp\left(-(0.01\,t)^{1.5}\right) + 0.5 \exp\left(-(0.04\,t)^{1.2}\right)$$

and, using (10.1), we find the transition rate

$$r(t) =$$
$$\frac{1.5 \cdot 0.01^{1.5} \cdot t^{0.5} \exp\left(-(0.01\,t)^{1.5}\right) + 1.2 \cdot 0.04^{1.2} \cdot t^{0.2} \exp\left(-(0.04\,t)^{1.2}\right)}{\exp\left(-(0.01\,t)^{1.5}\right) + \exp\left(-(0.04\,t)^{1.2}\right)}$$

Figure 10.1.3 illustrates the transition rates for this example. Both groups follow an increasing transition rate, but the transition rate for the population $r(t)$ is totally different, as it is bell-shaped (see also Blossfeld and Hamerle 1989b).

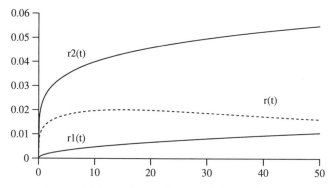

Figure 10.1.3 Mixture of two Weibull transition rates.

These examples show that the transition rate that is estimated for a population *can* be the result (a mixture) of quite different transition rates in the subpopulations. What are the consequences? First, this result means that one can *explain* an observed transition rate at the population level as the result of different transition rates in subpopulations. Of course, this will only be a sensible strategy if we are able to identify important subpopulations. To follow this strategy one obviously needs *observable* criteria to partition a population into subpopulations. Just to speculate about the fact that an observed transition rate *might* be the result of quite different transition rates will not further an explanation. Although there might be unobserved heterogeneity (and we can usually be sure that we were not able to include all important covariates), just to make more or less arbitrary distributional assumptions about unobserved heterogeneity will not lead to better models. On the contrary, the estimation results will be more dependent on assumptions than would be the case otherwise (Lieberson 1985). Therefore, we would like to stress our view that the most important basis for any progress in model building is sufficient and appropriate data.

There remains, however, the problem of how to interpret a time-dependent transition rate from a causal view. The question is: Can time be considered as a proxy for an unmeasured variable producing a time-dependent rate, or is it simply an expression of unobserved heterogeneity, which does not allow for any substantive interpretation?[5]

---

[5] There is, however, another aspect to this problem. From a purely descriptive point of view, a time-dependent transition rate provides some empirically relevant information about the population itself. Some researchers seem to assume that this is *not* the case. The argument runs as follows: Because a time-dependent transition rate could be the result of quite different transition rates in unobserved subpopulations, the transition rate for the population might only be "apparent." We agree with this reasoning insofar as there is always the possibility that the observed transition rate for a population could be the result of quite different transition rates in certain subpopulations. This sometimes produces an opportunity to *explain* the transition rate at the population level

10.2   Models with a Mixture Distribution

There have been several proposals to deal with unobserved heterogeneity in
transition rate models. The basic idea underlying these proposals is to incor-
porate an "error term" into the model specification. This is quite familiar from
traditional regression models, but specific problems arise if one tries to follow
this strategy in the specification of transition rate models. These problems become visible if we begin with the following general specification of a transition
rate model:

$$r(t) = f(x, \beta, \epsilon)$$

In this specification, the transition rate, $r(t)$, is a function of a vector of covariates, x, a vector of model parameters, β, to be estimated, and a stochastic
variable ϵ to represent an error term. In order to make such a model estimable
one needs additional specifications. First, one has to specify the functional
relationship $f(.)$. There are many options as already illustrated in previous
chapters of this book. But this is not enough. One also needs some assumptions about the distribution of ϵ.

This becomes clearer if we write our transition rate model as a regression
model, for instance, in the following way:[6]

$$\log(T) = x\beta + \epsilon$$

To simplify the argument we assume that the logarithm of the duration variable,
T, depends on a linear combination of covariates, $x\beta$, and, additively, on an
error term, ϵ. Depending on our assumptions about the distribution of ϵ,

---

by referring to the various transition rates in subpopulations. However, we do not agree with
the conclusion that the observed transition rate at the population level is only "apparent." It
remains an empirical fact. Otherwise there would be no point in *explaining* the transition rate
for the population. The conclusion should be quite different. Instead of using the examples
given previously to support speculation about "true" vs. only "apparent" time-dependencies in
the transition rate, statements about time-dependent transition rates should be made explicitly
dependent on specific populations. Then, there can be no contradiction in stating that there
are different transition rates for men and women, and that there is quite another transition rate
for a population consisting of men and women, for example. If, to follow this example, there
are constant, but different transition rates for both men and women, the transition rate for the
population consisting of men and women will decrease with time. Thus, the statement that there is
a decreasing transition rate for the population consisting of men and women will not become false
if we learn that this population consists of men and women and that transition rates for men and
women are time constant but different. The statement about the transition rate for the population
remains true and provides a more or less valuable *empirical* insight.

[6] Many authors have discussed the formal similarities between regression and transition rate
models; see, for instance, Lawless (1982) and Petersen (1990, 1991). See also the discussion of
SAS models in Blossfeld, Hamerle, and Mayer (1989).

this becomes a transition rate model. We can, for instance, assume that ϵ is normally distributed, $\epsilon \sim \mathcal{N}(0, \sigma^2)$, a common assumption in regression modeling. Consequently, T (conditional on the covariates) follows a log-normal distribution with density function

$$\frac{1}{t\,\sigma}\,\phi\left(\frac{\log(t) - \beta}{\sigma}\right)$$

(ϕ is used to denote the standard normal density function.) In fact, what we get is the log-normal transition rate model, as discussed in Section 7.5. However, then there is no longer an error term. What has happened? Our assumption about the error term in the regression model has become an assumption about the distribution of the duration variable T, so in a sense our transition rate model already contains an "error term"; it is, so to speak, the *distribution* of the duration variable T, *conditional* on the covariates. However, this formulation is somewhat misleading because the focus of the model has changed. In traditional regression modeling, the focus is on the *expectation* of the dependent variable, $E(T)$. This focus motivates reference to an "error term," meaning the residuals, in trying to explain the *expectation* of T, given the covariates x. The focus in transition rate models is quite different. It is *not* the expectation of T, but the *distribution* of T (i.e. the transition rate describing how the process in a population proceeds) if time goes on. We are not interested in how the expectation of T depends on covariates, but in how the distribution of T (i.e. the transition rate) depends on the covariates. In statistical terms, there is not much difference in these two modeling approaches, but in terms of substantive theory, there is quite a significant difference. The transition rate has a substantive meaning in event history modeling because it refers to a "propensity" of individuals to change states in a state space. It is, therefore, not just a statistical concept for making assumptions about an error term.

What would a transition rate model containing an *additional* error term look like? We could split, for instance, the error term ϵ into two components: $\epsilon = \epsilon_1 + \epsilon_2$. Written as a regression model, we then get

$$\log(T) = x\beta + \epsilon_1 + \epsilon_2$$

We can then make an assumption about the distribution of ϵ_1 to get a distributional form for T and finally arrive at a transition rate model containing an additional error term, ϵ_2. Of course, to make the model estimable, we also need a distributional assumption about ϵ_2. This is quite possible in purely formal terms, but we will obviously run into a problem. Having made distributional assumptions about ϵ_1 and ϵ_2, we have, in fact, made an assumption about $\epsilon = \epsilon_1 + \epsilon_2$. We have specified a mixture distribution for ϵ and, consequently, for T. Thus, we finally arrive at a mixture model for the duration variable and we have again lost our error term.

The essential point is that the whole procedure of splitting an error term into components is quite arbitrary. From an empirical point of view, we only have a single set of residuals that is *defined* by a model specification. It would be totally arbitrary to separate these residuals into two parts: one part to be interpreted as a description of the transition rate, the other part to be interpreted as an error term. If strong theoretical and empirical reasons were available to justify a specific distributional assumption about the transition rate, it could make sense to include an additional error term. But, at least in sociological research, this is almost never the case. In fact, we do not know of a single application where the researcher had strong a priori reasons (with respect to the given data) that could be used to justify the selection of a specific type of transition rate model.

Thus, it seems that there is no point in specifying and estimating transition rate models based on mixture distributions, at least in the current state of sociological research. However, this result is inconclusive. The fact remains that we almost never have sufficient reasons to decide for one specific transition rate model. Our estimation results will depend on the type of model. We have already discussed this previously, coming to the conclusion that the best strategy is always to estimate a broad variety of different models in order to find robust estimation results. Thus, if one looks at the problem from this perspective, mixture models might be helpful in another way. Although these models have no utility in separating an error term from a "true" transition rate, they broadly enrich the spectrum of models that can be used to look for robust estimation results. Thus, if the previously mentioned strategy is followed, there is some sense in using mixture models. They can be quite helpful in separating robust estimation results (i.e. estimation results that are to a large degree independent of a specific model specification) and "spurious" results, which might be defined by the fact that they heavily depend on a specific type of model.

For these reasons, we give a short technical discussion of mixture models in the following sections. There are, basically, two approaches. One type of approach begins with a fully parametric specification of the distribution of the error term. In particular, the use of a gamma distribution has been proposed (Tuma 1985).[7] This approach is discussed in the following section because it is implemented in TDA, and we provide some examples. Another approach, proposed by Heckman and Singer (1984), is based on a discrete mixture distribution and might be called semi-parametric because only very weak assumptions are necessary. Because this approach is currently not implemented in TDA, it is not discussed in this book.[8]

---

[7] In principle, any other distributional assumption resulting in correspondingly defined mixture models is possible. The gamma distribution is just a particularly convenient choice because the resulting mixture distribution is easily tractable.

[8] Trussell and Richards (1985) discussed their experience using this approach.

10.2.1 Models with a Gamma Mixture

In this section we follow the usual way of treating the error term in transition rate models. This is based on the assumption that there is a time-invariant unobserved constant specific for each individual. Furthermore, it is assumed that this unobserved constant can be represented as the realization of a random variable, identically distributed for all individuals and independent of observed covariates (Crouchley and Pickles 1987; Davies and Crouchley 1985). This error term is then multiplicatively connected with the transition rate. The idea is to make this random variable capture both individual heterogeneity and depart from the supposed shape of duration dependence (Galler and Pötter 1990).

To be more specific, it is assumed that the transition rate, $r(t \mid x, v)$, depends on a vector, x, of observed covariates and on a scalar stochastic term, v, which is not observed. Our question is how the variables comprising x influence the transition rate, but this cannot be observed directly. In any observed sample of episodes, the transition rate also depends on the values of v.[9]

The same is true for the associated density and survivor functions. The relation between transition rate, density, and survivor function must therefore be written as

$$r(t \mid x, v) \;=\; \frac{f(t \mid x, v)}{G(t \mid x, v)} \tag{10.2}$$

$$G(t \mid x, v) \;=\; \exp\left(-\int_0^t r(\tau \mid x, v)\,d\tau\right) \tag{10.3}$$

To find an estimation approach, we make some simplifying assumptions. First, that the transition rate can be expressed as

$$r(t \mid x, v) = r^u(t \mid x)\,v \qquad v \geq 0 \tag{10.4}$$

In fact, we assume that the component $r^u(t \mid x)$ of this expression, called the *underlying* rate, is parametrically given according to one of the standard parametric transition rate models discussed in chapters 4 and 7. The cumulative transition rate may then be written as

$$H(t \mid x, v) = v\,H^u(t \mid x) = v \int_0^t r^u(\tau \mid x)\,d\tau \tag{10.5}$$

The second basic assumption is that the stochastic term, v, follows a gamma distribution with expectation $E(v) = 1$. As implied by this assumption, the density function of v can be written as

$$f_v(v) = \frac{\kappa^\kappa\, v^{\kappa-1}}{\Gamma(\kappa)}\,\exp(-\kappa\,v) \qquad \kappa > 0$$

---

[9] This stochastic variable v corresponds to the error term ϵ_2, which has been introduced in the regression framework above. Because the regression model was formulated in terms of $\log(T)$, the error term now becomes $\exp(\epsilon_2)$, multiplicatively connected with the transition rate.

The variance of this distribution is $\text{Var}(v) = 1/\kappa$. The next step is to calculate the resulting mixture distribution for the observed durations. First, for the density and survivor functions, one gets

$$f(t \mid x) = \int_0^\infty f(t \mid x, v) \, f_v(v) \, dv$$

$$G(t \mid x) = \int_0^\infty G(t \mid x, v) \, f_v(v) \, dv$$

These mixtures are expectations according to the distribution of v. The calculation is easy because the gamma distribution implies the basic equality

$$\int_0^\infty \exp(-v\,s(t)) \, f_v(v) \, dv = \left[1 + \frac{1}{\kappa} s(t)\right]^{-\kappa}$$

which holds for any real valued function $s(t)$.[10] Therefore, using (10.3) and (10.5), the unconditional survivor function is

$$G(t \mid x) = \int_0^\infty \exp\left(-v\,H^u(t \mid x)\right) \, f_v(v) \, dv = \left[1 + \frac{1}{\kappa} H^u(t \mid x)\right]^{-\kappa} \qquad (10.6)$$

The unconditional density function can be found by differentiating the negative value of the unconditional survivor function, resulting in

$$f(t \mid x) = r^u(t \mid x) \left[1 + \frac{1}{\kappa} H^u(t \mid x)\right]^{-\kappa - 1} \qquad (10.7)$$

Finally, the unconditional transition rate is

$$r(t \mid x) = \frac{f(t \mid x)}{G(t \mid x)} = r^u(t \mid x) \left[1 + \frac{1}{\kappa} H^u(t \mid x)\right]^{-1} \qquad (10.8)$$

Multiple Origin and Destination States. So far we have derived a mixture model for episodes with one origin and one destination state. However, the extension to a situation with several origins and destinations is easy if a specific error term for each transition is assumed. The implementation of gamma mixture models in TDA is based on this assumption. More formally, for the transition from origin state j to destination state k, the model specification is

$$r_{jk}(t \mid x, v_{jk}) = r_{jk}^u(t \mid x) \, v_{jk} \qquad v_{jk} \geq 0$$

$r_{jk}^u(t \mid x)$ is the underlying rate used for model formulation. The error term v_{jk} is assumed to be specific for each transition and gamma distributed with unit expectation. In the same way, as was shown earlier for the single transition

---

[10] See, for instance, Lancaster (1990, p. 328).

case, one can finally derive expressions for the observed transition rates, which can be used for model estimations.[11]

Maximum Likelihood Estimation. The approach to deriving transition rate models with an additional gamma distributed error term can be summarized as follows. One starts with a parametrically given transition rate, as in (10.4), and assumes that the unobserved heterogeneity is gamma distributed with unit mean and variance $1/\kappa$. Then one derives the observed mixture distribution, described by $f(t \mid x)$, $G(t \mid x)$, and $r(t \mid x)$, given in (10.6), (10.7), and (10.8), respectively. This is for the single transition case, but an extension to the case of several transitions is wholly analogous. It follows that the log likelihood can be set up in the usual way. We only give the formula for the single transition case. With $\mathcal{N}$ and $\mathcal{E}$ denoting the sets of all episodes and of episodes with an event, respectively, the log likelihood can be written as

$$
\ell = \sum_{i \in \mathcal{E}} \log(r(t_i)) + \sum_{i \in \mathcal{N}} \log(G(t_i))
$$

$$
= \sum_{i \in \mathcal{E}} \log\left(r^u(t_i)\right) - \log\left(1 + \frac{1}{\kappa} H^u(t_i)\right) - \sum_{i \in \mathcal{N}} \kappa \, \log\left(1 + \frac{1}{\kappa} H^u(t_i)\right)
$$

Unfortunately, the usual way of applying the episode splitting method is no longer possible. Assume an episode $(0, t)$, starting at time zero and ending at time t, and assume that there is a covariate that changes its value at t_x $(0 < t_x < t)$. Then it would be quite possible to include this information into the calculation of the cumulated rate $H^u(t \mid x)$, which is needed for the calculation of the density and survivor functions of the unconditional distribution. However, the episode splitting method is only applicable in its usual form, if the calculation can be separated into two steps; the first step has the information about the $(0, t_x)$ split, and the second has information about the (t_x, t) split, but obviously the unconditional density and survivor functions cannot be calculated in these two distinct steps. Therefore, the current implementation of gamma mixture models in TDA does not allow for the use of split episodes.

Gamma Mixture Models in TDA. In principle, the approach of adding a gamma distributed error term can be used with any parametric transition rate model. However, TDA's capabilities are somewhat limited. The current version of the program only allows the estimation of gamma mixture models for the following "underlying" models: exponential, Weibull, sickle, log-logistic, and log-normal. To set up a command file to estimate one of these models with a gamma mixture is fairly easy. First, one can proceed as if he/she intends to estimate a model without a gamma mixture, and a command file is set up in the usual way as described in previous chapters. Then, to request estimation of the

---

[11] The mathematical derivation is given in Rohwer (1994, TDA-WP 5-5).

same model with an additional gamma distributed error term, one must only add the command

> *mix = 1;*

This command can be written into the command file or given on the command line. For instance, using the command file *ehd1.cf* (Box 4.1.1) with TDA as

> *tda cf=ehd1.cf > out*

would estimate a simple exponential model without a gamma mixture distribution (the estimation results would be written into the file *out*). Invoking TDA as

> *tda cf=ehd1.cf mix=1 > out1*

would instead estimate the same exponential model but now with an additional gamma distributed error term, and the results would be written into the output file *out1*.

10.2.2   Exponential Models with a Gamma Mixture

To illustrate the estimation of gamma mixture models with TDA, we first use an exponential model. The transition rate, now conditional on v, may be written as

$$r(t \mid v) = a\, v \qquad a, v \geq 0$$

The underlying model, already described in chapter 4, is the exponential, implying that

$$r^u(t) = a \quad \text{and} \quad H^u(t) = a\,t$$

The observed mixture distribution is described by

$$
\begin{aligned}
G(t) &= (1 + d\,a\,t)^{-\frac{1}{d}} \\
f(t) &= a\,(1 + d\,a\,t)^{-\frac{1}{d}-1} \\
r(t) &= a\,(1 + d\,a\,t)^{-1}
\end{aligned}
$$

d is the variance of the gamma distributed error term. Obviously, if $d > 0$, there will be a negative time-dependence, although the underlying rate is a time-independent constant.

The model has two parameters: a, the constant transition rate of the underlying exponential model, and d, the variance of the mixing gamma distribution. In the TDA implementation of this model, both parameters (the A- and D-terms of the model) can be linked to covariates by an exponential link function. The model formulation for the transition rate from origin state j to destination state k is

$$r_{jk}(t) = \frac{a_{jk}}{1 + d_{jk}\, a_{jk}\, t}, \quad a_{jk} = \exp\left(A^{(jk)}\alpha^{(jk)}\right), \; d_{jk} = \exp\left(D^{(jk)}\delta^{(jk)}\right)$$

Box 10.2.1   Estimation results of *ehd2.cf* with a gamma mixture distribution

```
Model: Exponential (Gamma mixture)

Maximum likelihood estimation
Maximum of log likelihood: -2442.13
Norm of final gradient vector: 2.1e-04
Last absolute change of function value: 3.7e-09
Last relative change in parameters: 9.1e-04
```

Idx	SN	Org	Des	MT	Var	Label	Coeff	Error	T-Stat	Signif
1	1	0	1	A	--	Const	-3.9869	0.3430	-11.6219	1.0000
2	1	0	1	A	V12	EDU	0.0873	0.0310	2.8108	0.9951
3	1	0	1	A	V20	COHO2	0.5707	0.1445	3.9503	0.9999
4	1	0	1	A	V21	COHO3	0.4163	0.1512	2.7529	0.9941
5	1	0	1	A	V22	LFX	-0.0046	0.0011	-4.2132	1.0000
6	1	0	1	A	V23	PNOJ	0.0850	0.0545	1.5594	0.8811
7	1	0	1	A	V10	PRES	-0.0321	0.0066	-4.8423	1.0000
8	1	0	1	D	--	Const	-0.8019	0.1837	-4.3659	1.0000

It is assumed that the first component of each of the covariate (row) vectors, $A^{(jk)}$ and $D^{(jk)}$, is a constant equal to one. The associated coefficient vectors, $\alpha^{(jk)}$ and $\delta^{(jk)}$, are the model parameters to be estimated.

To illustrate the model estimation, we use command file *ehd2.cf* shown in Box 4.1.4. The estimation results for an exponential model without a gamma-distributed error term are shown in Box 4.1.5. Now we estimate a mixture model. We can use the same command file, but TDA is now invoked as

$$tda\ cf=ehd2.cf\ mix=1 > out$$

Part of the output file (*out*) is shown in Box 10.2.1. Because the distribution of the error term is not linked with covariates, the model that we have actually estimated is

$$r(t) = \frac{a}{1 + d\,a\,t}, \quad a = \exp(A\alpha), \quad d = \exp(\delta_0)$$

In Box 10.2.1 estimates of the parameter vector α and an estimate of δ_0 are shown. Comparing these estimates with the results of the simple exponential model in Box 4.1.5 shows that there are no substantial changes in the estimated parameters. However, we get a quite significant estimate for the variance of the mixing gamma distribution: $\hat{d} = \exp(\hat{\delta}_0) = 0.448$. This is supported by the likelihood ratio test statistic to compare the two models, which is 47.7 with one degree of freedom. The result indicates that we have a decreasing transition rate, absorbed by the error term in relation to the assumption of a constant transition rate for the underlying model (see Figure 10.2.1). Of course, this does not prove that all deviations from a constant transition rate are a result of "unobserved heterogeneity." As already discussed at the beginning of this section, the utility of estimating a mixture model lies not in separating an error

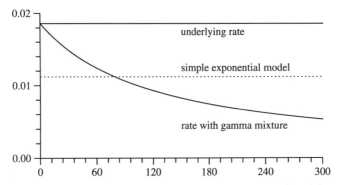

Figure 10.2.1 Transition rates estimated with an exponential model, without (dotted) and with (solid) a gamma mixture distribution. Model specification according to Box 4.1.5, all covariate values set to zero.

term from a "true" transition rate, but in providing some means for assessing the robustness of parameter estimates for *observed* covariates.

10.2.3   Weibull Models with a Gamma Mixture

For a second illustration, we use the Weibull model (see Section 7.3). The transition rate, now conditional on v, is

$$r(t \mid v) = r^u(t)\, v \qquad v \geq 0$$

The underlying transition rate and the cumulative rate are given by

$$r^u(t) = b\, a^b\, t^{b-1} \quad \text{and} \quad H^u(t) = (a\, t)^b$$

according to the standard Weibull model. The observed mixture distribution is described by

$$
\begin{aligned}
G(t) &= \left(1 + d\,(a\, t)^b\right)^{-\frac{1}{d}} \\
f(t) &= b\, a^b\, t^{b-1} \left(1 + d\,(a\, t)^b\right)^{-\frac{1}{d}-1} \\
r(t) &= b\, a^b\, t^{b-1} \left(1 + d\,(a\, t)^b\right)^{-1}
\end{aligned}
$$

The model has three parameters. a and b are the parameters of the underlying Weibull distribution; d represents the variance of the mixing gamma distribution. In the TDA implementation of this model, all three parameters (the A-, B-, and D-terms of the model) can be linked to covariates by an exponential link function. The model formulation for the transition rate from origin state j to destination state k is

$$r_{jk}(t) = \frac{b_{jk}\, a_{jk}^{b_{jk}}\, t^{b_{jk}-1}}{1 + d_{jk}\,(a_{jk}\, t)^{b_{jk}}}$$

Box 10.2.2   Estimation results of *ehg6.cf* with a gamma mixture distribution

```
Model: Weibull (Gamma mixture)

Maximum likelihood estimation
Maximum of log likelihood: -2410.71
Norm of final gradient vector: 7.5e-05
Last absolute change of function value: 7.3e-10
Last relative change in parameters: 2.0e-04

Idx SN Org Des MT Var  Label   Coeff    Error    T-Stat  Signif
---------------------------------------------------------------
  1  1   0   1  A --   Const   -3.4926  0.2953  -11.8272  1.0000
  2  1   0   1  A V12  EDU      0.0720  0.0266    2.7106  0.9933
  3  1   0   1  A V20  COHO2    0.4641  0.1205    3.8505  0.9999
  4  1   0   1  A V21  COHO3    0.4014  0.1284    3.1274  0.9982
  5  1   0   1  A V22  LFX     -0.0041  0.0008   -4.8731  1.0000
  6  1   0   1  A V23  PNOJ     0.1144  0.0470    2.4345  0.9851
  7  1   0   1  A V10  PRES    -0.0260  0.0053   -4.8769  1.0000
  8  1   0   1  B --   Const    0.6693  0.0880    7.6057  1.0000
  9  1   0   1  D --   Const    0.7833  0.1716    4.5648  1.0000
```

$$a_{jk} = \exp\left(A^{(jk)}\alpha^{(jk)}\right), \; b_{jk} = \exp\left(B^{(jk)}\beta^{(jk)}\right), \; d_{jk} = \exp\left(D^{(jk)}\delta^{(jk)}\right)$$

It is assumed that the first component of each of the covariate (row) vectors $A^{(jk)}$, $B^{(jk)}$, and $D^{(jk)}$ is a constant equal to one. The associated coefficient vectors $\alpha^{(jk)}$, $\beta^{(jk)}$, and $\delta^{(jk)}$ are the model parameters to be estimated.

To illustrate the model estimation, we use command file *ehg6.cf* shown in Box 7.3.3 (see Section 7.3 on Weibull models). The estimation results for a Weibull model without a gamma-distributed error term are shown in Box 7.3.4. Now we estimate a mixture model. We can use the same command file, but TDA is now invoked as

tda cf=ehg6.cf mix=1 > out

Part of the output file (*out*) is shown in Box 10.2.2. Because the distribution of the error term is not linked with covariates, the model that we have actually estimated is

$$r(t) = \frac{b\,a^b\,t^{b-1}}{1 + d\,(a\,t)^b}, \; a = \exp\left(A\alpha\right), \; b = \exp\left(\beta_0\right), \; d = \exp\left(\delta_0\right)$$

In Box 10.2.2 estimates of the parameter vector α and estimates of β_0 and δ_0 are shown. Comparing the estimates for α with the corresponding estimates in Box 7.3.4 (i.e. the simple Weibull model without a gamma mixture distribution) shows that there are no substantial changes. However, we do not only get a quite significant estimate for the variance of the mixing gamma distribution, $\hat{d} = \exp(\hat{\delta}_0) = 2.189$. The shape parameter of the underlying Weibull distribution has changed significantly as well. In the simple Weibull model it was $\hat{b} = 0.914$;

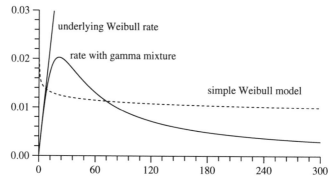

Figure 10.2.2 Transition rates estimated with a Weibull model, without (dotted) and with (solid) a gamma mixture distribution. Model specification according to Box 7.3.4, all covariate values set to zero.

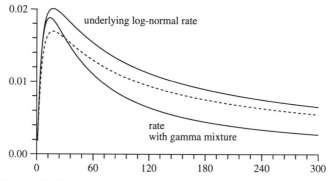

Figure 10.2.3 Transition rates estimated with a log-normal model, without (dotted) and with (solid) a gamma mixture distribution. Model specification according to Box 7.5.3, all covariate values set to zero.

now it is $\hat{d} = \exp(0.7833) = 1.953$. In fact, as shown in Figure 10.2.2, the transition rate has changed quite dramatically. Although the Weibull model only allows for monotonic increasing or decreasing transition rates, mixing the Weibull distribution with a gamma distribution allows for bell-shaped transition rates, and because this seems most appropriate for our data, such a rate can finally be estimated. The underlying Weibull transition rate is just an arbitrary part of the mixture distribution, or something like a residual to make the mixing distribution fit the data. This again demonstrates that one should be very careful in interpreting the various parts of a mixture distribution in theoretical terms.

These examples demonstrate that using a mixture model can significantly improve a model's capability to fit a given set of data with one of its possible time-dependent transition rates. As a by-product, this might result in more reliable parameter estimates for the covariates.

As a final example, Figure 10.2.3 shows the transition rates for a log-normal model with and without a mixing gamma distribution.[12] Because we already know that the log-normal distribution is appropriate for our data, we don't expect much improvement from using a mixture distribution. However, as seen in Figure 10.2.3, the final mixing distribution shows that the (population level!) transition rate is somewhat steeper than can be expressed with the simple log-normal model.

Specification of the Error Term

The main drawback of mixture models is that parameter estimates *can* be highly sensitive to the assumed parametric form of the error term. For example, Heckman and Singer (1982), who based the systematic part of the model on the same assumptions, estimated four different unobserved heterogeneity models: one with a normal, one with a log-normal, and one with a gamma distribution of the error term, as well as a model with a nonparametric specification of the disturbance. They found that the estimates provided by these models were surprisingly different. In other words, the identification problem might only be shifted to another level: Misspecification of the transition rate by neglecting the error term might be replaced by misspecification of the parametric distribution of the error term. Thus, a powerful theory would be needed with regard to the distribution of the stochastic error term. However, given the various sources of misspecification that are described later, it is very unlikely that any theory can provide solid guidance to a specific parametric distribution of the error term. In other words, misspecification is likely to occur.

This makes a semi-parametric specification of the error term attractive. Heckman and Singer (1982, 1984) proposed using a discrete distribution with a varying number of mass points to approximate the unknown distribution of the error term. Unfortunately, this solution again only shifts the identification problem to another level. This is because Trussell and Richards (1985) reported a strong dependence of the semi-parametric estimator on the choice of the duration dependence in transition rate models. Thus, again, a powerful argument would be needed to justify a specific parametric form of the duration dependence. However, as discussed in Section 7.1, this will be rarely the case in empirical applications (see also Heckman and Walker 1987).

Thus, a further step in trying to solve the identification problem would be to adopt a nonparametric specification of both the duration dependence and the unobserved heterogeneity term. However, it seems that these models

---

[12] The model is specified as shown in Box 7.5.3 (command file *ehg11.cf*); see Section 7.5 about log-normal models. The gamma mixture model is estimated by using the command file *ehg11.cf* with the additional command *mix=1*.

are only identifiable in the case of complete survivor functions for all values
of the covariates (Elbers and Ridder 1982). They are also very sensitive to
small perturbations in the values of the estimated survivor function (Galler
and Pötter 1990). Thus, given the common limitations of event history data
in practical research (censored information, measurement error), it seems impossible to estimate both duration dependence and unobserved heterogeneity
nonparametrically in one model (Galler and Pötter 1990).[13]

10.3   Discussion

So far we have discussed the topic of "unobserved heterogeneity." We have
tried to show that neglecting important covariates is, in fact, a serious source
of model misspecification. But we have also tried to show that there are no
simple remedies for this problem. In particular, transition rate models with a
mixture distribution do not provide a solution for the problems generated by
unobserved heterogeneity, but they can be quite helpful in our search for robust
parameter estimates. This is simply because these models provide a broader
range of possible shapes for the transition rate, so that they can better fit a given
set of data. The only empirically promising strategy to cope with unobserved
heterogeneity is to look for more and better data.

One should, however, not forget that unobserved heterogeneity is just one
source of problems in our search for useful and robust models. In fact, there
are many other problems of model specification that are no less important.
Therefore, it seems sensible to end this book by briefly drawing attention to
the most important problems.

(1) The most significant aspect of model specification is to find an appropriate
definition of the state space. For example, consider an investigation of women's
transition rates between the states "employed," "housewife status," and "unemployed" over the life course (Blossfeld in press). If women in part-time
and full-time employment behave differently and/or if covariates have distinct
effects that are dependent on the origin and destination states "full-time" and
"part-time employment," then a study neglecting the full-time and part-time
divide in the state space will produce omitted differences.[14] A further instructive example of misspecification of the state space was given in chapter 4, where
we demonstrated that estimating the effect of education on the job exit rate
is problematic because education has a positive effect on upward moves and a

---

[13] A possibly fruitful compromise between a fully nonparametric and a parametric specification of
the duration dependence could be a piecewise constant exponential model, as shown in chapter
5. This model could be mixed with a nonparametric specification of the unobserved error term.
However, if a larger number of dummy variables is used, the identification of this model, while
theoretically possible, would demand a large amount of exact data (see Galler and Pötter 1990).

[14] However, to some extent one could also include the differences of full-time and part-time
employment by using a dummy variable and some of its interaction effects with other covariates.

negative effect on downward moves. Thus, not taking into account differences in destination states mixes up the contradictory effects of education.

(2) It might not be possible to include all important variables in the model specification. As already stressed, the resulting parameter estimates are more or less dependent on the set of covariates actually used; and leaving out some important covariates is therefore an important source of misspecification.[15] For example, we have shown in some of our examples that the job exit behavior of men and women is, in some respects, quite different, but in many of our examples we did not take gender differences explicitly into account.[16] Therefore, this might be an important source of misspecification. In serious research, one would include covariates for gender differences and investigate the resulting changes in parameter estimates.

(3) Another important type of misspecification occurs if initial conditions at entry into the episode (in single and much more importantly in multi-episode models) are not taken into account. Differences at the beginning of the spells are normally the consequence of foregoing selection processes. As discussed previously, most sociological research is based on nonexperimental observations of highly selective processes, which may in themselves be influencing the estimated transition rate. Let us again take the job mobility example. It is very likely that (a) there is self-selection among individual employees depending in part on their preferences for specific jobs, (b) there is selection by employers through their hiring and personnel policies, and (c) there may be selectivity due to forces exogenous to the covariates included in the model (e.g. socioeconomic background, ethnicity, etc.). In short, various sorting processes have already taken place when individuals enter into a new job episode and they may massively influence the results of estimated transition rates. This is particularly true in models with multiple episodes where one should try to additionally control for the dependencies between successive episodes for each of the individuals (see Section 4.3). Although event history models allow for the inclusion of information about process history much better than cross-sectional or panel models, only a few researchers can contend that all relevant variables for the history of the process have been included in their models.

(4) Misspecification can result when important time-dependent covariates are not taken into account, or if time-dependent covariates are modeled as time-

---

[15] We do not speak of "biased" parameter estimates because, outside of descriptively defined estimation problems, the idea of unbiased estimation cannot be given a clear meaning. And without knowing the meaning of unbiased estimates, there is no sense in speculating about "biased" estimation. The problem is that our estimates are more or less dependent on model specification, so the question is how to find an appropriate model that may, in turn, heavily depend on its intended use.

[16] In fact, we did this because our example data set is small and, for didactical purposes, we wanted to use only one basic model throughout the book.

constant covariates, measured only once.[17] In chapter 6, we demonstrated that time-dependent covariates are observations of the sample path of parallel processes (at the individual level, the level of small groups, the intermediate level of organizations or households, or at the macrolevel of a society). Omitting these important processes, or including them only as time-constant covariates, is obviously a source of misspecification. Although we have argued that the genuine strength of event history models, at least compared to cross-sectional and panel models, is their ability to include these parallel processes appropriately, it could easily happen that important time-dependent covariates are neglected or must be neglected due to missing data. The effect of the time-dependent covariates may also be highly sensitive with regard to the points in time when they should change their value. This was demonstrated in Example 3 of Section 6.6, where the impact of pregnancy on entry into marriage for couples living in consensual unions was analyzed.

(5) Possible misspecification might occur if interaction effects are not taken into account. This is a serious point in many social science applications because often the relationship between the transition rate and any given (time-constant or time-dependent) explanatory variable is not the same across all values of the remaining covariates. When a transition rate model includes more than two covariates, then many interaction terms (also higher order terms) might become necessary. An instructive example for misleading estimation results due to an omitted interaction term was given in chapter 9, where we included marriage as a time-dependent covariate in the job exit rate model without taking into account that it has opposite effects on the job exit rate for men and women.

(6) Another problem that might result in misleading estimation results is measurement errors. In transition rate models, this problem not only concerns covariates, but also the information about starting and ending times of episodes (see the discussion in Sandefur and Tuma 1987).

(7) Quite another, but no less important, source of misspecification is the model type. As we have discussed in previous chapters of this book, there is a broad range of transition rate models that can be used for practical research. Using different types of models will probably lead to different estimates of the impact of covariates on the transition rate. As discussed in chapter 8, there are some methods of investigating whether a model fits the data, but these methods are quite limited. Based on maximum likelihood estimation, there are, in general, no conclusive statistical criteria that can be used for model selection. Thus, in practice, the most sensible strategy is to estimate and compare a variety of different models and find out to what degree the

---

[17] A serious source of misspecification is often a "one time" measurement of explanatory variables (normally at the time of a retrospective interview), which sometimes occurs even after the occurrence of the event being studied (see Sandefur and Tuma 1987).

estimation results are robust (i.e. do not depend on the selected model; see also Galler and Pötter 1992).

(8) Finally, the functional relationship between the various types of covariates just discussed (as well as duration dependence and possible interaction terms) and the transition rate might also be a source of misspecification. Normally, linear or log-linear functions to link model parameters to covariates are used. There are however many other possibilities, and estimation results might be dependent on the type of link function used to specify a model.

In summary, specification bias is pervasive in empirical social research. What can be recommended in such a situation—a situation that offers no satisfactory technical solution to settle the problem of model specification? First, it is important to remember that unobserved heterogeneity means that important information is omitted in the model or is not observable. Thus, if we have a clear hypothesis about what it is or could be that is not included in the model, then we can give the following advice: try to find better data that allow for representation of the important factors in the model. If we however have no idea about what is missing from the model, it would certainly be wrong to assume away the problem after diligently attempting to include a large number of variables in the covariate vector as controls. As shown convincingly by Lieberson (1985), this control variable approach will not merely lead to an underestimation or overestimation of the true relationship, but the true relationship in some circumstances will be more closely approximated before controls are applied rather than afterwards. A similar situation may occur if a stochastic error term is assumed to capture unobserved heterogeneity. Because, by definition, we do not have information about what is not observed, we are not able to assess assumptions about its distribution.

In particular, we do not believe that all the various sources of misspecification described earlier can be incorporated with just one stochastic error term. For example, including an error term into a job exit rate model does not bring us closer to a solution of the problem that education has a positive effect on upward moves and a negative effect on downward moves, and that this effect is at least based on the arguments available in the existing literature, without any specific meaning with regard to the job exit rate as such. Of course, such a conclusion can only be reached on the basis of theoretical considerations. In fact, our short discussion of possible sources of misspecification and the various examples in this book demonstrate that misspecification can at least be greatly reduced when event history model selection is theoretically guided. In our job mobility model, for example, an improvement in the model specification could simply be achieved by estimating it with regard to upward and downward shifts, differentiating for men and women, including parallel processes (e.g. family events, events at the level of the firm, changes in the macrostructure), as well as more appropriate information on the history of the process. The choice of a model is therefore not simply a technical decision made at the beginning of an analysis that can then be forgotten. Rather, the results critically depend on a theoretically guided model choice, and any differences among models can only be reconciled by a continuing awareness of the type of model used, and that interpretation may be contingent on the chosen model.

As stated by Manski (1993), identification of causal factors is not an all-or-nothing proposition. Very often, we may only have proxy variables or insufficient data to estimate the value of a parameter, but we may nevertheless be in a position to bound the parameter, to identify its direction of influence or its statistical significance. Sociological theory, at least at its current level of development, rarely predicts a specific value of coefficients. Most of the hypotheses that we have seen in empirical social science applications specify the influence direction of causal variables, or whether they have an effect at all. Thus, it seems that the fixation of sociologists on point estimation has inhibited appreciation of the usefulness of statements about bounds (Manski 1993). All in all, we need to develop a greater tolerance for ambiguity. As Manski (1993) expressed it, "social scientists often seem driven to draw sharp conclusions, even when these can be generated only by imposing much stronger assumptions than can be plausibly defended. Scientific reporting and policy analysis would be improved if we would face up to the fact that we cannot answer all of the questions that we ask."

Appendix A: Basic Information About TDA

TDA is a computer program specifically designed to analyze longitudinal (panel and event history) data. This appendix contains some basic information about the program that can be useful for understanding the examples given in the previous chapters.

TDA is written in the programming language C and can be compiled for many different computer platforms. Versions of the program for DOS-machines and UNIX workstations are currently available.[18] The program is distributed as *freeware* under the terms of the GNU General Public License and can be used and redistributed freely in accordance to this license.[19] The current version of the program that has been used for the examples in this book is 5.7. The full package consists of four standard DOS (1.4 MB) disks containing the program's source code, a makefile for UNIX workstations, an executable version for DOS-based machines, and the program's documentation (see below). The disk that accompanies this book only contains a DOS-executable version of the program, along with the example data and command files that have been used in this book; see Appendix B.

Manual and Online Help

Because TDA is a work in progress, a single manual does not exist. Instead, the documentation of the program is spread over a series of "TDA working papers" that become updated from time to time. Whenever one gets an actual version of the program, the current set of working papers is distributed along with the software. These working papers are available as PostScript files, so it is easy to make hard copies.

In addition to these working papers, TDA provides an online help option. To get this online help, invoke TDA as

> *tda help*

One can then select specific items from the help menu to find information about currently available options.

Command Files

TDA is a command-driven program. When invoking TDA, the user must provide an appropriate set of commands to be executed by the program. These

---

[18] The program's design relies on the assumption of a 32 bit processor. This is standard for almost all UNIX workstations. In the PC world, an 80386 processor is at least required.

[19] The disk that accompanies this book contains a file, named *COPYING*, which gives a full explanation of the GNU General Public License.

commands can be given on the command line when the program is invoked, or they can be put into a *command file* and TDA can be invoked as

    tda cf=name_of_command_file

- Command files are simple ASCII text files, so they can be created with any text editor. However, command files should not contain any control characters.

- Each command in a command file must be terminated by a semicolon (;). A command string may contain blank and newline characters. These characters are ignored (eliminated) before the command string is interpreted.[20]

- Empty lines and lines where the first non-blank character is a # or a * are interpreted as comments and ignored. Also any text after the terminating semicolon of a command string up to the end of the current line is ignored.

- The ordering of commands in a command file is generally of no importance. There is, however, one exception. Variables are built (and put into the internal data matrix) in the order of the commands used to define them. This is important when a variable has to be built with reference to other variables. Generally, only variables that have already been defined can be used to define other ones.

The Program's Output

TDA's output depends on the commands to be performed. There is always a *standard output* containing basic information about the performed job. As a default, this standard output is written to the terminal's screen. So when TDA is invoked as

    tda cf=name_of_command_file

the standard output of this job is written to the screen. It is possible, however, to redirect this output into a file. This can be achieved by invoking TDA as

    tda cf=name_of_command_file > out

In this example, the standard output is written into the file *out*. Instead of *out*, any other file name can be used.

Depending on the job, TDA creates additional output files. Names of these output files can be defined with the commands used to specify the job. For instance, the command

    ltb = ltb.out;

tells the program to perform a life table estimation and write the resulting life tables in the output file *ltb.out*. Again, instead of *ltb.out*, any other file name can be used, but note that already existing files with the same name are overwritten without warning.

---

[20] Note that when commands are given on the command line, they should not be terminated with a semicolon or contain any blank characters.

For further information about the program's calculations, a *protocol file* can be requested. The command is

pprot = name_of_protocol_file;

The contents of the protocol file depend on the performed job. For instance, if a model is estimated with the maximum likelihood method, the protocol file contains information about the iterative steps that have been used to find the maximum likelihood estimates.

Defining a Data Matrix

Like many other statistical packages, TDA is organized around the concept of a data matrix. A data matrix is a rectangular array of numerical entries, with rows corresponding to cases and columns corresponding to variables.

A data matrix is defined by two pieces of information. The first is about the number of rows (cases) of the data matrix. The command is

noc = number_of_cases;

The default is *noc=1000* or, when using an input data file, the number of records that are selected from this file.

The second is about the variables that should become part of the data matrix. The command to define a variable is

VName (Label) = expression;

VName is the name of the variable. Possible variable names are $V1,...,V32000$. *Label* is optional and, if provided, is used in the program's output tables. The right-hand side, *expression*, tells TDA how to create the variable.

TDA provides a lot of possibilities for defining variables. A full description is provided in the program's documentation. We only give a few examples here.

1. One can define variables by numerical constants. For instance, the command

   V1 = 99.9;

   defines a variable *V1* by assigning each of its components the constant value 99.9 (remember that a variable is actually a column vector where the number of components is equal to the number of cases in the data matrix).

2. Another possibility is to use information from an external data file to define variables. The syntax is

   VName = Cj;

   where *Cj* refers to the *j*th variable (column of numerical entries) in an external data file. (Further explanation is given later.)

3. A third elementary method to define variables is by using random numbers. For instance, the command

   V1 = rd(0,1);

defines a variable *V1* that is created by assigning each of its components a random number that is equally distributed in the (0, 1) interval.

4. In addition to such elementary methods of defining variables, one can use many mathematical and logical operators to create new variables. First, there are the elementary mathematical operators: $+, -, *, /$. For instance, the command

   V3 = *(V1 + V2)* / *2*;

   defines a new variable, *V3*, as the mean of the variables *V1* and *V2*. There are also many other mathematical operators, for instance:

   V2 = *sqrt(V1)*; *V2 is created as the square root of V1*
   V2 = *log(V1)*; *V2 is created as the logarithm of V1*
   V2 = *exp(V1)*; *V2 is created as the anti-logarithm of V1*

   Information about the available operators can be found in the program's documentation or in the online help menu.

5. There is almost no difference between arithmetical and logical operators. Therefore, logical constructs to define variables are somewhat different than compared to, say, SPSS or SAS. For instance, to define a variable *V3* to take the value 1 if the variables *V1* and *V2* are equal and 0 otherwise, the definition would be

   V3 = *eq(V1,V2)*;

   In the same spirit, the *if-then-else* operator has the syntax

   V4 = *if(V1,V2,V3)*;

   meaning that the variable *V4* is taken to be *V2* if *V1* is not equal to zero, and is otherwise taken to be *V3*. Alternatively, in this case, one could write

   V4 = *if V1 then V2 else V3*;

   to get a somewhat more familiar notation. Note that almost all operators can be used recursively so that it is possible, for instance, to have

   V20 = *if V1 then V10 else*
   if V2 then V12 else
   if V3 then V13 else V14;

6. There are some commands that use *logical variables*, where only two values are distinguished: zero (false) and not zero (true). It is important to note that *any* variable can be used as a logical variable, so this is not a specific type of variable but a context-dependent interpretation of variables. For instance, when using the operator *if(V1,V2,V3)*, the first variable (*V1*) is interpreted as a logical variable, meaning that the if-operator only distinguishes between two values, zero and not zero.

In general, logical variables can be easily combined if they are non-negative. For instance, to combine two logical variables with a logical

OR, one can use the mathematical + operator. For the logical AND, TDA uses a single point (.); for instance, the command

$V3 = V1 . V2;$

defines a new variable, $V3$, as the logical product of the variables $V1$ and $V2$, that is, $V3$ is given the value 1, if both $V1$ and $V2$ are not equal to zero and $V3$ is zero otherwise.

7. There is also a simple method to create dummy variables. For instance, the command

$V2 = V1[j1,j2,...];$

defines a new variable, $V2$, that takes the value 1, if variable $V1$ has one of the values $j1,j2,...$ and takes the value 0 otherwise. A somewhat extended version of this operator is

$V2 = V1[j1,,j2,...];$

Here, the variable $V2$ takes the value 1, if the variable $V1$ has a value in the range from $j1$ to $j2$.

As already mentioned, a full description of the available methods to build new variables is provided in TDA's online help. In addition, one can use the *calc* command to try out the working of operators. Invoking TDA as

tda calc

provides a small interactive calculator that allows to interactively build numerical expressions that contain any of TDA's operators to create variables.

Input Data Files

As a special resource to define a data matrix, one can use an input data file. These data files can have a free or a fixed format. As a default, TDA assumes a free format (i.e. numerical entries in the data file must be separated by at least one blank character). This convention defines the first entry in each record ($C1$), the second entry ($C2$), and so on, which can then be used to define variables for TDA's internal data matrix. The command to inform TDA about a data file is

dfile = name_of_a_data_file;

Given this command, one can define variables by referring to the numerical entries in the data file. This can be accomplished by using commands of the form

VName = Cj;

where Cj refers to the jth numerical entry in the records of the data file. For instance, the command

$V7 = C3;$

defines a variable, $V7$, which is created by assigning the values that are contained in the third position of the data file's records.

If an input data file has a fixed format, TDA needs some additional information as to where numerical entries in the data file records can be found. This information can be given with the command

$ffmt = w1,w2,w3,...;$

meaning that the first variable in the data file takes the first $w1$ (physical) columns; the second variable is placed in the following $w2$ columns, and so on. As an example, use any editor to create the following data file, say $t.dat$:

```
12345.1
6789.12
   1   -3
4 5 6e2
```

Assuming that there are three variables and that the first variable occupies the first two columns, the second variable the third column, and the third variable the remaining four columns, a command file to read this data file could be written as follows:

$dfile = t.dat;$
$ffmt = 2,1,4;$
$v1 = c1;$
$v2 = c2;$
$v3 = c3;$
$pdata = out.dat;$

In this example, we have used the $dfile$ command to inform TDA about the name of the data file, $t.dat$. Because it is a fixed format data file, we have used the $ffmt$ command to define the numerical entries in the data file's records. Then we have defined three variables by referring to the first, second, and third "logical" column in the data file. Finally, we have used the $pdata$ command to request that the internal data matrix be written into an output file $out.dat$. In this example, the output file, $out.dat$, would have the following contents:

```
12 3 45.1
67 8 9.12
1 -1 -3
4 5 600
```

Note that TDA's default in writing the output file is free format. This can be changed with the $dfmt$ command.

Input data files may have a fixed or a variable *record length*. As a default, TDA assumes that data files may have variable record length with a maximum of 20000 characters (bytes) per record.

In this case, each record must be terminated by an appropriate end-of-record (or end-of-line, EOL) character. The binary representation depends on the operating system. Under DOS, EOL is a carriage return–line feed sequence; in a UNIX environment, it is normally a single line feed character. If one is not sure about a data file, TDA's *dump* command to see what is in the file can be used. Invoking TDA as

    tda dump=name_of_a_file

shows the binary contents of the file (in a hexadecimal notation and an ASCII representation) in the program's standard output.[21] Another possibility is to invoke TDA as

    tda ccnt=name_of_a_file

providing a frequency distribution of the characters in the file. In particular, one gets information about the carriage return and line feed characters.

If the records of an input data file have a fixed length, an EOL character is not necessary, but the program must be informed about the record length. This can be done with the command

    dreclen = n;

where *n* is a positive integer. Then TDA reads the input file as a series of records, where each record consists of exactly *n* consecutive characters (including any EOL characters if present).

Missing Values

TDA can only handle numerical data; a data file to be used with TDA must not contain alphanumerical entries. So what happens if the program finds something in a data file that cannot be interpreted as a valid numerical value? This depends on what is actually found in the record's field where TDA expects a numerical entry. If there is an asterisk (*), a single dot (.), or (only with fixed format data files) a blank field, these entries are substituted by missing value codes. The default is -1, but this can be changed with the *mstar*, *mpnt*, and *mblnk* commands. If anything else is found, TDA's default reaction is exit with an error message. To avoid this, one must define a missing value code for these cases with the *mgen* command; or one has to exclude these records from the file (see below).

For instance, in the example data file *t.dat* shown earlier, the second variable (*C2*) in case number 3 has a missing value, a blank field. As a default, this is translated into -1. One could have used the command

    mblnk = value_to_be_substituted_for_blank_fields;

to change this default option.

Note that the term *missing value* refers to non-numerical entries in a data file that are translated into numerical values. The term has no statistical meaning for TDA. After the internal data matrix has been built, there are no longer any missing value codes, only numerical data. It is up to the user to decide about

---

[21] The output can be redirected into an output file with the *dmfile* command.

"substantive" missing values, for instance, to recode these values or to exclude cases containing missing values.

Selection of Data Matrix Cases

As a default, when using an external data file to build TDA's internal data matrix, the number of rows in the data matrix equals the number of records in the data matrix.[22] To be more precise, only *data records* are used to build the internal data matrix. A data file may contain comments; TDA regards each record in a data file that begins with a # character as a comment and skips these records when reading the file.[23]

There are several possibilities to select records. A simple command is

   rec = rec1 - rec2;

meaning that only records in the range from record number *rec1* up to and including record number *rec2* are used to build the internal data matrix. In this form of the command, all records—including comments—are used to count the records. Alternatively, one can use the *drec* command; then only data records are used to count records.

Another option is provided by the *dsel* and *vsel* commands. The syntax is

   dsel = expression;   and
   vsel = expression;

where *expression* defines a logical variable. The effect is that only records are selected to build the internal data matrix where the variable, defined by *expression*, has a value not equal to zero.

Both selection commands should be distinguished because they operate in different steps in the process of building the internal data matrix:

$$\boxed{\text{data file}} \xrightarrow{\textit{dsel}} \boxed{\text{data matrix}} \xrightarrow{\textit{vsel}} \boxed{\text{new data matrix}}$$

The *dsel* command is effective while TDA reads the data file. Because at this stage the data matrix is not available yet, one cannot use information about the data matrix to build the selection variable (*expression*) for the *dsel* command. It is possible, however, to use numerical constants, random numbers, and references to the numerical entries in the data file. For instance, the command

   dsel = gt(C1,0) . lt(C1,10);

would select only records from the input data file where the variable (data column) *C1* has values greater than 0 and less than 10. As another example, the command

---

[22] However, as already mentioned, the maximum number of records read from the data file is defined by the *noc* command with a default of 1000 records.

[23] TDA uses this feature sometimes when writing tables into an output file. Headers of the tables are preceded by a # character so that the file, containing the table, can subsequently be used as an input data file.

dsel = le(rd(0,1), 0.5);

would select a 50 % random sample from the input data file.

Contrary to the *dsel* command, the *vsel* command operates after the data file (if any) has been read to create the internal data matrix. The data matrix is then built in two steps. In a first step, it is built as if there were no *vsel* command and in a second step it is reorganized according to the *vsel* command (i.e. all rows are dropped from the data matrix where the *vsel* variable is zero). Because in the second step the input data file is already closed, one can only use V-variables to define the *vsel* selection variable. For instance, assuming that *V1=C1*, the command

vsel = gt(V1,0) . lt(V1,10);

would result in the same selection of data matrix rows as illustrated earlier with the *dsel* command. This way of record selection is however far less efficient than using the *dsel* command because the data matrix must be created in two steps. Therefore, the *dsel* command instead of the *vsel* command should be used whenever possible. The *vsel* command should only be used if one needs a reference to the variables in a data matrix to define an appropriate selection variable.

Writing Data Files

It is possible to write the contents of TDA's internal data matrix into an output file. The command is

pdata = name_of_an_output_data_file;

Given this command, the contents of the internal data matrix are written into the specified output file. As a default, the output file is written in a free format (i.e. numerical entries are separated by a blank character). As an option, one can specify the format to be used to write the output file with the *dfmt* command (information about this command is provided by TDA's online help). Furthermore, one can select variables to be written into the output file by using the command

keep = list_of_variables ;

Given this command, only the variables specified on the right-hand side are written into the output file.

In addition, one can use the command

dtda = name_of_a_file ;

to get a description of the output file, requested with the *pdata* command, which conforms to TDA's syntax for reading data files. [200zile then contains a definition of the variables that have been written into the output file and can subsequently be used as a command file to read the new data file.

If the data matrix contains episode data, that is, if one has explicitly defined episode data (see below), one can use the *pdate* command instead of the *pdata* command. Both commands work the same way, but when the *pdate* command is used, each record of the output file contains six additional variables: a case (episode) number, a serial number of the episode, two variables for the origin and destination states, and two variables for the starting and ending times of the episode.

Elementary Descriptive Statistics

There are a few commands to request basic descriptive information about the contents of the data matrix. The command *dstat* provides information about the minimum and maximum values, the mean, and the standard deviation for each variable in the data matrix.[24] The command

    corr = list_of_variables;

provides a correlation matrix for the variables specified on the right-hand side. And the command

    freq = list_of_variables;

provides the joint frequency distribution of the variables specified on the right-hand side. Note, however, that the *freq* command can only be used with integer-valued variables; floating-point variables are truncated to their integer values.[25]

Event History Data

TDA's internal data matrix can be used by different statistical procedures. Each of these procedures interprets the contents of the data matrix in a specific way. For instance, the OLS procedure for cross-sectional data interprets the data matrix as a set of cross-sectional data; some other procedures interpret the data matrix as a set of panel data, and statistical procedures for event history data interpret the data matrix as a set of single or multi-episode data.

For purposes of event history analyses, one must explicitly define how the contents of the data matrix should be interpreted as a set of episode data. There are two possibilities. First, one can define the data matrix as a set of single episodes; each row of the data matrix is interpreted then as the description of a single episode. This can be accomplished with the commands

    org   *= a_variable_containing_origin_states;*
    des   *= a_variable_containing_destination_states;*
    ts   *= a_variable_containing_starting_times;*
    tf   *= a_variable_containing_ending_times;*

---

[24] Optionally, one can use the command *dstat=list_of_variables* to get only the information about variables given on the right-hand side.

[25] It would be possible, of course, to multiply floating point variables by appropriate constants to obtain integer-valued variables.

Variables to be used with the *org* and *des* commands must only contain non-negative integer values, whereas variables to be used with the *ts* and *tf* commands must only have non-negative floating point values. Furthermore, the contents of these variables should be defined so that their difference equals the episode's duration.

In the case of multi-episode data, one has a set of units of analysis, each identified by a unique ID number, and for each unit one has a certain number of episodes to be distinguished by a serial (episode) number. As in the case of single episode data, it is assumed that each row of the data matrix describes a specific episode. Therefore, one again needs the four commands shown previously to define multi-episode data. In addition, two further commands are needed:

> *id = a_variable_containing_ID_values;*
> *sn = a_variable_containing_serial_numbers;*

The first of these commands defines how the episodes in the data matrix belong to the units of analysis, and the second provides a serial number for each of the episodes belonging to the same unit.

Case Weights

Most of TDA's statistical procedures can be used with *case weights*. The command to provide case weights is simply

> *cwt = name_of_a_variable;*

The variable to be given on the right-hand side must be contained in the internal data matrix and must only contain non-negative values. The effect of the *cwt* command depends on the statistical procedure. Case weights are used, for instance, in the calculation of basic descriptive statistics. In the case of model estimation with the maximum likelihood method, case weights (if provided) are used to weigh the individual contributions to the log likelihood in the following way:

$$\ell = \sum_{i+1}^{N} w_i \log(\ell_i)$$

In this formulation, ℓ_i is the contribution of the ith unit to the likelihood, and w_i is its case weight.

PostScript Plots

TDA provides some possibilities to create PostScript plots. This graphics language has been chosen to make the program independent of any specific graphics environment.[26] The currently available options are described in the

---

[26] *PostScript* is a trademark of Adobe Systems Inc.

TDA Working Paper 2–4, together with several examples that can easily be replicated. Many examples have also already been given in previous chapters.

One should note, however, that TDA's output is a file containing a description of a plot in the PostScript language. To actually see the plot, one needs a device (a terminal and/or a printer) that can understand PostScript. If one has access to a PostScript printer, one can get hard copies by sending the PostScript file to such a printer. However, because developing reasonable plots normally requires several trials, it is very helpful to have a program that gives previews on the screen of a terminal. An excellent program for this is GHOSTSCRIPT, distributed by the *Free Software Foundation*.

Appendix B: About the Accompanying Disk

This appendix describes the disk that accompanies this book. It is a standard DOS (1.4 MB) disk containing the example data and command files used in this book and a DOS-executable version of TDA (5.7). To save space, the files are put into two ZOO archives. The disk contains the following files:

1. *copying*, an ASCII file providing information about the GNU General Public License.

2. *zoo210.exe*, a DOS-executable version of Rahul Dhesi's ZOO archive program. It is a general purpose program to create and manage compressed archives.

3. *ehh.zoo*, a ZOO archive containing all data and command files discussed in this book.

4. *tda57.zoo*, a ZOO archive containing a DOS-executable version of TDA.

Installation

To run the software, you need a DOS-compatible PC with (at least) an 80386 processor and 2–4 megabytes of (extended) memory. For installation, proceed as follows:

1. Create a directory on your hard disk, for instance *C:TDA*, and copy the contents of the accompanying disk to this directory.

2. Execute *zoo210.exe* to get an executable version of the ZOO archive program. Note that *zoo210.exe* is a self-extracting archive. Executing this file results in two new files: *zoo.exe*, the executable version of the ZOO program, and *zoo.man*, a manual describing the ZOO program. (*zoo.man* is a plain ASCII file and can be sent to a printer to get a hard copy.)

3. Use *zoo.exe* to extract an executable version of TDA from the archive *tda57.zoo*. This can be done with the following command:

    zoo x tda57

    As a result, you should get three new files: *tda.exe*, a DOS-executable version of TDA, *dos4gw.exe*, a DOS-extender that is necessary to run *tda.exe*, and *tda.hlp*, an ASCII file to be used for TDA's online help option.

4. Check whether TDA can be executed on your machine. Just type: *tda*. You should get a short message about the actual version of the program and its syntax. Then try to type: *tda help*. You should then see TDA's help menu.

   Note that to be executable in a DOS environment, TDA requires a DOS-extender to gain access to extended memory. The DOS-extender *dos4gw.exe*, supplied on the disk, may conflict with other programs on your machine

273

that use extended memory. If any such conflicts occur, check your *config.sys* and *autoexec.bat* files and make sure that all possibly conflicting programs and drivers are turned off while working with TDA.

5. Next, extract the example data file, *rrdat.1*, and all of the example command files (*eh*.cf*), from the archive *ehh.zoo*. Just type:

   zoo x ehh

   As a result, you should get a single data file, *rrdat.1*, and a set of TDA command files: *ehh1.cf*, *ehh2.cf*, and so on. In fact, you should get all of the example command files discussed in this book.

6. Finally, check whether you can execute these command files on your machine. Try as a first example:

   tda cf=ehh2.cf

   The output should contain the table shown in Box 2.2.5 in Section 2.2. If this works, you can try out all the other examples discussed in this book.

References

Aalen, O. O. (1987). Dynamic modelling and causality. *Scand. Actuarial Journal, 12,* 177–190.

Aitchison, J., & Brown, J. A. C. (1973). *The lognormal distribution with special reference to its uses in economics.* Cambridge: Cambridge University Press.

Allison, P. D. (1982). Discrete time methods for the analysis of event histories. In S. Leinhardt (Ed.), *Sociological methodology* (pp. 61–98). San Francisco: Jossey-Bass.

Allison, P. D. (1984). *Event history analysis: Regression for longitudinal event data.* Beverly Hills: Sage.

Allmendinger, J. (1989a). *Career mobility dynamics: a comparative analysis of the United States, Norway, and West Germany.* Studien und Berichte no. 49, Max-Planck-Institut für Bildungsforschung, Berlin.

Allmendinger, J. (1989b). Educational systems and labor market outcomes. *European Sociological Review, 5,* 231–250.

Andreß, H.-J. (1985). *Multivariate Analyse von Verlaufsdaten.* Mannheim: ZUMA.

Andreß, H.-J. (1989). Recurrent unemployment—the West German experience: an exploratory analysis using count data models with panel data. *European Sociological Review, 5,* 275–297.

Andreß, H.-J. (1992). *Einführung in die Verlaufsdatenanalyse.* Köln: Zentrum für historische Sozialforschung.

Arminger, G. (1990). Testing against misspecification in parametric rate models. In K. U. Mayer & N. B. Tuma (Eds.), *Event history analysis in life course research* (pp. 253–268). Madison: University of Wisconsin Press.

Arminger, G., Clogg, C. C. & Sobel, M. E. (Eds.) (1995). *Handbook of statistical modeling for the social and behavioral sciences.* New York: Plenum.

Arminger, G., & Müller, F. (1990). *Lineare Modelle zur Analyse von Paneldaten.* Opladen: Westdeutscher Verlag.

Arrow, K. (1973). Higher education as a filter. *Journal of Public Economics, 2,* 193–216.

Barron, D. N. (1993). The analysis of count data: overdispersion and autocorrelation. In P. Marsden (Ed.), *Sociological Methodology* (pp. 179–220). San Francisco: Jossey-Bass.

Becker, G. S. (1975). *Human capital.* New York: Columbia University Press.

Becker, G. S. (1981). *A treatise on the family.* Cambridge: Harvard University Press.

Becker, R. (1993). *Staatsexpansion und Karrierechancen. Berufsverläufe im öffentlichen Dienst und in der Privatwirtschaft.* Frankfurt a.M. and New York: Campus.

Becker, R., & Blossfeld, H.-P. (1991). Cohort-specific effects of the expansion of the welfare state on job opportunities: a longitudinal analysis of three birth cohorts in the FRG. *Sociologische Gids, 4,* 261–284.

Bernasco, W. (1994). *Coupled careers. The effects of spouse's resources on success at work.* Amsterdam: Thesis Publishers.

Bilsborrow, R. E., & Akin, J. S. (1982). Data availability versus data needs for analyzing the determinants and consequences of internal migration: An evaluation of U.S. survey data. *Review of Public Data Use, 10*, 261–284.

Blau, P. M., & Duncan, O. D. (1967). *The American occupational structure*. New York: Wiley.

Bloom, D. E. (1982). What's happening to the age at first birth in the United States? A study of recent cohorts. *Demography, 19*, 351–370.

Blossfeld, H.-P. (1985). *Bildungsexpansion und Berufschancen*. Frankfurt a.M. and New York: Campus.

Blossfeld, H.-P. (1986). Career opportunities in the Federal Republic of Germany: A dynamic approach to the study of life-course, cohort, and period effects. *European Sociological Review, 2*, 208–225.

Blossfeld, H.-P. (1987a). Zur Repräsentativität der Sfb-3-Lebensverlaufsstudie. Ein Vergleich mit Daten aus der amtlichen Statistik. *Allgemeines Statistisches Archiv, 71*, 126–144.

Blossfeld, H.-P. (1987b). Labor market entry and the sexual segregation of careers in the FRG. *American Journal of Sociology, 93*, 83–118.

Blossfeld, H.-P. (1989). *Kohortendifferenzierung und Karriereprozeß. Eine Längsschnittstudie über die Veränderung der Bildungs- und Berufschancen im Lebenslauf*. Frankfurt a.M. and New York: Campus.

Blossfeld, H.-P. (1990). Changes in educational careers in the Federal Republic of Germany. *Sociology of Education, 63*, 165–177.

Blossfeld, H.-P. (1992). Is the German dual system a model for a modern vocational training system? *International Journal of Comparative Sociology, 33*, 168–181.

Blossfeld, H.-P. (1994). *Causal modeling in event history analysis*. Paper prepared for the XIII World Congress of Sociology (Bielefeld, July 1994). University of Bremen: mimeo.

Blossfeld, H.-P. (Ed.) (1995). *The new role of women. Family formation in modern societies*. Boulder: Westview Press.

Blossfeld, H.-P. (Ed.) (in press). *Between equalization and marginalization. Part-time working women in Europe and the United States of America*. Oxford: Oxford University Press.

Blossfeld, H.-P., & De Rose, A. (1992). Educational expansion and changes in entry into marriage and motherhood: The experience of Italian women. *Genus, 3-4*, 73–91.

Blossfeld, H.-P., De Rose, A., Hoem, J., & Rohwer, G. (1993). *Education, modernization, and the risk of marriage disruption: Differences in the effect of women's educational attainment in Sweden, West-Germany, and Italy*. Stockholm Research Reports in Demography, no. 76, Stockholm. [To appear in: K. Oppenheim Mason & A.-Magritt Jensen (Eds.), *Gender and family change in industrialized countries*. Oxford: Oxford University Press.]

Blossfeld, H.-P., Giannelli, G., & Mayer, K. U. (1993). Is there a new service proletariat? The tertiary sector and social inequality in Germany. In G. Esping-Andersen (Ed.), *Changing classes. Stratification and mobility in post-industrial societies* (pp. 109–135). London: Sage.

Blossfeld, H.-P., & Hamerle, A. (1989a). Using Cox models to study multiepisode processes. *Sociological Methods and Research, 17*, 432–448.

Blossfeld, H.-P., & Hamerle, A. (1989b). Unobserved heterogeneity in hazard rate models: a test and an illustration from a study of career mobility. *Quality and Quantity, 23*, 129–141.

Blossfeld, H.-P., & Hamerle, A. (1992). Unobserved heterogeneity in event history analysis. *Quality and Quantity, 26*, 157–168.

Blossfeld, H.-P., Hamerle, A., & Mayer, K. U. (1989). *Event history analysis*. Hillsdale, NJ: Lawrence Erlbaum Associates.

Blossfeld, H.-P., & Huinink, J. (1991). Human capital investments or norms of role transition? How women's schooling and career affect the process of family formation. *American Journal of Sociology, 97*, 143–168.

Blossfeld, H.-P., & Jaenichen, U. (1992). Educational expansion and changes in women's entry into marriage and motherhood in the Federal Republic of Germany. *Journal of Marriage and the Family, 54*, 302–315.

Blossfeld, H.-P., Klijzing, E., Pohl, K. & Rohwer, G. (1995). *Modeling parallel processes in demography: An application example of the causal approach to interdependent systems.* Paper prepared for the European Population Conference (Milano, September 1995). University of Bremen: mimeo.

Blossfeld, H.-P., Manting, D., & Rohwer, G. (1993). Patterns of change in family formation in the Federal Republic of Germany and the Netherlands: some consequences for solidarity between generations. In H. Becker & P. L. J. Hermkens (Eds.), *Solidarity between generations. Demographic, economic and social change, and its consequences* (Volume I, pp. 175–196). Amsterdam: Thesis Publishers.

Blossfeld, H.-P., & Mayer, K. U. (1988). Labor market segmentation in the FRG: an empirical study of segmentation theories from a life course perspective. *European Sociological Review, 4*, 123–140.

Blossfeld, H.-P., & Nuthmann, R. (1990). Transition from youth to adulthood as a cohort process in the FRG. In H. A. Becker (Ed.), *Life histories and generations* (pp. 183–217). Utrecht: ISOR.

Blossfeld, H.-P., & Rohwer, G. (in press). West Germany. In H.-P. Blossfeld (Ed.), *Between equalization and marginalization. Part-time working women in Europe and the United States of America*. Oxford: Oxford University Press.

Blossfeld, H.-P., & Shavit, Y. (1993). Persisting barriers: changes in educational opportunities in thirteen countries. In Y. Shavit & H.-P. Blossfeld (Eds.), *Persistent inequality* (pp. 1–23). Boulder: Westview Press.

Blumen, I., Kogan, M., & McCarthy, P. J. (1955). *The industrial mobility of labor as a probability process*. Ithaca: Cornell University Press.

Bollen, K. A. (1989). *Structural equations with latent variables*. New York: Wiley.

Breslow, N. (1974). Covariance analysis of censored survival data. *Biometrics, 30*, 89–99.

Brüderl, J. (1991a). *Mobilitätsprozesse in Betrieben. Dynamische Modelle und empirische Befunde*. Fankfurt a.M. and New York: Campus.

Brüderl, J. (1991b). *Bell-shaped duration dependence in social processes. A generalized log-logistic rate model*. University of Bern: mimeo.

Brüderl, J., & Diekmann, A. (1994). *The log-logistic rate model. Two generalizations with an application to demographic data.* München/Bern: mimeo.

Brüderl, J., Diekmann, A., & Preisendörfer, P. (1991). Patterns of intragenerational mobility: tournament models, path dependency, and early promotion effects. *Social Science Research, 20,* 197–216.

Campbell, D. T., & Stanley, J. C. (1963). *Experimental and quasi-experimental designs for research.* Chicago: Rand McNally.

Campbell, R. T., Mutran, E., & Nash Parker, R. (1987). Longitudinal design and longitudinal analysis. A comparison of three approaches. *Research on Aging, 8,* 480–504.

Carroll, G. R. (1983). Dynamic analysis of discrete dependent variables: A didactic essay. *Quality and Quantity, 17,* 425–460.

Carroll, G. R., & Delacroix, J. (1982). Organizational mortality in the newspaper industries of Argentina and Ireland: An ecological approach. *Administrative Science Quarterly, 27,* 169–198.

Carroll, G. R., & Mayer, K. U. (1986). Job-shift patterns in the FRG: The effects of social class, industrial sector, and organizational size. *American Sociological Review, 51,* 323–341.

Carroll, G. R., & Mosakowski, E. (1987). The career dynamics of self-employment. *Administrative Science Quarterly, 32,* 570–589.

Chamberlain, G. (1984). Panel data. In Z. Griliches and M. D. Intriligator (Eds.), *Handbook of econometrics* (Vol. 2, pp. 1247–1317). Amsterdam: North-Holland.

Clogg, C. C., & Arminger, G. (1993). On strategy for methodological analysis. *Sociological Methodology, 23,* 57–74.

Coale, A. (1971). Age patterns of marriage. *Population Studies, 25,* 193–214.

Coleman, J. S. (1964). *Introduction to mathematical sociology.* New York: Free Press.

Coleman, J. S. (1968). The mathematical study of change. In H. M. Blalock & A. Blalock (Eds.), *Methodology in social research* (pp. 428–478). New York: McGraw-Hill.

Coleman, J. S. (1973). Theoretical bases for parameters of stochastic processes. In R. E. A. Mapes (Ed.), Stochastic processes in sociology [monograph]. *The Sociological Review, 19,* 17–28.

Coleman, J. S. (1981). *Longitudinal data analysis.* New York: Basic Books.

Coleman, J. S. (1990). *Foundations of social theory.* Cambridge: Harvard University Press.

Coleman, J. S., & Hao, L. (1989). Linear systems analysis: macrolevel analysis with microlevel data. *Sociological Methodology, 19,* 395–422.

Courgeau, D. (1990). Migration, family, and career: a life course approach. In P. B. Baltes, D. L. Featherman, & R. M. Lerner (Eds.), *Life-span development and behavior* (pp. 219–255). Hillsdale, NJ: Lawrence Erlbaum Associates.

Courgeau, D., & Lelièvre, E. (1992). *Event history analysis in demography.* Oxford: Clarendon.

Cox, D. R. (1972). Regression models and life-tables. *Journal of the Royal Statistical Society, 34,* 187–220.

Cox, D. R. (1975). Partial likelihood. *Biometrika, 62,* 269–276.

Cox, D. R., & Snell, E. J. (1968). A general definition of residuals. *Journal of the Royal Statistical Society, B 30*, 248–275.

Cox, D. R., & Oakes, D. (1984). *Analysis of survival data.* London: Chapman and Hall.

Crouchley, R., & Pickles, A. R. (1987). An illustrative comparison of conditional and marginal methods for analysing longitudinal data with omitted variables. In R. Crouchley (Ed.), *Longitudinal data analysis* (pp. 177–193). Aldershot: Avebury.

Davies, R. B. (1987). The limitations of cross-sectional analysis. In R. Crouchley (Ed.), *Longitudinal data analysis* (pp. 1–15). Aldershot: Avebury.

Davies, R. B., & Crouchley, R. (1985). Control for omitted variables in the analysis of panel and other longitudinal data. *Geographical Analysis, 17*, 1–15.

Davis, J. A. (1978). Studying categorical data over time. *Social Science Research, 7*, 151–179.

Dex, S. (Ed.) (1991). *Life and work history analyses: Qualitative and quantitative developments.* London and New York: Routledge.

Diamond, I. D., & McDonald, J. W. (1992). Analysis of current-status data. In J. Trussell, R. Hankinson, & J. Tilton (Eds.), *Demographic applications of event-history analysis* (pp. 231–252). Oxford: Clarendon.

Diekmann, A. (1989). Diffusion and survival models for the process of entry into marriage. *Journal of Mathematical Sociology, 14*, 31–44.

Diekmann, A., & Mitter, P. (1983). The 'sickle hypothesis'. *Journal of Mathematical Sociology, 9*, 85–101.

Diekmann, A., & Mitter, P. (Eds.) (1984). *Stochastic modelling of social processes.* New York: Academic Press.

Diekmann, A., & Preisendörfer, P. (1988). Turnover and employment stability in a large West German company. *European Sociological Review, 4*, 233–248.

Diekmann, A., & Weick, S. (Eds.) (1993). *Der Familienzyklus als sozialer Prozeß.* Berlin: Duncker & Humblot.

Dierckx, P. (1975). An algorithm for smoothing, differentiation and integration of experimental data using spline functions. *Journal of Computational and Applied Mathematics, 1*, 165–184.

DiPrete, T. A. (1993). Industrial restructuring and the mobility response. *American Sociological Review, 58*, 74–96.

DiPrete, T. A., & Whitman, T. S. (1988). Gender and promotion in segmented job ladder systems. *American Sociological Review, 53*, 26–40.

Doeringer, P. B. (1967). Determinants of the structure of industrial type internal labor markets. *Industrial Labor Relations Review, 20*, 205–220.

Doeringer, P. B., & Piore, M. J. (1971). *Internal labor markets and manpower analysis.* Lexington: Heath Lexington.

Drobnič, S., & Wittig, I. (in press). Women's part-time employment and the family cycle in the United States. In H.-P. Blossfeld (Ed.), *Between equalization and marginalization.* Oxford.

Duncan, O. D. (1966). Methodological issues in the analysis of social mobility. In N. Smelser & S. M. Lipset (Eds.), *Social structure and social mobility* (pp. 51–97). Chicago: Aldine.

Eells, E. (1991). *Probabilistic causality*. Cambridge: Cambridge University Press.

Elbers, C., & Ridder, G. (1982). True and spurious duration dependence: The identifiability of the proportional hazard model. *Review of Economic Studies, 49*, 403–410.

Elder, G. H. (1975). Age differentiation and the life course. *Annual Review of Sociology, 1*, 165–190.

Elder, G. H. (1978). Family history and the life course. In T. K. Hareven (Ed.), *Transitions: the family and the life course in historical perspective* (pp. 17–64). New York: Academic Press.

Elder, G. H. (1987). War mobilization and the life course: a cohort of World War II veterans. *Sociological Forum, 2*, 449–472.

Engel, U., & Reinecke, J. (1994). *Panelanalyse*. New York: de Gruyter.

Erikson, R., & Goldthorpe, J. H. (1991). *The constant flux*. Oxford: Clarendon.

Esping-Andersen, G. (1990). *The three worlds of welfare capitalism*. Cambridge: Polity Press.

Esping-Andersen, G. (Ed.) (1993). *Changing classes*. London: Sage.

Esping-Andersen, G., Leth-Sørensen, S., & Rohwer, G. (1994). Institutions and occupational class mobility: Scaling the skill-barrier in the Danish labor market. *European Sociological Review, 10*, 119-134.

Faulbaum, F., & Bentler, P. M. (1994). Causal modeling: some trends and perspectives. In I. Borg & P. P. Mohler (Eds.), *Trends and perspectives in empirical social research* (pp. 224–249). Berlin: de Gruyter.

Featherman, D. L., Selbee, K. L., & Mayer, K. U. (1989). Social class and the structuring of the life course in Norway and West Germany. In D. I. Kertzer & W. K. Schaie (Eds.), *Age structuring in comparative perspective* (pp. 55–93). Hillsdale, NJ: Lawrence Erlbaum Associates.

Flinn, C. J., & Heckman, J. J. (1982). Models for the analysis of labor force dynamics. In R. Basmann & G. Rhodes (Eds.), *Advances in econometrics* (pp. 35–95). London: JAI Press.

Freedman, R. A. (1991). Statistical analysis and shoe leather. *Sociological Methodology, 21*, 291–313.

Freeman, J., Carroll, G. R., & Hannan, M. T. (1983). The liability of newness: Age dependence in organizational death rates. *American Sociological Review, 48*, 692–710.

Galler, H. P., & Pötter, U. (1990). Unobserved heterogeneity in models of unemployment. In K. U. Mayer & N. B. Tuma (Eds.), *Event history analysis in life course research* (pp. 226–240). Madison: University of Wisconsin Press.

Galler, H. P., & Pötter, U. (1992). Zur Robustheit von Schätzmodellen für Ereignisdaten. In R. Hujer, H. Schneider, & W. Zapf (Eds.), *Herausforderungen an den Wohlfahrtsstaat im strukturellen Wandel* (pp. 379–405). Frankfurt and New York: Campus.

Gardner, W., & Griffin, W. A. (1986). *A structural-causal model for analyzing parallel streams of continuously recorded discrete events*. Unpublished manuscript. University of Washington.

Glenn, N. D. (1977). *Cohort analysis*. Beverly Hills: Sage.

Goldthorpe, J. H. (1987). *Social mobility and class structure in modern Britain*. Oxford: Clarendon.

Goldthorpe, J. H. (1991). The use of history in sociology: Reflections on some recent tendencies. *British Journal of Sociology, 42*, 211–230.

Goldthorpe, J. H. (1994). *The quantitative analysis of large-scale data-sets and rational action theory: For a sociological alliance*. Oxford: Nuffield College (mimeo).

Goodman, L. A. (1973). Causal analysis of data from panel studies and other kind of surveys. *American Journal of Sociology, 78*, 1135–1191.

Grundmann, M. (1992). *Familienstruktur und Lebensverlauf. Historische und gesellschaftliche Bedingungen individueller Entwicklungen*. Frankfurt a.M. and New York: Campus.

Guo, G. (1993). Event-history analysis of left-truncated data. In P. Marsden (Ed.), *Sociological Methodology* (Vol. 23, pp. 217–242). San Francisco: Jossey-Bass.

Hachen, D. S. (1988). The competing risks model. *Sociological Methods and Research, 17*, 21–54.

Haller, M. (1989). *Klassenstrukturen und Mobilität in fortgeschrittenen Gesellschaften*. Frankfurt a.M. and New York: Campus.

Hamerle, A. (1989). Multiepisode spell regression models for duration data. *Applied Statistics, 38*, 127–138.

Hamerle, A. (1991). On the treatment of interrupted spells and initial conditions in event history analysis. *Sociological Methods & Research, 19*, 388–414.

Hamerle, A., & Tutz, G. (1989). *Diskrete Modelle zur Analyse von Verweildauer und Lebenszeiten*. Frankfurt: Campus.

Handl, J. (1988). *Berufschancen und Heiratsmuster von Frauen*. Frankfurt a.M. and New York: Campus.

Handl, J., Mayer, K. U., & Müller, W. (1977). *Klassenlage und Sozialstruktur*. Frankfurt a.M. and New York: Campus.

Hannan, M. T., & Freeman, J. (1989). *Organizational ecology*. Cambridge: Harvard University Press.

Hannan, M. T., Schömann, K., & Blossfeld, H.-P. (1990). Sex and sector differences in the dynamics of wage growth in the Federal Republic of Germany. *American Sociological Review, 55*, 694–713.

Hannan, M. T., & Tuma, N. B. (1979). Methods for temporal analysis. *Annual Review of Sociology, 5*, 303–328.

Hannan, M. T., & Tuma, N. B. (1990). A reassessment of the effects of income maintenance on marital dissolution in the Seattle-Denver income experiments. *American Journal of Sociology, 95*, 1270–1298.

Heckman, J. J., & Borjas, G. J. (1980). Does unemployment cause future unemployment? *Economica, 47*, 247–283.

Heckman, J. J., & Singer, B. (1982). The identification problem in econometric models for duration data. In W. Hildenbrand (Ed.), *Advances in econometrics* (pp. 39–77). Cambridge: Cambridge University Press.

Heckman, J. J., & Singer, B. (1984). A method of minimizing the impact of distributional assumptions in econometric models for duration data. *Econometrica, 52*, 271–320.

Heckman, J. J., & Walker, J. R. (1987). Using goodness of fit and other criteria to choose among competing duration models: a case study of Hutterite data. In Clogg, C. (Ed.), *Sociological Methodology* (pp. 247–307). San Francisco: Jossey-Bass.

Heckman, J. J., & Willis, R. J. (1977). A beta-logistic model for the analysis of sequential labor force participation by married women. *Journal of Political Economy, 85,* 27–58.

Heinz, W. R. (1991a) (Ed.). *Theoretical advances in life course research. Status passages and the life course,* Vol. 1. Weinheim: Deutscher Studien Verlag.

Heinz, W. R. (1991b) (Ed.). *The life course and social change. Status passages and the life course.* Vol. 2. Weinheim: Deutscher Studien Verlag.

Heinz, W. R. (1992) (Ed.). *Institutions and gate keeping in the life course. Status passages and the life course.* Vol. 3. Weinheim: Deutscher Studien Verlag.

Hernes, G. (1972). The process of entry into first marriage. *American Sociological Review, 37,* 173–182.

Hoem, J. M. (1983). Distortions caused by nonobservation of periods of cohabitation before the latest. *Demography, 20,* 491–506.

Hoem, J. M. (1985). Weighting, misclassification, and other issues in the analysis of survey samples of life histories. In J. J. Heckman & B. Singer (Eds.), *Longitudinal analysis of labor market data* (pp. 249–293). Cambridge: Cambridge University Press.

Hoem, J. M. (1986). The impact of education on modern family-union initiation. *European Journal of Population, 2,* 113–133.

Hoem, J. M. (1989). The issue of weights in panel surveys of individual behavior. In D. Kasprzyk, G. Duncan, G. Kalton, & M. P. Singh (Eds.), *Panel surveys* (pp. 539–565). New York: Wiley.

Hoem, J. M. (1991). To marry, just in case . . . : The Swedish widow's pension reform and the peak in marriages December 1989. *Acta Sociologica, 43,* 127–135.

Hoem, J. M., & Rennermalm, B. (1985). Modern family initiation in Sweden: Experience of women born between 1936 and 1960. *European Journal of Population, 1,* 81–111.

Hogan, D. P. (1978). The effects of demographic factors, family background, and early job achievement on age at marriage. *Demography, 15,* 139–160.

Hogan, D. P. (1981). *Transitions and social change: The early lives of American men.* New York: Academic Press.

Holland, P. W. (1986). Statistics and causal inference. *Journal of the American Statistical Association, 81,* 945–960.

Hsiao, C. (1986). *Analysis of panel data.* Cambridge: Cambridge University Press.

Huinink, J. (1987). Soziale Herkunft, Bildung und das Alter bei der Geburt des ersten Kindes. *Zeitschrift für Soziologie, 16,* 367–384.

Huinink, J. (1989). *Mehrebenenanalyse in den Sozialwissenschaften.* Wiesbaden: DUV.

Huinink, J. (1992). Die Analyse interdependenter Lebensverlaufsprozesse. In H.-J. Andreß, H. Huinink, H. Meinken, D. Rumianek, W. Sodeur, & G. Sturm (Eds.), *Theorie, Daten, Methoden. Neue Modelle und Verfahrensweisen in den Sozialwissenschaften* (pp. 343–367). München: Oldenbourg.

Huinink, J. (1993). *Warum noch Familie? Zur Attraktivität von Partnerschaft und Elternschaft in unserer Gesellschaft.* Habilitationsschrift, Freie Universität Berlin.

Huinink, J. (1995). Education, work, and family patterns of men: the case of West Germany. In H.-P. Blossfeld (Ed.), *The new role of women. Family formation in modern societies.* Boulder: Westview Press.

Hutchison, D. (1988a). Event history and survival analysis in the social sciences, part I. *Quality and Quantity, 22,* 203–219.

Hutchison, D. (1988b). Event history and survival analysis in the social sciences, part II (Advanced applications and recent developments). *Quality and Quantity, 22,* 255–278.

Hunt, M. (1985). *Profiles of social research. The scientific study of human interactions.* New York: Russell Sage Foundation.

Jöreskog, K. G., & Sörbom, D. (1993). *LISREL 8. Structural equation modeling with the SIMPLIS command language.* Chicago: Scientific Software International.

Kalbfleisch, J. D., & Prentice, R. L. (1980). *The statistical analysis of failure data.* New York: Wiley.

Kaplan, E. L., & Meier, P. (1958). Nonparametric estimation from incomplete observations. *Journal of the American Statistical Association, 53,* 457–481.

Kelly, J. R., & McGrath, J. E. (1988). *On time and method.* Newbury Park: Sage.

Kenny, D. A. (1979). *Correlation and causality.* New York: Wiley.

Kiefer, N. M. (1988). Economic duration data and hazard functions. *Journal of Economic Literature, 16,* 646–679.

Klijzing, E. (1992). Wedding in the Netherlands: First-union disruption among men and women born between 1928 and 1965. *European Sociological Review, 8,* 53–70.

Klijzing, E. (1993). A method for the simultaneous estimation of parallel processes in the human life course. *Studia Demograficzne, 3,* 111–124.

Krempel, L. (1987). *Soziale Interaktionen: Einstellungen, Biographien, Situationen und Beziehungsnetzwerke.* Bochum: Schullwig Verlag.

Lancaster, T. (1985). Generalized residuals and heterogeneous duration models with applications to the Weibull model. *Journal of Econometrics, 28,* 155–169.

Lancaster, T. (1990). *The econometric analysis of transition data.* Cambridge: Cambridge University Press.

Lauterbach, W. (1994). *Berufsverläufe von Frauen. Erwerbstätigkeit, Unterbrechung und Wiedereintritt.* Frankfurt a.M. and New York: Campus.

Lawless, J. F. (1982). *Statistical models and methods for lifetime data.* New York: Wiley.

Lazarsfeld, P. F. (1948). The use of panels in social research. *Proceedings of the American Philosophy of Sociology, 92,* 405–410.

Lazarsfeld, P. F. (1972). Mutual relations over time of two attributes: A review and integration of various approaches. In M. Hammer, K. Salzinger, & S. Sutton (Eds.), *Psychopathology* (pp. 461–80). New York.

Leridon, H. (1989). Cohabitation, marriage, separation: an analysis of life histories of French cohorts from 1968 to 1985. *Population Studies, 44,* 127–144.

Lieberson, S. (1985). *Making it count. The improvement of social research and theory.* Berkeley: University of California Press.

Lieberson, S. (1991). Small n's and big conclusions: An examination of the reasoning in comparative studies based on a small number of cases. *Social Forces, 70,* 307–320.

Liefbroer, A. (1991). The choice between a married or unmarried first union by young adults. A competing risks analysis. *European Journal of Population, 7*, 273–298.

Lomi, A. (1995). The population and community ecology of organizational founding: Italian co-operative banks, 1936-1969. *European Sociological Review, 11*, 75–98.

Magnusson, D., & Bergmann, L. R. (Eds.) (1990). *Data quality in longitudinal research.* Cambridge: Cambridge University Press.

Magnusson, D., Bergmann, L. R., & Törestad, B. (Eds.) (1991), *Problems and methods in longitudinal research: Stability and change.* Cambridge: Cambridge University Press.

Mahajan, V., & Peterson, R. A. (1985). *Models of innovation diffusion.* Beverly Hills: Sage.

Manski, C. F. (1993). Identification problems in the social sciences. *Sociological Methodology, 23*, 1–56.

Manting, D. (1994). *Dynamics in marriage and cohabitation. An inter-temporal, life course analysis of first union formation and dissolution.* Amsterdam: Thesis Publishers.

Marini, M. M. (1978). The transition to adulthood: sex differences in educational attainment and age at marriage. *American Sociological Review, 43*, 483–507.

Marini, M. M. (1984). Women's educational attainment and the timing of entry into parenthood. *American Sociological Review, 49*, 491–511.

Marini, M. M. (1985). Determinants of the timing of adult role entry. *Social Science Research, 14*, 309–350.

Marini, M. M., & Singer, B. (1988). Causality in the social sciences. In C. C. Clogg (Ed.), *Sociological Methodology* (pp. 347–409). San Francisco: Jossey-Bass.

Mason, K. O. et al. (1973). Some methodological issues in cohort analysis of archival data. American *Sociological Review, 38*, 242–258.

Mason, W. M., & Fienberg, S. E. (1985) (Eds.). *Cohort analysis in social research.* New York: Springer.

Mayer, K. U. (1987). Lebenslaufsforschung. In W. Voges (Ed.), *Methoden der Biographie- und Lebenslaufsforschung* (pp. 51–73). Opladen: Leske & Budrich.

Mayer, K. U. (1988). German survivors of World War II: the impact on the life course of the collective experience of birth cohorts. In M. W. Riley (Ed.), *Social structures and human lives. Social change and the life course* (pp. 229–246). Newbury Park: Sage.

Mayer, K. U. (Ed.) (1990). *Lebensverläufe und sozialer Wandel. Sonderheft 31, Kölner Zeitschrift für Soziologie und Sozialpsychologie.* Opladen: Westdeutscher Verlag.

Mayer, K. U. (1991). Life courses in the welfare state. In W. R. Heinz (Ed.), *Theoretical advances in life course research* (Vol. 1, pp. 171–186). Weinheim: Deutscher Studienverlag.

Mayer, K. U., Allmendinger, J., & Huinink, J. (Eds.) (1991). *Vom Regen in die Traufe: Frauen zwischen Beruf und Familie.* Frankfurt a.M. and New York: Campus.

Mayer, K. U., & Brückner, E. (1989). *Lebensverläufe und Wohlfahrtsentwicklung. Konzeption, Design und Methodik der Erhebung von Lebensverläufen der Geburtsjahrgänge 1929-31, 1939-41, 1949-51. Materialien aus der Bildungsforschung, Nr. 35.* Max-Planck-Institut für Bildungsforschung, Berlin.

Mayer, K. U., & Carroll, G. R. (1987). Jobs and classes: structural constraints on career mobility. *European Sociological Review, 3*, 14–38.

Mayer, K. U., Featherman, D. L, Selbee, L. K., & Colbjørnsen, T. (1989), Class mobility during the working life: A comparison of Germany and Norway. In M. L. Kohn (Ed.), *Cross-national research in sociology* (pp. 218–239). Newbury Park: Sage.

Mayer, K. U., & Huinink, J. (1990). Age, period, and cohort in the study of the life course: A comparison of classical A-P-C-analysis with event history analysis or farewell to Lexis? In D. Magnusson & L. R. Bergmann (Eds.), *Data quality in longitudinal research* (pp. 211–232). Cambridge: Cambridge University Press.

Mayer, K. U., & Müller, W. (1986). The state and the structure of the life course. In A. B. Sørensen, F. Weinert, & L. R. Sherrod (Eds.), *Human development and the life course* (pp. 217–245). Hillsdale, NJ: Lawrence Erlbaum Associates.

Mayer, K. U., & Schöpflin, U. (1989). The state and the life course. *Annual Review of Sociology, 15*, 187–309.

Mayer, K. U., & Schwarz, K. (1989). The process of leaving the parental home. Some German data. In E. Grebenik, C. Höhn, & R. Mackensen (Eds.), *Later phases of the family cycle. Demographic aspects* (pp. 145–163). Oxford: Clarendon.

Mayer, K. U., & Tuma, N. B. (Eds.) (1990). *Event history analysis in life course research.* Madison: University of Wisconsin Press.

Medical Research Council (1992). *Review of longitudinal studies.* London (mimeo).

Menken, J. (1985). Age and fertility: how late can you wait? *Demography, 22*, 469–483.

Meulemann, H. (1990). Schullaufbahnen, Ausbildungskarrieren und die Folgen im Lebensverlauf. Der Beitrag der Lebensverlaufsforschung zur Bildungssoziologie. In K. U. Mayer (Ed.), *Lebensverläufe und sozialer Wandel* (pp. 89–117). Opladen: Westdeutscher Verlag.

Michael, R. T., & Tuma, N. B. (1985). Entry into marriage and parenthood by young men and women: the influence of family background. *Demography, 22*, 515–543.

Mincer, J. (1974). *Schooling, experience, and earnings.* New York: National Bureau of Economic Research.

Mincer, J., & Polachek, S. (1974). Family investments in human capital: earnings of women. *Journal of Political Economy, 82*, 76–108.

Moreau, T., O'Quigley, J., & Mesbah, M. (1985). A global goodness-of-fit statistic for the proportional hazards model. *Applied Statistics, 34*, 212–218.

Murphy, M. (1991). *The family life cycle.* London: London School of Economics. Unpublished manuscript.

Namboodiri, K., & Suchindran, C. M. (1987). *Life table techniques and their applications.* New York: Academic Press.

Olzak, S. (1992). *The dynamics of ethnic competition and conflict.* Stanford: Stanford University Press.

Oppenheimer, V. K. (1988). A theory of marriage timing. *American Journal of Sociology, 94*, 563–591.

Papastefanou, G. (1987). *Familienbildung und Lebensverlauf. Eine empirische Analyse sozialstruktureller Bedingungen der Familiengründung bei den Kohorten 1929-31, 1939-41 und 1949-51.* Studien und Berichte no. 50. Max-Planck-Institut für Bildungsforschung, Berlin.

Petersen, T. (1986a). Estimating fully parametric hazard rate models with time-dependent covariates. *Sociological Methods and Research, 14*, 219–246.

Petersen, T. (1986b). Fitting parametric survival models with time-dependent covariates. *Applied Statistics, 35*, 281–288.

Petersen, T. (1988a). Analyzing change over time in a continuous dependent variable: Specification and estimation of continuous state space hazard rate models. *Sociological Methodology, 18*, 137–164.

Petersen, T. (1988b). *Incorporating time-dependent covariates in models for analysis of duration data*. CDE working paper.

Petersen, T. (1990). Analyzing event histories. In A. von Eye (Ed.), *Statistical methods in longitudinal research* (Vol. 2, pp. 259–288). New York: Academic Press.

Petersen, T. (1991). The statistical analysis of event histories. *Sociological Methods & Research, 19*, 270–323.

Pickles, A. R., & Davies, R. B. (1986). Household factors and discrimination in housing consumption. *Regional Science and Urban Planning, 16*, 493–517.

Pickles, A. R., & Davies, R. B. (1989). Inference from cross-sectional and longitudinal data for dynamic behavioural processes. In J. Hauer et al. (Eds.), *Urban dynamics and spatial choice behaviour* (pp. 81–104). New York: Kluwer Academic Publishers.

Piore, M. J. (1968). On-the-job training and adjustment to technological change. *Journal of Human Resources, 3*, 435–445.

Pötter, U. (1993). Models for interdependent decisions over time. In J. Janssen & C. H. Skiadas (Eds.), *Applied stochastic models and data analysis* (pp. 767–779). World Scientific Publishers.

Preisendörfer, P., & Burgess, Y. (1988). Organizational dynamics and career patterns: effects of organizational expansion and contraction on promotion chances in a large West German company. *European Sociological Review, 4*, 32–45.

Rindfuss, R. R., & Hirschman, C. (1984). The timing of family formation: structural and societal factors in the Asian context. *Journal of Marriage and the Family, 55*, 205–214.

Rindfuss, R. R., & John, C. S. (1983). Social determinants of age at first birth. *Journal of Marriage and the Family, 45*, 553–565.

Rodgers, W. L. (1982). Estimable functions of age, period, and cohort effects. *American Sociological Review, 47*, 774–787.

Rohwer, G. (1994). *TDA working papers*. Bremen: University of Bremen.

Rohwer, G. (1995). *Kontingente Lebensverläufe. Soziologische und statistische Aspekte ihrer Beschreibung und Erklärung*. Bremen: University of Bremen.

Rosenthal, L. (1991). Unemployment incidence following redundancy; the value of longitudinal approaches. In S. Dex (Ed.), *Life and work history analyses: Qualitative and quantitative developments* (pp. 187–213). London and New York: Routledge.

Sandefur, G. D., & Tuma, N. B. (1987). How data type affects conclusions about individual mobility. *Social Science Research, 16*, 301–328.

Sewell, W. H., & Hauser, R. M. (1975). *Education, occupation and earnings*. New York: Academic Press.

Shavit, Y., & Blossfeld, H.-P. (Eds.) (1993). *Persistent inequality. Changing educational attainment in thirteen countries*. Boulder: Westview Press.

Shingles, R. D. (1976). Causal inference in cross-lagged panel analysis. *Political Methodology, 3*, 95–133.

Singer, B., & Spilerman, S. (1976a). The representation of social processes by Markov models. *American Journal of Sociology, 82*, 1–54.

Singer, B., & Spilerman, S. (1976b). Some methodological issues in the analysis of longitudinal surveys. *Annals of Economic and Social Measurement, 5*, 447–474.

Singer, J. D., & Willett, J. B. (1991). Modeling the days of our lives: Using survival analysis when designing and analyzing longitudinal studies of duration and the timing of events. *Psychological Bulletin, 110*, 268–290.

Snyder, L. (1991). Modeling dynamic communication processes with event history analysis. *Communication Research, 18*, 464–486.

Sørensen, A. B. (1977). The structure of inequality and the process of attainment. *American Sociological Review, 42*, 965–978.

Sørensen, A. B. (1979). A model and a metric for the analysis of the intragenerational status attainment process. *American Journal of Sociology, 85*, 361–384.

Sørensen, A. B. (1984). Interpreting time dependency in career processes. In A. Diekmann & P. Mitter (Eds.), *Stochastic modelling of social processes* (pp. 89–122). New York: Academic Press.

Sørensen, A. B. (1986). Theory and methodology in social stratification. In U. Himmelstrand (Ed.), *The sociology of structure and action* (pp. 69–95). New York.

Sørensen, A. B., & Blossfeld, H.-P. (1989). Socioeconomic opportunities in Germany in the post-war period. *Research in Social Stratification and Mobility, 8*, 85–106.

Sørensen, A. B., & Sørensen, A. (1985). An event history analysis of the process of entry into first marriage. *Current Perspectives on Aging and Life Cycle, 2*, 53–71.

Sørensen, A. B., & Tuma, N. B. (1981). Labor market structures and job mobility. *Research in Social Stratification and Mobility, 1*, 67–94.

Spence, A. M. (1973). Job market signaling. *Quarterly Journal of Economics, 87*, 355–374.

Spence, A. M. (1974). *Market signaling.* Cambridge: Harvard University Press.

Sudman, S., & Bradburn, N. M. (1986). *Asking questions.* San Francisco: Jossey-Bass.

Tarone, R. E., & Ware, J. (1977). On distribution-free tests for equality of survival distributions. *Biometrika, 64*, 156–160.

Teachman, J. D. (1983). Analyzing social processes: life tables and proportional hazards models. *Social Science Research, 12*, 263–301.

Treiman, D. J. (1977). *Occupational prestige in comparative perspective.* New York: Academic Press.

Trussell, J., & Richards, T. (1985). Correcting for unmeasured heterogeneity in hazard models using the Heckman-Singer procedure. *Sociological Methodology, 15*, 242–276.

Tuma, N. B. (1980). *Invoking RATE.* Mannheim: ZUMA.

Tuma, N. B. (1985). Effects of labor market structure on job-shift patterns. In J. J. Heckman & B. Singer (Eds.), *Longitudinal analysis of labor market data* (pp. 327–363). Cambridge: Cambridge University Press.

Tuma, N. B., & Hannan, M. T. (1984). *Social dynamics. Models and methods.* New York: Academic Press.

Vaupel, J. A., & Yashin, A. I. (1985). The deviant dynamics of death in heterogeneous populations. *Sociological Methodology, 16,* 179–211.

Wagner, M. (1989a). *Räumliche Mobilität im Lebenslauf*. Stuttgart: Enke.

Wagner, M. (1989b). Spatial determinants of social mobility. In J. van Dijk, H. Folmer, & A. M. Herzog (Eds.), *Migration and labor market adjustment* (pp. 241–264). Dordrecht.

Wagner, M. (1990). Education and migration. In K. U. Mayer & N. B. Tuma (Eds.), *Event history analysis in life course research* (pp. 129–145). Madison: University of Wisconsin Press.

Wegener, B. (1985). Gibt es Sozialprestige? *Zeitschrift für Soziologie, 14,* 209–235.

Willett, J. B., & Singer, J. D. (1991). From whether to when: new methods for studying student dropout and teacher attrition. *Review of Educational Research, 61,* 4.

Wu, L. L. (1989). Issues in smoothing empirical hazard rates. *Sociological Methodology, 19,* 127–159.

Wu, L. L. (1990). Simple graphical goodness-of-fit tests for hazard rate models. In K. U. Mayer & N. B. Tuma (Eds.), *Event history analysis in life course research* (pp. 184–199). Madison: University of Wisconsin Press.

Wu, L. L., & Tuma, N. B. (1990). Local hazard models. *Sociological Methodology, 20,* 141–180.

Yamaguchi, K. (1991). *Event history analysis*. Newbury Park: Sage.

About the Authors

Hans-Peter Blossfeld is professor of sociology and social statistics at the University of Bremen and external professor of sociology and political sciences at the European University Institute, Florence. Since 1990 he has been editor of the *European Sociological Review*. He is particularly interested in developing and applying dynamic models based on longitudinal data and directs the international comparative project "Haushaltsdynamik und soziale Ungleichheit im internationalen Vergleich" (Household Dynamics and Social Inequality) at the Sonderforschungsbereich 186 "Statuspassagen und Risikolagen im Lebensverlauf" (Status Passages and the Life Course). His publications deal with modern methods of quantitative social research and statistical methods for longitudinal data. In substantive terms, he is interested in youth, family, and educational sociology; studies of the labor market; and research in demography, as well as social stratification and mobility. He has written several books including *Event History Analysis: Statistical Theory and Application in the Social Sciences* (with Alfred Hamerle and Karl Ulrich Mayer, 1989); *Persistent Inequality: Changing Educational Attainment in Thirteen Countries* (edited with Yossi Shavit, 1993); *The New Role of Women: Family Formation in Modern Societies* (1995); and *Between Equalization and Marginalization. Part-time Working Women in Europe and the United States of America* (forthcoming).

Götz Rohwer is assistant professor of sociology and statistics at the University of Bremen and was research fellow at the European University Institute, Florence. As a senior research scientist, he is a member of the project "Haushaltsdynamik und soziale Ungleichheit im internationalen Vergleich" (Household Dynamics and Social Inequality) at the Sonderforschungsbereich 186 "Statuspassagen und Risikolagen im Lebensverlauf" (Status Passages and the Life Course). He has written the program Transition Data Analysis (TDA), a program that estimates the sorts of models most frequently used with longitudinal data. He is interested in further development and application of statistical methods for longitudinal analysis. He has published several journal articles on social policy issues, demographic change, and labor market processes.

Index